D0065375

Physiological Correlates of Human Behaviour

Vol. III: Individual Differences and Psychopathology

Physiological Correlates of Human Behaviour

Vol. III: Individual Differences and Psychopathology

Edited by

Anthony Gale

Department of Psychology
University of Southampton
Southampton

John A. Edwards

Department of Psychology
University of Reading
Reading

1983

ACADEMIC PRESS

A Subsidiary of Harcourt Brace Jovanovich, Publishers

London   New York

Paris   San Diego   San Francisco

São Paulo   Sydney   Tokyo   Toronto

ACADEMIC PRESS INC. (LONDON) LTD.
24/28 Oval Road
London NW1

United States Edition published by
ACADEMIC PRESS INC.
111 Fifth Avenue
New York, New York 10003

British Library Cataloguing in Publication Data

Physiological correlates of human behaviour.
  Vol. 3
  1. Psychology, Physiological
  I. Gale, A.   II. Edwards, J. A.
  612'.8   QP360

  ISBN 0-12-273903-5
  LCCCN 82-73802

Typeset by Oxford Verbatim Ltd.
and printed in Great Britain by
St. Edmundsbury Press, Bury St. Edmunds, Suffolk

List of Contributors

J. *Beatty*, Department of Psychology, University of California, 8619 Franz Hall, Los Angeles, California 90024, USA.

R. *Blackburn*, Department of Psychology, Park Lane Hospital, School Lane, Maghull, Liverpool L31 1HW, UK.

M. S. *Buchsbaum*, Department of Psychiatry and Human Behaviour, California College of Medicine, University of California, Irvine, California 92717, USA.

P. *Crits-Christoph*, Department of Psychology, Box 11A Yale Station, Yale University, New Haven, Connecticutt 06520, USA.

J. A. *Edwards*, Department of Psychology, University of Reading, Earley Gate, Whiteknights, Reading RG6 2AL, UK.

H. J. *Eysenck*, Department of Psychology, Institute of Psychiatry, De Crespigny Park, Denmark Hill, London SE5 8AF, UK.

A. *Gale*, Department of Psychology, University of Southampton, Highfield, Southampton SO9 5NH, UK.

J. A. *Gray*, Department of Experimental Psychology, University of Oxford, South Parks Road, Oxford OX1 3UD, UK.

R. J. *Haier*, Butler Hospital, 345 Blackstone Boulevard, Providence, Rhode Island 02906, USA.

J. *Johnson*, National Institute of Mental Health, Bethesda, Maryland 20205, USA.

M. *Lader*, Institute of Psychiatry, De Crespigny Park, Denmark Hill, London SE5 8AF, UK.

J. G. *O'Gorman*, Department of Psychology, University of New England, Armidale, New England, Australia.

C. *Ray*, Department of Psychology, Brunel University, Uxbridge, Middlesex UB8 3PH, UK.

G. E. *Schwartz*, Department of Psychology, Box 11A Yale Station, Yale University, New Haven, Connecticutt 06520, USA.

J. *Strelau*, Institute of Psychology, University of Warsaw, Stawki 5/7, 00-183 Warsaw, Poland.

G. *Turpin*, Department of Psychology, Plymouth Polytechnic, Drake Circus, Plymouth, Devon, UK.

P. H. *Venables*, Department of Psychology, University of York, Heslington, York YO1 5DD, UK.

L. A. *Warwick-Evans*, Department of Psychology, University of Southampton, Highfield, Southampton SO9 5NH, UK.

M. *Zuckerman*, Department of Psychology, University of Delaware, Newark, Delaware 19711, USA.

Preface

All students of psychology are required to follow courses in physiological psychology, the biological bases of behaviour, or neuropsychology. Those who have an inadequate background training in biology experience some difficulty in coming to grips with terminology and are confused by anatomy and biochemistry. Others are also disenchanted by the fact that physiological psychology seems to focus largely upon animal behaviour, while many students are more concerned with the understanding of human behaviour. At some universities, human physiological psychology is studied, but typically as an advanced option or even only at postgraduate level. The study of physiological correlates of human behaviour over the last twenty years or so, has gone under the name of *psychophysiology*. It is a sad reflection of the state of psychological sciences that physiological psychologists and psychophysiologists rarely talk to each other. They attend different conferences and publish in different scientific journals. Few of the many excellent and comprehensive textbooks in physiological psychology cover more than the odd topic or two which has an immediate bearing upon those psychological processes studied by the experimental psychologist; and neuropsychology is only just beginning to establish links with experimental psychology. The present three volumes attempt to bridge some of the gaps and draw together disciplines which in our view should be working in collaboration. Thus we offer a unique combination of topics for the reader.

Physiological Correlates of Human Behaviour comes in three volumes because the sheer range of enquiry which now constitutes biological psychology inhibits a combination of all major topics under one set of covers. Even so, many topics which receive generous treatment in introductory textbooks, have been excluded. If space had allowed, we would have included chapters devoted to evolution, behavioural genetics, language, social psychophysiology, and sociobiology. We have tried, in selecting our contributions, to identify essentials, while filling major gaps in the available literature.

Moreover, this is not a series of textbooks, for range of treatment would of necessity have encouraged superficial coverage. Rather, we have commissioned internationally established authorities to prepare accessible, straightforward and yet critical accounts of the present state of the art. The aim has been to deal with a set of well defined research areas in depth, so that the reader can capture the full flavour and excitement of contemporary research.

Thus we hope that lecturers and postgraduate students, as well as under-graduates, will find this volume offers not only an introduction to biological research into human behaviour, but a spur and stimulus to further reading and research endeavour. Each of our authors has recommended additional readings, apart from the references provided within the text.

The term *correlates* which appears in our title, requires delicate and sensitive "unpacking". The business of relating subjective experience, behaviour and physiology is probably one of the most complex enterprises which human scientists will ever have to face. Some of our authors are bolder than others in staking their claims; this reflects the enthusiasm and zeal with which they tackle Nature. Sometimes it is necessary, like a thoroughbred racehorse, to wear blinkers and romp ahead. Others prefer a more painstaking and cautious approach to the finishing post. We hope that the different personalities and cognitive styles of our authors shine through. Indeed it is in the nature of science that the optimal approach to complex problems is to mix the broad brush with attention to fine detail. Virtually all our authors have written basic textbooks themselves or have made fundamental contributions to their disciplines. We owe them a profound debt of gratitude for staying so close to the briefs we gave them. By approaching leading authorities in their fields we know we have obtained for the reader's benefit not only a freshness and liveliness of approach but a far more authoritative and up-to-date account than we could have achieved on our own. We hope the reader will agree that they have managed to express very sophisticated problems in straightforward language yet without sacrificing complexity.

The three books in this series will be appropriate for courses in experimental psychology, individual differences, and psychopathology, as well as mainstream physiological psychology. Students of medicine and psychiatry will find that Volume III (*Individual Differences and Psychopathology*) in particular is highly relevant to their psychological studies.

We have already expressed our thanks to our authors. We must acknowledge the understanding of David Henderson of the Teaching Media Department at the University of Southampton, who in redrawing all our graphs and figures has exercised a satisfying combination of aesthetic virtue and technical skill. Liz Gale provided constant support to one of us and Marg Kuiack assisted and coaxed us through the final stages of preparation of the manuscript; to them also go special thanks.

June, 1983   Anthony Gale
University of Southampton   John Edwards

Contents

16. Psychophysiology, Psychopathology and the
    Social Environment
    G. Turpin

Contents of Other Volumes

VOLUME II: Attention and Performance

1 Introduction

*A. Gale
and J. Edwards*

Physiological Correlates of Human Behaviour draws together human and animal studies of the biological bases of behaviour. Volume I is devoted to basic issues, not only relating to the anatomy, physiology and biochemistry of the nervous system, but to problems of measurement and interpretation. What does it mean to say that this or that physiological event is a **correlate** of observed behaviour? How does one integrate data from physiological, behavioural and subjective domains of discourse? How does a physical event become a psychological stimulus? In Volume II we turn to problems of attention and performance, and our authors explore recent research showing how response to the environment is determined by the state of the individual. What psychological processes are reflected by observed changes in the brain and the autonomic nervous system? Thus Volume I and II are concerned with the description of *general* laws and the principles which govern behaviour. In Volume III we examine why people behave differently in apparently similar situations. Why is it that different individuals appear to be motivated by different factors, to perform more effectively than others and to be more or less resistant than others to the stresses which life imposes on us? All our authors share a common belief that the understanding of differences among individuals will include the solution to a number of biological puzzles. This does not mean that we shall find all the answers to questions about individual variations merely by examining the nervous system. Man has evolved over millions of years within a complex and changing environment. Thus, traits or attributes described in this volume (e.g. sensation seeking, anxiety, intelligence and so on) are shorthand descriptions of the individual's dispositions to respond in particular circumstances in particular ways. That is to say, individual variations have evolved as adaptations, hand in hand with the evolution of Man as a species. Thus, a complete description of individual variations must include Man, his environment and the interactions between Man and environment. Such a description will contain several basic characteristics:

PHYSIOLOGICAL CORRELATES OF HUMAN
BEHAVIOUR   ISBN 0-12-273901-9
*Copyright © 1983 by Academic Press Inc. (London) Ltd.
All rights of reproduction in any form reserved.*

readiness to respond in a particular fashion, appraisal of available stimuli, selection from among stimuli, reaction to stimuli, transformation of information about stimuli and the consequences of action, antecedent, synchronous and consequent bodily changes, conscious or sub-conscious reflection upon the environment and the consequences of action, adjustments of state, readiness to respond, appraisal . . . and so on in a continuous feedback loop. None of our authors attempts a complete description and, indeed, each one tends to emphasize a particular aspect at the expense of others, reflecting the way in which theory and research in this field have evolved over the last twenty years. However, taken together, our authors provide a representative sample of contemporary work, covering between them the full range of stages in the feedback loop.

Several of our authors refer to basic anatomical structures, functional brain systems and brain biochemistry. Reference is also made very frequently to classical conditioning procedures and to the standard psychophysiological techniques employed in the measurement of physiological responses in human subjects. Basic data on all these aspects are to be found in Volumes I and II.

Throughout this book the reader will find a remarkable consistency in the themes which emerge, even in apparently disparate subject areas. It will be useful for the reader, particularly if he is a student new to the field, to read the following summary of key themes and to return to it after reading any of the chapters in the book. From a learning point of view, such a strategy will enable the student to impose a coherent structure upon the material. We have identified similar key themes in Volumes I and II.

I. Key Themes

A. *Biological Origins*

Individual differences in both normal populations and among groups with psychiatric classifications reflect, in part, predispositions within the nervous system. Evidence for such a biological source of variation is derived from studies of genetic transmission of traits in both normal and clinical populations. The mode of such transmission is typically poorly understood, though it is seen to make its impact upon biological functioning. Such functioning may be explored by examining biochemical and electrophysiological processes in the nervous system. It is assumed that the functions under study are expressed as continuously distributed variables across the entire population, the clinical cases representing extremes of response. Thus, mechanisms studied in normals are relevant to the study of the abnormal and vice versa. Both biochemical and electrophysiological systems have been related to individual differences in personality within the general population, while anomalous responses have been observed in clinical groups.

B. *The Concept of Arousal*

This concept appears in various guises, either as a primary or important secondary factor, in most psychophysiological studies of personality. It is also implicated in various types of psychopathology, and distorted patterns of arousal are said to be the origin of several psychiatric disorders. When a concept is employed so extensively, a number of alternative implications may be drawn. The concept of arousal may indeed represent a fundamental principle governing the organism's interaction with its environment and influencing the manner in which information about the environment is stored and retrieved. Thus, the concept of arousal could be a candidate for a fundamental explanatory principle of human behaviour. Alternatively, the concept could be so over-used and so generally applied that it becomes like an over-inflated currency and has little exchange value. In other words, the concept of arousal could be employed to explain so many situations and states that it loses all explanatory power. In a review of individual differences research, Gale and Edwards (1984) point out that the term of arousal has been used in a variety of ways: as a *disposition* to respond, as a *source* of stimulation, as a *threshold* for response, as a *response* to stimulation, as an *endogenous* variation, as an *experienced* state, as a *correlate* or *consequence* of action, as a measure of *intensity* of action, or as a *drive* or motivator of action, and so on.

Setting aside these various contexts, there is ample evidence that, within the physiological domain, individual measures alleged to reflect arousal can move in opposite directions at the same time. For example, in the "intake" and "rejection" tasks devised by the Laceys (e.g. 1967), electrodermal responding occurs under both conditions, but heart rate decelerates in the former and accelerates in the latter. One cannot therefore argue that heart rate changes and electrodermal responses always reflect a common mechanism, either psychological or physiological. Thus, there are dangers associated with the use of the term *arousal* and the reader should be cautious in accepting its use without question. Nevertheless, whatever the future may hold for the concept, it is a fact that most of the authors in this volume have recourse to its use. Two associated concepts are the *optimum level of arousal* and disruption of *attention* through over- or under- arousal. The notion of an optimal level of functioning is of course quite common in biological systems and is associated with the notion of *homeostasis* and the maintenance of equilibrium in state. Again, the term "optimum level" has been used in a variety of ways, but there is some consensus among our authors that individuals fluctuate about particular optima and that their behaviour is designed to maintain a desirable equilibrium. Individuals vary in the equilibrium state which they find pleasurable or tolerable, and in the clinical case the optimal state may preclude normal functioning within the community at large. The effects of arousal upon attentional processes are seen in a variety of clinical conditions discussed in this volume. In the case of schizophrenia, disruption of attentional mechanisms is assumed by many theorists to underlie pathology and to be a basic causal factor. In anxiety and depression, however, influences upon attentional capacity are seen to be a secondary by-product of the basic pathology.

C. *Approach and Avoidance*

Within the interactive framework, mentioned above, which we have described as a feedback loop between the individual and the environment, there are factors which influence the willingness of the individual to act upon the environment. The notions of reward and punishment, and approach and avoidance are common to many theories of individual differences and psychopathology. This is clearly a complex matter since stimuli and situations will be appraised in terms of their potential rewarding or aversive properties and such appraisal will arise from complex origins, including possible biological biases within the organism, previous interactions with the environment, and past learning. Organisms cannot remain stationary and survive in a busy and changing environment; thus the elementary notion of approach and avoidance is an attractive one. It is not difficult to see how approach and/or avoidance must be presupposed before any action can be taken. Thus, this concept also is basic to biological accounts of human action, and some of our authors speculate about the brain mechanisms which may be implicated.

D. *Problems of Classification and Taxonomy*

Many of the descriptive concepts employed in personality research are not very far removed from vernacular use. This is acceptable so long as the concept in question, once taken over by science, is refined and clarified so that there is precision in its use, both within a theoretical framework and in the construction of experimental hypotheses. The psychometric tradition has ensured that standard procedures are available for the measurement of personality constructs and for the elaboration of theory. Unfortunately, not all theories benefit from a sound psychometric base, in which the reliability and validity of measurement instruments may be assumed. The position in psychopathology is more serious. While authorities in personality theory might dispute the meaning of factor structures and argue which factors are appropriate for psychophysiological research, there is controversy in psychiatry as to what *general* approach is appropriate for classification purposes. Thus, belief in a simple and straightforward medical model approach to mental illness can create the false impression that diagnosis is straightforward. We devote a special section below to problems of psychological research in the field of psychopathology. However, at this point, it is sufficient to say that patient groups employed in psychiatric research are rarely homogeneous. If that is the case, then it is unlikely that a simple relationship will be found between diagnosis and biological functioning. Zuckerman (Chapter 7) describes in some detail the procedures followed to establish appropriate measurement instruments for sensation-seeking traits. On the other hand, Strelau's account (Chapter 9) of Eastern European studies of personality indicates that questionnaire construction and development is in its infancy. Venables (Chapter 13) discusses problems of diagnosis in schizophrenia research in his searching examination of methodological and interpretative problems.

E. *Simulation of Real Life Events by Experiment*

People are pretty complicated and experiments are typically rather simple-minded. O'Gorman's review (Chapter 4) shows how difficult it is to come to straightforward conclusions in integrating research using the basic paradigm of habituation to explore individual differences. But such problems run right through this book. A particular difficulty in individual differences and psychopathology research is the meaning of the stimulus, its salience for the experimental subject. It is a mistake to think that the stimulus has the same meaning for the subject as it does for the experimenter. Yet within our feedback notion, appraisal of the stimulus is a crucial element in the feedback chain. Most of the research reviewed tends to be of a *correlational* nature. A subject is believed to have a particular score on a trait scale, and predictions are made concerning the correlation of such scores with psychophysiological indices scores. The notion of *process* is typically forgotten, and thus the emphasis shifts to fixed attributes of the individual and not to his interactions with the environment. This is the principal source of the very simple experimental paradigms used, and the reason why many of the experiments seem so unlike real life. Some of our authors (e.g. Eysenck, Chapter 2) insist upon using experimental procedures which are derived from mainstream experimental psychology, many of which are described in Volume II. Such an approach enables the individual differences researcher to call upon the complex theoretical frameworks which have been erected within experimental psychology. However, the majority of the procedures described in this

volume are *ad hoc* and devised to study a particular personality attribute or
particular aspect of pathology, in a particular laboratory. Such fragmenta-
tion makes it very difficult to move to the construction of general theories
based on commonly derived data. Both individual differences research and
psychopathology are in search of appropriate experimental paradigms which
enable systematic study of physiology and behaviour and yet manage to be
true to life. The Chapters by Crits-Christoph and Schwartz (15) and Turpin
(16), which study psychophysiological change in the psychotherapeutic context and in the patient's home, come closer to this ideal than do many of the
laboratory studies. Turpin's approach is particularly innovative.

F. *Dissociation between Physiology, Behaviour and Experience*

Among the many interpretative problems posed by the psychophysiological
approach are the frequent reports that data from these three domains of
description do not follow a straightforward parallel path. Thus, one cannot
infer that there is some central common process of which physiology,
behaviour and experience, as reported by the individual, are simple correlates, synchronous in time. This raises very fundamental issues, which are
discussed in detail in Volume I by Farrell and by Porges, Ackles and Truax.
One source of dissociation is the capacity of individuals to reflect upon their
own behaviour and upon physiological changes of which they are aware and
to modulate or interrupt them by voluntary control. Such control can occur
within the laboratory as well as in the real world and the experimenter is
deceiving himself if he feels that he is always able to bring his experimental
subjects under stimulus control. But the important issue is that, whatever the
source of dissociation, explanatory concepts must be adequate enough to
enable description of such complexity. Few of the concepts devised in personality research or in psychopathology can cope with the richness of the data
obtained.

G. *The Social Psychology of Psychological Research*

One of the problems the reader will have to face is that there is no general
theory of individual differences which gives comperehensive coverage of all
the data reviewed. It would be an ambitious task of course to construct such
a theory, but there are some very obvious obstructions which could be
removed. One difficulty is that researchers work away in isolation and
without acknowledging that others are dealing with very similar problems.
They also develop their own measuring instruments, which makes comparison of data between laboratories very difficult. Thus, the reader will find that

the same dependent variable (e.g. EEG alpha amplitude) has been correlated with a variety of individual difference variables (e.g. extraversion, intelligence, anxiety, schizophrenicity). A logical conclusion might be that it is foolish for a researcher to continue merely to follow up his own hunches, when there is evidence that other variables, in which he refuses to show interest, can account for a significant proportion of the variance of the dependent measure to which he is devoting his research life. Evidence is presented in this book which shows that some workers in the field (e.g. Zuckerman, Strelau) think it sensible to compare their work with that of others. But it is very rare in clinical research to find designs which include *several* patient groups, or several controls. This makes confident interpretation of data very difficult. We have called this recurrent theme a social psychological problem because it is certainly not a logical or a technical problem, but one of attitude and willingness on the part of researchers to face up to the complexity of research. In the case of clinical work, researchers seem to have a powerful motive to oversimplify, perhaps in the hope that they will thereby come closer to the relief of personal suffering in clinical patients.

H. *Ethical Problems*

We referred earlier to the problem of simulating real life in the laboratory. This is as much a matter of the *art* of experimentation as of the science of experimentation. The new paradigm is a mark of the ingenuity of the researcher. But there are limits to what can be done and these are often imposed by ethical considerations. For example, anxiety is difficult to study under laboratory conditions without causing distress. Thus, the study of patients suffering from anxiety is one of the principal sources of information about anxiety response in the population at large. Among the decisions which make up a research design in psychopathology are a number of ethical issues. One of these relates to the withholding of medication. It is never easy to come to a clear conclusion about costs and benefits, or ends and means. However, even the most ingenious research design is unlikely to overcome the problem of medication and its consequences for the interpretation of data. This is one of the grounds for investing resources in studies of high-risk groups. But again, there is the danger of studies of children at risk becoming self-fulfilling prophesies. The researcher must ask himself about the consequences of informing an individual that he is within an at-risk sample. The issue of ethics intersects with research, not only because most psychologists are caring persons who are motivated by a desire to understand and assist other human beings but, because ethical considerations do impose limits on the interpretation of data. Designs simply cannot be complete or thorough, and gaps in a design mean potential gaps in reasoning.

I. *The Potential Complexity of Individual Differences Research*

It will be apparent from all that we have said so far that we are not wholly satisfied with the present state of affairs. In bringing together the material in this book for the first time, we hope we have taken the first step towards an integration of both theory and research methodology. Hopefully, readers of this volume will themselves take up the challenge of developing an adequate framework for the psychophysiology of individual differences. An integrative theory will have to recognize the complexity of meshing together all the elements in the feedback loop which we described at the beginning of this introduction. That must mean a multivariate rather than a univariate approach to research design. As a general starting point, the Systems Theory approach described by Crits-Christoph and Schwartz, could form the basis for a new approach.

II. Special Problems with Research into Psychopathology

There are many pitfalls surrounding psychological research into mental illness. A major difficulty arises from the fact that, in psychiatry it is difficult to view people as an aggregation of separate parts. The person in distress shows many signs and symptoms, ranging across all the domains explored in this book: *subjective experience* is distorted, or in some sense overwhelming; the individual shows clear signs of *physiological* disturbance; and *behaviour* may be agitated, inhibited or bizarre. The clinician must view the person as a whole, taking all these aspects into account. Moreover, individuals live in *social contexts* and the person's interpretation of his emotional environment may play a role in inducing illness, make prognosis poor, or of course assist in recovery. Thus, it is likely to be misleading if the clinical researcher just pursues one interest in isolation from others; following the contents of one chapter in a textbook is unlikely to give an understanding of the interrelated whole. Seen in this light, our selection of topics makes sense. Lader provides a straightforward account of *physiological research* into anxiety and depression. Venables provides a *methodological critique* of the area of contemporary schizophrenia research. Warwick-Evans shows how biology, early upbringing, life stressors and the experience of stress and coping, cultural factors and cognitive, attitudinal and unconscious mechanisms could combine to induce *psychosomatic* disease. And Blackburn, Crits-Christoph and Schwartz and Turpin take us into a world where *social* variables are of considerable importance: *deviant behaviour* in our interaction with others; the *social interface* between client and therapist; and the social and emotional *domestic world* of the patient on a programme of *rehabilitation*. Thus we illustrate the power of psychophysiological approaches in applied contexts and the bearing of our theories and methods on issues of social concern.

While such a richness in scope is attractive, there are a number of fundamental problems which we shall summarize briefly; for without appreciating the difficulties involved, the reader might be misled into thinking we have ready answers.

(i) Several studies have shown psychiatric *diagnosis* to be unreliable. This is a complex issue since such unreliability might arise from the *methods* used, the nature of the *illness* itself, spontaneous changes in the *patients*, inadequate assessment by *psychiatrists*, or *interactions* between all or any of these factors. What is clear is that agreement on *type* of disorder or *degree* of disorder is not high, and therefore agreement on *prognosis* and *treatment* is likely to be low also.

While practice varies enormously, inspection of an individual patient's case record in many hospitals will make one wonder how any researcher can state his subjects' diagnosis with any confidence. Where assessment is based on several *samples* of the patient's behaviour and involves an approach in terms of different aspects of his life and experience then reliability increases; a brief interview of someone in a highly stressed state is unlikely to reveal a true or comprehensive picture of his view of the world. When one is dealing with someone in distress the need for clarity in definition and description becomes even more compelling.

(ii) An inspection of diagnostic glossaries or classification systems reveals that many symptoms are seen to be *common* to several disorders, and any individual patient is unlikely to exhibit a "pure" classification; the role and function of the same symptom in *different* contexts might be quite varied. Thus, a symptom *could* be a sign of disease (like spots in german measles) or it could be a behaviour which has *functional* equivalents; crying or refusing to eat for example could both serve the identical function of *seeking attention* yet within a medical model could be seen to reflect different symptomatology.

(iii) Many symptoms are *secondary*. Thus, depressive feelings may result from the *consequences* to self-esteem and interpersonal relations following an anxiety attack or a schizophrenic episode. Hospitalization *per se* takes the individual away from his normal environment, and in some circumstances can relieve him of a sense of personal responsibility or willpower to change his own life.

(iv) Some symptoms are incompatible with standard research procedures. Thus it is difficult to study *attentional* mechanisms in patients who, by virtue of their disorder, are unable to attend to the experimenter's instructions. Therefore it is likely that selection processes operate on some patient groups *before* they participate in experiments.

(v) Studies in which patients participate rarely involve *unmedicated* groups. This is just another illustration of the fact that the experimenter is addressing a *complex* pattern of events and their consequences. Frequently, the imperative to relieve suffering has severe consequences for the logic of research design.

(vi) A properly designed study must include *other* patient groups and appropriate control groups if any psychophysiological differences are to be attributed to a *particular* group or a particular condition. Control groups for psychiatric disorder are difficult to construct and investigators are often concerned with only one psychiatric condition and are therefore unlikely to wish to spend time testing other groups, however compelling such precautions may be from a *logical* point of view. Hospital diet, regimes for living and other aspects of *institutional* care also need to be controlled for as a source of variation.

(vii) The *experiment* itself is a very special social event (see Gale and Baker, 1981), and a laboratory, particularly one equipped with complex apparatus, is likely to induce anxiety and fear. Thus, *some* observed effects may be due to the *procedure*, or an *interaction* between the patient's *condition* and the procedure, rather than to the condition alone.

(viii) Many disorders have an identifiable *time course*, but others exhibit unpredictable fluctuations in severity and in symptom patterns over time. Indeed some conditions appear to be self-regulating, reflecting the nervous system's resilience and adaptiveness. Therefore, any group of patients is unlikely to be homogeneous for psychiatric state at the time of testing.

(ix) Experimenters who are used to administering *instructions* to students may assume that, to a large extent, the meaning and purpose of their instructions is understood. In our experience, however, institutionalized patients appear to treat *any* interaction with a professional of high status as *treatment* or *therapy*. Such an expectation is likely to colour the individual patient's whole approach to any task presented.

These nine considerations are rather crucial when one comes to examine any body of research data in psychiatry. Theory is all very well at the *macro* level but all theory if it is to be of use in the real world must be capable of empirical definition; that means the testing of specific hypotheses under conditions which allow for control. The analysis of experimental data involves consideration at the *micro* level; the fidelity of the data obtained is crucial to the corroboration or falsification of theory. Defective research designs yield measurement error and impose constraints upon the interpretation of data. The student should not be afraid, therefore, to express the view that particular studies are defective, or that an author's reasoning is not wholly logical or consistent. Inability to understand what one reads, or to be convinced by it, may reflect defects in the research itself and not in the thought processes of the reader. Clinical research is so complex and the desire to relieve human suffering so great, that researchers (who are after all, human beings themselves) frequently throw caution to the winds and let their enthusiasm grasp at answers which simply cannot cope with the data. Such wishful thinking has led to many explanatory devices in psychiatry and also to many new treatments, which after a few years seem to fall by the wayside. The reader has been warned!

References

Gale, A. and Baker, S. (1981). In vivo or in vitro? Some effects of laboratory environments, with particular reference to the psychophysiology laboratory. *In* "Foundations of Psychosomatics" (M. J. Christie and P. G. Mellett, eds). Wiley, Chichester.

Gale, A. and Edwards, J. (1984). Individual differences. *In* "Psychophysiology: Systems, Processes and Applications" (M. G. H. Coles, E. Donchin and S. W. Porges, eds). Guilford Press, New York.

Lacey, J. I. (1967). Somatic response patterning and stress: some revisions of activation theory. *In* "Psychological Stress: Issues in Research" (M. H. Appley and R. Trumbull, eds). Appleton Century Crofts, New York.

2 Psychophysiology and Personality: Extraversion, Neuroticism and Psychoticism

H. J. Eysenck

Abstract In this chapter we consider the three major dimensions of personality as they emerge from a multitude of descriptive studies of personality, and look at major theories of the underlying psychophysiological causes for the observed differences in behaviour. Also given is a brief review of the evidence regarding the theories in question. Extraversion–introversion appears to be related to differences in cortical arousal, mediated by the reticular formation, in the sense that introverts are characterized by greater resting levels of arousal. Neuroticism–stability appears to be related to differences in limbic system functioning, mediated by the autonomic system, in the sense that unstable people are characterized by excessive function of these variables. Psychoticism appears to be linked with certain hormonal and biochemical secretions, such as serotonin and dopamine metabolites and with sex hormones. There seems to be little doubt that personality traits have a firm basis in the individual's biological structure and functioning.

This chapter deals with the underlying neurophysiological and hormonal bases of the major dimensions of human personality. The first few paragraphs will introduce the descriptive aspects of the personality theory in question, and the reasons for suspecting a strong biological involvement in the determination of individual differences along the various dimensions in question. The rest of the chapter deals with the research that has been carried out to verify or disprove the biological theories associated with the personality model discussed.

I. The Trait Model: Extraversion and Neuroticism

Essentially all successful models of personality are **trait models**; in other words, they describe differences in human behaviour in terms of a number of

PHYSIOLOGICAL CORRELATES OF HUMAN
BEHAVIOUR   ISBN 0-12-273901-9

traits. These traits are usually found correlated together into higher order type concepts, such as extraversion, neuroticism and psychoticism. Trait concepts have been criticized by Gordon Allport (1937) on theoretical grounds, but in all his empirical work Allport and his students have nevertheless found it necessary to use trait concepts, very much like everyone else. Mischel (1976) has criticized the usefulness of trait concepts, and has advocated the importance of situational constraints on behaviour; this would seem an inappropriate dichotomy. All traits are manifested in situations and the situations are often specified directly in the very language of the trait nomenclature. Thus "sociability" relates to social situations, "persistence" relates to situations involving endurance, "impulsiveness" relates to situations involving spontaneous and non-thinking activity, etc. Eysenck and Eysenck (1980) have critically discussed the issues involved, and have come to the conclusion that the various criticisms of trait theory are not for the major part tenable.

On the whole, American authors prefer *lower level* trait concepts, like sociability, persistence and impulsiveness; British authors have on the whole preferred *higher order* concepts, i.e. type concepts based on the observed inter-correlations between traits. Figure 1 shows such a systematic higher order arrangement of two type-concepts, namely extraversion and neuroti-

Fig. 1 *Diagrammatic representation of two major axes of personality: extraversion versus introversion, and emotional instability versus stability (neuroticism).*

cism; shown on the periphery are the traits which are found to be correlated. In the centre are found the four Greek temperaments which historically preceded the more modern view of dimensions, but which clearly demarcate the four quadrants into which the two independent dimensions subdivide the person's space.

These two dimensions have been found in very large numbers of descriptive studies, often using factor analysis of intercorrelation matrices as the statistical tool. A third major dimension, also frequently found in large scale factor analytic studies of personality, is psychoticism (Eysenck and Eysenck, 1976). This refers to a dimension the high scoring end of which is characterized by personalities that are cold, egocentric, hostile, suspicious, impersonal and aggressive. The opposite pole is sometimes called, following Freud, "superego". Royce (1973) has summarized the very large literature leading to the postulation of these three major dimensions of personality. It is not suggested that these are the *only* major dimensions of personality, merely that at the present state of knowledge these are the ones which have been most frequently found in large scale studies of intercorrelations between traits on various human populations. These dimensions have emerged not only from analyses of questionnaires administered to English speaking Western groups but also from quite different cultures, including Japanese, Nigerian, Indian, Hungarian, Greek, Yugoslav and many other nationalities and cultures (Eysenck and Eysenck, 1980). Note also that similar dimensions have been found in animal populations, particularly monkeys (Chamove *et al.*, 1972). It should be further noted that these personality dimensions are intimately linked with various types of behaviour of social importance. Thus antisocial behaviour and criminality are often found correlated with high P, high N and high E scores; this has been found true not only in Western countries but also in Communist and Third World countries (Eysenck, 1977a). Neurosis is usually associated with high N and low E personality types; psychosis and psychopathy with high P scores; drug addiction with high P and high N; and so forth. Sexual behaviour, smoking behaviour, drinking behaviour and many other types of behaviour have been found associated in a predictable manner with these three major dimensions of personality (Wilson, 1981). There are various links mediating this relationship. These will be understood better once we have looked at the physiological bases of these personality dimensions.

II. Heredity

Before turning to our discussion of the psychophysiology of personality, however, let us consider one important determinant of personality, namely *heredity*. It used to be assumed until fairly recently that genetic factors played little part in the determination of differences in personality, but recent work has decisively contradicted this belief. Studies of identical twins brought up in separation, differences between monozygotic and dizygotic twins, studies of familial correlations and of adopted children have all demonstrated that the major dimensions of personality have a strong genetic basis, accounting for twice as much of the phenotypic variability as do environmental factors (Fulker, 1981). This is not the place to enter into the complex new methods of investigation and analysis that have been brought to bear on this topic in recent years; the fact of heritability is important because it suggests immediately that underlying individual differences in personality there must be biological factors of a psychophysiological or hormonal kind. Heredity cannot directly affect behaviour, it can only affect anatomical structures and physiological functions within the central nervous system, the autonomic nervous system, the hormonal system, or subsections of these systems. We turn, therefore, to theories and experiments in psychophysiology with the firm hope that these will throw some light on the nature and genesis of individual differences along the major personality dimensions.

III. Brain Mechanisms in Activation and Arousal

Let us first look at extraversion and neuroticism, because these dimensions have been prominent for a much longer time than psychoticism and theories regarding them are much more clearcut than those regarding psychoticism. Figure 2 shows in diagrammatic form a theory advanced by the present writer (Eysenck, 1967) to account for the major facts known about these dimensions. According to the theory, differences along the neuroticism-stability axis are produced by individual differences in the neurophysiology of the *limbic system* or *visceral brain*, the system which coordinates and governs the activities of the autonomic system in both its sympathetic and parasympathetic branches. Largely independent of this system, extraversion-introversion differences are determined by the *reticular formation-cortex* arousal loop, in the sense that extraverts tend to have lower resting arousal level than introverts. It is postulated that most of the time these two systems are indeed independent, but note that under conditions of strong limbic system activation there will be an overspill into the reticular formation, producing strong cortical arousal, so that under strong emotional stimulation it is impossible for the organism to remain in a state of low cortical arousal. For most of the time, of course, human beings are not in a state of high emotional arousal, and consequently for most of the time (including most laboratory investigations) the two systems are independent.

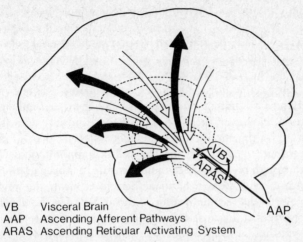

VB   Visceral Brain
AAP   Ascending Afferent Pathways
ARAS   Ascending Reticular Activating System

Fig. 2 *Diagram illustrating the hypothetical physiological basis of extraversion (reticular formation – cortical arousal) and neuroticism (limbic system or visceral brain).*

At first sight, the hypothesis that limbic system activation is responsible for individual differences in neuroticism may seem unlikely because of the well known facts that correlations between different measures of autonomic arousal are relatively poor, that there is considerable specificity of emotional reaction, and that correlations between autonomic measures and perceived emotionality are usually fairly low. This latter fact has given rise to the concept of desynchrony (Rachman and Hodgson, 1974; Hodgson and Rachman, 1974), in other words, the well substantiated fact that the three major aspects of emotional arousal (physiological, behavioural and intro- spective) tend to behave along rather independent lines.

While the facts are not in dispute, Thayer (1970) has suggested that the difficulties may be apparent rather than real. Using several different auto- nomic system variables, and recording individual reactions in these as well as giving state questionnaires of emotional arousal, he was able to show that, although the correlations between the physiological indices and between these indices and the questionnaires were all low, nevertheless, when the psychophysiological reaction scores were summed appropriately, they showed quite a high and acceptable correlation with the subject's emotional state, as recorded on the questionnaire. In other words, what seems to happen is that the individual is capable of *integrating* the input from several auto- nomic systems and interpreting this total input as emotional activation or arousal. Thus, experimental studies using only one autonomic input would not be expected to support the hypothesis strongly; what is needed are several different systems whose activation is measured simultaneously and combined in a meaningful fashion. When this is done results become much more positive.

A similar point may be made with respect to the arousal system; here too measurement of arousal by a single index, whether EEG, GSR, evoked potentials, or CNV is unlikely to give results as positive as the combination of measures. The great majority of studies, unfortunately, has been restricted to a single measure, so that we cannot point to much experimental evidence for this deduction. However, the logic of the theory, and such data as we possess strongly suggests that multiple measurement is better than single measurement with respect to cortical arousal as well as autonomic activation.

A very thorough review of the whole literature has been given by Stelmack (1981), and no attempt will be made here to replicate this review. Before turning to a brief discussion of some of the major areas, however, one point needs to be stressed, because it is of vital importance in testing deductions from the hypotheses outlined above. This point relates to what Pavlov called "transmarginal inhibition", a concept that is similar to the so-called Yerkes-Dodson Law, or the inverse-U shaped relationship between drive and performance. To explain briefly, Pavlov first of all postulated the "law of strength", according to which reaction (say the growth of a conditioned response) increased *pari passu* with the *strength* of the unconditioned stimulus (see Chapter 9 by Strelau). By and large, of course, this is true, but he found that beyond a certain point the relationship became inverted, so that *further increase in the strength of the stimulus produced a weakening in the reaction.* He labelled this process "transmarginal inhibition" or "protective inhibition", his hypothesis being that the nerve cells of the subject were protecting themselves against too strong stimulation by evoking some form of inhibition. The neurophysiology underlying this concept is of course very unrealistic, but the phenomenon itself has been observed many times, in many different connections. A single example may suffice to illustrate its relevance to the measurement of extraversion–introversion.

On the hypothesis that introverts have a higher arousal level than extraverts, and that arousal facilitates Pavlovian conditioning, it has been predicted that introverts would condition better than extraverts (Eysenck, 1957). Using eyeblink conditioning to test this hypothesis, Eysenck and Levey (1972) tested groups of extraverts and introverts with a relatively weak puff strength (3 psi) and found the predicted relationship (Fig. 3). On Pavlovian principles, we should find an inversion of this relationship if we increase the strength of the puff to something like 6 psi, and when this was done Eysenck and Levey (1972) did indeed report that extraverts showed better conditioning that introverts (Fig. 4). In other words, there is a point in the continuum relating to strength of the unconditioned stimulus, where transmarginal inhibition reverses the relationship observed at lower levels. This, of course, is

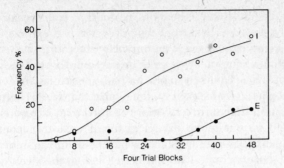

Fig. 3 *Rate of eyelid conditioning for introverts and extraverts under conditions of weak UCS, partial reinforcement and short CS–UCS interval.*

just an illustration; many other examples are found in the literature (Eysenck, 1967).

IV. The Evidence

Turning now to the actual evidence for or against the theory linking extraversion and arousal, we must first of all discuss EEG differences between the groups. This is because the concept of arousal has been intimately linked with the frequency and amplitude of alpha waves on the EEG, high arousal being linked with fast, low amplitude waves and lack of arousal with slow, high

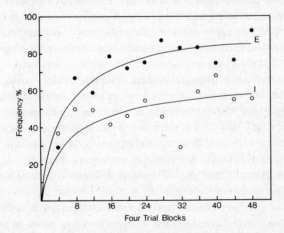

Fig. 4 *Rate of eyelid conditioning for extraverts and introverts under conditions of strong UCS, 100% reinforcement and long CS–UCS interval.*

amplitude waves. We would therefore expect that under resting conditions introverts would show the former type of waves and extraverts the latter. Gale (1973) has given a review of the fairly large literature on this topic which should be consulted in order to appreciate the complexity of the problem. As he points out, "There have been more than a dozen studies of this relationship and they have yielded three classes of outcome. Extraverts have been shown to be less aroused than introverts, more aroused than introverts, or equally aroused. . . . Can one make any sense out of such discrepant findings?" (p. 217). Gale suggests a generalization which takes into account the different *conditions* under which the EEG has been taken in the investigations summarized by him. "My general proposition is that when extraverts are either too bored with the procedure or too interested with the task, they will be more aroused than introverts. That is to say, a moderate level of arousal is required to optimize on the personality differences in this context. Where the extravert is too bored (habituation tasks, or simply lying with eyes closed) boredom leads to self-arousal, possibly involving imagining, which its turn activates the EEG. Where tasks are interesting (performing arithmetic problems, watching the Archimedes Spiral, talking to the experimenter) the extravert becomes aroused. With moderately arousing tasks (opening and shutting eyes upon instruction, or a simple eyes closed recording procedure in a laboratory which does not preclude sound of the experimenter's activities) the extraverted subject is more able to obey the instruction to relax and keep his mind clear." (p. 245). Gale gives a table showing that in three studies where the conditions are highly arousing, extraverts show greater arousal; in six studies where the conditions are likely to produce very low arousal, again extraverts show greater arousal. There are seven studies in which conditions are moderately arousing, and in all of these introverts show greater arousal. This outcome fits in very well with the notion of *transmarginal inhibition*, high arousal in the testing situation producing "protective inhibition" in the introvert but not the extravert.

The notion that experimental conditions which lack any arousing qualities should produce high arousal in extraverts may need an explanation. We may see the sort of thing that happens in an experiment on sensory deprivation reported by Tranel (1961). On the basis of our hypothesis, we would expect that introverts would be able to tolerate sensory deprivation better than extraverts. Studying 20 extraverts and 20 introverts, Tranel found that: "As a group, extraverts tolerated the isolation conditions significantly better than introverts in terms of time spent in the room." He also, however, discovered the reason for this unexpected result. Subjects had been instructed to lie quietly on their couch, to estimate the time every half hour and not to go to sleep. "In general the extraverts reacted by ignoring the instructions . . . while the introverts reacted by attempting to adhere rigidly to instruction." The mean number of movements observed per minute was 0·38 for the extraverts and 0·23 for the introverts; the difference would have been much greater if some extraverts had not reacted by going to sleep. "All of the extraverts who spoke during isolation, with one exception, mentioned difficulty in keeping awake. None of the introverts mentioned such a difficulty." Tranel describes the behaviour of the extravert thus: "Extraverts largely ignored the instruction to lie quietly. They moved about quite freely and this movement was part of their coping behaviour. In other words, extraverts reverted to a form of self-stimulation in the form of tapping, moving, or exploration of the surroundings. They seemed to be much more concerned with devising ways to endure the situation than with following the instructions." Thus, conditions resembling sensory deprivation (such as those under which some EEG records were taken) are so intolerable to extraverts as to produce protective behaviour on their part which in turn is arousing, and produces EEG patterns characteristic of arousal. Looked at it in this way all the seemingly contradictory results fall into place.

Another EEG measure which has been used is the so-called CNV (contingent negative variation). An experiment by O'Connor (1980) illustrates very well the relationship between arousal and personality, and also the inversion due to the law of transmarginal inhibition. Subjects, i.e. groups of extraverts and introverts as determined by questionnaire responses, were tested under two conditions, one arousing, the other one not. The arousing condition consisted of smoking a cigarette (nicotine is well known to have stimulant pharmacological properties), while the non-arousing situation consisted of sham smoking, i.e. the subject manipulating an unlit cigarette. The CNV was used as a measure of arousal, and the prediction is shown in Fig. 5. Extraverts

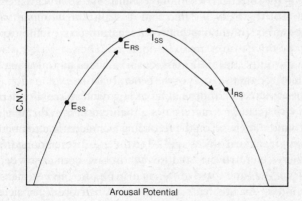

Fig. 5 *Diagram illustrating the theory linking arousal potential in introverts and extraverts with CNV measurement of arousal. (SS – sham smoking; RS – real smoking).*

are predicted to show lower CNV arousal than introverts under sham smoking conditions, i.e. $I_{SS} > E_{SS}$. After smoking a cigarette, however, extraverts would show an increase in CNV arousal, whereas introverts, due to the action of transmarginal inhibition, would show a decrement, as indicated by the arrows in Fig. 5. This is precisely what happened in the experiment, at a high level of significance; introverts showed greater arousal than extraverts under low arousal conditions, but after smoking a cigarette extraverts showed higher arousal than introverts.

Cortical evoked potentials are another EEG measure which has been studied in relation to extraversion–introversion. Stelmack (1981), in his review, points out that increased levels of cortical activity for introverts, inferred from the somatosensory evoked potential, have been reported by various authors, but there are also some negative findings.

There are many reasons for the apparent contradictions, thus for instance Stelmack et al. (1977) found the expected differences between extraverts and introverts with low frequency auditory stimulation, but not with high frequency auditory stimulation. Much greater attention will have to be paid to stimulus parameters before we can say that we fully understand the relationship between personality and the evoked potential.

Quite a different line of research has been concerned with the orienting response, which is usually accepted as an important precursor of the conditioning process. Here again, while the majority of studies are favourable, some are unfavourable to the hypothesis, as in the case of the EEG. As Stelmack points out, "it appears that conditions which favour differentiating between extraversion groups with the electrodermal measures of the OR can be described as moderately arousing, a consideration which may serve as a rough guide in the selection of stimulus conditions." In other words, here too, as in the case of the EEG, we find that it is absolutely imperative to have regard to stimulus conditions and other parameters of the experimental procedure if positive results are to be obtained. The similarity between these electrodermal studies, and the EEG ones summarized by Gale, is exactly what would be predicted on the basis of the general theory.

Other measures of electrodermal recording which have shown differences between introverts and extraverts along theoretically predictable lines have often been found to depend on the recording technique or circuitry employed and the type of transformations applied to the measures obtained. Significant differences between introverts and extraverts have been observed with both tonic and phasic measures, with differences in phasic response measures more frequently noted. As Stelmack points out, "differences in electrodermal activity between introverts and extraverts have been demonstrated with both simple auditory stimuli of moderate intensity and visual stimulation, and usually under non-stress conditions, where more than passive participation is required. Electrodermal activity is typically greater for introverts than extraverts. Differences in phasic response, in particular with introverts showing more persistent electrodermal responses to repetitive stimulation, has been the effect most frequently observed . . . there is also some evidence that introverts demonstrate high skin conductance levels and greater frequency of nonspecific responses than extraverts. These observations imply differences in basic arousal processes and suggest that the effect is not exclusively stimulus bound."

Another series of studies has been concerned with the pupillary response. The iris muscle that circumscribes the pupillary aperture is reciprocally innervated by the autonomic nervous system and the effects of this system are particularly dominant in the pupillary light reflex. With the onset of a light stimulus, activity of primarily parasympathetic origin can be inferred from an initial rapid constriction phase that is then moderated by increasing sympathetic opposition, while the rapid redilation at the offset of the stimulus signals parasympathetic relaxation followed by slower redilation that is due to peripheral sympathetic activity. Introverts have been found to have larger tonic pupil size prior to stimulation (Frith, 1977; Stelmack and Mandelzys, 1975), which would support the association of introversion with higher levels of cortical arousal. The less intensive pupillary constriction during the pupillary light reflex for extraverts (Holmes, 1967; Frith, 1977) may also be interpreted along the same lines, but rather less unequivocally.

While on the whole the evidence in favour of the hypothesis linking arousal with introversion is reasonably convincing, studies of the hypothesis linking neuroticism with the limbic system have been rather more ambiguous. There are many reasons for this. One of these is the difficulty of inducing high autonomic activation under laboratory conditions, which would usually be regarded as unethical. Thus, we have to rely on quite mild degrees of stimulation which may not be sufficient for practical purposes. Second, we have the difficulties associated with the law of initial value, which tells us that increases in autonomic activity are dependent on the initial state of the organism; this is seldom similar for high and low N scorers under laboratory conditions of testing. Third, we have ceiling conditions which make it impossible for high N scorers to obtain higher levels after successful autonomic stimulation than low N scorers. Possibly the most successful way of discovering differences in autonomic functioning between high and low N scorers is to look at the terminal phase of the experiment, i.e. the length of time needed after stimulation to reach base level again. Here longer periods seem to be required by high N scorers than by low N scorers (Eysenck, 1967).

As an example of the kind of results found, we may refer to a study by Kelly and Martin (1969), who reported significant differences between neurotic patients and control groups differing in degree of neuroticism for tonic levels of heart rate, blood pressure and blood flow during an unstressful control period, a result consistent with expectations of high sympathetic activity for high neuroticism subjects who have experienced chronic or reactive anxiety states. No differences in these measures were evident during a stressful mental arithmetic task, a failure presumably due to ceiling effects associated with the obvious agreement of the results with the law of initial value. A review of similar studies employing anxiety–neurotic patients (Lader, 1969) also suggested that patient groups are generally autonomically less reactive than controls and draws attention to the possible limiting of responsiveness due to initially raised pre-stimulus levels in patient groups.

Along similar lines, using normal subjects, Katkin (1975) has observed that under high stress conditions (that of shock) no differences between groups emerged when these are defined in terms of manifest anxiety scores, but that under moderate levels of stress (mild ego-involving threat) subjects with high trait anxiety showed greater increase in number of electrodermal responses than subjects with low trait anxiety scores. Mention of these two different stressors (shock and ego threat) suggests another possibility, discussed by Saltz (1970), namely that pain-induced stress may have quite different and indeed opposite results. Thus, the studies that have been done in this field require to be evaluated with respect to the type of stress imposed; neuroticism according to Saltz, is related to failure-induced stress, but not to pain-induced stress.

V. Brain Mechanisms and Behaviour

Having looked in some brief outline at the experimental support for the general hypotheses of physiological bases for neuroticism and introversion–extraversion, we must next look at the links between these bases and the types of behaviour which originally gave rise to the descriptive concept of extraversion and neuroticism. In the case of neuroticism the relation is a fairly direct one; the items on a questionnaire defining neuroticism are items directly describing strong emotional reactions which persist longer than usual, are easier to evoke than usual, and are stronger than normal. In addition, however, we must bear in mind than in the Hullian system anxiety has the status of a drive, and that Spence, in particular, has been arguing, with the support of a large body of experimental data, that anxiety-neuroticism drive is very important in producing individual differences in learning. Thus, the learning of stimulus–response sequences already having some habit strength would be facilitated by high anxiety, while the learning of stimulus–response sequences having low response probabilities would be made more difficult by high anxiety. A detailed discussion of these hypotheses and the evidence relating to them is given by Eysenck (1973), who on the whole comes to the conclusion that much of the evidence supports Spence's view.

Turning to the relationship between arousal and the social consequences of extraversion–introversion, we have two major links. The first of these has already been mentioned, in connection with the Eysenck and Levey experiment on conditioning. If under most ordinary conditions introverts form conditioned responses more strongly, more easily, and more lastingly than extraverts, then all those behaviour patterns controlled by conditioning contingencies would be expected to show differences in favour of introverts. This would account for the connection between introversion and neurosis (introverts condition the emotional behaviours characteristic of neurosis more readily than do extraverts – Eysenck, 1977a). If we assume, as the author does, that socialized behaviour is acquired through a Pavlovian conditioning process responsible for the creation of a "conscience" (Eysenck, 1977b), then the difficulties that extraverts have in forming strong conditioned responses would be responsible for their more antisocial and even criminal type of behaviour. These suggestions will of course sound much more dogmatic than they are meant to, because of the lack of space to develop the theories in question; readers will have to look at the actual research evidence in order to find the support given there to these hypotheses.

A rather different connection is made in terms of the relationship between level of arousal and hedonic tone (Fig. 6). There is much evidence to show that very low sensory input (sensory deprivation), associated with very low arousal, and very high intensity sensory input (pain), leading to very high levels of arousal, are both unpleasant and produce negative hedonic tone. Preferred levels of sensory stimulation, and of arousal, are intermediate, as

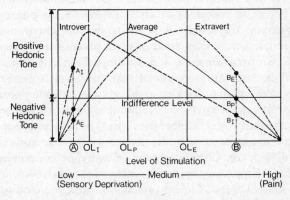

Fig. 6 *Relationship between level of stimulation and hedonic tone, for the general population, introverts and extraverts.*

shown by the central curve in the diagram. When identical conditions of sensory stimulation impinge on organisms differing in their resting level of arousal, then the resulting curve would be displaced to the left (in the case of introverts) or to the right (in the case of extraverts). This would equally displace the optimal level of stimulation (O.L.) from the general population mean in the centre to the left or right respectively. Sensory stimulation at extremes, such as points A and B, would be at the indifference level of hedonic tone for the average person, but would be positive or negative respectively for extraverts and introverts (Eysenck, 1967.)

We would thus postulate that extraverts would seek strong sensory stimulation, whereas introverts would seek to avoid it. This may account, for instance, for the sociability of extraverts; other human beings produce strong arousal in most people and extraverts seek this arousal, while introverts wish to avoid it. There is much evidence along all these lines (Eysenck, 1980) as well as regarding the obvious experimental deductions to be made from Fig. 6, namely that introverts would be more tolerant of sensory deprivation, extraverts of physical pain.

VI. Biological Bases of Psychoticism

There is no more space to delve into the complexities of the situation, which inevitably cannot be discussed in a brief chapter such as this. We must turn finally to a discussion of what is known about the biological bases of our last personality variable, namely psychoticism. A continuum of this kind was postulated originally because much work had shown that psychoses are not *qualitatively* differentiated from normal states, but tend to blend imperceptibly into odd and unusual personalities, and finally into normal human behaviour. Psychiatric research, much of it German, has indicated the existence of a psychotic "Erbkreis", i.e. genetic connections between the different types of functional psychosis, such as schizophrenia and manic depressive illness, and also between these and psychopathy, alcoholism, criminality, drug addiction, and various types of odd and unusual behaviour. These connections were found by looking at the relatives of schizophrenic or manic depressive probands, where it was found that these relatives showed these aberrations in much larger number than would be expected by chance. (Note that the relatives of psychotic probands did not show neurotic behaviour to any greater extent; this is strong support for the hypothesis that psychosis and neurosis are quite separate types of disorder – Eysenck, 1972).

We have several clues as to the direction in which to look for biological correlates of psychoticism. One of these is obviously the fact that psychotics, particularly schizophrenics, are characterized by certain biological features which would be expected to be found in high P scorers. Thus schizophrenics are differentiated from non-schizophrenics by serotonin level, and it has been found that psychoticism is significantly correlated with serotonin metabolites in normal groups (Schalling, personal communication). Similar findings have been made with respect to dopamine metabolites and to MAO (ibid.).

Schizophrenia has also been found to be associated with the human leucocyte antigen (HLA) system (McGuffin, 1979). Some recent unpublished work has shown that, in schizophrenic groups, those with HLA had much higher psychoticism scores than those not having HLA. These lines of evidence strongly support a biological basis of psychoticism.

Another line of research originated from the fact that males tend to have much higher P scores than females. This is in good agreement with the behavioural connotations of high P, it is in good agreement with the fact that criminals tend to be mostly male, and also that psychosis is related to maleness. We would consequently expect sex hormone differences between high and low P scorers, and while the evidence is not conclusive it is certainly suggestive of such a relationship (Eysenck and Eysenck, 1976). Unfortunately, psychoticism scales have only been in existence for a few years, so that not enough is known about the biological foundations of psychoticism to say much more than this; clearly the field is in a very interesting state and much research will no doubt be done in the near future to clarify these issues.

Many other chapters in this book deal with issues relevant to this chapter, particularly the chapters by Gray, Zuckerman, Buchsbaum *et al.*, Strelau, O'Gorman, Blackburn, and Lader. What is beginning to emerge is a model of personality (Eysenck, 1980) which covers a good deal of ground, which is internally consistent and which links experimental psychology, social psychology and physiological psychology through the intermediate concept of personality. By also bringing into the picture genetics, biochemistry, and other biological sciences, this set of theories attempts to put forward a proper biosocial model of man which neglects neither the social nor the biological side of human nature, and tries to integrate both with whatever is known about the psychology of human beings.

VII. Summary

In this chapter, we have looked at some of the evidence linking physiological and hormonal functioning with the major personality dimensions. On the whole, the conclusion seems to be that there is good support for the major hypotheses linking these two areas, but it must also be added that there are many difficulties in the way of finding experimental support for deductions from the theories in question. The existence of curvilinear relations of a prominent kind (Pavlov's law of transmarginal inhibition, the Yerkes-Dodson law, the law of inverse-U relation) is one such example. Others are the law of initial value, the law of ceiling effects, the rules concerning desynchrony of physiological, behavioural and verbal indices of emotion, and many others. Attempts at verification of hypotheses linking personality and psychophysiology must be very careful in taking parameter values into account which can often be derived from knowledge of these laws; when this is not done, the outcome of experiments cannot be predicted, and the results are not clearly related to theory. Research seems to be moving into a better understanding of these general rules of procedure, and it is to be hoped that future work will clarify many of the anomalies which still cloud some of the issues in this field. This qualification does not affect our main conclusion, namely that *no clear understanding of individual differences can be gained without close attention to the role of psychophysiological variables.*

Further Reading

Eysenck, H. J. (ed.), (1981). "A Model for Personality". Springer Verlag, New York.
  A full account of the present position with respect to the various aspects of the writer's personality theory is given in this edited book. This includes a summary chapter on the psychophysiology of personality, and another one on genetics and personality research. An earlier presentation of the model is given in:
Eysenck, H. J. (1967). "A Biological Basis of Personality". C. C. Thomas, Springfield.
Nebylitsyn, V. D. and Gray, J. A. (1972). "Biological Bases of Individual Differences". Academic Press, New York and London.
  Another directly relevant book, which is concerned also with the Pavlov–Teplov–Nebylitsyn system of personality description and its relation to Western systems.
Hobson, J. A. and Brazier, M. A. (eds.), (1980). "The Reticular Formation Revisited". Raven Press, New York.
  This book provides an up-to-date detailed discussion of the reticular formation.
Fulker, D. W. (1981). The genetic and environmental architecture of psychoticism, extraversion and neuroticism. *In* "A Model for Personality" (H. J. Eysenck, ed.). Springer Verlag, New York.
  Fulker discusses in a critical manner the genetics of personality. He also provides an excellent introduction to modern methods of biometrical genetical analysis. For a textbook treatment of these methods, see:
Mather, K. and Jinks, J. L. (1971). "Biometrical Genetics". Chapman and Hall, London.
  The following two books present reprints of important papers in this general area:
Eysenck, H. J. (1976). "The Measurement of Personality". Medical and Technical Publications, Lancaster.
Prentky, R. A. (1979). "The Biological Aspects of Normal Personality". Medical and Technical Publications, Lancaster.
  A general review of extraversion–intraversion is given by Morris in:
Morris, L. W. (1979). "Extraversion and Introversion". Hemisphere, New York.

Eysenck, H. J. and Eysenck, S. B. G. (1969). "Personality Structure and Measurement". Routledge and Kegan Paul, London.
This book provides a thorough discussion of the descriptive basis of the personality system used in this chapter.

References

Allport, G. W. (1937). "Personality: A Psychological Interpretation". Constable, London.

Chamove, A. S., Eysenck, H. J. and Harlow, H. F. (1972). Personality in monkeys: Factor analysis of rhesus social behaviour. *Q. J. Exp. Psychol.* **24**, 496–504.

Eysenck, H. J. (1957). "The Dynamics of Anxiety and Hysteria". Routledge and Kegan Paul, London.

Eysenck, H. J. (1967). "The Biological Basis of Personality". C. C. Thomas, Springfield.

Eysenck, H. J. (1972). An experimental and genetic model of schizophrenia. *In* "Genetic Factors in Schizophrenia" (A. R. Kaplan, ed.), 504–515. C. C. Thomas, Springfield.

Eysenck, H. J. (1973). Personality, learning and anxiety. *In* "Handbook of Abnormal Psychology" (H. J. Eysenck, ed.), 2nd edn. Pitman, London.

Eysenck, H. J. (1977a). "You and Neurosis". Maurice Temple Smith, London.

Eysenck, H. J. (1977b). "Crime and Personality". Routledge and Kegan Paul, London.

Eysenck, H. J. (ed.), (1981). "A Model for Personality". Springer Verlag, New York.

Eysenck, H. J. and Eysenck, S. B. G. (1976). "Psychoticism as a Dimension of Personality". Hodder and Stoughton, London.

Eysenck, H. J. and Eysenck, S. B. G. (1980). Culture and Personality Abnormalities. *In* "Culture and Psychopathology" (I. Al-Issa, ed.). University Park Press, New York.

Eysenck, H. J. and Levey, A. (1972). Conditioning, introversion–extraversion, and the strength of the nervous system. *In* "Biological Bases of Individual Behaviour" (V. O. Nebylitsyn and J. A. Gray, eds). Academic Press, New York and London.

Eysenck, M. W. and Eysenck, H. J. (1980). Mischel and the concept of personality. *Br. J. Psychology* **71**, 191–204.

Frith, C. D. (1977). Habituation of the pupil size and light responses to sound. Paper presented at APA meeting, San Francisco.

Fulker, D. W. (1981). The genetic and environmental architecture of psychoticism, extraversion and neuroticism. *In* "A Model for Personality" (H. J. Eysenck, ed.). Springer Verlag, New York.

Gale, A. (1973). The psychophysiology of individual differences: Studies of extraversion and the EEG. *In* "New Approaches in Psychological Measurement" (P. Kline, ed.), 211–156. Wiley, New York.

Hodgson, R. and Rachman, S. (1974). Desynchrony in measures of fear. *Behav. Res. Therapy* **12**, 319–326.

Holmes, D. G. (1967). Pupillary response, conditioning and personality. *J. Personality Soc. Psychol.* **5**, 98–103.

Katkin, E. S. (1975). Electrodermal lability. *In* "Stress and Anxiety: Vol. 2" (I. G. Sarason and C. D. Spielberger, eds), 141–176. Wiley, New York.

Kelly, D. and Martin, I. (1969). Autonomic reactivity, eyelid conditioning and their relationship to neuroticism and extraversion. *Behav. Res. Therapy* **7**, 233–244.

Lader, M. H. (1969). Psychophysiological aspects of anxiety. *In* "Studies of Anxiety" (M. H. Lader, ed.), 53–61. Headley Brothers, Ashford, Kent.

McGuffin, P. (1979). Is schizophrenia an HLA-associated disease? *Psychol. Med.* **9**, 721–728.

Mischel, W. (1976). "Introduction to Personality". Holt, Rinehart and Winston, New York.

O'Connor, K. (1980). The contingent negative variation and individual differences in smoking behaviour. *Personality Individ. Diff.* **1**, 57–72.

Rachman, S. and Hodgson, R. (1974). Synchrony and desynchrony in fear and avoidance. *Behav. Res. Therapy* **12**, 311–318.

Royce, J. R. (1973). The conceptual framework for a multifactor theory of individuality. *In* "Multivariate Analysis and Psychological Theory" (J. R. Royce, ed.). Academic Press, London and New York.

Saltz, E. (1970). Manifest anxiety: Have we misread the data? *Psychol. Rev.* **77**, 568–573.

Stelmack, R. M. (1981). The psychophysiology of extraversion and neuroticism. *In* "A Model for Personality" (H. J. Eysenck, ed.). Springer Verlag, New York.

Stelmack, R. M. and Mandelzys, N. (1975). Extraversion and pupillary response to affective and taboo words. *Psychophysiology* **12**, 536–540.

Stelmack, R. M., Achorn, E. and Michaud, A. (1977). Extraversion and individual differences in auditory evoked response. *Psychophysiology* **14**, 368–374.

Thayer, R. E. (1970). Activation states as assessed by verbal report and four psychophysiological variables. *Psychophysiology* **7**, 86–94.

Tranel, N. (1961). The effects of perceptual isolation on introverts and extraverts. Unpublished Ph.D. thesis. Washington State University, Washington, D.C.

Wilson, G. (1981). Personality and social behaviour. *In* "A Model for Personality" (H. J. Eysenck, ed.). Springer Verlag, New York.

3 Anxiety, Personality and the Brain

J. A. Gray

Abstract The study of personality is inextricably linked to the study of the general laws of behaviour. Pavlov applied his theory of general laws of behaviour to the task of accounting for differences between the behaviour of individual dogs. Anxiety and susceptibility to anxiety may be seen to reflect nervous system properties common to animals and Man. Drugs which alleviate anxiety in both animals and man may be used to study the mechanisms underlying anxiety, by observing their mode of action within the brain. It is assumed that the neural processes antagonized by these drugs, themselves form the neural bases underlying anxiety. It is postulated that there is a Behavioural Activation System and a Behavioural Inhibition System in the brain and that anti-anxiety drugs act upon the latter to produce their behavioural effects. Anxiety in animals consists of a central state elicited by threats of punishment, frustration or failure, and by novelty and uncertainty. The evidence suggests that anti-anxiety drugs reduce the flow of noradrenergic and serotonergic impulses to the septo-hippocampal system under conditions of stress. A theory of anxiety is described, which maps the functions of the Behavioural Inhibition System onto the septo-hippocampal system and connected structures. This system is thought to act as a comparator, checking predicted against actual events, and to be able to interrupt motor execution programmes. The system also modulates the control of exploratory behaviour. Such a model may be integrated with both animal and human data, particularly from the field of clinical anxiety.

I. Individual Differences

An objection that is sometimes voiced against the biological approach to behaviour is that the existence of differences between individuals makes the development of a lawful science of behaviour impossible. The existence of individual differences is undeniable, but the inference drawn from them is false. It would have some validity only if the individual differences were random (although, even in this case, the objection would not be insurmountable, as the example of modern physics shows). But in fact observed indi-

PHYSIOLOGICAL CORRELATES OF HUMAN
BEHAVIOUR   ISBN 0-12-273901-9

vidual differences are anything but random. On the contrary, they produce reliable patterns which have been described in considerable detail by workers using the technique of factor analysis and allied methods of multivariate statistics (see H. J. Eysenck, this volume). These patterns allow one to predict, from knowledge of how two individuals differ on one or a few items of behaviour, how they will differ across a very wide range of other such items. The existence of such consistent patterns of individual differences itself calls for explanation within the framework of a scientific account of behaviour.

The general structure of such explanations has been agreed (although rarely made explicit) since Pavlov's pioneering work in this field. It supposes that there are general laws that apply to all individuals within a given species; that these laws arise from the general features of the systems that control behaviour in this species; and that differences between individuals within the species are due to different parameters of the functioning of one or other component in these systems. The features of the systems that are common to the species may be taken to define a machine which generates species-specific behaviour, including the ways the species learns; by varying the parameters of operation of components in the machine, we can then produce "machines with personality".

It follows from this analysis that the study of personality is inextricably related to the study of the general laws of behaviour: the two enquiries are opposite sides of the same coin. Nonetheless, it is possible to start from one side or the other. Pavlov, for example, first developed an account – his theory of conditioned reflexes – of the general behaviour and modes of learning of the dog, and then applied this theory to the task of accounting for the differences between individual dogs. More recently, Teplov and Nebylitsyn in Moscow have extended this approach by using Pavlov's theory of general canine behaviour to predict – often with considerable success – individual differences in a variety of aspects of human performance. In contrast to this approach, Western work on the biological basis of individual differences has generally started with a thorough description of the patterns of individual differences (most commonly in terms of factors or dimensions derived from factor analysis) and has then attempted to generate a theory of underlying processes, common to all members of the species, which would account for these patterns. The most notable exponent of this approach is Eysenck.

The approach I shall describe here is in some ways a compromise between those of Pavlov and Eysenck. On the one hand, it takes the factor-analytic description of personality in Man (but modified somewhat from Eysenck's preferred description) as defining the patterns of individual differences that require explanation; but, on the other, it generates this explanation from direct investigations of the behaviour and physiology of animals. Thus, like Pavlov, I assume not only that there is a system common to all men, but also that the general features of this system exist in other mammals. The particular problem to which I have applied this approach concerns the psychology and physiology of anxiety and of the personality correlates of susceptibility to anxiety. In terms of Eysenck's descriptive framework, these correlates are high neuroticism combined with high introversion (low extraversion); see Eysenck, this volume. Individuals with this cluster of personality traits are far more likely than others to complain of conditions which involve anxiety, such as phobias, obsessive-compulsive neurosis, anxiety state and neurotic depression (Marks, 1969).

II. Anxiety

Note, however, that, whereas factor analysis can give a more or less definitive answer to the question, "what is the minimum number, N, of independent factors required to account for a given pattern of individual differences?", it cannot determine where in the resulting N-dimensional space the factors should be located (the problem of rotation). Thus, in our particular case, factor analysis cannot tell us whether Eysenck's particular rotation of factors in the 2-dimensional space he uses to describe individual differences related to susceptibility to anxiety has more biological reality than any other. If his rotation is correct (that is, closest to putative underlying causal processes), it follows that, to explain individual differences in susceptibility to anxiety, we must account for two things: high neuroticism and high introversion. But we may produce a simpler problem by rotating his factors by approximately 45° and thus creating one dimension (trait anxiety) which directly relates to high susceptibility to anxiety, and a second (orthogonal to the first) which is independent of susceptibility to anxiety (Fig. 1). This rotation is neither more nor less arbitrary than Eysenck's (though it has been preferred by a number of American workers in the field of personality, including in various ways Cattell, Guilford and the Spences). Resolution of this issue cannot come from consideration of parsimony alone, but rather from consideration of which (if any) rotation can be allied to a theory which accounts for all or most of the data. Two particular arguments which suggest that the rotation shown in Fig. 1 may have this merit concern physiological treatments of anxiety to which I shall return later. For the moment, we shall simply take the rotation shown in Fig. 1 as a descriptive device defining our problem: what causes high values on the trait of Anxiety?

In keeping with the general strategy outlined above, this question can temporarily be converted into the allied question: what is the nature of the general state of anxiety, common in some degree to all individuals? This question can itself be asked in two ways. First, one may enquire into the

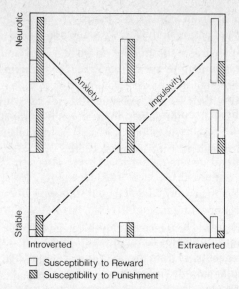

Fig. 1 *Proposed relationships of: (i) susceptibility to signals of reward and susceptibility to signals of punishment; to (ii) the dimensions of introversion–extraversion and neuroticism. The dimensions of anxiety and impulsivity (diagonals) represent the steepest rate of increase in susceptibility to signals of punishment and reward, respectively.*

psychological nature of anxiety. This is tantamount to asking for a black-box description – what Hebb called a "conceptual nervous system" – of the features of a machine which can generate anxious behaviour. Second, one may enquire into the physiological basis of anxiety. Since we know that the systems which control behaviour are largely in the brain (although important roles are also played by the endocrine system and other peripheral physiological mechanisms), this is tantamount to asking about the brain mechanisms that generate anxious behaviour. The two types of enquiry – into the conceptual and the real nervous systems – are closely related, and neither can afford to ignore advances made by the other. Note that, once one begins to ask about brain mechanisms, experiments with animals are virtually indispensable. This in turn requires that one identify "anxious behaviour" in animals – no easy feat.

A vital aid in resolving this problem and allowing one to investigate both the psychology and the physiology of anxiety in animals is the existence of drugs which alleviate anxiety in Man. Provided one can show that the behavioural effects of these drugs are consistent with the hypothesis that they alleviate anxiety in animals as well, one can use them as tools which have every probability of acting in essentially the same ways when used clinically in

Man or experimentally in animals. Furthermore, one can then proceed to ask about their mode of action in the brain, on the assumption that the neuronal processes which they reverse when altering behaviour in the direction of reduced anxiety would have constituted (had they proceeded unchecked) the neural basis of anxiety.

It is fashionable to treat the anti-anxiety drugs as though they consist exclusively of the benzodiazepines, such as Valium (diazepam) or Librium (chlordiazepoxide). It should be noted however that, before these drugs were introduced in the early 1960s for the treatment of anxiety, the barbiturates (e.g. sodium amytal or amylobarbitone) were often used for this purpose; and, before any of these drugs were introduced into medical practice, a very effective reduction in anxiety could be (and still is) produced by alcohol in its many guises. It is important that anxiety can be treated by these very different families of chemicals. This fact allows one, as it were, to "triangulate" the critical behaviour and neural changes which constitute anti-anxiety action, and thus to segregate these from the additional "side effects" produced by the different particular anti-anxiety drugs. Thus, in what follows, statements about the anti-anxiety drugs, unless qualified, may be taken to apply to all members of this group, not just to the benzodiazepines.

I have reviewed the behavioural effects of the anti-anxiety drugs elsewhere (Gray, 1977). Many hundreds of studies have been conducted, in species ranging from goldfish to chimpanzee. A major conclusion which emerges is that there is rarely any need to qualify a description of the behavioural effects of the anti-anxiety drugs with respect to species: insofar as the data allow one to judge, they produce essentially the same effects in all species studied. This conclusion is supported by biochemical research, which has demonstrated that the same receptor that binds the benzodiazepines in mammals, including Man, is also present in fish. Thus, assuming that the behavioural changes produced in animals by the anti-anxiety drugs are indeed due to a reduction in anxiety, we may conclude that anxiety and its neural basis are phylogenetically relatively old.

However, the assumption that the anti-anxiety drugs reduce anxiety in animals, or that it is even meaningful to talk in this way, cannot be made lightly or without justification. Support for this assumption comes from consideration of the nature of the changes that the anti-anxiety drugs in fact produce in animal behaviour. Although very diverse experimental paradigms have been used to describe these changes both within and between species, it turns out to be fairly simple to summarize them in an economical formula, as outlined below.

The anti-anxiety drugs counteract the behavioural effects of three classes of stimuli: stimuli associated with punishment, stimuli associated with the omission of expected reward ("frustrative non-reward"), and novel stimuli.

Furthermore, they counteract all the major kinds of behavioural change produced by these stimuli: i.e. inhibition of ongoing behaviour (and especially instrumental, that is, reinforced, behaviour); increased attention to environmental (and especially novel) stimuli; and an increased level of arousal (Gray, 1977). Finally, they do *not* affect behaviour elicited by other classes of reinforcing stimuli, including primary punishment and primary frustrative non-reward. These findings are summarized in Fig. 2. This postulates that there is a behavioural inhibition system (BIS) upon which the anti-anxiety drugs act to produce their behavioural effects. The BIS is activated by the adequate inputs listed to the left of the figure and produces the outputs listed to the right. Thus, activity in the BIS constitutes anxiety. On this view, and in less technical language, anxiety in animals consists of a central state elicited by threats of punishment, frustration or failure, and by novelty or uncertainty. This formulation is clearly plausible also as a description of anxiety in Man, thus giving us grounds for supposing that anxiety exists in animals and in a form closely comparable to that taken by the human emotion.

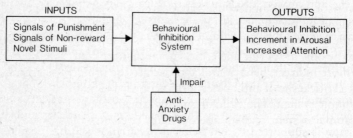

Fig. 2 *The behavioural inhibition system.*

III. The Brain and Anxiety

The evidence above suggests that it is possible to study the physiological basis of anxiety in experimental animals. It suggests also that a way to tackle this problem is to investigate the manner in which the anti-anxiety drugs exert their effects. There are two main ways in which this has been done. The first concentrates on the drug as drug: it asks, for example, how the drug affects neurones, where it is distributed in the brain, whether it acts on specific receptors, and so on. The second is, from a pharmacological point of view, more indirect: it concentrates on the behavioural effects of the drug, and attempts to find other manipulations of the brain which produce similar effects. The two approaches are complementary, as each alone suffers from inevitable limitations.

Important advances in the direct study of anti-anxiety drug action have come from the demonstration of a specific, high-affinity receptor for the benzodiazepines located on neural mechanisms in the brain (Braestrup and Nielsen, 1980), and the establishment of a probable relation between this receptor and the effectiveness of action of the inhibitory neuro-transmitter, γ-aminobutyric acid (GABA). It is clear, however, that occupancy of the benzodiazepine receptor is not an essential prerequisite of anti-anxiety drug action, since the barbiturates and alcohol have essentially the same behavioural effects as the benzodiazepines yet do not bind to this receptor. A better case can be made for the view that an essential step in anti-anxiety drug action is facilitation of GABA-ergic transmission, since this is produced by the barbiturates as well as the benzodiazepines. This view faces difficulties, however, in the universal role played by GABA as an inhibitory transmitter throughout the brain (and the similarly ubiquitous distribution of benzodiazepine receptors); this suggests that facilitated GABA-ergic trans-mission might have general sedative or anti-convulsant effects on behaviour (as is indeed produced by both benzodiazepines and barbiturates, especially at high doses) rather than the highly specific behavioural profile that is characteristic of anti-anxiety drug action at low doses. Thus, if anti-anxiety action depends on facilitated GABA-ergic transmission, a proposition for which the psychopharmacological evidence is in any case equivocal, this is likely to be only at specific and critical points in the brain.

The more indirect, behavioural approach to the problem suggests that, if there is a critical site of anti-anxiety drug action in the brain, this is likely to lie in the limbic system. The structures most strongly implicated are the septo-hippocampal system and its afferents and efferents (Elliott and Whelan, 1978; Gray, 1982). As shown in detail by Gray (1982), there is a substantial overlap between the profile of behavioural change observed after septal and hippocampal lesions, on the one hand, and administration of anti-anxiety drugs on the other. This pattern of results has given rise to the hypothesis (Gray, 1970a, 1982) that the anti-anxiety drugs act on the septo-hippocampal system to produce *those changes which are critical for their anti-anxiety effects* (as distinct, say, from the sedative or anti-convulsant effects that they may also produce).

One way to test this hypothesis is to look at the effects of the anti-anxiety drugs in animals which have sustained lesions to part of the septo-hippocampal system. If this system mediates the behavioural effects of the drugs, they should be attenuated or altered. Experiments of this kind have not provided convincing support for the hypothesis. An alternative possibility is that the anti-anxiety drugs act on critical afferents to the septo-hippocampal system. There is evidence to support this possibility with respect to two pathways: the noradrenergic afferents to the septo-hippocampal system from the locus coeruleus, and the serotonergic afferents from the raphe nuclei.

Activity is increased in both of these pathways by stress and this increase is counteracted by anti-anxiety drugs, although the latter effect is clearer for noradrenergic than for serotonergic fibres. Furthermore, destruction of either pathway, most often produced by local injection of a specific neurotoxin (6-hydroxydopamine in the case of the ascending noradrenergic pathway, 5, 6- or 5, 7-dihydroxytryptamine in the case of serotonergic fibres), gives rise to certain critical behavioural changes also seen after injection of anti-anxiety drugs. Thus, for example, destruction of the dorsal ascending noradrenergic bundle, which innervates the septo-hippocampal system, causes increased resistance to extinction, while impairment of central serotonergic transmission increases resistance to punishment. In addition, destruction of the dorsal ascending noradrenergic bundle produces a pattern of electrophysiological change in the septo-hippocampal system that is characteristic of anti-anxiety drug action. It is possible, therefore, that the critical action of the anti-anxiety drugs that underlies their anti-anxiety behavioural effects consists in a reduction in the flow of noradrenergic and serotonergic impulses to the septo-hippocampal system under conditions of stress. This hypothesis is not in conflict with the biochemical and neurophysiological evidence indicating that these drugs enhance GABA-ergic transmission, since such enhancement might inhibit the firing of cells in the locus coeruleus and/or the raphe nuclei, both of which probably receive GABA-ergic afferents.

If we accept this hypothesis, it is possible to gain further insight into the nature of anxiety by asking what functions are performed by the septo-hippocampal system and its noradrenergic and serotonergic afferents. This is an active and controversial area of research. There is general agreement that the septo-hippocampal system acts in some way as a comparator (Elliott and Whelan, 1978), but the particular tasks to which this function is applied remain a matter of considerable dispute. I have recently reviewed the evidence which concerns these issues, and have attempted to wed the notion that the septo-hippocampal system functions as a comparator, to the hypothesis that it forms a critical node in the neural substrate of anxiety (Gray, 1982). I give here a brief outline of the ensuing theory; but the reader should note that it has not yet had the opportunity to face critical analysis from other workers in the field.

IV. A Theory of Anxiety

The theory maps the functions of the BIS, as outlined in Fig. 2, onto the septo-hippocampal system and connected structures; but at the same time it proposes specific ways in which these brain regions act so as to respond appropriately to the adequate stimuli for anxiety (i.e. the inputs listed to the left of Fig. 2). As well as the septal area and hippocampus themselves, the theory allots functions to the ascending noradrenergic and serotonergic afferents to these regions: to the Papez circuits, i.e. the outflow from the subicular area (itself in receipt of afferents from area CA 1 of the hippocampus), to the mamillary bodies in the hypothalamus, to the anterior thalamus, to the cingulate cortex and back to the subicular area; to the neocortical input to the hippocampus from the entorhinal area of the temporal lobe; to the prefrontal cortex, which projects to the entorhinal area and cingulate cortex; and to the particular pathways by which these structures are interrelated. The central task of this overall system is to compare, quite generally, actual with expected stimuli. The system functions in two modes. If actual stimuli are successfully matched with expected stimuli, it functions in "checking" mode, and behavioural control remains with other (unspecified) brain systems. If there is discordance between actual and expected stimuli or if the predicted stimulus is aversive (conditions jointly termed "mismatch"), it takes direct control over behaviour, now functioning in "control" mode.

In control mode, the outputs of the BIS (Fig. 2) are operated. First, there is an immediate inhibition of any motor programme which is in the course of execution. This inhibition is not envisaged as taking place at the level of individual motor commands, but rather as an interruption in the function of higher-level systems concerned with the planning and overall execution of motor programmes.

Second, the motor programme which was in the course of execution at the time that "mismatch" was detected is tagged with an indication which, in English, might read "faulty, needs checking". This has two further consequences.

(i) On future occasions the relevant programme is executed with greater restraint (more slowly, more easily interrupted by hesitations for exploratory behaviour, more readily abandoned in favour of other programmes, etc.).

(ii) The tagged motor programme is given especially careful attention the next time it occurs. That is to say, the system exercises particularly carefully its basic function of checking predicted against actual events. It is supposed that in performing this function the system is able to subject each stimulus in the environment to an analysis that ranges over many dimensions (e.g. brightness, hue, position, size, relation to other stimuli, etc.). The dependencies between the subject's responses and behavioural outcomes can similarly be subjected to multi-dimensional analysis (e.g. a turn in a rat's T-maze can be classified as left-going or white-approaching).

Third, the system initiates specific exploratory and investigative behaviour designed to answer particular questions that arise from the operation of the comparator (e.g. is it left-going or white-approaching which gives rise to mismatch?). Like the inhibition of ongoing motor programmes, it is not supposed that this function is exercised directly at the point of motor output, but rather that the system modulates the control of exploratory behaviour carried out by other brain systems. Among the environmental stimuli for which the system commands a special search in this way, an important class is constituted by those which themselves predict disruption of the subject's plans, i.e. stimuli which are associated with punishment, non-reward or failure.

These, then, are the major consequences of mismatch; and, given that the BIS is most active under these conditions, this is the time at which anxiety will be greatest. But the system is also continuously active at times when there is agreement between predicted and actual events; if it were not, mismatch would go undetected. Furthermore, it is supposed that the system is able to identify certain stimuli as being particularly "important" and requiring especially careful checking. In this connection the role played by the ascending noradrenergic and serotonergic inputs to the hippocampus is of particular importance. Physiological experiments have shown that impulses coming from the entorhinal cortex to the hippocampus and thence to the subicular area must pass through a "gate" in the dentate gyrus and area CA 3 of the hippocampus proper. With stimulus repetition such impulses either habituate quickly or become consolidated and enhanced. It seems, furthermore, that impulses are more likely to pass the dentate/CA 3 gate if they are associated with events of biological importance to the animal, such as those associated with the delivery of food or footshock. There is also evidence that the passage of impulses in the hippocampal formation is facilitated by the simultaneous occurrence of noradrenergic or serotonergic inputs to the hippocampus. The action of noradrenergic afferents in particular can apparently be characterized as increasing the signal-to-noise ratio of hippocampal neurones, allowing them to respond more effectively to sensory information (of neocortical origin) entering the system from the entorhinal cortex. In accordance with these data, the author's theory of anxiety attributes to the noradrenergic and serotonergic afferents to the septo-hippocampal system the role of labelling such sensory information as "important, needs checking", as outlined above.

Applied to human clinical syndromes, this theory of anxiety can explain most naturally the symptoms of obsessive–compulsive neurosis (Rachman and Hodgson, 1979), especially those that involve excessive checking of potential environmental hazards. In this respect it contrasts with earlier theories of anxiety based on animal experiments, which have usually found their most natural application to phobic symptoms. However, phobic symptoms can also be readily understood within the present theory, which attributes them to the inhibition of motor programmes, as described above.

Pharmacotherapy of anxiety is seen as depending essentially on a reduction in the intensity of noradrenergic and serotonergic signals reaching the septo-hippocampal system; this, given the theory outlined above, would tend to diminish the subject's tendency to check the environment for threat. The effectiveness of behaviour therapy in cases of anxiety is seen as depending on manipulations of schedules of presentation of phobic stimuli which maximize the rate of habituation (Watts, 1979); the critical site of habituation, according to the theory, lies in the hippocampal formation (Vinogradova, 1975).

In Man, a particularly important role in anxiety is apparently played by the prefrontal and cingulate regions of the neocortex. Destruction of each of these areas has been used successfully in the treatment of anxiety (Powell, 1979). Within the present theory the role of these regions is twofold. First, they supply to the septo-hippocampal system information about the subject's own ongoing motor programmes; this information is essential if the septo-hippocampal system (together with the Papez circuit) is to generate adequate predictions of the next expected event to match against actual events. Second, they afford a route by which language systems in the neocortex can control the activities of the limbic structures which are the chief neural substrate of anxiety. In turn, these structures, via subicular and hippocampal projections to the entorhinal cortex, are able to scan verbally coded stores of information when performing the functions allotted to them in the theory outlined above. In this way, it is possible for human anxiety to be triggered by largely verbal stimuli (relatively independently of ascending monoaminergic influences), and to utilize in the main verbally coded search strategies to cope with perceived threats. It is for this reason, if the theory is correct, that lesions to the prefrontal and cingulate cortices are effective in cases of anxiety which are resistant to drug therapy (Powell, 1979).

V. The Anxious Personality

In principle the extension of this theory to the personality correlates of anxiety is simple: it proposes merely that, the greater the reactivity of the behavioural inhibition system as described above, the more susceptible is the individual to anxiety (Gray, 1970b). This assumption underlies the model shown in Fig. 1. Note that the rotation of Eysenck's axes indicated in this figure is better able to handle two key features of the data reviewed above. The anti-anxiety drugs and lesions to the prefrontal and cingulate cortex reduce anxiety. In terms of Eysenck's theory, and empirically, this means that they reduce scores on both his personality dimensions, neuroticism and introversion. It is possible of course that these changes reflect, as his theory must hold, two independent effects on underlying causal processes. But it is more likely that the drugs and lesions affect only one causal process related to anxiety, but that this is then imperfectly refracted into two changes (reduced neuroticism and reduced introversion) because of an imperfect alignment between Eysenck's preferred location of the dimensions of personality and the underlying biological reality.

Although the application of the writer's theory of anxiety to the personality correlates of anxiety is in principle simple, in practice much remains to be done to spell out and test the predictions made by such an extension. That the endeavour may well be worth while is indicated by the available data relating to one particular prediction where the present theory and Eysenck's part company. This concerns the relative ease with which introverts and extraverts form conditioned responses. It is a critical postulate of Eysenck's theory that introverts condition better than extraverts irrespective of the nature of the reinforcement (Gray, 1970b). In contrast, the model shown in Fig. 1 predicts that introverts will condition better than extraverts when aversive unconditioned stimuli are used, but that extraverts will condition better than introverts when appetitive stimuli are used. The available data support the present theory on this point (Gray, 1981). However, much remains to be done before the present theory can be regarded as a serious alternative to Eysenck's in the field of personality.

In a book devoted to the physiological correlates of human behaviour, one final comment is worth making. Fowles (1980) has recently reviewed evidence which suggests that, in Man, the level of skin conductance is closely related to the operation of the behavioural inhibition system. This is consistent with the known effects of the anti-anxiety drugs and of lesions to the septal area on this measure of autonomic reactivity. Unfortunately, however, there is a dearth of data on the factors that affect skin conductance in animals. Investigations of this problem are urgently needed if we are to increase the confidence with which we can make extrapolations from animals to Man. As the reader has seen, the validity of the arguments pursued in this chapter is critically dependent on our ability to make such extrapolations.

Further Reading

Gray, J. A. (1979). "Pavlov". Fontana Paperbacks, London.
    An introduction to the master's work both on conditioned reflexes and the biological basis of personality.
Nebylitsyn, V. D. (1972) "Fundamental Properties of the Human Nervous System". Plenum, New York.
    An application of Pavlovian theory to human personality.
Eysenck, H. J.(1967). "The Biological Basis of Personality". C. C. Thomas, Springfield.
    The best statement of Eysenck's theory of introversion–extraversion.

Eysenck, H. J. (ed.), (1981). "A Model for Personality". Springer-Verlag, New York.
A recent consideration and critique of Eysenck's theory of introversion–
extraversion.
Gray, J. A. (1982). "The Neuropsychology of Anxiety: An Enquiry into the Functions
of the Septo-Hippocampal System". Oxford University Press, Oxford.
A thorough statement of the physiological background to my own theory. There is a
précis of this book in *Brain and Behavioural Sciences* (1982) **5**, 469–534, along
with multiple reviews and commentaries.
Marks, I. M. (1969). "Fears and Phobias". Heinemann, London.
A good review of the clinical phenomena that require explanation.
Rachman, S. and Hodgson, R. (1979). "Obsessions and Compulsions". Prentice-Hall,
New York.
A good review of the most intriguing of the anxiety-related syndromes.

References

Braestrup, C. and Nielsen, M. (1980). Benzodiazepine receptors. *Arzneimitt-elforschung* **30**, 852–857.
Elliott, K. and Whelan, J. (eds), (1978). "Functions of the Septo-Hippocampal
System". CIBA Foundation Symposium No. 58 (new series). Elsevier, Amsterdam.
Fowles, D. (1980). The three arousal model: implications of Gray's two-factor learn-
ing theory for heart rate, electrodermal activity and psychopathy. *Psycho-physiology* **17**, 87–104.
Gray, J. A. (1970a). Sodium amobarbital, the hippocampal theta rhythm and the
partial reinforcement extinction effect. *Psychol. Rev.* **77**, 465–480.
Gray, J. A. (1970b). The psychophysiological basis of introversion–extraversion.
Behav. Res. Therapy **8**, 249–266.
Gray, J. A. (1977). Drug effects on fear and frustration: possible limbic site of action of
minor tranquilizers. *In* "Handbook of Psychopharmacology" (Iversen, L. L.,
Iversen, S. D. and Snyder, S. H., eds), Vol. 8, pp. 433–529. Plenum, New York.
Gray, J. A. (1981). A critique of Eysenck's theory of personality. *In* "A Model for
Personality" (Eysenck, H. J., ed.). Springer-Verlag, New York.
Gray, J. A. (1982). "The Neuropsychology of Anxiety: An Enquiry into the Functions
of the Septo-Hippocampal System". Oxford University Press, Oxford.
Marks, I. M. (1969). "Fears and Phobias" Heinemann, London.
Powell, G. E. (1979). "Brain and Personality". Saxon House, London.
Rachman, S. and Hodgson, R. (1979). "Obsessions and Compulsions". Prentice-Hall,
New York.
Vinogradova, O. S. (1975). Functional organization of the limbic system in the process
of registration of information: facts and hypotheses. *In* "The Hippocampus: Vol. 2
– *Neurophysiology and Behaviour*" (Isaacson, R. L. and Pribram, K. H., eds),
pp. 3–69. Plenum, New York.
Watts, F. N. (1979). Habituation model of systematic desensitization. *Psychol. Bull.*
86, 627–637.

4 Habituation and Personality

J. G. O'Gorman

Abstract Measures of individual differences in habituation of physiological responses have been employed in personality research in two ways. The first assumes that the measure of habituation provides an index of psychophysiological functioning relevant to the efficiency of performance in attentional tasks. The second attempts to account for individual differences in habituation in terms of subject characteristics, such as temperament traits and social-cognitive factors. Studies adopting each of these approaches are reviewed and the conclusion reached is that, while both are necessary, results from the first of these have to date proved more promising.

I. Introduction

Habituation, broadly defined, is the decrement in response that occurs when a stimulus is repeatedly presented. The phenomenon is readily demonstrated by presenting a simple sensory stimulus (e.g. 2 s of a 1 kHz tone at 70 dBA) two to three times a minute while recording electrodermal activity. When data from a number of subjects studied in this way are pooled, response magnitude is observed to decline over trials to an asymptote, with the greatest decrement occurring early in the stimulus series. A plot of magnitude against the logarithm of stimulus number yields a linear function, the slope of which can be used to estimate the rate of habituation (Lader and Wing, 1966). Alternatively speed of habituation can be estimated from the number of trials required to reach asymptote, which is commonly defined as two or three consecutive response failures. Once habituated the response can be reinstated by varying the parameters of the stimulus (e.g. decreasing its intensity), an effect which is taken to imply that the process underlying habituation is separable from other decremental processes, such as fatigue of the effector system.

A good deal is known about the stimulus factors which influence habituation and reinstatement of a number of physiological responses. For example, intensity of the stimulus and its frequency of presentation are major

PHYSIOLOGICAL CORRELATES OF HUMAN
BEHAVIOUR   ISBN 0-12-273901-9

determinants of the rate and speed of habituation. The exact functions depend on which of these measures are used and on the response system studied (see Graham, 1973). All responses do not habituate at the same rate or speed (e.g. Dykman, *et al.*, 1959; Koriat, *et al.*, 1973), and for some responses (vascoconstriction in the finger, EEG abundance) there is doubt about the existence of an habituation effect (Furedy, 1971; Gale, 1973). Habituation is also influenced by instructions to the subject, with suggestions of threat or requirements to respond to the stimulus in some way reducing the rate or speed of habituation (see O'Gorman, 1977).

Knowledge of the stimulus determinants of habituation has been used to develop a number of theories of the processes underlying it. Sokolov (1969), for example, proposed that habituation is a function of cortical inhibition of sub-cortical arousal, controlled by a system which analyses the novelty of stimulus events. More recently, Maltzman (e.g. 1979) and Bernstein (e.g. 1979) have argued that habituation depends on the subject's evaluation of the significance of the stimulus. These theories, in stressing the high-level processing of the stimulus during habituation, attribute considerable importance to what might first appear a simple phenomenon.

Given the relative ease with which habituation can be demonstrated, the amount known about it, and its presumed theoretical importance, it is perhaps not surprising that personality researchers have shown a good deal of interest in the differences in rate and speed of habituation which individuals exhibit. Two major questions have guided this research interest. Do individual differences in habituation of physiological responses provide useful information about individual human behaviour? What personality factors account for variation in speed and rate of habituation? The purpose of the present chapter is to review the evidence and issues which attempts to answer these questions have raised.

The two questions dictate the use of somewhat different research strategies. Identification of individual differences in speed or rate of habituation as an index of personality leads to the use of these measures as quasi-independent variables. That is, subjects are selected who show rapid or slow rates of habituation. Physiological, behavioural or psychometric differences between these subject groups are then studied. Since speed or rate of habituation is a characteristic of the subject and as such cannot be manipulated in the sense that a stimulus property can, it is better described as a quasi- than a true independent variable. The distinction is of some significance because subjects selected in terms of differences in habituation may differ in a number of other respects and these differences rather than the characteristics of slow or rapid habituation may be responsible for any observed variation in the dependent variable.

The question of which personality factors account for individual differences in habituation casts measures of speed and rate of habituation in the role of dependent variables to be studied in relation to predetermined characteristics of subject samples, such as sex differences, status on a personality trait, or cognitive styles, which are the quasi-independent variables in this research design. Although both research strategies are essentially correlational in nature, the different questions addressed recommend that studies relevant to each be reviewed separately.

II. Habituation as an Index of Personality

Drawing on the results of a number of earlier studies, Crider and Lunn (1971) proposed that speed of habituation of electrodermal responsiveness to simple auditory stimuli was an index of an important dimension of individual differences which, following Mundy-Castle and McKiever (1953), they termed electrodermal lability. In support of this hypothesis, they reported that: (i) speed of habituation of the skin potential response (SPL) and the frequency of non-stimulus evoked or non-specific responses (NSRs) in this system were reasonably stable characteristics of subjects when tested in sessions spaced a week apart; (ii) both indices intercorrelated within the limit set by their respective stability coefficients; and (iii) both in turn correlated with scores on a psychometric measure of extraversion, and particularly with the impulsivity component of that dimension.

A year later, Nebylitsyn's work on "properties of the nervous system" was published in English translation, one chapter of which was devoted to reviewing the work of Soviet researchers on individual differences in habituation of electrodermal, EEG and vasomotor responses. On the basis of his review, Nebylitsyn proposed that speed of habituation was a referent index of the property (dimension) of nervous system functioning termed dynamism of inhibition, i.e. the speed of generation of inhibitory processes (see Chapter 9 by Strelau). Two implications followed directly from this hypothesis: (i) speed of habituation should predict individual differences in performance on tasks which involve the generation of inhibitory potentials; and (ii) speed of habituation should be unrelated to referent indices of properties hypothesized to be independent of dynamism of inhibition, notably speed of acquisition of CRs (or "conditionability"), which reflects dynamism of excitation, and lower sensory thresholds (or "arousability"), which reflect strength-sensitivity.

Both the hypotheses of Nebylitsyn and Crider & Lunn provide a rationale and an empirical basis for the study of habituation measures as indices of personality, but raise a number of issues, few of which can be satisfactorily resolved on the evidence available to date. The first and perhaps most basic issue has to do with the measurement of individual differences in habituation and involves the stability and consistency of rate and speed measures as characteristics of individuals. Several studies (e.g. Bull and Gale, 1973; Siddle and Heron, 1976) support the hypothesis of Crider and Lunn (1971) that speed and rate of habituation of electrodermal responses are relatively stable measures over intervals of at least three months. An important exception to this generalization, however, is the report of Koriat *et al.* (1973), which indicates stability coefficients as low as $0 \cdot 19$ for a one-day interval, though there are certain features of their study which might account for this atypical finding (see O'Gorman, 1977).

With this one qualification, there is considerable evidence of stability of habituation measures, at least for the electrodermal system, but the question of the consistency of these measures over variations in stimulus conditions has yet to be explored systematically. The only substantial evidence reported to date on this point argues against consistency. Stelmack *et al.* (1979) found that speed of habituation of SCR, HR and vasomotor responses to visual stimuli correlated poorly across variations in hue and emotional significance of the stimuli. Whether consistency is more pronounced when simple auditory stimuli of the sort employed by Crider and Lunn (1971) are varied in intensity, pitch, and temporal characteristics has yet to be determined. The question of consistency is important since, if estimates of individual differences in habituation vary with the stimulus conditions imposed in their determination, there is a clear need to standardize these conditions so as to permit cross-laboratory comparisons of results.

The second issue concerns the construct validity of measures of habituation, i.e. the extent to which different measures of habituation intercorrelate and in turn are separable from other measures of general reactivity and change within any particular response system. Unless at least some measures of habituation can be shown to correlate highly and not to be redundant with simpler measures of responsiveness such as mean magnitude of response to a stimulus series, the claim that a unique characteristic of the subject is being assessed by measures of habituation is without foundation. The evidence bearing on this issue is mixed.

Measures of speed and rate of habituation of SCR have been found to relate highly when the latter is determined by the method made popular by Lader and Wing (1966), and both in turn relate to frequency of NSRs (e.g. Siddle and Heron, 1976). Whether this pattern of covariation of habituation speed, rate, and NSR frequency reflects the operation of the one underlying process as Crider and Lunn (1971) proposed or the operation of separate though interacting processes as others (e.g. Munday-Castle and McKiever, 1953; Lader and Wing, 1966) have argued is yet unclear. Under some circumstances, the commonly observed correlation between habituation and NSR frequency has not been found (e.g. Geer, 1966; Katkin and McCubbin, 1969), and further study of the conditions under which such a dissociation occurs would seem warranted.

Even less clear is the extent to which measures of habituation are redundant with other measures of responsiveness. Crider and Lunn's (1971) summary of the evidence pointed to dissociation of speed of habituation from resting level and possibly amplitude measures of electrodermal activity. Bull and Gale (1973), however, reported moderate to high correlations among a number of features of skin conductance activity, a result consistent with Bundy and Mangan's (1979) view on the physiology of the effector system responsible for this activity. Martin and Rust (1976) attempted to resolve the issue by factor analysing a number of measures of skin conductance obtained for two independent samples of subjects. These authors interpreted their results as support for a general dimension of reactivity common to all measures of skin conductance, but interestingly, in the larger and possibly more representative of their samples, two reasonably clear factors emerged, one of which would have some claim to being identified as the electrodermal lability factor proposed by Crider and Lunn. The first factor loaded SCR magnitude and mean SCL, whereas the second loaded rate of habituation of SCR and rate of decline of SCL. The two factors correlated less than $0 \cdot 1$, and it was the second factor that accounted for more of the variance in NSR frequency and the total number of stimulus-evoked responses during the habituation series, a close correlate of speed of habituation. Replication of this factor pattern is necessary, however, before concluding that speed and rate of habituation reflect an aspect of functioning independent of general reactivity of the system.

Relationships between measures of habituation and change in responsiveness resulting from stimulus manipulations such as those employed in conditioning have been the subject of several investigations. It will be recalled that Nebylitsyn's (1972) hypothesis proposed that speed of habituation and speed of CR acquisition are independent. It does, however, predict a relationship between speed of habituation and speed of formation of a conditioned discrimination and speed of CR extinction, since these are both considered to reflect dynamism of inhibition. Some support for Nebylitsyn's hypothesis comes from a study of discriminative conditioning reported by Öhman and Bohlin (1973), which compared the performance of subjects differing in speed of SCR habituation and in initial amplitude of SCR. Habituation speed, but not initial amplitude, was found to predict extinction, but not acquisition, of SCRs to the CS and in the pre-UCS interval. Although Öhman and Bohlin's study is but one of a number of studies which need to be considered in a full appreciation of this issue, and one which has not gone unchallenged (Solanto and Katkin, 1979), it serves well to demonstrate the strategy of investigating differential relationships among measures of reactivity, habituation and indices of change.

The third issue concerns the predictive validity of measures of habituation against criteria of individual differences in behaviour of some social significance. If measures of habituation interrelate only among themselves and with one or two other measures of physiological responsiveness, their value for personality research is limited. Both the hypotheses of Crider and Lunn (1971), and Nebylitsyn (1972) imply, however, that relationships between speed of habituation and more molar aspects of personality functioning should be found. The data relevant to trait correlates of habituation are discussed below, but without pre-empting that discussion it should be noted here that results to date have not been encouraging. One possible explanation is that, as Nebylitsyn (1972) argued, indexes of nervous system properties, such as speed of habituation, may be more useful in predicting the operating efficiency of individuals under conditions of task demand ("operative reliability" in Nebylitsyn's terms) rather than the typical behaviour of individuals as summarized by psychometric measures of temperament.

If Nebylitsyn is correct in this surmise, the best place to look for evidence of predictive validity is at the behavioural level and, in fact, at this level a number of interesting relationships with speed of SCR habituation have been reported. Subjects habituating rapidly have been found to show greater resistance to distraction (Siddle and Mangan, 1971), greater decrement in a vigilance task (Coles and Gale, 1971; Crider and Augenbraun, 1975; Hastrup, 1979; Sostek, 1978; Siddle, 1972), more omission errors in a discriminative reaction time task (Voicu and Olteanu, 1972; Voronin, et al., 1959), earlier onset of sleep with monotonous stimulation (Bohlin, 1973; Voronin et al., 1959), and greater response to systematic desensitization (Lader et al., 1967). If Crider and Lunn's hypothesis of the interchangeability of speed of habituation and frequency of NSRs as indexes of electrodermal lability were accepted, this list of relationships would be lengthened by including the results of studies that have used the NSR frequency index. Notably, a relationship with effectiveness of biofeedback training for producing HR change reported by Katkin and Shapiro (1979) would be added to the list. Although these relationships have not always been replicated (see, for example, Klorman's 1974 failure to replicate the relationship with response to systematic desensitization), the network of covariation in which measures of habituation have been located to date is impressive.

While it is no doubt of interest to widen this network in future studies by including other behavioural tasks, a more urgent requirement is the more precise definition of the limits of this covariation. If the pattern of relationships with measures of habituation becomes too diffuse, it will be difficult to attach any specific meaning to these measures. It is necessary therefore that speed and rate of habituation be shown to predict some but not other aspects of individual performance, so as to sharpen the theoretical interpretation of these measures.

The problem is illustrated by the differing interpretations placed on the relationship between speed of habituation and vigilance decrement by Crider (1979) and Katkin (1975). Crider interprets the relationship as a consequence of individual differences in the arousal level of subjects, whereas Katkin maintains that it is differences in perceptual sensitivity that are involved. Both claim support for their interpretations in the differential relationships between speed of habituation and estimates of sensitivity and criterion setting, derived using the methodology of signal detection theory from performance measures during the vigil. The use of this methodology with other paradigms devised by experimental psychologists to study attentional processes (e.g. discriminative reaction time, dichotic listening) may serve in future studies to clarify the basis of relationships between individual differences in habituation and individual differences in operating efficiency. The encouragement for such a programmatic attack on the problem is certainly available in the results obtained to date.

III. Personality Correlates of Habituation

Studies that have cast the habituation measure in the role of dependent variable have been approached from one of two theoretical perspectives. The first of these involves the assumption that variation in measures of habituation can be accounted for in terms of biologically-based temperament factors, such as extraversion and emotionality, which influence responsiveness to the environment by virtue of their relationship to central arousal level. From the other perspective, individual differences in habituation are viewed as a function of the subject's perceptual-cognitive activity in relation to the stimulus, which depends on habits of responding to or stylistic differences in processing environmental events. Studies from each of these perspectives are reviewed in turn.

A. *Trait Correlates*

Mundy-Castle and McKiever (1953) proposed that speed of SRR habituation was related to the temperament dimension of secondary function (a dimension similar to extraversion), and Lader and Wing (1966) demonstrated that anxiety patients' SCR habituated slowly, if at all. Most subsequent research on the trait correlates of measures of habituation has followed these precedents and examined the influence of extraversion and anxiety.

A major issue in this research has been the extent to which the two dimensions can be considered independent in their influence on habituation. Eysenck (e.g. 1967) proposed that extraversion (E) and neuroticism (N) are orthogonal factors when assessed psychometrically, and that anxiety scales such as the MAS (Taylor, 1953) represent a factor oblique to E and N. The use of the MAS thus raises difficulties of interpretation, in that any relationships observed may be due to the overlap of anxiety with E or with N or with both these factors. However, the neuropsychological model Eysenck (1967) presented to account for differences in E and N allows for the interaction of these dimensions, although as Gale (1973) observed it does not specify precisely enough the conditions under which independent or joint influence of E and N is to be expected. It is perhaps not surprising, therefore, that the data on relationships between E and N and measures of habituation are so mixed.

Mangan and O'Gorman (1969) reported that both E and N interacted in influencing speed of SRR habituation but that, when differences in N were controlled by selecting subjects with low scores on this scale, habituation was a function of E, with extraverts habituating more rapidly. This result is consistent with the correlations between E and speed of habituation reported by other researchers (e.g. Crider and Lunn, 1971; Marton, 1972), and received support from the results of Stelmack et al. (1979). These authors reported two studies in which subject samples varying in E but homogenous with respect to N were compared in terms of speed of habituation to visual stimuli. In both studies extraverts were found to habituate SCR more rapidly than introverts.

As well as these positive findings a number of null results must also be noted. A well-controlled study by Coles et al. (1971) showed that speed of SCR habituation was a function of N rather than E, with subjects with high scores on N habituating more slowly. Sadler et al. (1971) also reported that N rather than E was the determinant of speed of SRR habituation, but in their study it was the high N and not the low N subjects who habituated rapidly.

Studies of MAS-defined anxiety rather than N suggest no relationship between this measure and SCR habituation. Katkin and McCubbin (1969) reported that subjects with high scores on the MAS did not differ from subjects with low scores on this scale in rate of SCR habituation to auditory stimuli of either high or moderate intensity. A partial replication of the study by Hirschman and Brumbaugh-Buehler (1975) yielded the same null result for MAS and these findings are given additional support by Neary and Zuckerman (1976) and Epstein and Fenz (1970). A relationship between the anxiety dimension and habituation of vasomotor responses has, however, been reported in several studies. McGuinness (1973) found that subjects with high scores on the IPAT anxiety scale, which correlates highly with MAS, habituated the finger blood volume response more slowly than subjects with low scores on this scale. This result is supported by the findings of Koepke and Pribram (1967) and Jackson and Barry (1967).

It is difficult to draw together these divergent results, but several explanations for the divergence can be suggested. The first is that extraversion and emotionality may influence habituation in different response systems. Differences in E may be primarily responsible for individual differences in habituation of electrodermal responses, whereas emotionality may influence habituation of cardio-vascular responses. Reasons for such differential patterning have been suggested elsewhere (O'Gorman, 1977).

A second line of argument is that E interacts with stimulus factors in determining individual differences in habituation. The complexities which this possibility raises are well illustrated in the work of Wigglesworth and Smith (1976) and Smith and Wigglesworth (1978), which examined the role of stimulus intensity in moderating the influence of E on SCR habituation. In their first experiment (Wigglesworth and Smith, 1976) no significant main effects for E or N in determining speed of habituation were obtained, nor were the interactions between the personality variables and stimulus intensity significant. There was, however, an effect of E on a measure of dishabituation, with extraverts showing no disturbance of habituation as a consequence of the interpolation of a new stimulus in the habituation series. The second experiment (Smith and Wigglesworth, 1978) replicated this effect of E on dishabituation, and in addition revealed an interaction between E and stimulus intensity in determining speed of habituation. At an intensity of 100 dB, but not at intensities of 60 or 80 dB, extraverts habituated more rapidly than introverts. The authors were cautious in interpreting this result, noting the specific conditions under which it was obtained and their failure to demonstrate it in their earlier study. However, interactions between E and stimulus intensity have been reported by other researchers (e.g., Fowles *et al.*, 1977) and future investigations of the relationship between E and habituation might benefit therefore from a closer consideration of the influence of stimulus parameters such as intensity and frequency of stimulus presentation.

A third possible explanation for the conflict of evidence to date is that the personality sphere has not been sufficiently well-defined for psychophysiological investigation. Although there is a reasonable consensus among theorists that dimensions of extraversion and emotionality appear repeatedly in factor analyses of self-report and trait ratings, there is no consensus that these are the only major dimensions, that Eysenck's E and N scales are the best measures of them, or that the orthogonal factor solution which gives rise to E and N is the optimal solution for summarizing the interrelationship among traits. A full discussion of these arguments is beyond the scope of the present chapter, but two implications should be noted.

The first is that if there are other major dimensions in the temperament sphere apart from E and N, for example Eysenck's psychoticism factor (P; Eysenck and Eysenck, 1976), Cattell's (1972) UI 22 or UI 23, and if these also partly account for individual differences in habituation, then failure to control for their effects in studies of the relationship between E and habituation may produce ambiguous results. The argument is given credence by the report of Neary and Zuckerman (1976) that differences in sensation seeking, a component of P according to Eysenck, influence speed of SCR habituation. Differences in habituation between groups of subjects selected so as to differ in terms of E might therefore be obscured if these groups differ also in sensation seeking.

The second implication of this uncertainty about the dimensionality of the trait domain is that the impulsivity component rather than the sociability component of differences in E may be the true correlate of speed of habituation, and as a consequence measures of E may be insufficiently sensitive instruments for research on trait correlates of habituation. That is, subject groups which differ in E may not show differences in habituation if the differences in E are due to sociability rather than impulsivity. The observation of Crider and Lunn (1971) that impulsivity measures correlated most strongly with speed of habituation gives this suggestion substance.

Future research on trait correlates of habituation might thus be directed to an examination of what Cattell considers the first-order factors in the trait domain rather than, as has been the common practice to date, examination of the second-order factors of extraversion and emotionality. Hybrids of the traits which give rise to the major dimensions of extraversion and emotionality might provide a better account of variance in speed and rate of habituation than the major dimensions have provided to date.

B. *Social-Cognitive Factors*

A variety of factors have been investigated by researchers who view individual differences in habituation as a consequence of the perceptual-cognitive activity of their subjects. Rather than attempt to catalogue each of these factors and their relationships with measures of habituation, discussion will be confined to just two, sex of subject and locus of control.

Maltzman *et al.* (1979) argued that "the cognitive styles or patterns of thinking ... that are a consequence of the different kinds of past experiences acquired by males and females" (p. 219) should result in different patterns of responsiveness for the sexes in the habituation paradigm. They compared rates of habituation of SCR and vasomotor responses to word stimuli for males and females. In the first but not in the second of their two experiments, males were found to show significantly greater responsiveness to the stimuli in both systems, but there was little evidence of differences between the sexes in rates of habituation. Other researchers have fared little better in attempting to relate sex differences to measures of habituation. Kimmel and Kimmel (1965) reported that females habituated SCR at a more rapid rate than males. McGuinness (1973), on the other hand, observed that females habituated finger vasoconstriction more slowly than males.

At least part of the reason for these conflicting findings with a variable as objectively determined as sex of subject is suggested by the results of a study by Friedman and Meares (1979). They investigated speed of SCR habituation for females at different points in the menstrual cycle, and classified their subjects into those taking oral contraceptives, those ovulating regularly as determined by temperature and urine analyses, and those with anovulatory cycles. Comparisons of speed of habituation between the three groups so formed revealed a complex interaction between subject group and phase of cycle. For example, subjects ovulating regularly habituated more rapidly on days prior to than following ovulation. The complexity of these results clearly calls for further investigation, but it serves to indicate the problems of interpretation of sex differences in habituation and the possible confounds introduced when data for males and females are not analysed separately.

The second example of research on social-cognitive factors in relation to habituation is that concerned with the attitudinal variable of locus of control, a generalized belief or expectancy about the individual's efficacy in influencing the environment. Berggren *et al.* (1977) predicted that internally-oriented subjects (internals), because of their better control over attentional processes, would habituate more rapidly than externally-oriented subjects (externals) to a non-signal stimulus and, unlike externals, would show different rates of habituation to signal and non-signal stimuli. The results of the two studies they reported were consistent with these predictions. In the first experiment, internals took fewer trials to habituate SCR to a non-signal tone than externals. In the second, this relationship was replicated and it was further shown that, when subjects were required to perform a motor response to the tone, speed of habituation decreased for internals but showed little change for externals.

Their conclusion is weakened, however, by the results of Lobstein *et al.* (1979), who failed to find a significant relationship between locus of control and speed of SCR habituation using highly similar stimulus parameters including, importantly, the use of a non-signal stimulus. If anything, the results of Lobstein *et al.* suggested that externals habituated more rapidly than internals. Admittedly there were differences between the two studies in terms of the questionnaires used to assess locus of control. More importantly perhaps, in view of the earlier discussion of the potentially confounding effect of sex differences, both studies employed male and female subjects and, whereas Lobstein *et al.* found that females tended to habituate more rapidly than males, Berggren *et al.* found the reverse. An interaction of sex of subject, locus of control, and speed of habituation is thus implied by these findings and needs to be examined more carefully in future studies.

Research on individual differences in social-cognitive factors in relation to habituation has yet to establish a corpus of replicable relationships. It has, however, alerted researchers to the fact that, as Gale (1973) and Maltzman (e.g. 1979) have both observed, the habituation paradigm when used with human subjects is far more complex than it first appears. The lack of stimulus control over the subject which characterizes studies of habituation (see Gale, 1973) means that the implicit sets which subjects bring with them or generate in the experimental situation are likely to be a major, and commonly uncontrolled, source of variance in studies of this kind. Future research might benefit, therefore, from attempts to assess, control, or manipulate these subject sets.

Assessment might be accomplished by the routine administration of attitude and mood questionnaires to subjects prior to or at the conclusion of the study and by having subjects rate their reactions to the stimulus and experimental setting. Control might be achieved by the use of more meaningful stimulus material (see Gale, 1973), or by embedding the conventional tone series in a more demanding task. Iacono and Lykken (1979) suggested, for example, that subjects be presented with stimulation they find interesting (e.g. passage of prose or drama) and be instructed to ignore the tone series. Habituation to tone would thus provide a less ambiguous and more ecologically valid estimate of physiological response decrement to irrelevant stimulation. Manipulation of subject set could be achieved by variation in instruction or by variation in incentives as Bernstein (e.g. 1979) suggested. Whichever tactic is chosen, it would seem unwise to ignore the potential intrusion of subject set in future studies of individual differences in habituation.

IV. Conclusion

In retrospect, the use of speed or rate of habituation as an index of individual differences rather than as a dependent variable in personality research has proved the more successful strategy, to judge from the results obtained to date. More progress has been made, for example, in studying differences in performances on attentional tasks as a function of differences in speed of habituation than in attempts to account for differences in habituation in terms of E and N. Although this assessment would seem to imply that future research should concentrate on the predictive efficiency of measures of habituation, the question of what accounts for individual differences in habituation of course remains.

An uncritical division of subjects into rapid and slow habituators, for the purpose of determining differences in performance between these groups, may lead researchers to neglect the sensitivity of speed of habituation to stimulus and situational factors and the attitudes and expectancies of subjects which they control. As a consequence, the covariance between measures of habituation and performance may be too readily explained in terms of a neurophysiological process common to both (e.g. inhibitory control of arousal), and the possibility overlooked that it is due to the influence of temperament or to the shared meaning that subjects attribute to the experimental situations in which the two types of measures are obtained.

V. Summary

Experimental personality research employing the habituation paradigm has been reviewed from the point of view of the use of measures of rate or speed of habituation as either quasi-independent or dependent variables in the research design. The questions which each of these research strategies addresses and the issues they raise are somewhat different. Studies employing measures of habituation as quasi-independent variables are concerned with the generalizability and differential predictive validity of these measures. That is, to what extent is it possible to predict individual differences in performance on complex tasks from knowledge of individual differences in speed of habituation, and is this predictability unique to the habituation measure or simply a by-product of its relationship with general physiological reactivity? Studies which have used measures of habituation as dependent variables are concerned with the temperament and social-cognitive characteristics of subjects that account for observed variation in rate or speed of habituation. That is, the interest is in the explanation of individual differences in habituation in terms of personality factors.

Results to date suggest that the first of these research strategies has been the more fruitful. Speed of habituation of electrodermal response has been found to be a relatively stable characteristic of subjects, and one which relates to frequency of NSRs within that system and to efficiency of performance in a range of attentional tasks. The consistency of this measure and its relationships with other measures of reactivity and change within the electrodermal system remain open questions, as does the specific meaning that can be placed on the pattern of covariation of this measure and measures of performance.

Research on the personality correlates of individual differences in habituation has yet to provide an unequivocal pattern of results. The temperament dimension of extraversion may relate to speed of habituation, but not all studies have replicated earlier reports that extraverts habituate more rapidly than introverts. Possible interactions between differences in extraversion and the parameters of the stimulus employed in habituation may account for the discrepancies in results, or the difficulty may lie in the current uncertainty about the proper psychometric description of the temperament domain.

Results for other personality factors that might account for differences in habituation are no less ambiguous. Sex of subject and differences in locus of control have been found in some but not all studies to relate significantly to measures of SCR habituation. Although ambiguous, these data are considered of value in sensitizing researchers to the potential influence of subject set in studies of personality employing the habituation paradigm.

Further Reading

Crider, A. (1979). The electrodermal response: Biofeedback and individual difference studies. *Int. Rev. Appl. Psychol.* **28**, 37–48.
Part of this review is devoted to a consideration of research on electrodermal lability as a dimension of individual differences.

Gale, A. (1973). The psychophysiology of individual differences: Studies of extraversion and the EEG. *In* "New Approaches in Psychological Measurement" (P. Kline, ed.), pp. 211–256. Wiley, New York.
Includes a review of studies of individual differences in habituation of EEG responses and a critical evaluation of the habituation paradigm in experimental research in personality.

Graham, F. K. (1973). Habituation and dishabituation of responses innervated by the autonomic nervous system. *In* "Habituation" (H. V. S. Peeke and M. J. Herz, eds), Vol. 1, pp. 163–218. Academic Press, New York and London.
Presents a thorough review of the literature to that date on stimulus determinants of habituation of human physiological responses; the question of individual differences is not directly addressed.

Katkin, E. S. (1975). Electrodermal lability: A psychophysiological analysis of individual differences in response to stress. *In* "Stress and Anxiety" (I. G. Sarason and C. D. Spielberger, eds), Vol. 2, pp. 141–176. Wiley, New York.
A review of Katkin's research and that of his colleagues on individual differences in electrodermal responsiveness, including rate of habituation; should be read in conjunction with Crider's paper.

Nebylitsyn, V. D. (1972). "Fundamental Properties of the Human Nervous System". Plenum, New York.
Presents a summary of neo-Pavlovian differential psychophysiology which includes a theoretical discussion of speed of habituation as a dimension of personality.

O'Gorman, J. G. (1977). Individual differences in habituation of human physiological responses: A review of theory, method, and findings in the study of personality correlates in non-clinical populations. *Biol. Psychol.* **5**, 257–318.
A detailed summary of the evidence to that date on the social-psychological and trait correlates of measures of habituation.

References

Berggren, T., Öhman, A. and Fredrikson, M. (1977). Locus of control and habituation of the electrodermal orienting response to nonsignal and signal stimuli. *J. Personality Soc. Psychol.* **35**, 708–716.

Bernstein, A. S. (1979). The orienting reflex as novelty and significance detector: Reply to O'Gorman. *Psychophysiology* **16**, 263–273.

Bohlin, G. (1973). The relationship between arousal level and habituation of the orienting reaction. *Physiol. Psychol.* **1**, 308–312.

Bull, R. H. C. and Gale, M. A. (1973). The reliability of and interrelationships between various measures of electrodermal activity. *J. Exp. Res. Personality* **6**, 300–306.

Bundy, R. S. and Mangan, S. M. (1979). Electrodermal indices of stress and cognition: Possible hydration artifacts. *Psychophysiology* **16**, 30–33.

Cattell, R. B. (1972). The interpretation of Pavlov's typology, and the arousal concept, in replicated trait and state factors. *In* "Biological Bases of Individual Behaviour" (V. D. Nebylitsyn and J. A. Gray, eds), pp. 141–164. Academic Press, London and New York.

Coles, M. G. H. and Gale, A. (1971). Physiological reactivity as a predictor of performance in a vigilance task. *Psychophysiology* **8**, 594–599.

Coles, M. G. H., Gale, A. and Kline, P. (1971). Personality and habituation of the orienting reaction: Tonic and response measures of electrodermal activity. *Psychophysiology* **8**, 54–63.

Crider, A. (1979). The electrodermal response: biofeedback and individual difference studies. *Int. Rev. Appl. Psychol.* **28**, 37–48.

Crider, A. and Augenbraun, C. B. (1975). Auditory vigilance correlates of electrodermal response habituation speed. *Psychophysiology* **12**, 36–40.

Crider, A. and Lunn, R. (1971). Electrodermal lability as a personality dimension. *J. Exp. Res. Personality* **5**, 145–150.

Dykman, R., Reese, W. G., Galbrecht, C. R. and Thomasson, P. J. (1959). Psychophysiological reactions to novel stimuli: Measurement, adaption, and relationship of psychological and physiological variables in the normal human. *Ann. N. Y. Acad. Sci.* **79**, 43–107.

Epstein, S. and Fenz, W. D. (1970). Habituation to a loud sound as a function of manifest anxiety. *J. Abnorm. Psychol.* **75**, 189–194.

Eysenck, H. J. (1967). "The Biological Basis of Personality". C. C. Thomas, Springfield, Illinois.

Eysenck, H. J. and Eysenck, S. B. G. (1976). "Psychoticism as a Dimension of Personality". Hodder and Stoughton, London.

Fowles, D. D., Roberts, R. and Nagel, K. E. (1977). The influence of introversion/extraversion on the skin conductance response to stress and stimulus intensity. *J. Res. Personality* **11**, 129–146.

Friedman, J. and Meares, R. A. (1979). The menstrual cycle and habituation. *Psychosom. Med.* **41**, 369–381.

Furedy, J. J. (1971). The nonhabituating vasomotor component of the human orienting reaction: Misbehaving skeleton in OR theory's closet. *Psychophysiology* **8**, 278.

Gale, A. (1973). The psychophysiology of individual differences: Studies of extraversion and the EEG. *In* "New Approaches in Psychological Measurement" (P. Kline, ed.), pp. 211–256. Wiley, New York.

Geer, J. H. (1966). Effect of interstimulus intervals and rest-period length upon habituation of the orienting response. *J. Exp. Psychol.* **72**, 617–619.

Graham, F. K. (1973). Habituation and dishabituation of responses innervated by the autonomic nervous system. *In* "Habituation" (H. V. S. Peeke and M. J. Herz, eds), Vol. 1, pp. 163–218. Academic Press, London and New York.

Hastrup, J. L. (1979). Effects of electrodermal lability and introversion on vigilance decrement. *Psychophysiology* **16**, 302–310.

Hirschman, R. and Brumbaugh-Buehler, B. (1975). Electrodermal habituation and subjective response: Effects of manifest anxiety and autonomic arousal. *J. Abnorm. Psychol.* **84**, 46–50.

Iacono, W. G. and Lykken, D. T. (1979). The orienting response: Importance of instructions. *Schizophrenia Bull.* **5**, 11–14.

Jackson, B. T. and Barry, W. F. (1967). The vasomotor component of the orientation reaction as a correlative of anxiety. *Percept. Mot. Skills* **25**, 514–516.

Katkin, E. S. (1975). Electrodermal lability: A psychophysiological analysis of individual differences in response to stress. *In* "Stress and Anxiety" (I. G. Sarason and C. D. Spielberger, eds), Vol. 2, pp. 141–176. Wiley, New York.

Katkin, E. S. and McCubbin, R. J. (1969). Habituation of the orienting response as a function of individual differences in anxiety and autonomic lability. *J. Abnorm. Psychol.* **74**, 54–60.

Katkin, E. S. and Shapiro, D. (1979). Voluntary heart rate control as a function of individual differences in electrodermal lability. *Psychophysiology* **16**, 402–404.

Kimmel, H. D. and Kimmel, E. (1965). Sex differences in adaptation of the GSR under repeated applications of a visual stimulus. *J. Exp. Psychol.* **70**, 536–537.

Klorman, R. (1974). Habituation of fear; effects of intensity and stimulus order. *Psychophysiology* **11**, 15–26.

Koepke, J. E. and Pribram, K. H. (1967). Habituation of the vasoconstriction response as a function of stimulus duration and anxiety. *J. Comp. Physiol. Psychol.* **64**, 502–504.

Koriat, A., Averill, J. R. and Malmstrom, E. J. (1973). Individual differences in habituation: Some methodological and conceptual issues. *J. Res. Personality* 88–101.

Lader, M. H. and Wing, L. (1966). "Physiological Measures, Sedative Drugs, and Morbid Anxiety". Oxford University Press, London.

Lader, M. H., Gelder, M. G. and Marks, I. M. (1967). Palmar skin conductance measures as predictors of response to desensitization. *J. Psychosom. Res.* **11**, 283–290.

Lobstein, T., Webb, B. and Edholm, O. (1979). Orienting responses and locus of control. *Br. J. Soc. Clin. Psychol.* **18**, 13–19.

Maltzman, I. (1979). Orienting reflexes and significance. A reply to O'Gorman. *Psychophysiology* **16**, 274–282.

Maltzman, I., Gould, J., Barnett, O. J., Raskin, D. and Wolff, C. (1979). Habituation of the GSR and digital vasomotor components of the orienting reflex as a consequence of task instructions and sex differences. *Physiol. Psychol.* **7**, 213–220.

Mangan, G. L. and O'Gorman, J. G. (1969). Initial amplitude and rate of habituation of orienting reaction in relation to extraversion and neuroticism. *J. Exp. Res. Personality* **3**, 275–282.

Martin, I. and Rust, J. (1976). Habituation and the structure of the electrodermal system. *Psychophysiology* **13**, 554–562.

Marton, M. L. (1972). The theory of individual differences in neo-behaviourism and in the typology of higher nervous activity. *In* "Biological Bases of Individual Behaviour" (V. D. Nebylitsyn and J. A. Gray, eds), pp. 221–235. Academic Press, London and New York.

McGuinness, D. (1973). Cardiovascular responses during habituation and mental activity in anxious men and women. *Biol. Psychol.* **1**, 115–123.

Mundy-Castle, A. C. and McKiever, B. L. (1953). The psychophysiological significance of the galvanic skin response. *J. Exp. Psychol.* **46**, 15–24.

Neary, R. S. and Zuckerman, M. (1976). Sensation seeking, trait and state anxiety, and the electrodermal orienting response. *Psychophysiology* **13**, 205–211.

Nebylitsyn, V. D. (1972). "Fundamental Properties of the Human Nervous System". Plenum, New York.

O'Gorman, J. G. (1977). Individual differences in habituation of human physiological responses: A review of theory, method, and findings in the study of personality correlates in non-clinical populations. *Biol. Psychol.* **5**, 257–318.

Öhman, A. and Bohlin, G. (1973). Magnitude and habituation of the orienting reaction as predictors of discriminative electrodermal conditioning. *J. Exp. Res. Personality* **6**, 293–299.

Sadler, T. G., Mefferd, R. B. and Houck, R. L. (1971). The interaction of extraversion and neuroticism in orienting response habituation. *Psychophysiology* **8**, 312–318.

Siddle, D. A. T. (1972). Vigilance decrement and speed of habituation of the GSR component of the orienting reaction. *Br. J. Psychol.* **63**, 191–194.

Siddle, D. A. T. and Heron, P. A. (1976). Reliability of electrodermal habituation measures under two conditions of stimulus intensity. *J. Res. Personality* **10**, 195–200.

Siddle, D. A. T. and Mangan, G. L. (1971). Arousability and individual differences in resistance to distraction. *J. Exp. Res. Personality* **5**, 295–303.

Smith, B. D. and Wigglesworth, M. J. (1978). Extraversion and neuroticism in orienting reflex dishabituation. *J. Res. Personality* **12**, 284–296.

Sokolov, E. N. (1969). The modelling properties of the nervous system. *In* "Handbook of Contemporary Soviet Psychology" (M. Cole and I. Maltzman, eds), pp. 671–704. Basic Books, London.

Solanto, M. V. and Katkin, E. S. (1979). Classical EDR conditioning using a truly random control and subjects differing in lability level. *Bull. Psychonom. Soc.* **14**, 49–52.

Sostek, A. J. (1978). Effect of electrodermal lability and payoff instructions on vigilance performance. *Psychophysiology* **15**, 561–568.

Stelmack, R. M., Bourgeois, R. P., Chien, Y. C. and Pickard, C. W. (1979). Extraversion and the orientation reaction habituation rate to visual stimuli. *J. Res. Personality* **13**, 49–58.

Taylor, J. A. (1953). A personality scale of manifest anxiety. *J. Abnorm. Soc. Psychol.* **48**, 285–290.

Voicu, C. and Olteanu, T. (1972). Study of the correlation between flexibility of attention and dynamism of nervous processes. *In* "Biological Bases of Individual Behaviour" (V. D. Nebylitsyn and J. A. Gray, eds), pp. 325–333. Academic Press, New York and London.

Voronin, L. G., Sokolov, E. N. and Bao-Khua, U. (1959). Type features of the orientation reaction in man. *Vop. Psikhol.* **6**, 73–88. Cited in: Lynn, R. "Attention, Arousal and the Orientation Reaction". Pergamon Press, Oxford.

Wigglesworth, M. J. and Smith, B. D. (1976). Habituation and dishabituation of the electrodermal orienting reflex in relation to extraversion and neuroticism. *J. Res. Personality* **10**, 437–445.

5 Perspectives on Pain

C. Ray

Abstract Pain has both sensory and emotional aspects, each of which is integral to the quality of the experience. It can be treated in a variety of ways, including both somatic and psychological forms of therapy. The relationship between pain and injury is not a simple one, and patients often present with pain that does not have a clear, physical origin. In such cases pain is sometimes attributed to psychological rather than somatic sources. Another distinction sometimes made is that between the pain state and the subjective and overt response to pain. Both of these distinctions are difficult to maintain in practice, and may be difficult to justify in principle. Doubts about their utility are reinforced by recent neuro-physiological analyses of pain processing. The gate-control theory suggests that somatic and psychological factors interact, and that the system is a complex and dynamic one. The theoretical understanding of pain has direct implications for the care of the patient with chronic pain.

Pain is a difficult area to research, because of its subjective nature and because of ethical considerations that inevitably limit the kinds of studies that can be undertaken. There have nevertheless been considerable developments in the understanding of pain over the last three decades, to which both laboratory experiments and clinical observations have contributed. There are a number of different kinds of questions that can be addressed, and a number of levels at which answers might be sought. This chapter describes some of the frameworks within which pain has been analysed. An approach which emphasizes physiological aspects of pain processing represents one of these perspectives, but at the same time embraces several issues raised within other perspectives.

I. Pain Research

For most people pain is an affliction that occurs only from time to time, causing more or less disruption depending upon its intensity, but for some it is an enduring handicap that limits and distorts their lives. The psychological

PHYSIOLOGICAL CORRELATES OF HUMAN
BEHAVIOUR   ISBN 0-12-273901-9

salience of pain, or the possibility of pain, thus varies from individual to individual. It does, however, have a shared significance in the abhorrence it generally elicits, and this response is so common that those who find pain acceptable are likely to be regarded with either awe or suspicion. It sometimes seems that physical suffering is a "useless evil" (Buytendijk, 1962). There are many specific situations in which this is certainly true, with terminal illness providing a striking example, and there are situations also where pain promotes responses that could be maladaptive and reduce chances of survival. Nevertheless, in certain circumstances pain does have a recognizable biological function. It is often a signal that damage is occurring or has occurred, and it motivates us to withdraw from harm and to nurse the injury.

The development of a psychological understanding of pain has been hindered by several methodological constraints. A central problem is that of carrying out empirical research and producing data that have external validity, given the ethical considerations that have to be taken into account when designing studies in this area. Work with animals can provide interesting insights and hypotheses and may be the only way in which some neurophysiological and biochemical hypotheses can be directly tested. There are likely, though, to be important differences between human beings and other animals in the origins, experience and implications of pain, and for most purposes data from human subjects is to be preferred. It is possible to induce pain experimentally in the laboratory, employing voluntary subjects, by applying heat, cold, pressure or electrical stimulation. The investigation can be carried out under strictly controlled conditions, and the subjects' responses carefully monitored. This kind of study has generated an extensive literature. However, the validity of much of this laboratory work is questionable (Beecher, 1959). It has a number of limitations. Firstly, its standardized and artificial procedures may not adequately reproduce the quality of many naturally-occurring pains: the stimulation may be similarly noxious but differ in other subtle respects. Secondly, the setting is a protected one in which the subject knows the limits of the pain to which he will be subjected; he knows that its intensity will be bearable, and that it will last for the time of the experimental session only. Thirdly, the pain is threatening only because of its immediate unpleasantness; it is easily accounted for and does not imply the possibility of illness or long term damage. Fourthly, subjects who take part in pain experiments have presumably given their informed consent, and are willingly exposing themselves to pain; the reactions of such volunteers will probably not be the same as those of a truly random sample. Finally, in a situation in which his responses are explicitly the focus of interest, the subject may be motivated to appear "tough" and not admit to pain at levels at which he feels others might disclaim this. All of these considerations could bias the data. Their interpretation will be problematic, and caution must be exercised in generalizing conclusions drawn from this artificial situation to those that occur naturally. Research carried out in clinical settings does not suffer from the same drawbacks, but in several respects it is at a disadvantage when compared with laboratory research. There may be problems in systematically observing the subjects and recording their responses, and it may be impossible to specify the nature and intensity of the "stimulus" with any degree of precision. Moreover, while there are ethical difficulties in deliberately inflicting pain for the purpose of laboratory experiments, there is also a question of whether it is justifiable to add to the existing troubles of pain patients by asking them to participate in a research programme. This applies particularly if the methodology requires the infliction of additional pain, or foregoing the possibility of pain relief.

A second problem encountered in the course of research is that of actually measuring degree of pain. The experience is a private and subjective one, yet its measurement requires that it be rendered public and objective. Methods that have been used in assessing clinical pain include determining the impact upon the patient's physical and social activities, personal relationships and psychological well-being. A rather different approach is to ask the subject to compare the intensity of his pain with that of a standardized one that is artificially induced; an estimate of the former in relation to the individual's pain tolerance on the artificial stimulus can then be derived (Sternbach *et al.*, 1974). Cross-modality matching tasks have been employed in assessing experimentally-induced pain, with subjects comparing the intensity of a variable pain stimulus with the magnitude of some other kind of stimulus (Tursky, 1976). Physiological changes associated with arousal and distress may also be monitored, instead of or in conjunction with a judgemental task. The most feasible and commonly employed procedure is, however, the relatively direct one of asking for a description of the pain. There are many ways in which such self-reports may be elicited. Subjects may be asked to report the presence or absence of pain and their ability to tolerate further increments, or they may be required to rate the intensity of the experience on one of the many forms of verbal and numerical scales available (Scott and Huskisson, 1976). In some contexts the researcher may be as interested in the quality as in the intensity of the pain, and may ask subjects to describe this by selecting appropriate adjectives from a number of descriptive categories (Melzack and Torgerson, 1971). Such measures of pain are interrelated, and it is difficult to determine their relative validity given the lack of an acceptable objective criterion of pain. The one selected by the investigator will depend upon the setting in which the measure is to be used, the pain source, and the aspect of the pain experience which he wishes to tap.

A number of perspectives have been employed in the theoretical explanation of pain. These have governed the character of the questions asked and the level at which answers are sought. Some have tried to analyse semantically and phenomenologically the nature of the experience; some have been pragmatically concerned with finding ways of treating pain effectively; some have been focused upon the genesis of pain and the factors to which it may be attributed; some have taken a psychosocial approach and looked at the individual's response to pain. No perspective can, however, afford to ignore physiological aspects of pain and the way in which it is processed by the nervous system. Models of the mechanisms involved in pain processing not only offer an additional perspective, but present theories and ideas that are relevant to all frameworks.

II. The Meaning of Pain

Pain does not fit neatly into the categories we use for describing similarly subjective experiences. It is not really a sensation, in the way we talk of visual or auditory sensations. With these we can assume the independent existence of the object of the experience; there is something actually to be seen or to be heard. This is not so for pain which has an internal referent only. A prick from a needle, a blow from a hammer, a bruise or a cut, can give rise to pain, but it is their effects and not they themselves which are experienced. In any case, a concept of pain as a sensation does not convey the unpleasant and vivid nature of the experience, and this is surely integral to its nature. It has at times, in fact, been suggested that pain is more similar to an emotion than to a sensation. Feeling pain would thus be analogous to feeling fear or anger. Again, however, the analogy is far from satisfactory, only here it is the sensory quality of the pain experienced that is lacking. In practice, most theorists have assumed that pain has both sensory and emotional aspects which interact to produce a qualitative "gestalt". Their dual importance is illustrated by cases of patients who, after undergoing a prefrontal lobotomy, report a kind of pain when given appropriate stimulation, but without the distress and unpleasantness normally associated with the experience. Similar effects can be produced by certain drugs.

Beecher (1959) suggested that the same set of sensations may or may not give rise to pain depending upon the context within which they are experienced, and that sensory and emotional aspects of the stimulus are processed in sequence. Where the context is benign in terms of its psychological meaning, even quite intense stimulation may be tolerated without distress. He provided the example of American soldiers who had been wounded in battle and admitted to hospital with severe injuries, but did not complain of pain. He argued that their relief at being removed from the arena, and satisfaction with the role they had played, may have positively coloured the psychological context in which the experience would have been interpreted. This specific explanation has, however, been questioned (Carlen *et al.*, 1978). It can be argued that the situation would, on the contrary, have been highly threatening in view of the long term consequences of some of the injuries sustained, and that this anxiety would have outweighed other positive factors.

An alternative explanation might be sought in the high degree of arousal and involvement in the situation undoubtedly felt by soldiers prior to and at the time of injury. The example is often quoted of sportsmen who pursue the race or the game in spite of and even without awareness of quite serious injuries. An intense concentration directed toward other concerns may block the processing of the emotional component necessary for the experience of pain. Leventhal and Everhart (1979) have suggested that any potentially painful stimulus will be simultaneously analysed for its physical qualities, such as intensity and location, and for its emotional implications. Whether or not the stimulus is experienced as painful will depend upon the form in which it is *primarily* encoded: whether employing objective schemata relating to information features or emotional schemata relevant to the evaluation of threat. Subtle changes in the situation may bias the form of encoding toward one or the other set of schemata (Leventhal *et al.*, 1979).

III. Treatment of Pain

Before this century such treatments that were offered for the relief of pain were primarily physical or opiate-based. Apart from massage, hot fomentations might be applied to the affected part, blisters raised on the skin's surface or whelts inflicted by dry cupping. The latter entailed using a pump or flame to withdraw air from a glass, and then drawing the glass across the skin. Recent thinking has indicated that there may be sound principles underlying such practices, although they were not at the time recognized. The modern equivalent is transcutaneous electrical stimulation, which is applied at the site of the pain or at a related trigger area. Its effectiveness in the treatment of some syndromes has been ascribed to an inhibitory effect of sensory input on pain processing. Acupuncture might work in a similar way. Here stimulation is provided by needles which are inserted under the skin in precisely determined locations that may be remote from the site of the pain, and vibrated either manually or by the passage of an electric current. There may be a component of suggestion provided by the preparation for the procedure and the subject's expectations, and psychological factors probably contribute too, even if they do not completely explain, the success of the therapy (Chaves and Barber, 1974). Other physical methods now employed include surgery and the injection of chemical blocking agents into the nerve root. Surgical techniques, whether peripheral or central, can be disappointing in their outcome (Noordenbos, 1959), and because of their irreversibility are not often used. Nerve blocks are less drastic and can have a long term effect, relieving pain for periods of days or even permanently. It is speculated that they may work by disrupting abnormal patterns of pain processing and permitting normal patterns to be re-established.

Opium has long been used in the treatment of pain, and morphine and its derivatives still have a role to play. The role is generally a limited one, because of the likelihood of establishing an addiction if the drugs are used regularly or in quantity, but they are very effective and induce a general feeling of well-being by way of a bonus. Minor tranquillizers and anti-depressants act centrally, like the narcotic drugs, but without the same risk of addiction. They do not directly influence pain but reduce psychological distress, and by this means can modify the way in which the former is experienced. Perhaps the most commonly employed agents are those that act peripherally, rather than centrally, by reducing inflammation. It is these that most people turn to for self-medication in response to minor and short term pains, but they can help too in relieving the chronic pain associated with conditions like arthritis.

Psychological approaches to the treatment of pain also have a history. Suggestions of analgesia or pain relief have been implicit in most forms of treatment, and may account for any benefits claimed or demonstrated in the absence of other plausible explanations. Placebo effects are indeed a useful component of most current therapies, including those which have a sound scientific rationale (Beecher, 1955). Some people will react more strongly to suggestion and placebos than others, the influence depending upon the setting and upon the subject's expectations. The potency of suggestion can be greatly enhanced by hypnosis. Most people are familiar with stage demonstrations of an enhanced ability to tolerate pain while hypnotized, but are less well aware that hypnosis has been quite commonly used in clinical situations to increase resistance to clinical pain and to complement or replace the use of anaesthetics (Hilgard and Hilgard, 1975). The nature of the trance has been hotly debated (for example, Sarbin and Anderson, 1964), but it seems that when in this state pain may be processed at a "conscious level" without being consciously acknowledged.

Many informal or "naive" ways of coping with pain have incorporated elements of behavioural and cognitive techniques, although it is only recently that they have been systematically developed and evaluated. Behaviour therapy focuses on the individual's overt behaviour, and not on the subjective experience of pain. Evaluation and treatment is directed at what the person *does*. Verbal reports of pain, although technically behaviour, are essentially reflections of an inner experience, and are given a secondary role (Fordyce *et al.*, 1973). The patient's behaviour is monitored before therapy proper begins. Reinforcement programmes are then designed by the therapist, with the cooperation of the patient and his family. The goal of these is to decrease the occurrence of undesirable behaviour, such as complaining, inactivity or an excessive use of medications, and to increase the frequency of desirable and healthy behaviours. A behavioural approach does seem to be effective in changing the patient's activities, helping him to lead a relatively normal life in spite of a chronic condition. It does not, however, alter verbal reports of what it feels like "inside". Cognitive therapies, in contrast, attempt to alter the pain as experienced rather than behaviour and have been applied in situations in which short term pain is anticipated rather than in cases of chronic pain. The subject can be taught to use various self-statements and cognitive strategies which distract him from pain or restructure its meaning and relevance. Using these methods the individual can be psychologically "inoculated" against pain, so that tolerance is increased and distress reduced (Leventhal *et al.*, 1979; Turk, 1978). The success of these strategies may depend upon the subject's confidence in his ability to cope, and on his general orientation to the pain rather than on their specific semantic content (Girodo and Wood, 1979).

IV. Determinants of Pain

Both theorists and therapists are concerned with describing the causes of pain, when considering pain as a general phenomenon and when presented with specific instances. While there is obviously a close association between pain and tissue damage, the relationship is a very imperfect one. Actual injury is not a necessary condition, and if the description of the experience given by the individual is similar to descriptions of pain that occurs after injury then this can be taken as a sufficient criterion for labelling the experience as pain (IASP Sub-committee, 1979).

In many clinical conditions pain may have a clearly somatic origin, while a satisfactory physiological explanation is nevertheless lacking. These include phantom limb pain. The phantom in itself is an unexplained phenomenon. It does not occur where the limb has been lost by absorption, as in leprosy, nor in children under the age of three (Simmel, 1966). This suggests that it may represent a "neural memory" of the limb and, indeed, pain is most likely to occur where it was experienced before the amputation. The neuralgias and causalgias provide other examples of pain which persists after injury.

It sometimes happens that a patient presents with pain but it is difficult to find any evidence of physical disease or disorder whether current or historical. The pain may then be regarded as psychogenic or functional, which implies that it has its origins in the needs and personality of the sufferer. Freud explicitly regarded pain as having a symbolic function, arguing that it can serve the individual by permitting the indirect expression of a suppressed drive. Engel (1959) suggested that there is a "pain-prone personality" who has a family background of violence and punishment, feels hostility against himself, and uses pain to assuage his guilt. Many studies have shown that chronic pain patients have personality profiles that are consistent with such theories, being more neurotic than those of control groups (Sternbach, 1974). They tend to be more anxious and depressed, and to have higher scores on measures of hypochondriasis. There is, however, a problem in interpreting these findings. There is a highly plausible alternative hypothesis which cannot be dismissed, namely that long term pain *gives rise to* emotional disturbances and to a focus upon the body and bodily symptoms.

Most cases of chronic pain will probably reflect the influence of both somatic and psychological factors. The therapist may wish to determine the relative influence of these, in order to guide the diagnosis of the underlying condition and the treatment appropriate to this. Were the pain to be primarily psychogenic, and this could be unambiguously determined, the search for an organic disorder would be in vain, and the patient might benefit instead from a psychological analysis of the meaning of his pain and psychotherapeutic support. There are, however, two considerations to be noted. Firstly, the pain symptoms may be treated independently of the underlying disorder, and may be equally responsive to somatic or psychological approaches to therapy regardless of their origin. The practical implications of distinguishing between somatogenic and psychogenic pain may therefore be limited, once a diagnosis has been made and if the condition resists treatment. Secondly, pain would generally be described as psychogenic on the basis of an absence of evidence for a somatic explanation, rather than on the basis of positive evidence for a psychological influence. This practice could result in pain being psychologically attributed when a somatic basis exists but is undetected, and could reduce the chance of the latter subsequently being detected.

V. Responses to Pain

Many cultures, Eastern ones in particular, have rites and ceremonies that involve the infliction of injury by the person himself or by some other. There may be little evidence of any experience of pain during the ritual (Kosambi, 1967), yet responses in other settings appear normal. Variations according to the situation are in fact quite common in all cultures, although the range may not be as great as this. For example, where pain is expected this expectation can enhance the intensity of the pain experience (Epstein, 1973), and toler-ance increases with the degree of control the sufferer can exert, or thinks he can exert, over the situation (Ball and Vogler, 1971). Furthermore, if we observe the behaviour of another in the same situation as ourselves, his reactions as we see them will influence our own. Studies have been carried out in which a subject is given a series of electric shocks, in the presence of a confederate of the experimenter who is supposedly receiving the same shocks. Where the confederate is instructed to appear "tolerant" and not to express pain in any way, subjects report that they experience less pain and are more willing to tolerate additional shock (Craig, 1978).

Laboratory investigations show that there are large differences between individuals in their levels of threshold and tolerance (Clark, 1976), and that these differences are relatively stable. Apparent tolerance of pain varies with sex and age (Belville *et al.*, 1971; Notermans and Tophoff, 1975; Woodrow *et al.*, 1972): women and the young show a more extreme response when compared with men and older people respectively. The relationship between personality traits, such as neuroticism and extraversion, and response to pain has been extensively researched, but the results have been inconsistent. There is a tendency for extraverts to be more tolerant, and for those who score high on neuroticism scales to be less so, but these relationships are unstable and are affected by specific characteristics of the situation.

Differences between individuals are paralleled by differences between cultures. There are cultural norms which govern the way in which pain is perceived and the behaviour considered to be appropriate. These norms are internalized by the individual member of the culture and exemplified by him even when he is not in this setting. In one study, patients of American, Jewish, Italian and Irish descent were observed while in hospital (Zborowski, 1969). The Italians and Jews were more reactive to pain, while the Old Americans and the Irish were relatively stoical in their behaviour. Although patients of Italian and Jewish origin expressed their pain similarly, the focus of their concern was not the same. It appeared that the Jewish patients were less worried about the pain than about the condition underlying it, while the reverse was true of the Italians. Laboratory studies involving the artificial induction of pain have produced findings consistent with these (Sternbach and Tursky, 1965).

Responses to pain can be compared with responses to illness in general. Illness and illness behaviour are often distinguished on the grounds that two individuals can have the same disease or, indeed, be in the same state of health, and yet react differently to this (Mechanic and Volkhart, 1960; Mechanic, 1977). It follows that, if the intention is to assess objective states of illness or health, it is necessary to look beyond behaviour. In the case of pain it could similarly be argued that two people may be exposed to the same pain but vary in their response. One person might appear greatly distressed, and the influence of pain on his life be apparent in a number of ways. Someone else may be a stoic by comparison, and be relatively unaffected. The concept of illness behaviour is actually a compound. It comprises, on the one hand, the subjective appraisal of the symptoms as they are interpreted by the individual and reacted to emotionally; on the other hand, it refers to overt behaviour, which includes change in social, work and physical activities. The model implied by extending this analysis to pain and pain behaviour is represented in Fig. 1.

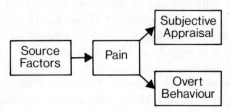

Fig. 1 *Pain behaviour.*

How satisfactory is the status of the concept of "pain" within this model? Since it excludes a subjective component, it seems that it is here regarded as an *objective* state, analogous to one of bodily need or deprivation. Such deprivation states can to an extent be assessed independently of experience and behaviour, using indices such as blood sugar level and body weight, and are assumed to exist independently of these. A man can be physically starving without feeling hungry. This is not so in the case of pain, which is essentially a subjective phenomenon defined by the quality of the experience. It is nonsense to say that somebody is in pain but does not feel pain. Moreover, as our understanding of the physiological aspects of pain processing increases, so the boundaries between the somatic and the psychological, the objective and the subjective, become increasingly blurred.

VI. Neurophysiology of Pain

The traditional model of pain assumed that stimuli which impinge on pain receptors travel a direct route along specific neural pathways to specific cells and tracts of the spinal cord, from where they are conveyed to the pain centres of the brain. Later refinements of the basic model suggested that touch sensations are mediated by large fibres, while the small fibres are responsible for the passage of pain impulses, and the possibility was raised of several small fibres converging cumulatively onto one central cell. A historical survey of such physiological models is presented in Melzack (1973). There was little empirical evidence for these models as they stood, and clinical and experimental observations have cast doubt upon their adequacy. One principal objection is the fact that none can account for the widely acknowledged influence of psychological and social factors. A more sophisticated analysis was put forward in the 1960s, and this has had a considerable impact in the last decade. It is the gate-control theory of Melzack and Wall (1965). According to this model, impulses travel along nerve fibres to the dorsal horns of the spinal cord, from where they are transmitted to the centre. The activity of these transmission cells is, however, modulated by a process that acts like a gate, and this is thought to be mediated by the substantia gelatinosa of the dorsal horns. Inputs from large fibres tend to close the gate, while inputs from smaller fibres open it, so that output depends upon the ratio of large and small fibre activity. Moreover, output can also be affected by descending inhibitory influences from the brain, described as a "central biasing mechanism". This mechanism influences not only the activity of the gate but transmission at other synapses between the spinal cord and the brain.

Melzack and Casey (1968) recognize a sensory-discriminative, a motivational-affective and a cognitive-evaluative dimension of pain, and suggest that these represent not only phenomenological aspects of the subjective experience but different neural pathways ascending from the dorsal horns to the brain. The first of these dimensions, the sensory-discriminative, is linked with the rapidly conducting pathways which project to the somatosensory thalamus and cortex. The second, the motivational-affective, is associated with more slowly conducting pathways which project to the medial reticular areas of the brainstem and to the limbic system. It is proposed that the cognitive-evaluative system is the most rapidly conducting, and that this projects to the neocortex; here impulses are analysed with respect to past experiences and knowledge of the current situation. This analysis can in turn influence processing in both of the other systems, thus affecting sensory and emotional aspects of the pain experience and responses.

The theory has generated many hypotheses, and among these are possible explanations for the efficacy of methods of therapy such as transcutaneous electrical stimulation and acupuncture. Input to the central biasing mechanism would influence activity of the gate and it is suggested that stimulation of peripheral trigger points might have this effect. This could cause a selective as well as a general anaesthesia, since stimulation of points within reticular areas can produce analgesia in discrete parts of the body (Balagaru and Ralph, 1973). Where long term effects are obtained, these may be attributed to the disruption of reverberatory circuits that prolong pain in the absence of further intense inputs, and to the normalization of physical activity that results from the relief of pain and restores peripheral input. The influence of anaesthetic blocks can be accounted for in similar terms. Where cells in the spinal cord or brain are deprived of input, this may result in abnormal physiological activity in response to many different kinds of stimuli, and these may generate pain. Again nerve blocks may interrupt such patterns and allow the restoration of normal inputs.

The model is complex, but can account for complex phenomena. The physiological evidence has been reviewed and discussed by Wall (1979), and some aspects continue to be revised and elaborated. Other avenues of research and explanation are now opening with developments in the psychopharmacology of pain, and attempts can be made to relate these to the gate-control theory. Naturally-occurring peptides which are similar to morphine (the endorphins and the enkephalins) are plentiful in both the substantia gelatinosa and analgesia-producing brainstem areas. Moreover, naloxone blocks the action of brainstem areas sensitive to morphine (Akil *et al.*, 1976), and also inhibits the effect of transcutaneous electrical stimulation and acupuncture (Mayer *et al.*, 1976). It seems that communication within the pain processing system is regulated by both neurophysiological and chemical structures and processes.

VII. The Control of Pain

The gate-control theory proposes a complex and dynamic organization of mechanisms and processes, and could not have been formulated without a detailed conceptual analysis of pain processing to specify clearly what it was that had to be explained and the kinds of hypothetical mechanisms that would be required. Conceptual and neurophysiological descriptions are intertwined and their relationships explicit, and it is this feature that gives the model its particular force.

A central implication of the theory is the extent to which both somatic and psychological factors affect different stages of pain processing and interact at all stages beyond the periphery. It is these interactions which determine whether or not pain is perceived and the quality of the response. Psychological factors can modulate the activity of the gate, alongside somatic ones, and subsequently determine how the signals are evaluated, the stimulus defined and its motivational and emotional implications decided. Pain signals can thus arise in response to stimuli that would not commonly have this potential, while noxious stimuli may be treated neutrally and not give rise to pain. In these circumstances it is difficult to maintain a clear distinction between pain that has a somatic origin and pain that has a psychological origin, since any experience of pain will inevitably comprise elements of both, and their relative influence would be difficult to determine. The distinction between pain and pain behaviour presents a similar difficulty. Within the framework of this model, pain is not recognized and does not exist until a stage at which psychological influences are active. We cannot point to any basic *pain* signals which are input to an interpretive system, since objective and subjective aspects of the stimulus are analysed interactively. There is thus no somatic state of pain to which a psychological element is then subsequently added, and pain is in a truly fundamental sense to be regarded as a psychosomatic phenomenon.

There is, nevertheless, a temptation to employ these distinctions in our thinking. We are all concerned to explain the phenomena that have significance for us, and these explanations commonly take the form of causal attributions. They provide working models of the world which reduce uncertainty and provide guidelines for behaviour. The categorization of specific instances of pain into somatogenic and psychogenic, and the differentiation between pain and the response to it, serves this function. However, like other "naive" causal models, it simplifies a complex situation and in doing so may have undesirable implications for the treatment of the pain patient. The attribution of pain to psychological factors carries with it a number of interrelated risks. First, there may be a tendency to see the pain as somehow more imaginary than real, even though rationally one accepts an experiential definition of pain. Secondly, there is the possibility of attributing responsibility to the individual for the fact that he is in pain, and blaming or resenting him accordingly. Thirdly, we are perhaps more likely to regard the pain as within the control of the individual, and abdicate therapeutic responsibility. The attribution of personal responsibility for pain is most clearly illustrated by Szasz' description of "l'homme douloureux" who makes a "career of suffering" (1968). He suggests that chronic and intractable pain is often a sign that the patient wishes, albeit unconsciously, to occupy the sick role. Szasz does not claim that the pain is imaginary, and acknowledges its real and vivid nature from the patient's point of view. He does, however, assert that it is the patient's life rather than his body which is unwell, and suggests that the physician's responsibility lies primarily with those whose trouble is physical.

Current approaches to the care of the patient with chronic pain tend in practice to be pragmatic and flexible, and treatment is unlikely to be determined by rigid preconceptions such as these. It is true that there is a greater emphasis today upon the patient's own efforts and contribution to therapy (Sternbach, 1974; Wooley *et al.*, 1978), but this does not derive from suppositions about any particular balance of contributing somatic and psychological factors. Patients are encouraged to take an active role within the doctor–patient relationship rather than to rely upon the physician's expertise and directions, and to regard the latter as a partner in the treatment enterprise rather than as sole agent. This approach does seem to have advantages, and it is welcome to the extent that it acknowledges the real importance of psychological factors without discounting the sufferer's report of his experience, and to the extent that it emphasizes the possibility of personal control without putting too great a burden of responsibility on the patient. On the other hand, a high degree of support from the therapist and others will be necessary to give the patient courage and the will to cope. An implication of personal failure would be likely to increase the stress associated with intractable pain and hence act against the possibility of change. The ideal relationship between the therapist and the patient would therefore be one which provides the latter with the incentive to help himself, but within a framework of support and reassurance which is not conditional upon the progress of the treatment.

Further Reading

Melzack, R. (1973). "The Puzzle of Pain". Penguin, Harmondsworth.
Sternbach, R. A. (1974). "Pain Patients: Traits and Treatment". Academic Press, London and New York.
  Both of these books provide a general introduction to physiological, psychological and social aspects of pain and its treatment.
Weisenberg, M. and Tursky, B. (eds), (1976). "Pain: New Perspectives in Therapy and Research." Plenum.
Sternbach, R. A. (ed.), (1978). "The Psychology of Pain". Raven Press.
  These latter two books are collections of papers, which identify conceptual and methodological issues and controversies at a more sophisticated level.

References

Akil, H., Mayer, O. J. and Liebeskind, J. C. (1976). Antagonism of stimulation-produced analgesia by naloxone, a narcotic antagonist. *Science* 191, 961–962.
Balagaru, S. and Ralph, T. (1973). The analgesic effect of electrical stimulation of the diencephalon and mesencephalon. *Brain Res.* 60, 369–379.
Ball, T. S. and Vogler, R. E. (1971). Uncertain pain and the pain of uncertainty. *Percept. Mot. Skills* 33, 1195–1203.
Beecher, H. K. (1955). The powerful placebo. *J. Am. Med. Ass.* 159, 1602–1606.
Beecher, H. K. (1959). "Measurement of subjective responses". Oxford University Press, New York.
Belville, J. W., Forrest, W. H., Miller, E. and Brown, B. W. (1971). Influence of age on pain relief from analgesics. A study of postoperative patients. *J. Am. Med. Ass.* 217, 1835–1841.
Buytendijk, F. J. J. (1962). "Pain: Its Modes and Functions". University of Chicago Press, Chicago.
Carlen, P. L., Wall, P. O., Nadvorna, H. and Steinbach, J. (1978). Phantom limbs and related phenomena in recent traumatic amputations. *Neurology* 28, 211–217.

Chaves, J. F. and Barber, T. S. (1974). Acupuncture analgesia: a six-factor theory. *Psychoenergetic Systems* 1, 11–21.

Clark, W. C. (1976). Pain Sensitivity and the report of pain. *In* "Pain: New Perspectives in Therapy and Research" (M. Weisenberg and B. Tursky, eds). Plenum, New York.

Craig, K. D. (1978). Social modelling influences on pain. *In* "The Psychology of Pain" (R. A. Sternbach, ed.). Raven Press, New York.

Engel, G. L. (1959). "Psychogenic pain" and the pain-prone patient. *Am. J. Med.* 26, 899–918.

Epstein, S. (1973). Expectancy and magnitude of reaction to a UCS. *Psychophysiology* 10, 100–107.

Fordyce, W. E., Fowler, R. S. Jr., Lehmann, J. F., De Lateur, B. J., Sand, P. L. and Trieschmann, R. B. (1973). Operant conditioning in the treatment of chronic pain. *Arch. Phys. Med. Rehabil.* 54, 399–408.

Girodo, M. and Wood, D. (1979). Talking yourself out of pain: the importance of believing that you can. *Cognitive Therapy and Research* 3, 23–33.

Hilgard, E. L. and Hilgard, J. R. (1975). "Hypnosis in the Relief of Pain". Kaufmann, Los Altos.

IASP Subcommittee on Taxonomy (1979). Pain terms: a list with definitions and notes on usage. *Pain* 6, 249–252.

Kosambi, D. D. (1967). Living prehistory in India. *Sci. Am.* 216, 105.

Leventhal, H. and Everhart, D. (1979). Emotion, pain and physical illness. *In* "Emotions and Psychopathology" (C. E. Izard, ed.). Plenum, New York.

Leventhal, H., Brown, D., Shacham, S. and Engquist, G. (1979). Effects of preparatory information about sensation, threat of pain and attention on cold pressure distress. *J. Personality Soc. Psychol.* 37, 688–714.

Mayer, D. J., Price, D. D., Barber, J. and Rafii, A. (1976). Acupuncture analgesia: evidence for activation of a pain inhibitory system as a mechanism of action. *In* "Advances in Pain Research and Therapy" (J. J. Bonica and D. Albe-Fessard, eds), Vol. 1. Raven Press, New York.

Mechanic, D. (1977). Illness behaviour, social adaptation and the management of illness. *J. Nerv. Ment. Dis.* 165, 79–87.

Mechanic, D. and Volkart, E. H. (1960). Illness behaviour and medical diagnosis. *J. Health Hum. Behav.* 1, 86–94.

Melzack, R. (1973). "The Puzzle of Pain". Penguin, Harmondsworth.

Melzack, R. and Casey, K. L. (1968). Sensory, motivational and central control determinants of pain: a new conceptual model. *In* "The Skin Senses" (D. Kenshalo, ed.). C. C. Thomas, Springfield, Illinois.

Melzack, R. and Torgerson, W. S. (1971). On the language of pain. *Anaesthesiology* 34, 50–59.

Melzack, R. and Wall, P. D. (1965). Pain mechanisms: a new theory. *Science* 150, 971–979.

Noordenbos, W. (1959). "Pain". Elsevier/North Holland, Amsterdam.

Notermans, S. L. H. and Tophoff, M. M. W. A. (1975). Sex differences in pain tolerance and pain apperception. *In* "Pain: Clinical and Empirical Perspectives" (M. Weinberg, ed.). Mosby, St. Louis.

Sarbin, T. R. and Anderson, M. L. (1964). Role – theoretical analysis of hypnotic behaviour. *In* "Handbook of Hypnosis" (J. Gorden, ed.). Macmillan, New York.

Scott, J. and Huskisson, E. C. (1976). Graphic representation of pain. *Pain* 2, 175–184.

Simmel, M. L. (1966). Developmental aspects of body schema. *Child Development* 37, 83–96.

Sternbach, R. A. (1974). "Pain Patients: Traits and Treatment". Academic Press, New York and London.

Sternbach, R. A. and Tursky, B. (1965). Ethnic differences among housewives in psychophysical and skin potential responses to electric shock. *Psychophysiology* 1, 241–246.

Sternbach, R. A., Murphy, R. W., Timmermans, G., Greenhoot, J. H. and Akeson, W. (1974). Measuring the severity of clinical pain. *Adv. Neurol.* 4, 281–288.

Szasz, T. S. (1968). The psychology of persistent pain: a portrait of L'homme douloureux. *In* "Pain" (A. Soulairac, J. Cahn and J. Charpentier, eds). Academic Press, New York and London.

Turk, D. C. (1978). Application of coping-skills training to the treatment of pain. *In* "Stress and Anxiety" (C. D. Spielberger and I. G. Sarason, eds), Vol. V. Halsted Press, New York.

Tursky, B. (1976). The development of a pain perception profile: a psychological approach. *In* "Pain: New Perspectives in Therapy and Research" (M. Weisenberg and B. Tursky, eds). Plenum, New York.

Wall, P. D. (1979). On the relation of injury to pain. *Pain* 6, 253–264.

Woodrow, K. M., Friedman, G. D., Siegelaub, A. B. and Collen, M. F. (1972). Pain tolerance: differences according to age, sex and race. *Psychosom. Med.* 34, 548–556.

Wooley, S. C., Blackwell, B. and Winget, C. (1978). A learning theory model of chronic illness behaviour: theory, treatment, and research. *Psychosom. Med.* 40, 379–401.

Zborowski, M. (1969). "People in Pain". Jossey-Bass, San Francisco.

6 Cortical Correlates of Intelligence

A. Gale
and J. Edwards

Abstract Throughout the history of mental testing, authorities in the field of intelligence have claimed that intelligence tests measure some general, all-round, innate ability which relates to variables of social significance. With the discovery of the electroencephalogram, which measures electrical activity in the brain, there arose the possibility of direct measurement of this inherited characteristic. During the 1940s and 1950s dozens of studies were reported, using a variety of populations including children, adults, the aged and subnormals. There was controversy over the interpretation of the research findings. The event related potential (ERP) research of the 1960s and 1970s has revived interest in cortical correlates of intelligence and generated new theories of intellect tied to models of brain function. All these studies must be seen against a background of political and moral debate, which has affected the capacity of psychologists for disinterested and scientific examination of research. It is now clear that substantial correlations may be obtained between measured intelligence and measures of cortical activity. However, there is uncertainty over the meaning of such correlations, the conditions under which they are produced and the reasons for frequent failures to replicate them. We argue that mere correlational studies are not enough and that research will be improved by drawing together work on intelligence (as a trait) with work on information processing.

I. Introduction

It is not easy to make sense out of research into electrocortical correlates of intelligence. Firstly, the research combines two very technical fields of expertise and there is controversy over method and interpretation in both mental measurement and EEG and ERP research. For example, textbooks on IQ (e.g. Butcher, 1968) typically provide an account of the controversy over appropriate mathematical treatment of test scores, how to derive factors, and how to interpret the factor structure which emerges. Given the way in which mental tests are constructed and standardized, some psychologists hold a

PHYSIOLOGICAL CORRELATES OF HUMAN
BEHAVIOUR   ISBN 0-12-273901-9

very pragmatic view and refuse to speculate beyond the operational procedures employed. For them intelligence is simply what intelligence tests
measure. Thus, the tests say no more than "this individual has gained this
score which, given the tests employed, places him in this percentile point of
the population sampled . . .". Alternative views apply meaning to test scores,
referring to intellectual *processes*, individual differences in cognitive style and
the ways in which inherent differences in IQ have an impact on social
mobility and social class. Thus, significant correlations between IQ scores
and subsequent examination performance may be interpreted in two ways.
IQ and examinations could tap a common intellectual function, or IQ scores
could merely reflect the educational system upon which the examinations are
based, or indeed be attainment tests themselves. Problems relating to the
measurement and interpretation of EEG and ERP correlates of cortical
functions are considered in Vol. II. Again, there is controversy as to what is
being measured, how to measure it and what it means in psychological terms.

It follows that the reader should familiarize himself/herself with basic
materials on the nature of intelligence and its measurement, with particular
reference to the problems raised over the factorial analyses of test scores (see
Kline, 1979). Without such an understanding he/she will come nowhere near
to appreciating the difficulties in the field; many of the researchers whose
work we review appear to assume that intelligence is a unitary trait, that it is
genetically transmitted in a straightforward manner and that electrophysiological measurement will reveal the phenotype which reflects the
genotype. They also seem to assume on occasion that processes involved in
intellectual activity are describable in simple and reducible terms. This leads
to the second difficulty for the reader, for considerable controversy surrounds
the concept of intelligence because of the debate over inter-ethnic comparisons (Eysenck and Kamin, 1981). If you read the work of Eysenck and Kamin
you feel yourself being pulled in one direction and then the other. The
emotion surrounding the debate undermines your capacity to examine the
issues in a dispassionate and disinterested fashion.

There can be no doubt that psychometrics is the most powerful psychological tool to be contributed to society so far, particularly in its capacity to
predict academic performance and its use in personnel selection and evaluation. Because of its power, its use bears responsibilities; psychologists have
seen that their work can have influence on social policy, and that the issues
raised by testing can be as emotive and political as those relating to nuclear
energy, pollution and armament. We are aware that the search for an
electrophysiological correlate of the IQ could be seen to reinforce arguments
in favour of biological differences between groups, but such an implication is
false. Callaway (1973) shows his irritation with this debate: "IQ testing has
become a political issue with the resulting generation of much learned

academic gibberish. People continue to argue about whether or not IQ tests are culturally biased, and some suggest AEP measures may be 'culture-free'. The whole argument seems absurd; as an extreme example, consider how culturally determined prenatal and perinatal nutrition can affect gross brain development. Even at the subtle psychological level we suspect that habitual modes of cognitive functioning influence AEP measures. Thus, like most other behaviour, AEP's will reflect genetic, biological and social influences" (p. 557). We cite Callaway at length because he is both right and wrong. There are *few* extreme hereditarians or extreme environmentalists (although more of the latter); most of the participants in the debate are indeed interactionists. The controversies are rarely over the two extreme positions, but over (i) the partitioning of variance between heredity, environment and their interactions, and (ii) issues relating to the nature of the interactive process and the limits of modifiability. Long ago, Anastasi (1958) identified these as the "how much" and the "how" arguments. It is certainly logically possible to separate out biologically and experientially determined aspects of the ERP and to allocate differential variance. Whether ERP's are better candidates in this respect than traditional paper and pencil tests is, we agree, a matter of considerable doubt.

Fear of abuse of psychometric devices is matched by a concern at the use to which psychophysiological instrumentation might be put. Traditional IQ tests may be powerful, but their capacity to predict performance *other* than academic success in examinations is relatively weak. We also know from Terman's longitudinal studies that IQ alone is not the best predictor but needs to be taken together with tests of personality and emotional stability (Terman and Oden, 1959). It is questionable whether psychophysiological measurement can *replace* paper and pencil tests for such purposes, particularly where in North American tradition sub-test profiles are seen to be of more value in selection and occupational guidance than the score for *g* favoured by past British orthodoxy. Without wishing to question the motives of those who have set about marketing devices for measuring mental efficiency, it surely is likely in psychological terms that those who have a *commercial* interest in such machines are more likely to have a *set* to look upon their own research more favourably; commercial involvement cannot always be compatible with the disinterested view which characterizes the archetypal scientist. It is encouraging to note that Ertl (1971) has not shirked from publishing non-significant findings, even though he manufactured Neural Efficiency Analysers for general use.

Thus we see that there are several sources of potential bias in this field. The reader who seeks a balanced view should refer to the book of Loehlin *et al.* (1975), the proceeds of which are used to promote inter-ethnic harmony, and whose chapters and appendices were shown to parties to the race and IQ controversy prior to publication. Another volume, by Vernon (1979) is equally objective in its evaluation of the evidence. The truth is that, while there is considerable evidence of within-ethnic heritability of IQ and evidence of within-group relationships between IQ and variables of social significance, the logical leap to *between-group* comparisons simply cannot be made. Equally important is the *residual* variance; whatever value is placed upon the *heritability* estimate is quite sufficient in an interactive model to allow for considerable variation in resultant behaviour in the individual. It is social policy and not psychology which determines the resources available to ensure all individuals develop within a psychologically satisfactory environment, and there is plenty of evidence that individuals change in a positive direction when removed from impoverished environments (Clarke and Clarke, 1976). For an excellent discussion of problems of genetic modelling in the field of individual differences see Eaves and Young (1981); and Roubertoux (1983), who reviews genetic studies relating to the transmission of psychophysiological variables. Over and above these more tangible issues, however, is the fact that the concept of intelligence has undergone some dramatic changes in emphasis (Butcher, 1968). Just as the polygraph and the microcomputer are now commonplace in psychophysiological laboratories, so mainframe computers have taken away the mystique which surrounded factor analysis in its infancy; now thousands of test score results may be processed and infinite numbers of factorial solutions be assessed in matters of hours rather than months or years. Thus the faith earlier workers placed upon particular factorial solutions and the zeal and enthusiasm generated by months of hand calculation has been diluted. The work of the Piaget school, in revealing qualitative differences in intellectual process with age, has modified notions of constancy of the IQ, while the use of large computers for studies of artificial intelligence and the growth of cognitive psychology, has shifted the emphasis to *process* rather than stable dispositions. Even within the psychometric tradition, Guilford (e.g. 1967) has emphasized the dynamic nature of the interaction of his 120 factors. In psychophysiology and in experimental neuropsychology studies of hemispheral specialization clearly indicate that solutions to intellectual problems may be arrived at by very different routes. Finally, although creativity research has come to a comma if not a complete full stop, it has focused attention yet again on the need to consider variability in the ways in which various forms of competent behaviour emerge.

Thus although there is evidence (i) that IQ has a strong hereditary component, (ii) that it has striking retest reliability, and (iii) that the EEG has both reliability and strong hereditary determination, it does *not* necessarily follow that by correlating one with the other some simple relationship will emerge. Before correlating two variables, one is well-advised to know something of the *functional* significance of at least one of them. Combining the unknown with the unknown does not necessarily increase human knowledge in a systematic fashion.

We have written this lengthy introduction to the topic because we believe not only that research in this field has remained virtually stationary in conception for more than forty years, but that psychophysiological endeavours have fallen behind parallel trends and developments in the study of intellectual process. Thus we hope this review becomes out of date as soon as possible. Attention to our cautionary remarks is essential. The present authors' view is that the confusion in the field reflects, in part at least, the refusal of researchers to tolerate complexity. The reader would be well served by referring to a classic paper by Miles (1957) which is referred to in most British texts on intelligence. Miles draws the distinction between *real* and *nominal* definitions. To list a set of attributes is not to imply that the attributes in combination form an *entity*. Thus humid, cold, wet and equatorial describe attributes of the world's weather. It is unlikely, however, that God will ever think it worthwhile to attach electrodes to the North and South Poles in order to reveal some electrophysical correlate of a thing called "the Weather". The early psychometric testers claimed their factors were only mathematical devices for characterizing clusters of related attributes. We would not be writing this chapter if we did not believe that physiology and behaviour are related; that does not commit us to the view that such relationships need be simple. Indeed since behaviour is patently complex, it is likely that factors correlated with it will also be complex.

II. EEG and Test Intelligence

We begin our review with a quartet of papers, all published in the *Psychological Bulletin*, beginning with a major review by Ellingson (1956) and followed by a debate between Ellingson (1966) and Vogel and Broverman (1964, 1966). Ellingson has been a major critic of EEG studies and the attempt to relate the EEG to psychological processes. His 1956 review was concerned with a range of phenomena: sleep, stimulation (including photic driving), hypotheses concerning the functional characteristics of alpha activity, voluntary movement, conditioning, learning and memory, hypnosis, emotion, personality, and intellectual processes including intelligence, mental effort and imagery. This was therefore a typically impressive and wide ranging *tour de force* of a review, which provided an authoritative background to Ellingson's observation that "The weight of evidence indicates that the alpha rhythm is unrelated to test intelligence" (p. 18). The discussion of intelligence occupies one column only of a very long paper, indicating the paucity of studies in the field and the lack of coherent findings. Ellingson's conclusion was in line with earlier more substantial reviews of the topic by Lindsley (1944) and Ostow (1950).

Vogel and Broverman (1964) set out to qualify this unanimous and negative view. They accuse Lindsley, Ostow and Ellingson of selectivity, claiming that there was a continuous stream of papers equal in quantity and quality to those reviewed, but which reported positive results. They review studies of the EEG and intelligence in the feeble-minded, children, normal adults, the aged and those with brain disease. While pointing out that several studies might have confounded with age, they conclude that EEG characteristics had been shown to relate to degree of Mental Age (MA) among feeble-minded children in a majority of studies, particularly when *non*-occipital placements were employed and the focus was not wholly upon simple measures of alpha activity. As regards normal children, outcomes again varied. However, they conclude that positive findings might be masked when the EEG is correlated with IQ rather than MA; studies with null results tended not to hold Chronological Age (CA) constant. They cite a study by Netchine and Lairy (1960) showing a significant negative correlation with alpha frequency at 5–6 years, which inverts sign and becomes significant again at 9 years through to 12 years. Studies by Lindsley and others had failed to control for age. Among adults, only Mundy-Castle's laboratory (e.g. Mundy-Castle, 1958) had obtained significant findings; this group had been unique in using the Wechsler scales to measure intelligence. It is logically possible of course for the Wechsler scales to share variance with other IQ tests and with aspects of the EEG, but for the EEG not to share variance with those other tests. In relation to studies with the aged, Vogel and Broverman point out that the ideal study involves controls for age, health and pre-geriatric intellectual level; no study satisfied these requirements. As with child studies, MA and CA were often confounded. So far as brain disease is concerned, they cite studies indicating clear evidence of specific EEG abnormalities combined with specific intellectual loss, e.g. hemispheral differences in relation to verbal and performance scores. Thus they conclude that except for normal adults the burden of evidence for an association between the EEG and measured intelligence is positive. They argue that intelligence becomes progressively differentiated and elaborated with age, making it easier to detect relationships in children, where intelligence is more unitary in nature. Moreover, if such differentiation implies differential topographical fluctuations, then occipital measurement alone (relatively successful in children) is unlikely to be successful in the case of adult subjects. They plead for a much more sophisticated approach to the analysis of the EEG, involving topography and a wide range of frequencies. Since sex differences in the EEG had been frequently reported, they cautioned against computing correlations for mixed sex populations. (We should note that since there are established sex differences in developmental rate and attainment, even age-related sex samples cannot be compared directly and their use might be misleading; Tanner, 1962). Of the several dozen studies reviewed, only one had employed an *active* task involving "intelligent" behaviour; while they do not deny MA:EEG correlates might be revealed at rest, they claim such differences as there are will be accentuated during processes which reflect the behaviour sampled by IQ tests.

Thus we have two very extensive and closely argued reviews of the same subject area, but coming to diametrically opposed conclusions.

Ellingson (1966) came back with a sharp rejoinder. He challenged the view that studies of subjects with brain damage or EEG abnormalities will illuminate problems relating to normal functioning. Abnormal EEG's and deficits in intelligence certainly can be observed in the same population, but their association neither implies correlation nor generality to other contexts. He draws attention to the fact that the EEG measures employed are often eccentric or at least unique to the laboratory in question, unstandardized and possibly unreliable. Few studies had employed experimenters blind to the hypothesis that IQ and EEG would be correlated or to the subject's score on the IQ test. Retarded subjects are retarded for a variety of reasons and should not be cast indiscriminately within the same population. He then examines in detail several of the studies cited by Vogel and Broverman (1964).

Unfortunately, the Vogel and Broverman (1966) reply is equally sharp, but clearly better informed. They have little quarrel over methodological points; but they do take Ellingson to task over his rejection of individual studies, citing chapter and verse in a very detailed fashion. It is unfortunately clear that Ellingson had failed to read the papers in question with due care. The reader is invited to make careful scrutiny of these four papers; our view is that the Vogel and Broverman (1964, 1966) arguments and supporting data are powerful and that Ellingson's arguments owe more to rhetoric than reason. The key points are as follows. (i) Ellingson claims it is improper to include in these studies subjects with abnormal EEG's. Vogel and Broverman point out that estimates of abnormality can vary between 15% and upwards in a "normal" population. Thus the definition of abnormal EEG is itself unreliable. (We should note that Gibbs and Gibbs' (1963) estimate of EEG abnormality in adolescents would exclude more than 30% of subjects from any study!). (ii) In the studies of retarded groups, subjects were indeed selected on the basis of objective criteria and distinctions were drawn between subcategories (i.e. subjects were not lumped together as Ellingson alleged). (iii) That is only one of more than a dozen errors of fact of which Vogel and Broverman accuse Ellingson. (iv) Even so, they challenge his view that an actuarial balance sheet is a means of deciding the truth or falsehood of a scientific assertion. If there are competent and well-designed replications with similar results, then they can only be overturned by systematic analysis: "To summarize, Ellingson's critique of Vogel and Broverman, 1964 is based almost entirely on error" (p. 104). (v) Finally, they draw attention to Ellingson's conviction that "the EEG is such a primitive bioelectric function of neural tissue and as such, cannot be expected to relate to higher functions such as intelligence or personality". They charge Ellingson with the responsibility for inhibiting EEG research in this field, by asserting this a priori view in review articles. It is presumably this alleged prejudice which limited his selection and interpretation of the existing literature.

It is refreshing to find that men of science are not free of passion. These articles are particularly angry and irritable in style and one suspects that there were more bitter accusations before the editorial blue pencil did its work. We have devoted considerable attention to these reviews because the issues today still remain very much the same.

III. List of Requirements for EEG/ERP and IQ Research

(i)   Care is needed in the assessment of intelligence; a global score, derived from only one IQ test, is quite unsatisfactory. Moreover, there is reason to believe that different sub-scales (e.g. verbal versus performance; fluid versus crystallized intelligence) might relate to different hemispheres, different electrode placements and of course, different experimental tasks and contexts.

(ii)   Single EEG channels are insufficient. Multiple recording is essential and EEG parameters should reflect reliable and well-established methods of measurement. A topographical analysis may not only reveal differential discriminability but differential *patterning* in terms of magnitude, sign and the conditions under which particular effects hold.

(iii) Heterogenous groups, representing the full ability range, should be used. Extreme groups may be different in a *variety* of ways and special populations may give special effects; in neither case may the outcome truly reflect processes in the criterion variable.

(iv)   Age must be controlled for or partialled out.

(v)   Subject sex, particularly in developmental studies, must be controlled for.

(vi)   Subjects should perform tasks which have prima-facie relevance to the processes underlying IQ test scores.

(vii) Experimenters should be blind to test score both at the time of recording and the time of scoring, particularly if the data selection schedule is not automatic.

(viii)   Elaborate analysis is required for determining the interrelationships between EEG parameters and IQ items and sub-scales.

(ix)   Reliability estimates should be obtained of all measures employed.

(x)   There are always possibilities of confounding, for example, institutional life influences on experimental groups, sex and age characteristics of subjects.

(xi)   Since most tasks employed involve experimental control of *attention* and since attentional regulation is required to perform well in IQ tests, it is always possible that what is measured (particularly in extreme group designs) is an EEG correlate of attention, i.e. it is a correlate of both IQ test performance and capacity to satisfy laboratory demands. While attentional control is clearly not unrelated to intelligent performance, few would assert that it is *synonymous* with intelligence.

All these issues of methodology and inference must be borne in mind when considering more contemporary work. Vogel and Broverman suggest that the lack of confirmation of the EEG/IQ relation "has been due less to a failure to find relationships which have been sought than it has been due to a failure to initiate research".

The late 1960s and the 1970s witnessed a revival of work on this most important topic, with a shift towards evoked potential work. This resurgence was regrettably accompanied by both the equivocal pattern of findings derived from spontaneous rhythm research and the associated errors in both method and interpretation.

IV. More Recent Research

Traditional studies relating IQ to aspects of the EEG still appear. For example, Petersen *et al.* (1976) present a complicated study in which children who are "normal", according to a number of criteria, constitute a large sample of more than 200 subjects. The study included sub-groups on the basis of social class, which was its main focus, and there were in addition sub-groups classified on the basis of EEG characteristics. Generally, they found little relation between EEG and IQ, although in one case a male sample with abnormal EEG (i.e. 14 and 6 Hz wave spike) had a *higher* IQ than the normal EEG controls!

Undoubtedly the most impressive of spontaneous EEG studies is that of Giannitrapani (1969), who explored EEG frequency and IQ making three assumptions: (i) Frequency will be positively related to IQ; (ii) frequency will increase during mental tasks; and (iii) there will be greatest hemispheral differentiation during mental work. A sample of only 18 subjects was used with IQ scores ranging from 93–143 (WAIS) and an age range of 21–45 years. Frontal, temporal, parietal and occipital leads were sampled from both hemispheres. Conditions were rest (eyes closed) and mental multiplication. Experimenters were blind to the hypotheses and records were scored independently by two scorers. Reliability coefficients were presented. Analysis of variance (ANOVA) was computed for conditions, area, period (into task) and IQ (two groups: middle and high). Also Spearman's Rho was calculated for verbal, performance and full IQ scores, taken separately. Strangely, conditions had no significant effect (this may have been due to fixed order) and there was no major effect for IQ and conditions; the left hemisphere showed a higher frequency. Brain areas produced significant effects for IQ; there was a crossover effect such that high IQ subjects had a higher parietal frequency in the left hemisphere and a higher occipital frequency in the right hemisphere, with the reverse holding for the middle IQ group. Several correlations are presented between (i) mathematics minus rest and (ii) left hemisphere scores for frequency, and IQ such that the higher the IQ the *lower* the difference between conditions and the *larger* the differences between hemispheres. We shall see later that in an ERP study by Shucard and Horn (1973) it is alleged greater *differences* between conditions for brighter subjects are evidence of greater *flexibility*; thus every possible finding can always find a plausible explanation! Some of the correlations in the Giannitrapani study are extraordinarily high, given that this is a psychophysiological study and N is so small; it is indeed unusual in EEG studies for treatment effects to be swamped by individual difference effects; the reverse is usually the case, particularly when a rest period with eyes closed is being compared with an active and involving task. Thus the correlation between full IQ score and a collapsed score for frontal-parietal-temporal minus occipital EEG (taking individual signs into account) is 0·72 and several other correlations exceed 0·5, the sign varying in accordance with the crossover effects in Area:IQ relations revealed in the ANOVA. Alpha index is also correlated with WAIS scores.

Does this study overcome objections made to previous work? On the positive side there is adequate topological sampling and this reveals how differences in direction of relation can occur, making it quite clear that negative findings or even positive findings based on one or two channels cannot be trusted. On such grounds alone we should be grateful for this study. Similarly, more than adequate formal requirements are satisfied for measurement and statistical analysis. The small sample and the limited choice of tasks are weaknesses. More important criticisms, on the basis of earlier studies are as follows.

(i) Age is not controlled for and may have been confounded; for example, some subjects might have been both younger and less intelligent.

Younger subjects *could* have been trained nurses and older subjects established medical colleagues.
(ii) Was arousal controlled for? The significant correlation between alpha index and IQ suggests high IQ subjects were more relaxed.
(iii) The greater difference between hemispheres for *brighter* subjects indicates possibly *less* difficulty in mental computation i.e. more focused attention; this is reflected in *increased* differentiation of parietal activation (specific to calculation) and decreased *occipital* differential activation (reflecting general, non-specific activation).

Such criticisms may seem unduly carping. The Giannitrapani study was conducted in a most scrupulous fashion and presents perhaps the most powerful set of data in the literature. Given the revival of studies of hemispheral differentiation of psychological function, this clearly represents one of the ways forward. We turn now to studies of event related potentials.

V. ERP Studies of Test Intelligence

A study by Shucard and Horn (1972) is notable for its care and attention to detail. Referring to the early ERP work by Ertl and associates (e.g. Ertl and Shafer, 1969), Shucard and Horn point out that those studies were characterized by selective subgroups (including extremes) and gross measures of the IQ, and were not integrated within a coherent theory. In contrast, they employ a wide-ranging sample in which they attempt to control for occupation, social class, age and sex; a battery of 16 tests, with particular focus on the distinction between fluid and crystallized intelligence (see Cattell, 1963); include controls for speed; and vary attentional requirements. Their ERP measurement was limited to only one left and one right hemisphere channel (F3-P3 and F4-P4, the latter replicating Ertl's favoured placement). Three treatments were used in fixed order: reaction time to a light stimulus, counting the number of light stimuli, and lying quietly and attending to the stimuli (intrinsic attention). We should note the authors do not refer to the pitfalls of fixed order designs, where for example fatigue might be confounded with type of task. Their *general* finding (supported in terms of *sign* in virtually all their correlations) was that long ERP latency was associated with low ability, short latency with high ability. This is quite in line both with Ertl's theory and his findings (see pp. 91–92 below). The majority of their correlations were in the region of -0.15 ($p<0.05$ at $r=0.195$ for their sample of 100). Contrary to the expectations of Vogel and Broverman, condition 3, involving least response, yielded a higher proportion of significant correlations, which also tended to be larger in magnitude.

It is not easy to make a simple verbal characterization of the mass of data presented; it does appear, however, that ERP correlations held with larger groupings of test scores, i.e. partialling out of sub-scales reduced the magnitude of the correlation. They suggest that one might wish to interpret their task-times-ability finding as an indication that "bright subjects . . . tend to maintain alertness, even during the rather boring intrinsic activation condition . . . this implies that short evoked potential latency represents in part, intellectual alertness" (p. 66). However, subjective reports indicated that brighter subjects felt less alert during the more boring tasks. This they claim supports the view that brighter subjects are more *flexible*, i.e. can allocate attention appropriately to tasks making different demands on them than can duller subjects. The present authors find the presentation of several dozen correlations quite confusing and cannot understand why the data were not subjected to some higher order factor analysis to see if a patterning of factors emerged. While Shucard and Horn are clearly and openly not satisfied with the alternative interpretations of their findings, it is difficult to see how the study constitutes a great advance in our knowledge. We should note also that correlations of about 0·2, whether statistically significant or not, account for less than 5% of the overall variance. It remains open whether their correlations reflect anything directly to do with intelligence or rather the ease with which brighter persons adapt to laboratory conditions. In a follow-up study, which procedurally appears to be identical, Shucard and Horn (1973) examined difference scores (i.e. ERP values between conditions). Of 22 correlations five were found to be significant (range 0·21 to 0·25). These held only for fluid intelligence. Again they claim that the results indicate the brighter subjects are more "modifiable and show greater plasticity in their response". Given the tiny size of these correlations we are most sceptical about their bearing upon IQ. One only needs a small common variance on a factor common to IQ and ERP (capacity to relax in the laboratory?), which may be antecedent to or consequent causally upon IQ, to yield such modest evidence of a "relationship". Such a criticism is particularly relevant to the studies of Ertl (e.g. 1971) where extreme groups are employed, for the possibility of confounding with other variables is enhanced. Indeed, in the 1971 study Ertl failed to show an effect, for an enormous sample, in comparing high and low IQ subjects but using a Fourier transform rather than his latency measure. Similar criticisms can be directed at a study by Rhodes *et al.* (1969). They found late components of the ERP to be higher in bright children, who also showed hemispheral differences. However, as we shall see below, replications of Ertl's work by Hendrickson yield extremely high correlations, which it is difficult to dismiss on the grounds of artefact.

A paper by Everhart *et al.* (1974) is of interest because it seems frankly antagonistic to Ertl. Unable to obtain a technical manual or a diagram of Ertl's commercially available Neural Efficiency Analyser (NEA) they subjected the machine to rigorous testing to discover what exactly it measured! They report (i) relative consistency of score over six trials, (ii) that the NEA measures background EEG and not visual ERP's (Callaway ,1975, suggests the two are in fact confounded but in a reasonable fashion), and (iii) correlations based on two samples of 20 and 47 subjects, between WAIS and NEA scores as high as $-0·5$ for verbal scores and $0·54$ for digit symbols. In all five from fourteen correlations were significant, with a correlation of $-0·43$ for the full score. In view of the scepticism expressed by these authors and their reluctance to consider their findings of any value, we must conclude that this is a study clearly in support of Ertl's views and data, albeit perhaps a reflection of ongoing EEG rather than ERP, but derived in favour of Ertl in the most hostile of circumstances. Ertl's claims are discussed below.

A. *The Neural Efficiency Hypothesis*

Callaway (1975) provides an excellent and balanced summary of the first ten years of ERP's and IQ. His discussion is logical, involves rigorous analysis of previous work, and gives a detailed account of his own studies. The early work of Chalke and Ertl (1965) is characterized as being associated with a straightforward hypothesis: "fast minds should have higher IQ's – fast brains should produce short-latency AEP's and fast minds should be the companions of fast brains" (p. 43). He then points out that the history of the research proved to be far from simple. Ertl's work is criticized on several grounds: (i) use of a peculiar bipolar electrode placement (or placements, since information on location is ambiguous); (ii) an unusual definition of latency ("Ertl's definition of latency can result in the identification of events that are given the same name but are quite different from subject to subject", p. 45); Ertl's method is based on a zero-cross-type metric rather than the usual peak-type; (iii) use of Pearson's *r* on extreme groups, and (iv) insensitivity (because of a strong biological commitment) to age and arousal state of subjects. Nevertheless, in spite of these problems, Callaway finds Ertl's data to be impressive; he presents a table from Ertl and Schafer (1969) based on 566 schoolchildren, yielding correlations on WISC, PMA and Otis in the $-0·35$ region. He cites supporting evidence from several other studies using visual ERP frequency analysis. He also presents detailed accounts of work from his own laboratories involving both visual and auditory ERP's. On the negative side is a major and publicly funded study by Davis (1971), carried out in association with Ertl, and what Callaway calls quasi-failure to replicate by Engel and Henderson (1973). Failure to replicate in their study *could* have been due to differences in electrode placements and latency measurement; an effect was found by Engel and Henderson when black and white subjects were treated within a multiple correlation. Thus we see there are data both anti- and pro- Ertl's view, using visual ERP's; brighter subjects have shorter latency, reflecting in his theory, faster brainpower.

However, an important difficulty arises for the theory when it comes to measurement of auditory ERP's. Callaway found that auditory ERP measures that correlated negatively with age correlated *positively* with IQ score! This finding undermines the neural efficiency hypothesis of Ertl, since brighter children by definition have higher IQ scores like those of older children. Brainpower and neural speed cannot hold for visual ERP's in one direction and auditory ERP's in the reverse direction and at one and the same time be seen to be a fundamental property of intelligence, reflected in ERP's. Hendrickson (1972) found the reverse, i.e. auditory and visual effects were the same, while Rust (1975) using two samples of 84 and 212 subjects found no relation with auditory ERP's. Callaway is unable to reconcile these contradictory findings and cites studies by Ertl himself (1969) and Straumanis *et al.* (1973) using Downs syndrome and control children, showing *shorter* auditory ERP latencies for *duller* children.

In concluding his extensive and detailed review, Callaway rejects the neural efficiency hypothesis. Nor can a version of the Shucard and Horn (1973) boredom interpretation stand, since it fits visual ERP data but not auditory ERP data, where shorter latency goes with habituation while longer latency goes (in several studies) with higher IQ. Callaway sees studies which vary task demands and, in particular, manipulations which cause the latency/IQ correlation to vanish, to hold most promise for future research.

B. *The Hendrickson Theory*

We have tried to present a balanced view. We have not cited all the studies available because that would not really help us in our appraisal. Before summarizing the overall position we consider two very recent studies by the same workers, which exhibit correlations of an extraordinary magnitude, in one case barely short of the retest reliability coefficients of either IQ or EEG! These are studies by Hendrickson and Hendrickson (1980) and Blinkhorn and Hendrickson (1982). The Hendricksons' theory is delightfully simple.

> "The theory proposes that higher intelligence is a function of lower error rates in the central nervous system, and that in consequence of the way information is coded and transmitted in the brain the effect of error is to reduce both the number and the amplitude of excursions from the zero point in the AEP trace. Therefore, differences in IQ should be manifested in AEP traces as differences in complexity, which can be captured in a simple measure involving no more than the measurement of the length of the trace over a standard epoch. This measure we refer to as the "string" measure, since in effect one treats an AEP trace like a piece of string and measures its straightened length."

Hendrickson and Hendrickson obtained a correlation of 0·77 from 254 children aged 14 to 16 years, using the full WAIS IQ scale. More impressive perhaps is the study of Blinkhorn and Hendrickson where, using advanced students, correlations between score on the Advanced Progressive Matrices and the string measure was 0·53, for 33 subjects. Test scores were derived before the EEG study and unknown to the experimenter. Since a variety of test scores were available, a total of 54 correlations was computed, with only three significant. Nevertheless, Blinkhorn and Hendrickson claim that, if the correlation obtained is corrected for full range IQ score, it would be in the region of 0·70 and 0·84, i.e. very similar in magnitude to the earlier study. We should note that these data are for auditory presentation of simple tones and that Blinkhorn and Hendrickson wish to eschew the use of complex tasks.

> "The string measurement procedure involves the subject in no decisions, makes no apparent demands on memory, involves no difficult discriminations, uses stimulus intensities very far above threshold . . . whilst one can see the point of constructing cognitive models to account for large correlations between the latter and IQ, there appears to be no place for such models in accounts of string-IQ correlations, given the mindless nature of the "task" involved."

With this pair of papers we must end our review, for the research has come full circle.

VI. Conclusion

As time goes on and more and more experimenters dabble with electro-cortical measures and traditional IQ measures, evidence accumulates to demonstrate a correlation between the two variables. But the position is little different from that reviewed by Vogel and Broverman. Very many studies have shown modest effects while equally competent studies show reverse findings or null effects. However, the signposts for future work are pretty clear. What is needed is a study involving repeated measurement on a group of subjects; incorporating spontaneous EEG and ERP; using visual and auditory ERP's; standard, Ertl and Hendrickson measures of response; multichannel topographical recording for both EEG and ERP; and a variety of tasks, ranging from Hendrickson's "mindless" tone presentations to complex problem solving. Topographical analysis would be aided by measures of coherence between locations since Surwillo (1971) and others have suggested that the amount of brain involvement in tasks is a function of ability. Until all the existing research has been incorporated into such a common design, a programme which would not be difficult to execute, there will be lingering doubt and anxiety as to whether the EEG and IQ are correlated in a direct and simple fashion. Certainly, it seems difficult to dismiss findings like those of Giannitrapani (1969) or Hendrickson and Hendrickson (1980) with their enormous effects, on any of the grounds which have been given in relation to other studies. It must be considered remarkable that responses to a paper and pencil test can correlate so readily with what Ellingson called "a primitive bioelectric function of neural tissue". On balance, time appears to show that Vogel and Broverman were correct in their predictions for the future. However, we still have a long way to go before the functional significance of these relationships, is clearly understood even if the pattern of findings becomes consistent. Correlations yes, but process no. Blinkhorn and Hendrickson may generate robust data but they do not produce sound arguments. It may well be that correlations of considerable magnitude appear under straightforward testing conditions, but it must then be shown (i) why it is they do *not* appear under complex conditions (if that indeed is the case) and (ii) how evoked potential changes of this sort are involved in processes which lead to more efficient performance. Moreover, since the string measure of Hendrickson and Hendrickson (1980) appears to resemble at least the account of NEA given by Everhart *et al.* (1974), it is surely incumbent upon Hendrickson to explain to us how it is that the measure succeeds on some occasions and fails on others, and why it is that her findings for auditory potentials appear to be so different from those of authorities like Callaway and, on occasion, Ertl himself.

Finally, there is a feature common to virtually all the work on this topic. Workers have set out to demonstrate that aspects of brain activity relate to a dimension of psychological significance, i.e. intelligence. But elsewhere in this volume we see that the same aspects of the EEG, for example alpha amplitude, relate to other dimensions of psychological significance such as extraversion–introversion. If all such variables are seen to correlate in a similar way with the same aspects of the electrocortical measure then one possible logical conclusion is that they all share variance with some factor which *may* be psychologically trivial. One essential requirement if work is to progress is to include *all* such measures in an appropriate design, so that at the very least each correlated factor can be partialled out systematically. Alternatively, a multivariate approach would enable higher order factors to be derived which in turn might lead to the creation of a general model of brain function. With such a model we shall be able to make sense of findings in this review. Indeed, the generation of further correlational data, in the absence of a general and testable model of brain function, strikes us as wasteful of research effort and research funding. If indeed measures of electrocortical activity can be shown to vary systematically with well validated psychometric measures under theory-related test conditions, we *could* be on the threshold of major discoveries. Sources of error in this field of research have remained almost constant for thirty years. Is it unfair to appeal for a change in research strategy for the 1980s?

Further Reading

Vernon, P. E. (1979). "Intelligence: Heredity and Environment". Freeman, San Francisco.
  An up-to-date and balanced account of controversies surrounding the measurement of intelligence, and the effects of genetic and environmental factors in determining individual attainments.
Andreassi, J. L. (1980). "Psychophysiology: Human Behavior and Physiological Response" Oxford University Press, New York.
  Summarizes key research findings in psychophysiology. The sections on intelligence provide a comprehensive coverage, but lack a critical framework.
Callaway, E. (1975). "Brain Electrical Potentials and Individual Psychological Differences" Grune and Stratton, New York.
  A highly critical and authoritative account of electrocortical studies. Although there are many packed pages of research findings, Callaway's frank and entertaining style of presentation, makes the book a pleasure to read.

References

Anastasi, A. (1958). Heredity, environment, and the question "How?" *Psychol. Rev.* **65**, 197–208.
Blinkhorn, S. F. and Hendrickson, D. E. (1982). Averaged evoked responses and psychometric intelligence. *Nature* **295**, 596–597.
Butcher, H. J. (1968). "Human Intelligence: Its Nature and Assessment". Methuen, London.
Callaway, E. (1973). Correlations between average evoked potentials and measures of intelligence. *Arch. Gen. Psychiat.* **29**, 553–558.
Callaway, E. (1975). "Brain Electric Potentials and Individual Psychological Differences". Grune and Stratton, New York.
Cattell, R. B. (1963). Theory of fluid and crystallized intelligence: a critical experiment. *J. Educ. Psychol.* **54**, 1–22.
Chalke, F. C. R. and Ertl, J. P. (1965). Evoked potentials and intelligence. *Life Sci.* **4**, 1319–1322.
Clarke, A. M. and Clarke, A. D. B. (1976). "Early Experience: Myth and Evidence". Open Books, London.
Davis, F. B. (1971). The measurement of mental capability through evoked potential recording. *Educ. Rec. Res. Bull.* No. 1.
Eaves, L. and Young, P. A. (1981). Genetical theory and personality differences. *In* "Dimensions of Personality: Papers in Honour of H. J. Eysenck (R. Lynn, ed.), pp. 129–180. Pergamon Press, Oxford.
Ellingson, R. J. (1956). Brain waves and problems of psychology. *Psychol. Bull.* **53**, 1–34.
Ellingson, R. J. (1966). Relationship between EEG and test intelligence: a commentary. *Psychol. Bull.* **65**, 91–98.

Engel, R. and Henderson, N. B. (1973). Visual evoked responses and IQ scores at school age. *Dev. Med. Child Neuro.* **15**, 136–145.

Ertl, J. P. (1969) Neural efficiency and human intelligence. Final Report, US Office of Education Project, No. 9–0105.

Ertl, J. P. (1971) Fourier analysis of evoked potentials and human intelligence. *Nature* **230**, 525–526.

Ertl, J. P. and Schafer, E. W. P. (1969). Brain response correlates of psychometric intelligence. *Nature* **223**, 421–422.

Everhart, J. D., China, C. L. and Auger, R. A. (1974). Measures of EEG and verbal intelligence: an inverse relationship. *Physiol. Psychol.* **2**, 374–378.

Eysenck, H. J. and Kamin, L. (1981). "Intelligence: The Battle for the Mind". Penguin, Harmondsworth.

Giannitrapani, D. (1969). EEG average frequency and intelligence. *Electroenceph. Clin. Neurophysiol.* **27**, 480–486.

Gibbs, F. A. and Gibbs, E. L. (1963). Fourteen and six per second positive spikes. *Electroenceph. Clin. Neurophysiol.* **15**, 553–557.

Guilford, J. P. (1967). "The Nature of Human Intelligence" McGraw-Hill, New York.

Hendrickson, D. E. (1972). An examination of individual differences in cortical evoked response. Unpublished Ph.D. Thesis, University of London.

Hendrickson, D. E. and Hendrickson, A. E. (1980). The biological basis of individual differences in intelligence. *Personality and Individual Differences,* **1**, 3–33.

Kline, P. (1979). "Psychometrics and Psychology". Academic Press, London and New York.

Lindsley, D. B. (1944). Electroencephalography. *In* "Personality and Behaviour Disorders" (J. McV. Hunt, ed.) Vol. 2, pp. 1033–1103. Ronald, New York.

Loehlin, J. C. Lindzey, G. and Spuhler, K. P. (1975). "Race Differences in Intelligence". Freeman, New York.

Miles, T. R. (1957). Contributions to intelligence testing and the theory of intelligence. I. On defining intelligence. *Br. J. Educ. Psychol.* **27**, 153–165.

Mundy-Castle, A. C. (1958). Electrophysiological correlates of intelligence. *J. Personality* **26**, 184–199.

Netchine, S. and Lairy, G. C. (1960). Ondes cérébrales et niveau mental: quelques aspects de l'évolution génétique du trace EEG suivant le niveau. *Enfance* **4**, 427–439.

Ostow, M. (1950). Psychic function and the electroencephalogram. *Arch. Neurol. Psychiat.* **64**, 385–400.

Petersen, I., Sellden, U. and Bosaeus, E. (1976). The relationship between IQ, social class and EEG findings in healthy children investigated by child-psychiatric methods. *Scand. J. Psychol.* **17**, 189–197.

Rhodes, L. E., Dustman, R. E. and Beck, E. C. (1969). The visual evoked response: a comparison of bright and dull children. *Electroenceph. Clin. Neurophysiol.* **27**, 364–372.

Roubertoux, P. (1983). Genetic correlates of personality and temperament: the origins of individual differences. *In* "The Biological Bases of Personality and Behavior" (J. Strelau, F. Farley and A. Gale, eds). Hemisphere, New York.

Rust, J. (1975). Cortical evoked potential, personality and intelligence. *J. Comp. Physiol. Psychol.* **89**, 1220–1226.

Shucard, D. W. and Horn, J. L. (1972). Evoked cortical potentials and measurement of human abilities. *J. Comp. Physiol. Psychol.* **81**, 59–68.

6. Correlates of Intelligence

Shucard, D. W. and Horn, J. L. (1973). Evoked potential amplitude change related to intelligence and arousal. *Psychophysiology* 10, 445–452.

Straumanis, J. J., Shagass, C. and Overton, D. A. (1973). Auditory evoked responses in young adults with Down's syndrome and idiopathic mental retardation. *Biol. Psychiat.* 6, 75–80.

Surwillo, W. W. (1971). Human reaction time and period of the EEG in relation to development. *Psychophysiology* 8, 468–482.

Tanner, J. M. (1962). "Growth and Adolescence" (2nd Edn). Blackwell, Oxford.

Terman, L. M. and Oden, M. H. (1959). "Genetic Studies of Genius: Vol. V – The Gifted Group at Mid-Life". Stanford University Press, Stanford, California.

Vernon, P. E. (1979). "Human Intelligence: Heredity and Environment". Freeman, San Francisco.

Vogel, W. and Broverman, D. M. (1964). Relationship between EEG and test intelligence: a critical review. *Psychol. Bull.* 62, 132–144.

Vogel, W. and Broverman, D. M. (1966). A reply to "Relationship between EEG and test intelligence: a commentary". *Psychol. Bull.* 65, 99–109.

7 Sensation Seeking: a biosocial dimension of personality

M. Zuckerman

Abstract This chapter describes how a personality test was developed to measure a trait called sensation seeking; and how the construct and test were validated by correlation with peer ratings, many kinds of life experiences, volunteering behaviour, responses to confinement situations, comparisons of risk-taking groups with control groups, vocational interests and social attitudes. The biological basis of the trait was investigated through genetic, biochemical and psychophysiological studies. The results suggest that this trait in humans and other species is affected by inherited biological traits that affect the reactivity of brain systems which influence the seeking and internal regulation of stimulation.

I. Introduction

A biosocial theory of the type espoused in this chapter rests on certain assumptions which are better stated at the outset. A *basic* dimension of human personality is likely to be based upon variations in biological structure and consequent physiological functions. Since biological structure has evolved slowly, we should see differences in the variations of similar behaviours in non-human species which are related to the same biological characteristics as they are in humans.

Consistent differences in biological function between organisms may be regarded as biological traits. A highly reactive autonomic nervous system, for instance, is an example of a biological trait. When such autonomic reactions typically occur in response to certain intensities or qualities of stimulation we may speak of a psychophysiological trait. Such a trait may influence a behavioural trait, such as disorganization under stress, which may be one component of a personality trait, such as anxiety or emotionality. Social influences interact with biological traits to influence their forms of behavioural expression. Social influence may result in autonomic reactivity being conditioned to specific kinds of social situations in one person and to specific kinds of physical threats in another. But the strength of the biological trait will also influence the likelihood of aversive conditioning and its strength and persistence.

Biological traits are likely to be strongly heritable, although pre-natal physical influences and post-natal social influences may modify inherited biological dispositions. An example of the former is the way that pre-natal hormone influences from the mother may interact with chromosome directed gonadal development to produce certain atypical sex-role behaviours and interests in girls (Ehrhardt et al., 1968). An example of the latter is the way in which prolonged stress may lower testosterone levels in males, thereby changing dominance, sexual and aggressive behaviours linked to the hormone levels. A prolonged experience of sensory deprivation tends to result in a slowing of characteristic levels of waking brain activity and this alteration of brain activity is related to a post-confinement loss of motivation for behavioural activity (Zubek, 1969).

Biological traits affect behavioural reactions to the environment and pro-longed or repeated environmental stimulation, or absence of stimulation, may affect biological traits. However, biology is essentially conservative (not in a political sense) and biological traits, as opposed to states, are not likely to be changed by transient or weak environmental influences.

II. First Biological Model of Sensation Seeking

The earlier theory of sensation seeking (Zuckerman, 1969; Zuckerman et al., 1964) assumed that differences in biological traits, such as reactivity of the reticulo-cortical arousal system, influenced what quantities and qualities of stimuli were characteristically sought after, or avoided, by individuals. The biological trait of strength of cortical excitation and inhibition was assumed to be partly inherited and partly influenced by levels of stimulation during early development as well as current levels of stimulation. The biological part of this theory has been recently modified for reasons that will become clearer with the discussion of the biological correlates of sensation seeking. A newer biological model will be presented at the end of this chapter.

A. *Sensation Seeking Scales*

The first version of the Sensation Seeking Scale (SSS) was developed to study individual differences in reaction to the experimental situation of sensory deprivation. Sensory deprivation is a situation in which subjects are deprived of at least visual and auditory stimulation by confining them in dark soundproof rooms or suspending them in water-tanks (with a breathing apparatus), for periods of time which have ranged from 30 minutes to two weeks (Zubek, 1969). Individuals showed marked differences in reaction to such sensory restriction.

We reasoned that one source of such differences in reaction might be the individual's own characteristic need for stimulation, or their *optimal level of stimulation*. This idea of an optimal level of stimulation for all persons is a relatively old one in psychology (see Zuckerman, 1979, for a discussion of the history of the construct), and a few theorists had suggested that there might be consistent individual differences in the optimal level of stimulation, but none had developed a measure of this hypothetical personality trait.

There are several ways to develop a personality scale. One method is to contrast individuals who seem to embody the extreme characteristics of the trait and to see how they respond to questionnaire items. Items which reliably differentiate the two criterion groups are selected for the scale. This *empirical* method of scale development has the disadvantage of including many items which may differentiate the criteria groups but are not central to the trait. If, for example, I selected items which differentiated highly anxious from non-anxious groups, the items would reflect more than anxiety. They would also reflect general neurotic traits, such as lack of self-regard, which are often found in anxious persons but are not intrinsically part of the anxiety construct.

Instead of using the empirical method to develop a sensation seeking scale we used a *rational* approach combined with an *internal consistency* method called factor analysis.

First items were written to embody what we thought might reflect the expressions of the trait in behaviour, attitudes and preferences. Items reflecting preferences for intense, novel, complex and changing experiences were paired with choices reflecting preferences for moderate, familiar, simple and constant experience. A desire to try new activities which might be risky were contrasted with a conservative attitude of avoiding risk (not necessarily out of fear but from good "common sense").

At this point a personality scale is nothing but a hypothesis, for there is no guarantee that the rationally constructed items have any relationship to each other except in the mind of the test constructor. Even if subjects do respond in some more or less consistent manner to the items at one testing session, and after a period of intervening time, there is no assurance that their responses to the test will actually reflect the trait as measured by their overt reactions in daily life. The first hurdle to scale construction is that of *reliability*, and the second is that of *validity*. Reliability is relatively simple to assess compared to validity. If the test is developed to assess a construct that is set within a theoretical framework, there are almost an infinite number of validity tests which could be proposed. A failure of any one of these tests could be due to a lack of validity for the instrument, an erroneous deduction from the theory linking the instrument and the situation in which it is tested, or a flaw in the theory itself. While a cumulation of positive findings using the test instrument supports the *construct validity* (Cronbach and Meehl, 1955) of the instrument *and* the theory from which it is devised, a preponderance of negative results suggests that either the instrument or the theory is in need of modification; or worse, one or both are hopelessly invalid and should be consigned to the enormous scrap-heap of tests and theories which have accumulated in the psychological literature.

B. *Development of the Sensation Seeking Scales (SSS)*

Factor analysis is a method for determining the reliable dimensions that exist within a set of data. In the case of test development it indicates if there is a central cluster of items in a test, or several such groupings of related items. In our application of this method to our rationally derived items we did discover a central dimension running through items with diverse kinds of content. These results were encouraging, since it was not certain that there would be any relationship between responses to these items.

However, subsequent factor analyses revealed that the dimension which we tentatively labelled "general sensation seeking" contained more than one dimension pertaining to more specific modes of seeking sensation. Factor analyses of the response of subjects in America, England and the Netherlands have all shown the same four dimensions of sensation seeking (Zuckerman, 1971, 1979).

(*i*) *Thrill and adventure seeking*   These items express a desire to engage in certain kinds of physical activities, like parachuting or scuba diving, that are risky but promise certain kinds of physical sensations, such as those produced by defiance of gravity or speeding.

(*ii*) *Experience Seeking*   These items suggest the desire to seek new experience through the senses and the mind, using either external stimuli (music, art, travel), alteration of the mind through drugs, or engaging in a nonconformist style of life with unusual kinds of friends.

(*iii*) *Disinhibition*   These items describe a social-hedonistic orientation, with the pursuit of sensation through parties, drinking and sex.

(*iv*) *Boredom Susceptibility*   These items, unlike the items on the other scales, do not reflect a preference for anything but variety and change. They do express a dislike of routine activities and work and boring people. They also suggest a restless reaction to a lack of stimulus variety.

C. *Reliability of the SSS*

The question of reliability is essentially the question of response consistency. If there is no consistency of response to the items of a scale taken on one occasion (internal reliability), or between the score on the scale taken on two occasions (retest reliability), we cannot expect to find validity for the scale as a predictor of some other reliable phenomenon. If we wanted, for instance, to measure the differences in running speed of several athletes but we used a stopwatch that varied considerably from one instance of use to another, we would not be able to detect differences which might actually exist between the speeds of the different runners. The SSS has shown both good internal and retest reliability, particularly for the Total score on form V of the scale. The retest reliability of 0·94 for this 40 item scale taken twice by the same persons, with a 3-week interval between testings, indicates that about 88% of the variation in scores on this test is reliable over the three week period of time.

D. *Validity*

The difficulty of proving the *construct validity* of a test has been discussed previously. When there is no single criterion against which a test may be assessed, we must demonstrate the effectiveness of the test in its relations to a variety of outcomes and other phenomena external to the test itself. There is a large body of data demonstrating the validity of the SSS (see Zuckerman, 1979) which can only be summarized here since the main focus of this chapter is on the biological correlates of the SSS which provide a special kind of validity related to our understanding of the fundamental nature of the trait called "sensation seeking."

The SSS is correlated with the variety of sexual and drug experience reported by college students and non-college populations. The test is also related to reported cigarette smoking and alcohol use, although for these habits the correlation is not as high and is limited to certain of the SSS sub-scales. In general, the riskier and more unconventional the habit, the more it is likely to be related to sensation seeking.

Sensation seeking, as measured by the SSS, predicts who will volunteer for unusual kinds of activities such as hypnosis, sensory deprivation experiments, encounter groups, gambling activities and meditation training. Although high sensation seekers may volunteer for certain kinds of low stimulation activities, such as sensory deprivation and meditation-training, they are more likely than lows to become restless in such activities and give them up if they do not provide the novel kinds of inner experience they expected to find. Sensation seekers do not seek external stimulation for its own sake, but do so for the changes it can produce in internal sensations and feelings.

Among groups of persons distinguished from the general population by their voluntarily enjoying activities such as parachuting, scuba diving and fire fighting we find a high proportion of sensation seekers. It is interesting that such persons score high on all of the SS scales, not just the thrill and adventure seeking sub-scale which contains relevant items. This shows the generality of the sensation seeking trait. A study of the actual behaviour of subjects in certain situations conceived of as risky by fearful persons (i.e. exposure to a snake, looking over a high open parapet, sitting in darkness in a strange room) show that the low sensation seekers are more likely to become fearful in such situations.

High sensation seekers prefer occupations which are more stimulating and varied in their activities. Female low sensation seekers are interested in the conventional female occupations while highs are more likely to be interested in occupations that are less sex-role stereotyped.

Sensation seeking is strongly expressed in values and attitudes. As one might expect, low sensation seekers are conservative and highs are more liberal and hold more permissive attitudes toward a variety of activities. Lows are more conventionally religious. In the area of psychopathology the sensation seeking trait is related to certain disorders whose symptoms are behaviourally congruent with the idea of a highly active, unconventional, variety seeking person. Manic–depressives and psychopathic personalities both score high on the SSS, and the manic does so even when he or she is not in the manic-state. Low SSS scores are found in withdrawn, behaviourally inactive types of schizophrenics.

E. *Demographic Factors*

Males, as a group, score higher on the SS scales, particularly on the thrill and adventure seeking and disinhibition sub-scales. Of course when we speak of population differences like this, even when they are highly statistically significant, there is still a large amount of overlap in the distributions of scores. It is comparable to stating that men are, on the average, taller than women. Some women are taller than the average man and some men are shorter than the average woman. But the fact that there is overlap in the distributions on a variable does not invalidate a biological explanation of the difference. Certainly the differences in average heights of men and women within a given society are not likely to be due to different patterns of child rearing or exercise. Rather this difference is a genetically encoded growth pattern characteristic of our species, but with variations in individual expression.

Age is another demographic factor that is strongly related to sensation seeking. The trait measured by the SSS reaches a peak in the late teens or early 20s and seems to decline thereafter. These findings are particularly true for thrill and adventure seeking and disinhibition, the same two sub-scales that show the largest sex differences.

Education, socio-economic status, socio-economic background and national-cultural differences are less important determinants of SS scores, and what differences there are on these variables are primarily found in females. These findings have suggested that social factors may influence sensation seeking in females more than in males.

This might suggest that some females are more likely to hide their true sensation seeking tendencies or desires from their peers or not express them in open behaviour. But actual correlations between scores on the SSS and ratings of the subject by his or her peers show an equal amount of relationship. The correlations between test scores and peer ratings of the trait are $+0\cdot50$ for both males and females. This is a relatively good correlation between observers' ratings and a questionnaire measure. The fact that it is not a perfect $1\cdot0$ correlation simply means that a trait is not always observable in behaviour; it does not mean that one method of measuring a trait is necessarily better than another. The disadvantage of the peer-rating is that it is tied to the particular observers making the ratings and therefore cannot provide a standardized measurement across different studies.

F. *Biological Factors*

1. *Genetics*

It has been suggested that sensation seeking may be in part governed by biological traits which have evolved and been shaped by natural selection. What kind of behavioural traits can we find in other species which might represent the intermediate stages of this evolution? One obvious candidate is the tendency to explore a novel environment. In rodents we see marked differences in this tendency between various inbred strains, and marked individual differences within strains. The experimental test used with rodents is usually their behaviour in an open-field or arena. Some animals move quickly into such an open-field and explore it. Others are reluctant to explore it and when they do they stay close to the periphery of the arena like humans who station themselves close to the wall at a crowded cocktail party. These "wall-flower" rodents are likely to show emotional reactivity rather than behavioural reactivity, as indicated by their copious defecations, a sign of emotional discharge. Behavioural reactivity and emotional reactivity are partially independent factors although somewhat negatively correlated.

Selective breeding studies have shown that both factors may be selectively bred into mice. Crossbreeding of high and low exploratory strains produces animals that are intermediate in behavioural reactivity. This suggests that the behavioural trait is polygenic, that is, it is under the control of many genes rather than single dominant or recessive genes.

Humans cannot be selectively bred, although studies revealing correlations between the SSS scores of husbands and wives indicate that humans do a certain amount of self selection in choosing marital partners. To assess the genetic contribution to the trait in humans Fulker *et al.* (1980) used the method of comparing similarities in SSS scores of identical and fraternal twins. A sophisticated biometrical method revealed that heredity contributed about 58% of the variability in the test-measured trait, and 69% if we correct for the unreliability of the test measure. This is a high figure for a personality trait, which approaches the higher figures found for tests of intelligence and other cognitive traits.

2. Biochemical correlates of sensation seeking

Except for a few simple reflexes, we do not inherit complex behavioural traits as "pre-wired" circuits. Learning experiences probably account for the "wiring", but a greater readiness to learn or be conditioned by experience may be created by inherited differences in reactivity of certain circuits in our nervous system. The reactivity of such neuronal systems is regulated by biochemicals which are necessary for the transmission of the nerve impulses in these systems. Levels of such biochemicals, inherent in the structure of the neurones, may produce the readiness to learn, or not to learn, certain kinds of behaviour.

(*i*) *Gonadal (sex) hormones* The sex hormones are a good example of biochemicals which indirectly regulate or direct behaviour. Besides accounting for growth of sexual organs and secondary sexual characteristics during puberty they play a necessary, if not sufficient, role in the complex sexual behaviour of humans. Although psychological sex arousal can occur without them, physiological arousal is, at most, weak in their absence.

Since one of the characteristics of high sensation seekers is their greater variety of sexual experience, it was thought possible that they might be found to have higher levels of sex hormones than low sensation seekers. Such results have been found in several studies of males (Daitzman *et al.*, 1978; Daitzman and Zuckerman, 1980), with similar findings in one small sample of females. High sensation seekers were found to have higher levels of testosterone, oestradiol and oestrone than low sensation seekers. The latter two hormones are called "female" sex hormones because they are found in greater quantity in post-pubescent females, but they are also found in lesser quantity in males.

The results suggest that the total quantity of sex hormones, rather than the male hormone testosterone alone, plays some role in the sensation seeking trait. If this is true the relationship between sex hormones and the SSS cannot fully explain the sex differences found on the SSS.

(*ii*) *Monoamine-oxidase (MAO)* Apart from their effects on parts of the central nervous system regulating sexual behaviour, sex hormones also produce a general activation of behaviour or "drive". This may be accomplished directly or through an inhibitory effect on a regulator of other brain chemicals which also have general arousal effects. The gonadal hormones act as inhibitors of monoamine-oxidase (MAO).

MAO is a brain enzyme (found in other parts of the body as well) which regulates the levels of chemicals called monoamines. The monoamines are neurotransmitters that are heavily concentrated in certain areas of the limbic system which regulate emotions, drives, and general activity.

Some theories of endogenous depression and mania attribute these clinical disorders to deficiencies (depression) or excesses (mania) of certain monoamines, particularly noradrenaline, at the time the behavioural symptoms appear. As mentioned previously, high sensation seeking trait levels are found in manic–depressives. Low MAO levels have also been found to be characteristic of these persons, even when they are not in the manic state. It is possible that low MAO levels produce a lack of natural protection against the accumulation of high levels of monoamines, which in turn may trigger the manic attack. One type of anti-depressant drug lowers MAO levels and is particularly useful for activating depressives who are not subject to manic swings of mood. But given to a manic–depressive in the depressed phase, such drugs may trigger a manic episode.

But low MAO levels are found in many persons who are not manic, including the biologically-related well relatives of the manic–depressive. In fact, the distribution of platelet MAO levels in the general population is a normal one, with no sharp break in the distribution between low and high levels. Platelet MAO seems to be a reliable biological trait and, as such, may represent one of the substrates of sensation seeking. Two studies (Murphy *et al.*, 1977; Schooler *et al.*, 1978) have shown reliable negative relationships between SSS scores and platelet MAO in males, and one also found the relationship in females. Two others have not found a statistically significant relationship, but the direction of the relationship was the same: high sensation seekers tend to have *low* MAO levels and low sensation seekers tend to have high MAO levels.

The finding of low MAO levels in high sensation seekers is consistent with the findings of high sociability, some criminal activity and greater likelihood of drug use in low MAO subjects from a "normal" population. It is also consistent with the finding of low MAO levels in male monkeys, in a monkey colony, who displayed greater social, dominance, sexual, aggressive and playful behaviour.

The finding that women have *higher* MAO levels than men is consistent with the finding that men score higher on the SSS, since low MAO is associated with high SSS scores within both sexes. This intriguing pattern of convergence between biological, behavioural and psychological traits and human psychopathology (mania and psychopathy) suggests that regulation of the monoamines, and the levels of the monoamines themselves, may be central to the trait. This will be discussed further at the end of this chapter.

(*iii*) *Endorphins* Endorphins are recently discovered morphine-like peptides (endorphin = endogenous morphine) in the brain. Studies have suggested that they may play a role in protection against pain, and over-stimulation or over-arousal. It has been suggested that an excess of these peptides may play a role in schizophrenia and that a lack of them may make one particularly susceptible to the temptations of the exogenous opiates. If high levels of endorphins dampen activity and arousal, we might expect *low* sensation seekers to have such high levels. Of course one could make the opposite prediction from a behaviour compensation hypothesis: that is, the hypothesis that high sensation seekers are under-aroused. But no evidence is available supporting the hypo-arousal hypothesis for high sensation seeking.

There is no substitute for data on a question like this. A group of Swedish investigators (Johansson *et al.*, 1979) measured one type of endorphin from cerebrospinal fluid and found a significant negative relationship between SSS scores and endorphin levels; low sensation seekers had higher levels of endorphins and high sensation seekers had lower levels. Since there has been no reported replication of this finding, speculation on its significance may be premature. It is interesting to note that young heroin users tend to be higher sensation seekers than other delinquents.

3. *Psychophysiological correlates of sensation seeking*

The original theory of sensation seeking (Zuckerman, 1969; Zuckerman *et al.*, 1964) was based on an optimal level of arousal construct which suggested that high sensation seekers felt and functioned better at higher levels of cortical arousal than low sensation seekers. The deductions from this theory to measures of *arousal* and arousability were not clear. High sensation seekers might be chronically aroused and require more intense or novel stimulation to reach the same optimal level of arousal as lows. High sensation seekers might have a weak reaction to stimulation and therefore might require more intense or novel stimulation to provide a stronger response; they might be less *arousable*. A third possibility was that higher sensation seekers have stronger responses to novel stimulation which create higher optimal levels of arousal, i.e. the level reached by a novel stimulus may set a higher discrepancy between that level and the subsequent level of arousal created by a habituated, non-novel stimulus. The high sensation seeker would be the type of person who is always nostalgic for the excitement of first experiences, which of course cannot be repeated except by changing the experience. In conditioning terminology this is called the disinhibitory effect of a novel stimulus on a reaction which has habituated in response to a repeated stimulus. This is certainly a problem in routine repetitious kinds of work, and sometimes in marriage as well.

(*i*) *Orienting and defensive reflexes* Neary and Zuckerman (1976) first studied the electrodermal OR in relation to sensation seeking. In this and subsequent studies, some using measures of other kinds of physiological arousal including cortical (EEG), no evidence was found that high sensation seekers have low basal levels of arousal when they are not being stimulated. Nor did we find that they were hypo-arousable in response to novel stimuli of moderate intensity. Quite to the contrary, it was discovered that high sensation seekers have a *stronger* electrodermal OR to novel stimulation, but do not differ from lows in their response to subsequent repetitions of the stimulus. The most plausible hypothesis seemed to be that high and low sensation seekers differ in the optimal levels of arousal produced by novel stimulation, but not in basal or general optimal levels of arousal.

This conclusion about basal arousal was further reinforced by the finding in a study by Carrol et al. (1982), in which the level of arousal was manipulated by drugs, using amphetamine as a stimulant and diazepam as a depressant. An optimal level of arousal theory would predict that high sensation seekers would feel and perform most efficiently under the influence of the stimulant drug, while low sensation seekers would feel and perform more efficiently when relaxed by the depressant drug. The results did not support this hypothesis. Both high and low sensation seekers showed more positive mood and performed better on motor and learning tasks under the influence of the stimulant than under the influence of the depressant drug.

The orienting reflex is the alerting response seen in response to a moderate stimulus which is novel and of unknown significance. Another kind of arousal is seen in reaction to more intense or painful stimulation, or stimulation with aversive significance. The defensive reflex (DR) cannot be distinguished from the OR using a uniphasic electrodermal response, but it can be measured using the biphasic heart rate reaction. Heart rate acceleration in the first 10 s after a stimulus is presented defines a DR, whereas deceleration is characteristic of an OR. Dutch investigators (Orlebeke and Feij, 1979) have found that differential OR–DR reaction in heart rate is apparent in the reactions of subjects scoring high or low on the SSS-disinhibition sub-scale. Low disinhibitors show a DR and highs more typically show an OR heart rate reaction to an auditory stimulus of moderately high intensity on the first few trials it is presented. The DR reaction may be comparable to the extreme emotional response of mice when they are presented with the stimulation of novel environment. Heart rate acceleration is more typically associated with fear arousal although it is sometimes associated with other types of emotional reactions.

(*ii*) *Average evoked potential (AEP)*   Our initial theory of sensation seeking concerned cortical arousal. While studies of peripheral arousal (e.g. skin conductance and heart rate) are of interest, it was even more crucial to measure the cortical response itself. A short article in *Science* by Buchsbaum (1971) alerted us to the development of a new method of measuring brief cortical reactivity as an individual difference measure, and to the possibility that it was related to sensation seeking.

The average evoked potential (AEP) is obtained by presenting a brief stimulus to the subject many times and measuring the brain waves (EEG) during each presentation. These results are fed into a computer, which averages the EEG potential for all of the stimulation presentations at various points of time after the stimulus presentation. What emerges is a clear picture of the wave form typical for the response to that stimulus presentation (see Chapter 8 for a further description of this method).

Buchsbaum measured the individual's characteristic AEP's at each of four stimulus intensities. While a simple psychophysiological function would show that all individuals' responses increase in proportion to the stimulus intensity, the matter was not that simple. In both cats and humans some individual subjects show this positive increase in brain response with increasing stimulus intensity, but others show little increase, and others actually show a decrease in response, particularly at the highest intensity. The former types are called *augmenters* and the latter are called *reducers*. Actually the responses do not allow separation at any point into two clear types; the distribution of the slope measure used to define the continuum is a reasonably normal one. Individuals are reliable (consistent) in their characteristic *augmenting–reducing* function (see Chapter 8 by Buchsbaum, Haier and Johnson).

Zuckerman *et al.* (1974) studied the relationship between the AEP and sensation seeking using a modification of Buchsbaum's method. Augmenting–reducing of the AEP was related to sensation seeking, but particularly to one of the subscales: *disinhibition*. High disinhibitors tended to be augmenters and lows tended to be reducers. This study was replicated (von Knorring,

1980) in Sweden. In this study, as in the Zuckerman *et al.* study, disinhibition showed the highest relationship with augmenting of the AEP.

Disinhibition is also the scale most highly related to gonadal hormones, one of the two scales related to endorphins and is the scale related to strength of the DR. *High* disinhibitors have high levels of gonadal hormones and low levels of endorphins. Low disinhibitors have low levels of gonadal hormones, high levels of endorphins, strong defensive reflexes (DRs) and they are reducers of the AEP. Disinhibition (at the low end) seems to be based upon a nervous system that is highly geared to defend against or reduce the intensity of stimulation. The endorphins may be the source of the reducing reaction since their primary function seems to be to dampen central nervous system reactivity to pain. High disinhibitors seem to lack this "built-in" protection against overstimulation, which may explain why they find alcohol and other depressant drugs so attractive. Given their love of social stimulation, high disinhibitors need some kind of "brake" to prevent stimulation from augmenting into manic hyper-excitability. Depressant drugs keep them "cool" while they seek stimulation. The intensity aspect of stimulation seems more involved in disinhibition, while the novelty of stimulation is more important in the general and thrill and adventure types of sensation seeking.

III. A New Biological Model

A collection of findings, such as those presented in this chapter, is useless unless the data can be ordered within a theory or model. The model should then lead to new predictions and tests.

The earlier theory was largely speculation and suggested that people seek stimulation in order to maintain a level of arousal that is optimal for the particular individuals. The newer theory suggests that, while individuals may be characterized by the levels of stimulation they seek, arousal produced by the stimulation is not the reward but a secondary effect. In fact, how much central arousal is produced by a given stimulus depends on characteristics of the nervous system it is acting upon.

Arousal itself produces internal stimulation and variation in this stimulation that is as important to the sensation seeker as variation in external stimulation. The sensation seeking drug abuser uses drugs which take him "up" and drugs which bring him "down", and he can enjoy all types of states, although both high and low sensation seekers tend to feel best when "up" rather than "down".

Our current conception of the biological bases of sensation seeking is based on the assumption that we inherit structural differences in the neurones' capacities to produce, utilize and metabolize chemical neurotransmitters.

Some of these neurotransmitters affect the sensitivity of the reward systems of the brain: systems where self-stimulation seems inherently rewarding. External stimulation can also produce these rewarding effects, probably through the same systems. In particular, it has been suggested that the firing of these systems is dependent on the release of the *central* catecholamines, noradrenaline and dopamine. High levels of a regulator like MAO in some individuals may reduce the amount of these neurotransmitters which are available for neural transmission. The net result will be that a given amount of novel or complex stimulation will be less rewarding for such individuals.

Individuals with high levels of central catecholamines will be more sensitized to the reward potential of stimulation, but there is a danger inherent in their over-responsive reward systems. The lack of long-term regulators like MAO, and immediate dampeners of stimulation like the endorphins, produces a vulnerability to over-stimulation. High sensation seekers of the disinhibitor type impulsively seek more stimulation than is good for them. A positive feedback of stimulation, releasing greater amounts of neurotransmitters, can produce manic-like states. Alcohol is the agent most used to supply the required dampening of the nervous system, although other drugs may be used for the same purpose.

Tests of this biological model are hampered by the difficulty of measuring the brain amines and enzymes in an intact human organism. However a number of methods have been developed to measure the metabolites of monoamines from urine, blood and cerebrospinal fluid, and levels of these metabolites may be used in the initial approaches to a testing of the model in humans.

More direct approaches may be pursued using animals where measures of brain amines and enzymes may be done post-mortem after experimental observations or observations of natural behaviour have been made.

The reader may justifiably ask where is the "social" in this "biosocial" theory? I must admit to a neglect of this part of the theory. In this respect I am unlike other theorists who have focused on social and promised the biological data for the future. It would certainly be interesting to know if sensation seeking children have parents who reward such exploratory behaviour in their children, and conversely if low sensation seekers are discouraged from seeking stimulation by overprotective parents. But even if such results are found we will not know if the parents had their influence through their genes, their example, their direct reinforcement of behaviour, or some combination of these. Only adoptive child studies, of the type being done for schizophrenia and criminality, can answer these questions. The results for criminality, some of which can be assumed to be related to disinhibitory sensation seeking, suggest that we cannot assume a simple modelling or reinforcement hypothesis to explain socially deviant behaviour. A biological readiness exists before the child is exposed to models or rewarded or punished for behaviour. The effects of such exposure or reinforcement may be stronger, and dependent on inherited potentialities.

IV. Summary

A basic personality dimension is presumed to rest in part on inherited biological characteristics that affect subsequent reactions to the environment. A personality scale was developed to measure the propensity to seek or avoid novel, intense and complex stimulation. The construct validity of the scale was assessed against a variety of risk-taking life experiences and behaviours.

Evidence of a strong genetic influence was obtained from twin studies. Data from psychophysiological studies showed that high sensation seekers showed strong reactions (orienting reflex) to novel stimuli, while lows showed arousal of a defensive nature. Data from studies of the evoked potential revealed that high sensation seekers have a strong nervous system, i.e. one capable of responding to high intensities of stimulation, while lows show strong neural inhibition in response to such intense stimulation.

The reactivity of the central nervous system is hypothesized to be a function of levels of biochemicals, which sensitize or dampen neural reactivity, including: gonadal hormones, monoamines in the brain, the enzyme monoamine oxidase which regulates the levels of these monoamines, and endorphin levels which directly dampen neural reactivity. It remains for future research to explicate the way in which such inherited biological traits interact with social experience to produce the manifestations of the trait in behaviour.

Further Reading

Zuckerman, M. (1979). "Sensation seeking: Beyond the optimal level of arousal". Lawrence Erlbaum Associates, Hillsdale, New Jersey.
This book is the primary source reference for the subject. It describes the theoretical background of the construct of sensation seeking, how the author's own interest in the topic developed from experimental studies of sensory deprivation, the development of the scales used to measure the trait, and the research using the test between 1962 and 1979. The book also presents the old and new biological models for sensation seeking.
Zuckerman, M. (1978). Sensation seeking: The biological need for high stimulation. *Psychology Today*, February, 1978.
This magazine article is a less technical treatment of the topic. It provides an informative introduction to the topic for the undergraduate student of psychology, or for those interested persons with less background in psychology.

Zuckerman, M. (1974). The sensation seeking motive. *In* "Progress in experimental personality research" (B. A. Maher, ed.), Vol. 7. Academic Press, New York and London.

This chapter provides a good summary of how the research on sensation seeking developed from the author's research on sensory deprivation. It describes the research on sensation seeking up to 1974 and the earlier conception of an optimal level of arousal.

Zuckerman, M. (1976). Sensation seeking and anxiety, traits and states, as determinants of behaviour in novel situations. *In* "Stress and anxiety" (I. G. Sarason and C. D. Spielberger, eds), Vol. 3. Hemisphere, Washington, D.C.

This chapter develops a theory of how sensation seeking and anxiety (conceived of as independent traits and states) interact in situations as a function of the novelty and appraised riskiness of the situations to produce approach or withdrawal behaviour.

Zuckerman, M. (1979) Sensation seeking and risk taking. *In* "Emotions in personality and psychopathology" (C. E. Izard, ed.). Plenum, New York.

This chapter further develops the theory of sensation seeking and risk-taking behaviour, described in the previous reading, and provides some empirical studies testing the model. The chapter also describes the role of sensation seeking in certain types of psychopathology, including the manic–depressive disorder, delinquency, anti-social personality disorder and schizophrenia. An early statement of the new biological theory of sensation seeking is also included.

Zuckerman, M. (1978). Sensation seeking. *In* "Dimensions of personality" (H. London and J. Exner, eds). Wiley, New York.

This chapter describes the Sensation Seeking Scale development through form IV and the development of the state scale of sensation seeking. It also describes the research on the scales up to 1978 including some of the new biochemical studies not included in the earlier research summary (reference 3).

Zuckerman, M., Buchsbaum, M. S. and Murphy, D. L. (1980). Sensation seeking and its biological correlates. *Psychol. Bull.* **88**, 187–214.

This article is a review of sensation seeking and the biological phenomena associated with it. The article shows convergent findings in sensation seeking behaviour of humans and other animals that is correlated with the same biological factors that correlate with the Sensation Seeking Scale. It also reviews convergent findings relating the biological factors to human psychopathology and age and sex differences.

References

Buchsbaum, M. (1971). Neural events and the psychophysiological law. *Science* **172**, 502.

Carrol, E. N., Zuckerman, M. and Vogel, W. H. (1982). A test of the optimal level of arousal theory of sensation seeking. *J. Personality Soc. Psychol.* **42**, 572–575.

Cronbach, L. J. and Meehl, P. E. (1955). Construct validity in psychological tests. *Psychol. Bull.* **52**, 281–302.

Daitzman, R. and Zuckerman, M. (1980). Disinhibitory sensation seeking, personality and gonadal hormones, *Personality Individ. Diff.* **1**, 103–110.

Daitzman, R. J., Zuckerman, M., Sammelwitz, P. H. and Ganjam, V. (1978). Sensation seeking and gonadal hormones. *J. Biosoc. Sci.* **10**, 401–408.

Ehrhardt, A. A., Epstein, R. and Money, J. (1968). Fetal androgens and female gender identity in the early-treated adrenogenital syndrome. *Johns Hopkins Med. J.* **122**, 160–167.

Fulker, D., Eysenck, S. B. W. and Zuckerman, M. (1980). The genetics of sensation seeking. *J. Personality Res.* **14**, 261–281.

Johansson, F., Almay, B. G. L., von Knorring, L., Terenuis, L. and Aström, A. (1979). Personality traits in chronic pain patients related to endorphin levels in cerebrospinal fluid. *Psychiat. Res.* **1**, 231–239.

Knorring, L. von (1980). Visual evoked responses and platelet monoamine oxidase in patients suffering from alcoholism. *In* "The Biological Effects of Alcohol" (H. Begleiter ed.). Plenum, New York.

Murphy, D. L., Belmaker, R. H., Buchsbaum, M. S., Martin, N. F., Ciaranello, R. and Wyatt, R. J. (1977). Biogenic amine related enzymes and personality variations in normals. *Psychol. Med.* **7**, 149–157.

Neary, R. S. and Zuckerman, M. (1976). Sensation seeking, trait and state anxiety, and the electrodermal orienting reflex. *Psychophysiology* **13**, 205–211.

Orlebeke, J. F. and Feij, J. A. (1979). The orienting reflex as a personality correlate. *In* "The orienting reflex in humans" (H. D. Kimmel, E. H. van Olst and J. F. Orlebeke eds). Lawrence Erlbaum Associates, Hillsdale, New Jersey.

Schooler, C., Zahn, T. P., Murphy, D. L. and Buchsbaum, M. S. (1978). Psychological correlates of monoamine oxidase in normals. *J. Nerv. Ment. Dis.* **166**, 177–186.

Zubek, J. P. (1969). Physiological and biochemical effects. *In* "Sensory deprivation: Fifteen years of research" (J. P. Zubek, ed.) Appleton-Century-Crofts, New York.

Zuckerman, M. (1969). Theoretical formulations: I. *In* "Sensory deprivation: Fifteen years of research" (J. P. Zubek, ed.). Appleton-Century-Crofts, New York.

Zuckerman, M. (1971). Dimensions of sensation seeking. *J. Consulting Clin. Psychol.* **36**, 45–52.

Zuckerman, M. (1979). "Sensation seeking: Beyond the optimal level of arousal". Lawrence Erlbaum Associates, Hillsdale, New Jersey.

Zuckerman, M., Kolin, E. A., Price, L. and Zoob, I. (1964). Development of a sensation-seeking scale. *J. Consulting Psychol.* **28**, 477–482.

Zuckerman, M., Murtaugh, T. M. and Siegel, J. (1974). Sensation seeking and cortical augmenting–reducing. *Psychophysiology* **11**, 535–542.

8 Augmenting and Reducing: Individual Differences in Evoked Potentials

M. S. Buchsbaum,
R. J. Haier and J. Johnson

Abstract Individual differences in the perception of stimulation can be conceptualized as a function of sensory inhibition. The evoked potential measure of augmenting/reducing supports this characterization on the basis of correlates with sensation-seeking behaviours, pain tolerance and vulnerability to psychopathology. Furthermore, demographic, genetic and reliability data indicate that evoked potential augmenting/reducing may be a trait-like feature, although the lack of cross modal correlations needs further clarification. Topographic mapping may help identify specific or general brain areas related to sensory inhibition. Whether or not sensory inhibition as measured by the evoked potential is a fundamental basis for personality or other complex behaviour awaits further research.

"I did not know before," continued Bingley immediately, "that you were a studier of character. It must be an amusing study."

"Yes, but intricate characters are the most amusing. They have at least that advantage."

"The country," said Darcy, "can in general supply but a few subjects for such a study. In a country neighbourhood you move in a very confined and unvarying society."

"But people themselves alter so much, that there is something new to be observed in them forever."

Jane Austen, 1811
Pride and Prejudice

PHYSIOLOGICAL CORRELATES OF HUMAN
BEHAVIOUR   ISBN 0-12-273901-9

A quiet weekend in the country is restful and relaxing for some, but something from which escape cannot be too soon for others. Any setting may be boring or relaxing, or it may be stimulating or overwhelming; in fact individual differences in the perception of stimulation are well-known for pain, taste, noise and social contact.

Early interest in individual differences emphasized experiential factors in cognitive abilities and personality. Galton's study of genius and Wundt's study of reaction time outlined the origins of differential psychology later to be known as the psychology of individual differences. More recently interest in individual differences has extended to the physiological level, in an effort to understand the underlying basis of behavioural differences.

Asenath Petrie (1960) began her pioneering research in individual differences in pain and suffering with the belief that "contrasting reactions to pain were based solely on differences in the control demanded by the culture or by the individual himself. The possibility that culture and will-power constitute the total explanation of this variation seemed even more improbable when it became clear that a person's tolerance for pain could be permanently increased by surgical methods that altered his personality" (Petrie, 1978). Petrie identified two contrasting response styles to stimulation, and classified individuals into either "augmenters" or "reducers" based on their performance on a kinesthetic figural after-effects task (KFA). Augmenters were those individuals who typically judged the magnitude of a standard stimulus as larger after kinesthetic stimulation; reducers judged the standard as markedly reduced. Augmenters were found to evidence a special sensitivity to pain, while reducers evidenced a notable tolerance (Petrie *et al.*, 1958; Petrie, 1960). Subsequent studies have supported these conclusions (Ryan and Foster, 1967). On the basis of these findings, Petrie (1960) suggested that the tolerance for pain shown by "reducers" might be due in part to their tendency to diminish the intensity of stimulation they receive. This puts them at a disadvantage in sensory deprivation, where they may reduce the already limited available stimulation. Petrie (1960) has found that augmenters could tolerate more hours in a tank-type respirator than reducers, who could not tolerate this condition as well. On the other hand, augmenters could be pushed in the reducing direction by bombarding them with continuous loud noise (Petrie *et al.*, 1962).

From these and other studies, Petrie (1978) argued that the KFA was an index of a general central nervous system mechanism modulating the intensity of incoming sensory stimulation. Although this measure of perceptual style has been widely studied (see review by Barnes, 1976) varying degrees of construct validity have been observed.

Investigators using the KFA in their research have cited two major difficulties with it. The first is its test–retest reliability. Because the augmenting/reducing score is a difference measure, its reliability is statistically reduced below that of the constituent psychophysical measures. A second and related problem stems from the relative complexity of the task. The sequence of judgments required by the task brings into play individual perceptual differences in anchor, order and anticipatory effects. These aggregate effects were termed "stimulus governance" by Petrie. The task itself involves joint position, vibratory and tactile modalities, making study of its neural substrates arduous. Petrie's own model suggests a method of resolution for these problems. If reducers are modulating incoming stimuli more strongly than augmenters, the responses to brief lights, tones, or shocks should be attenuated. Petrie (1978) postulates that this attenuation might be true for all intensities of stimulation. Others have suggested that the attenuation is especially marked at higher stimulus intensities (Buchsbaum, 1976, 1979). This view and its relationship to Pavlov's concept of the "strength of the nervous system" are discussed in detail elsewhere (Barnes, 1976; Buchsbaum, 1976; and Chapter 9 by Strelau).

The regulation of sensory input lends itself to neurophysiological investigation if unique electrical signals from specific sensory stimuli of differing intensities are non-invasively recorded from human subjects. The average evoked potential technique, developed subsequent to Petrie's initial work, has allowed just such studies.

Evoked potentials can be recorded from subjects stimulated by light flashes, tones, electric shocks or any sensory event which has a fast enough onset to produce adequate synchrony of brain response. Differences between individuals in the way evoked potentials change with increasing stimulus intensity appear especially striking. Reliable individual differences in the way EPs change with stimulus intensity are so dramatic that the technique appeared appropriate for the investigation of Petrie's hypothesis (Figs 1–3). One could anticipate that reducers have smaller amplitude evoked potentials than augmenters, especially at high stimulus intensities, since they appear less responsive to incoming stimulation. Thus, the sensory inhibition postulated by Petrie's hypothesis might be identified in electrical signals as a general and trait-like feature of the central nervous system.

In this chapter we will review evidence concerning the concept of augmenting/reducing as an evoked potential measure of sensory inhibition. This will complement earlier reviews focusing on psychophysics (Buchsbaum, 1976), clinical correlates (Buchsbaum, 1978), depression and sensory homeostasis (Buchsbaum, 1979), and biological aspects of sensation seeking (Zuckerman *et al.*, 1980). Demographic information and recent data on pain sensitivity, cortical topography and psychiatric vulnerability are added in this review.

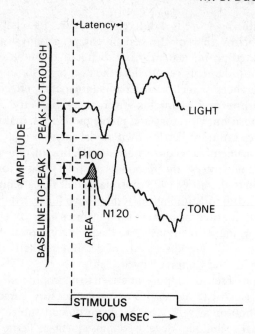

Fig. 1 *Typical evoked potentials recorded from vertex (Cz), for onset of a light and tone. These are the average of 64 stimulus presentations. The typical triphasic wave is shown with a positive component at 100 ms after the stimulus (termed P100), a negative at 100–140 (N120) and a broad positive at 200 ms. The components are labelled with P or N for positive and negative, and a number indicating the typical number of milliseconds from stimulus onset to the component peak. Note similarity of wave form between auditory and visual modalities in vertex recordings. Three measurement techniques are shown, peak-to-trough from P100 to N120, pre-stimulus baseline to peak, and area integration. All three have advantages. Pre-stimulus baseline to peak yields a measure of a single discrete event uncontaminated with N120, but tends to have lower test–retest values. Area measures can be applied at a fixed latency and yield the highest test–retest values and can be applied by computer even to ambiguous waveforms.*

I. The Augmenting/Reducing Continuum

In the EP method of defining the augmenting–reducing dimension four intensities of light flashes, or tones, are presented in randomized blocks of the same intensity or in completely randomized order (see Buchsbaum *et al.*, 1973). The augmenting measure we have most frequently used is the slope of the best fit linear regression line between the stimulus intensities and the EP at

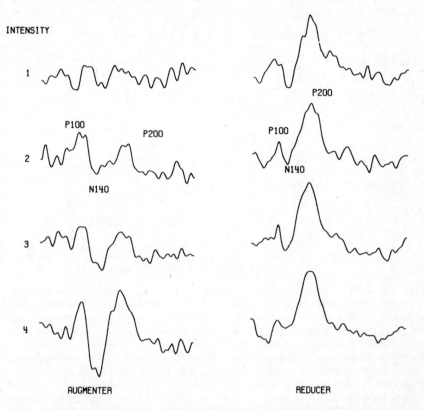

Fig. 2 *Typical visual evoked potentials illustrate augmenter and reducer response to four intensities of light (at 2, 30, 80 and 240 foot lamberts). The curves show 500 ms of average activity recorded between Cz (vertex, the midline point on the head on a line joining the two ears and right ear) (Buchsbaum, 1974). The components used to define the augmenting/reducing dimension are the positive component at 76–112 ms (P100) and a negative one at 90–150 ms (N120, sometimes termed N140).*

The augmenter shows P100–N140 increasing in amplitude with increasing stimulus intensity. The reducer shows a maximum amplitude at the 30–80 foot lambert range, with a progressive decrease. These individuals would be given positive or negative amplitude intensity slopes by any of three measurement techniques: P100–N140 measured from P100 to N140, from a pre-stimulus baseline to P100, and an integration of the area between 76 and 112 ms. P200 tends to show a general increase in size in most individuals.

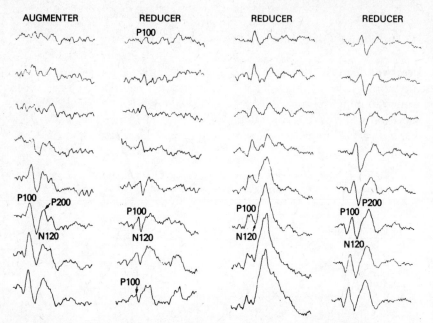

Fig. 3 *Individual differences in response to differing stimulus intensities are complex. Here, 8 stimulus intensities were presented to extend the range from 0·02 to 800 foot lamberts. Thus, the 3 lowest and the highest intensities are outside the range shown in Fig. 2. Far left (first column) A typical augmenter-P100 component increases steadily across over 50 000 fold increase in stimulus intensity. Note that P100 amplitude parallels P200 throughout the intensity range. This subject shows minimal EP at lowest intensities, consistent with sensory insensitivity for minimal levels of stimulation in augmenters. Left (second column) Reducer subject reaches greatest P100–N120 excursion at sixth curve (80 foot lamberts) and then shows decline. P100 is largest at weakest intensities, consistent with low level sensitivity in reducers, hypothesized by Buchsbaum and Silverman (1968). Right (third column) Another reducer reaches peak excursion for P100–N120 at second intensity and declines thereafter although P200 shows a large increase. Far right (last column) Almost equal P100–N120 amplitudes over entire intensity range is reducer pattern which yields 0·0 amplitude/intensity slope.*

each of the intensities (Fig. 2). A high positive slope represents augmenting, an increased cortical response with increasing stimulus intensity; low or negative slopes represent reducing and are usually produced by decrements in response at the higher stimulus intensities. Other techniques for assessing stimulus intensity effects include multivariate measures and specific decision free rules for peak identification.

II. Individual Differences and Evoked Potentials

Like the fingerprint the evoked potential curve shows a tremendous variety of waveforms in individuals (Fig. 4). Conventional neurophysiology initially tended to minimize the value of scalp evoked potentials and to attribute the variation to artifacts or poor control of stimulus delivery. However, even under the meticulous stimulus delivery control possible in animal experiments (e.g. Lukas and Siegel, 1977) individual differences are still prominent.

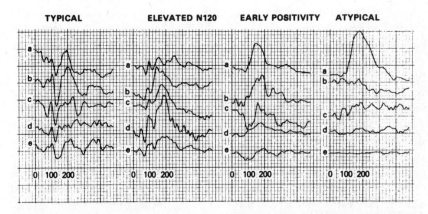

Fig. 4 *Individual variation in visual EP waveform. EPs at 80 foot lamberts in 20 subjects are shown in four categories. The "typical" EP shows a positive at 100 ms, a negative at 120 ms, and a large broad positive peak at 190–240 ms (which may have two or more wavelets, especially on the ascending slope). N120 is the most negative point on these curves. The "elevated N120" is similar but N120 may be above the initial baseline and, therefore, negative only with respect to P100. About 58% of 225 normal subjects showed these two forms. The "early positivity" may show a single or multiple positive points, swinging negative around 100 ms and is a relatively uncommon variation. Atypical forms are rare (less than 10% incidence) and idiosyncratic. Five examples are shown: (a) resembles some EPs constructed by averaging across individuals with a very small or non-existent P100 and giant P200; (b) and (c) show tiny P100–N120–P200 forms; and (d) and (e) scarcely show an EP at vertex, although EP is present at occiput. This unusual recording was also obtained in a pair of identical twins (Buchsbaum 1974). Thus, while many subjects have a recognizable and unambiguous P100 and N120 within an appropriate latency range, in some subjects these components are not clearly discernible. The area integration technique can be determined for every subject, every intensity, and on an empirical basis yields somewhat higher test–retest values for slopes than techniques involving visual identification of components (Buchsbaum, 1976).*

A. *Test–Retest Reliability*

Buchsbaum and Pfefferbaum (1971) found a substantial retest reliability of 0·70 for the slope measure of augmenting–reducing with a test–retest interval of two or more months. Similar reliabilities were found by others utilizing pharmacological control of pupillary diameter. There were also no differences in mean slopes over that interval. Thus, on the basis of this evidence the EP augmenting–reducing measure shows the characteristics of a reliable trait.

B. *Recording Artifacts*

There is no substitute for good recording, adequate number of EP trials, and controlled stimulus delivery. For visual EP's, changes in pupillary diameter, electrical eye blink signals and occlusion of stimulus input, by blinking or eye diversion, are the most critical to consider. Pupillary diameter seems to have little effect on vertex EPs in humans (Buchsbaum, 1978), nor is visual–reducing reliability affected by pilocarpine stabilization. Eye movement or blink electrical activity also has little effect on Cz and posterior locations. Topographic maps clearly show separate anterior and posterior elements in the 100–150 ms ranges. Our maps (Fig. 6) of reducing show the negative slope area confined to central polysensory cortex, a distribution not clearly explicable on the basis of ocular potentials. Not unexpectedly, considering these anatomic features, studies comparing EP results in trials edited and unedited for eye artifacts have revealed no significant impact of editing (e.g., McCarthy and Donchin, 1981). Little EOG artifact was found in the 100–150 ms time range in a similar stimulus intensity paradigm. Eye movement subtraction procedures yield trivial changes in amplitude/intensity slope test–retest correlations for the P100–N120 region.

C. *Topographic Mapping*

EP reducing has been most prominent when EPs are recorded over an area sometimes termed polysensory cortex (Cz), whereas recordings over primary visual areas (Oz) tend to show more uniform and linear amplitude/intensity slopes (Buchsbaum and Pfefferbaum, 1971). This raises the question of whether differences between augmenters and reducers could reflect individual differences in the scalp distribution of the components, rather than merely quantitative reduction. To investigate this, we have developed a technique for representing EP data as a topographic map. Sixteen EEG leads are recorded and amplitude intensity slope calculated for each. The 16 slope values are then used to interpolate values over the entire scalp area as described elsewhere (Buchsbaum *et al.*, 1982). Figures 5 and 6 present data from an augmenter and a reducer and their corresponding cortical maps.

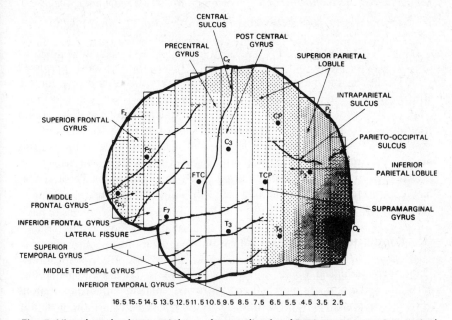

Fig. 5 *Visual evoked potential map for amplitude of P100 component in a typical subject. EPs recorded from 16 EEG leads and value for each spot on surface determined by interpolation (Buchsbaum et al., 1982). Darker areas indicate higher amplitude P100 at 30 foot-lamberts, using area integration measurement (see text and Fig. 1). Note how parieto-occipital sulcus forms anteroposterior border of EP component. Little frontal amplitude is recorded, and temporal areas are the lowest.*

D. *KFA and Augmenting/Reducing*

The perceptual style of augmenting–reducing has been assessed both with the KFA and the evoked potential. The extent to which these two disparate techniques measure the same trait has been assessed in three ways: correlational studies in groups, examination of extreme individuals, and construct validation of Petrie's theory with EP variables. Buchsbaum and Silverman (1968) found a rank order correlation of $0 \cdot 63$ between P100 amplitude intensity slope and the KFA score. Others have all found significant correlations using similar techniques. Similarly, Schooler *et al.*, (1976), using our EP technique, found a significant correlation ($r = 0 \cdot 41$) with the P100 slope among schizophrenics. Using the method of extreme groups, Buchsbaum and Pfefferbaum (1971) located ten EP extreme augmenters and ten extreme reducers with evoked potential recordings in 66 normal male college students, and noted a significant difference in KFA scores (see Schooler *et al.*, 1976).

Construct validity is supported by the corroboration of findings obtained in KFA studies with other studies using EPs. Just as the previously discussed pain studies using the KFA have shown reducers to be pain tolerant, EP studies have related both visual (von Knorring, 1974) and electric shock (Buchsbaum *et al.*, 1980; Davis *et al.*, 1979) reducing to psychophysical pain tolerance. In clinical studies Petrie *et al.* (1963) found schizophrenics to be reducers on the KFA, although not all clinical studies have confirmed this finding (Kuster *et al.*, 1975). Others (Davis *et al.*, 1979) have also found evidence of EP reducing in schizophrenics. On the basis of this, Petrie (1974) has recognized the advantages of a neurophysiological measure.

III. Population Distribution, Age and Sex

Data were analysed on 209 individuals drawn from a series of studies (primarily age and sex matched groups for psychiatric patient populations and psychopharmacological studies). Volunteers were white, generally middle class, suburban residents, paid to be control subjects and screened for recent drug taking and major visual problems. There were 138 males and 71 females aged between 17 and 65. EPs were recorded and measured as in Buchsbaum (1974). P100 amplitude/intensity slopes for the visual EP had a mean of $0 \cdot 79 \mu$v/log foot lambert; SD = $1 \cdot 08$, with a range of $-2 \cdot 65$ to $4 \cdot 32$. The median was $0 \cdot 57$; Quartile 1 was $0 \cdot 12$ and Quartile 3 was $1 \cdot 46$. Reducing, as defined by an amplitude/intensity slope of $0 \cdot 00$ or less, was found in $19 \cdot 6\%$ of the sample. Augmenting, as defined by an amplitude/intensity slope of $1 \cdot 00$, was found in $33 \cdot 4\%$ of the sample. Thus, the amplitude/intensity slope has a relatively normal distribution slightly skewed (skewness $0 \cdot 50$) to the left. About 80% of individuals show some increase in amplitude with increasing intensity, although we have previously used the $1 \cdot 00$ criterion to identify robust augmenters.

As reported in a previously independent series of experiments examining the EPs of normal males and females (Buchsbaum *et al.*, 1974), higher slopes (augmenting) are found in individuals under 17 years. The age effect, however, was of marginal significance in this sample (age by sex ANOVA, $F = 2 \cdot 08$; $df = 4, 199$; $p < 0 \cdot 08$). Neither a significant main effect for age nor an interaction for age by sex was found, although the previously reported larger amplitude at all intensities was found for females. Thus, between the ages of about 21 and 55, neither age nor sex effects appear as important explanations of individual differences in normal individuals. In our previous study (Buchsbaum *et al.*, 1974), higher amplitude/intensity slopes were found in females although more intense stimulation and briefer flashes of light were used.

A reversal of this pattern of sex differences was found by Silverman *et al.* (1973) in a group of adolescent (ages 14–17) delinquents. While controls showed the pattern of lower AER slopes (reducing) in males, male delinquents showed higher slopes (augmenting) than either the delinquent females or normal males. The delinquent females did not differ from the control females, however, with both showing moderately positive slopes. Buchsbaum *et al.* (1973) had found sex differences in primary affective disorders in the USA with females having higher slopes than males. However, in groups of affective disorders and controls in Israel (Gershon and Buchsbaum, 1977) and Sweden, no significant sex differences were found in either patients or controls. Thus, sex differences found on augmenting–reducing are not entirely consistent from one group to another, with differences varying as a function of clinical diagnosis, age and perhaps ethnic group.

IV. Genetics

Although there are great individual differences in EP shape and amplitude, identical twins have extremely similar EPs while fraternal twins do not (see review by Gershon and Buchsbaum, 1977). This pattern is seen in augmenting–reducing as well; adult identical twins had similar amplitude/intensity slopes ($r = 0.71$) in contrast to fraternal twins ($r = 0.09$).

In data collected on the families of normal controls and psychiatric patients with affective disorders, Gershon and Buchsbaum (1977) noted similar intraclass correlations in the offspring–offspring (0.30) and sibling–sibling (0.29) comparisons, both higher than the correlations observed in dizyotic twin pairs. Assortative mating (individuals and their spouses have similar amplitude/intensity slopes) was also observed (intraclass $r = 0.32$).

V. Behavioural Correlates

If augmenting/reducing is a general trait-like measure of sensory inhibition as suggested earlier, then we might expect it to be correlated with behavioural measures beyond those ordinarily associated with psychophysical intensity judgments. Stimulus seeking behaviours would appear particularly relevant.

In both animal and human studies, augmenting EPs have been associated with sensation seeking traits. Two studies (Hall *et al.*, 1970; Lukas and Siegel,

1977) have reported relationships between augmenting/reducing in cats and their rated behavioural characteristics. In both studies cats who were judged to be more exploratory, active, aggressive and responsive to novel stimuli, on the basis of ratings by observers blind to the neurophysiological data, were also classified as augmenters on the basis of their EP patterns. On the other hand, reducer cats tended to be socially avoidant and unreactive to novel stimuli.

Sensation seeking activities, such as motorcycle riding, alcohol use and skydiving, are inventoried on the Sensation Seeking Scale of Zuckerman *et al.* (1974). Three studies have shown sensation seeking to be related to EP augmenting (Buchsbaum, 1971; Coursey *et al.*, 1975; Zuckerman *et al.*, 1974). The sensation seeking sub-scale which showed the significant correlation with augmenting in the Zuckerman *et al.* (1974) study was disinhibition although Coursey *et al.* (1975) found that the general scale related to augmenting. The disinhibition scale contains items expressing a need to seek stimulation through an extraverted pattern of partying, drinking and seeking variety in sexual partners. Zuckerman has suggested that it measures the more psychopathic type of sensation seeking. The disinhibition scale also shows the highest correlation with the hypomania scale on the MMPI (see Chapter 7 by Zuckerman).

Smoking was found to enhance reducing in one study of nine smokers after 12 to 36 hours of abstinence (Hall *et al.*, 1973), and a specific perception-related factor that makes tobacco especially attractive was suggested. However, Knott and Venables (1978) found no significant amplitude/intensity effects of smoking or smoker/non-smoker differences, although some amplitude effects did reach significance. However, willingness to volunteer for studies requiring tobacco abstinence may distort these results.

Coursey *et al.* (1975) investigated the relationships between sleep disorder (insomnia), the EP augmenting/reducing measure and various personality measures (including the sensation seeking general scale). Insomniac subjects showed more reducing and lower sensation seeking scores than the controls. With the effects of age partialled out, the sensation seeking general scale proved to be the most significant predictor of sleep efficiency while the EP relationship did not. Augmenting tended to correlate negatively with depression trait measures although the correlations were not significant.

VI. Pain Tolerance

Petrie *et al.* (1958) found reducers, as identified on the KFA, to be pain tolerant, as previously discussed. This has been confirmed by some, but not all, subsequent studies (see review by Buchsbaum, 1976). Pain sensitivity has also been related to EP augmenting for both visual and somatosensory stimulation. Von Knorring (1974) found augmenters on the visual EP to be less tolerant to electric shocks administered to their forefingers. Depressed patients reporting the experience of pain on questionnaires also tended to be augmenters (von Knorring, 1975, 1978). High visual EP amplitude/intensity slopes (augmenting) have also been found to be associated with significantly lower levels of fraction one endorphins (von Knorring et al., 1979). Augmenting on a pre-drug session also predicted which individuals would report side effects from the drug Zimelidine, a relatively specific serotonin uptake inhibitor.

Somatosensory EPs, like visual EPs, also increase with increasing stimulus intensity (see Buchsbaum, 1976) and show reliable individual differences (Buchsbaum and Davis, 1979). Electrical stimulation of the finger, forearm (Sitaram et al., 1977) and tooth pulp (Chen and Chapman, 1980), as well as laser stimulation of the forearm (Coger et al., 1980), have shown an association between pain sensitivity and EP amplitude. Chronic pain patients appeared to have lower amplitude intensity slopes (Mushin and Levy, 1974). We have recorded EPs to four intensities of brief electric shock administered to the forearm (Sitaram et al., 1977) in a randomized sequence one second apart (resembling the visual EP paradigm). Individuals who are pain tolerant on a psychophysical pain assessment show lower amplitude intensity slopes (Buchsbaum et al., 1980; placebo data in Buchsbaum et al., 1977a; Buchsbaum et al., 1981).

In pharmacological studies, we have observed that somatosensory EPs at unpleasant stimulus intensities are diminished in amplitude by analgesic drugs such as morphine, whereas low intensity responses are unchanged (Davis et al., 1980). Interestingly, naloxone and naltrexone (Davis et al., 1978; Buchsbaum et al., 1977a), both antagonists of opiates and of endogenous opiate-like substances, increase EP amplitude at the high intensities in relatively pain insensitive individuals. Thus, EP amplitude appears to correlate both with pain responsiveness and pharmacological effects.

Evoked potential measures of pain response may provide additional advantages which supplement exclusive reliance on the analysis of subjective reports. (i) Psychomotor performance is unnecessary, permitting the testing of unconscious, disturbed, paralysed patients, or individuals in whom pain perception is disturbed. For example, chronic pain patients showed lower correlations between EP amplitude and psychophysical ratings than normal controls (Coger et al., 1980). (ii) Cortical localization (Fig. 6) of somatosensory processing may be possible (e.g. Duff, 1980). (iii) Such specific EP parameters may be more closely related to pharmacological effects than variables based on self report.

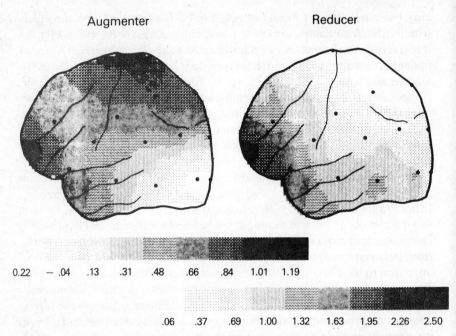

Fig. 6 *Topographic map of augmenter and reducer subjects chosen on the basis of Cz amplitude/intensity slope. Gray scale numbers in microvolts/log foot lambert are midpoints of range; reducer showed negative slope at Cz. Note central and superior parietal location of amplitude/intensity slope differences. Occipital area which has larger amplitude (see Fig. 5) does not show especially high slope values in either subject.*

VII. Cross-modal Correlations in Augmenting/Reducing

The question of whether individuals maintain the same perceptual style in all sensory modalities is important to understand the level of operation of the postulated inhibitory mechanisms (Nebylitsyn, 1972). We have examined the correlation between visual and somatosensory EP augmenting in 96 normal volunteers who were administered the four intensity procedures with EEG averaged from Cz. The amplitude/intensity slope correlation for P100 was only $0 \cdot 15$ ($p < 0 \cdot 10$, 1-tailed). Visual/auditory correlations were also assessed in 22 normal volunteers who received four intensities of lights and four intensities of tones randomly intermixed. EPs were recorded twice, once while subjects counted lights and once while subjects counted tones (Buchsbaum, 1978). Thus, we could compute cross modality correlations for attended stimuli (visual EP while counting lights and auditory EP while counting tones) which proved to be $r = 0 \cdot 125$, as well as for unattended stimuli (visual EPs while counting tones and auditory EPs while counting lights) which was $r = 0 \cdot 09$. Similarly Kaskey *et al.* (1980) found no correlation between visual and auditory EP amplitude/intensity slopes for Cz P100–N120 data.

The lack of cross modal correlations is surprising in view of the prediction of pain tolerance from visual EPs and the visual EP/personality correlations. The primacy of the visual system in man, individual differences in modality preference, and differences in cortical topography, especially between visual and auditory areas, may partially explain this lack of correlation.

VIII. Psychopathology

The most consistent clinical correlate of augmenting is with bipolar manic–depressive psychosis (Buchsbaum *et al.*, 1973; Buchsbaum *et al.*, 1977b; Gershon and Buchsbaum, 1977). Male unipolar depressive patients tend to be reducers and the females tend to be augmenters, but not to the same degree as bipolar disorders (Buchsbaum *et al.*, 1973). Augmenting patterns have also been found among the relatives of patients with affective illnesses, even though these relatives do not have the affective disorder themselves (Gershon and Buchsbaum, 1977). Older (over 49) patients may be more likely to be augmenters (von Knorring, 1978). Alcoholics who have a relative with bipolar affective illness tend to be augmenters as well (Martin *et al.*, 1978). Because of this possible genetic link, augmenting has been found in several unselected groups of alcoholics (Coger *et al.*, 1976; von Knorring, 1976). Among alcoholics, EP augmenting predicted high alcohol acquisition behaviour in a laboratory study of inpatients (Ludwig *et al.*, 1977). Alcoholics were more likely to reduce when given alcohol in a sensory overload condition than normal controls (Buchsbaum and Ludwig, 1980). Alcohol also produced reducing in normal controls for auditory EPs at 50–80 dB (Pfefferbaum *et al.*, 1979).

The augmenting pattern in the manic–depressive is a consistent trait, not entirely dependent upon the clinical condition at the time the AER is measured (Buchsbaum *et al.*, 1973). In one study, bipolar manic–depressives tended to show the augmenting pattern whether or not they were in the manic state (Buchsbaum *et al.*, 1973). However, some change during mania (von Knorring, 1978) or just preceding a switch into mania may occur (Buchsbaum *et al.*, 1977a). Using auditory stimuli Friedman and Meares (1979) found amplitude but not slope changes with depressive mood. Lithium, which prevents manic swings of the cycle, can also change an augmenting pattern of EPs in such patients to a reducing one (Buchsbaum *et al.*, 1971), and augmenters tend to show more clinical response to lithium than reducers (Buchsbaum *et al.*, 1971; Buchsbaum *et al.*, 1979).

In comparison to normals and patients with bipolar affective disorders, off medication acute schizophrenics tended to be reducers for visual (Landau *et al.*, 1975) and somatosensory EPs (Davis *et al.*, 1979). These findings are consistent with the finding of Shagass (1972) that indicated that acutes had low amplitudes, particularly at stronger stimulus intensities, as well as with the shape of the amplitude/intensity curve illustrated by Rappaport *et al.* (1975). In a larger group of patients, the correlation of augmenting with chronicity was $0 \cdot 40$ with age, race, sex and drug status partialled out (Schooler *et al.*, 1976). Augmenting and chronicity were also found in schizophrenics with a family history of schizophrenia, as compared to those without a family history of schizophrenia (Asarnow, *et al.*, 1978). Acute schizophrenics with reducing patterns have a good prognosis for improvement during hospitalization (Landau *et al.*, 1975), suggesting a protective function for reduction. This adaptive aspect of reducing in schizophrenia has been extended by von Knorring *et al.* (1978).

While schizophrenics seem to have reduced N120 components with auditory EPs (see Buchsbaum, 1977), they do not seem to clearly reduce with increased stimulus intensity in paradigms where no task is given (Pfefferbaum *et al.*, 1980). Attentional effects appear to predominate. The lack of similarity between visual and auditory EP results in schizophrenia discussed below is consistent with the lack of cross-modal correlations.

A case of multiple personality was studied by Larmore *et al.* (1977). This 35-year old woman from a rural Kentucky background displayed four personalities. Alicia, the delusional entity of being a Satanic agent, was a moderate augmenter, whereas "Alicia-Faith," the first of the personalities to split off and "the absorber of physical and emotional pain," was a reducer.

A. *Vulnerability to Psychopathology*

The evoked potential has been studied as a predictor of psychiatric vulnerability. In one study (Buchsbaum *et al.*, 1976) college volunteers were screened for extreme monoamine oxidase (MAO) activity, because of the role MAO plays in metabolizing neurotransmitters (like dopamine and serotonin) which are thought to be related to affective disorders or schizophrenia. The students were clasified into four "biological" sub-groups: low MAO with augmenting (LA); high MAO with reducing (HR); low MAO with reducing (LR); and high MAO with augmenting (HA). The groups were then compared with respect to the frequency of MMPI profiles indicating psychopathology. Overall, 79% of the students in the combined LA and HR groups revealed MMPI evidence of psychopathology, whereas only 49% of the LR and HA groups showed similar evidence ($p < 0.05$; Haier *et al.*, 1980a).

This pattern was replicated in a second independent study of male college volunteers screened for extreme or normal MMPI scores (Haier *et al.*, 1980a). These students were classified into the same four biological subgroups according to MAO activity and augmenting/reducing. Each individual was interviewed by a psychiatrist, who administered a structured psychiatric interview which systematically inquires about information necessary to make a diagnosis (Spitzer *et al.*, 1978). The findings of this analysis revealed that affective disorders were more frequent in the LA and HR groups than in the LR and HA groups (52% versus 6%: $p < 0.005$). A follow-up of these students showed that the LA and HR combinations were predictive of new episodes of major depression and/or hypomania during the 18 months after the initial interviews (Haier *et al.*, 1980b). In the combined LA and HR groups, 67% had subsequent episodes of these affective disorders compared to 18% of LR and HA students ($p < 0.012$). This follow-up also suggested that individuals in the LA and the HR groups (particularly the LA group) who did not meet the RDC for any affective disorder at the initial interview were more likely to have an episode of major depression and/or hypomania during the subsequent 18 months than such individuals in the LR and HA groups.

The stimulus-seeking correlates of MAO (i.e. low MAO is related to high stimulus-seeking) demonstrated both in students (Schooler *et al.* 1978) and in monkeys (Redmond *et al.*, 1979) and the characterization of augmenting/reducing as a dimension of sensory inhibition (Buchsbaum, 1976; Lukas and Siegel, 1977; Zuckerman *et al.*, 1974) suggest a vulnerability/protective model for consideration (Haier *et al.*, 1980a). In this model the four biological combinations (LA, LR, HA, HR) are described as types of individuals based on the presence or absence of stimulus-seeking and sensory inhibition. Low MAO/augmenting individuals are hypothesized as high sensation seekers who lack sensory protection (with the possible correlate of over-arousal). High MAO/reducers are low sensation seekers with strong sensory inhibition (under-arousal may be associated with this combination). Both the LA and HR groups or "quadrants" are associated with vulnerability to psychopathology, especially depression. In the remaining two groups, a congruence or balance is hypothesized between high sensation seeking with sensory inhibition (LR) and low sensation seeking with the lack of sensory inhibition (HA). In fact, the LR and the HA combinations may be "protective" in the sense that few individuals in these groups meet the RDC for psychopathology. The problem of specificity between possible biological "markers" of psychopathology and diagnostic categories is discussed elsewhere (Buchsbaum and Haier, 1978).

Further Reading

Petrie, A. (1978). "Individuality in Pain and Suffering" 2nd edn. The University of
    Chicago Press, Chicago.
    This second edition of Petrie's classic work on augmenting/reducing reviews KFA
    research.
Barnes, G. E. (1976). Individual differences in perceptual reactance: a review of the
    stimulus intensity modulation individual difference dimension. *Can. Psychol. Rev.*
    17, 29–52.
Buchsbaum, M. S. (1976). Self-regulation of stimulus intensity augmenting/reducing
    and the average evoked response. *In* "Consciousness and Self Regulation, Advances
    in Research" (G. E. Schwartz and D. Shapiro, eds), pp. 101–135. Plenum, New
    York.
    More detailed information on stimulus intensity and evoked potential is found here.
Zuckerman, M., Buchsbaum, M. S. and Murphy, D. L. (1980). Sensation seeking and
    its biological correlates. *Psychol. Bull.* **88**, 187–214.
    A review of the trait of sensation-seeking and the biological phenomena associated
    with it.

References

Allison, T., Matsumiya, Y., Goff, G. D. and Goff, W. R. (1977). The scalp tomography
    of human visual evoked potentials. *Electroenceph. Clin. Neurophysiol.* **42**, 185–
    197.
Asarnow, R. F., Cromwell, R. L. and Rennick, P. M. (1978). Cognitive and evoked
    response measures of information processing in schizophrenics with and without a
    family history of schizophrenia. *J. Nerv. Ment. Dis.* **166**, 719–730.
Barnes, G. E. (1976). Individual differences in perceptual reactance: A review of the
    stimulus intensity modulation individual difference dimension. *Can. Psychol. Rev.*
    17, 29–52.
Buchsbaum, M. S. (1971). Neural events and the psychophysical law. *Science* **172**,
    502.
Buchsbaum, M. S. (1974). Average evoked response and stimulus intensity in identical
    and fraternal twins. *Physiol. Psychol.* **2**, 365–370.
Buchsbaum, M. S. (1976). Self-regulation of stimulus intensity: augmenting/reducing
    and the average evoked response. *In* "Consciousness and Self Regulation: Advances
    in Research" (G. E. Schwartz and D. Shapiro, eds), pp. 101–135. Plenum, New
    York.
Buchsbaum, M. S. (1977). The middle evoked response components and schizo-
    phrenia. *Schizophr. Bull.* **3**, 93–104.
Buchsbaum, M. S. (1978). The average evoked response technique in differentiation of
    bipolar, unipolar and schizophrenic disorders. *In* "Psychiatric Diagnosis:
    Exploration of Biological Criteria" (H. Akiskal, ed.), pp. 411–432. Spectrum, New
    York.
Buchsbaum, M. S. (1979). Neurophysiological reactivity, stimulus intensity modulation
    and the depressive disorders. *In* "The Psychobiology of the Depressive Disorders:
    Implications for the Effects of Stress" (R. A. Depue, ed.), pp. 221–242. Academic
    Press, New York and London.

Buchsbaum, M. S. and Davis, G. C. (1979) Application of somatosensory event-related potentials to experimental pain and the pharmacology of analgesia. *In* "Human Evoked Potentials" (D. Lehmann and E. Callaway, eds), pp. 43–54. Plenum, New York.

Buchsbaum, M. S. and Haier, R. J. (1978). Biological homogeneity, symptom heterogeneity and the diagnosis of schizophrenia. *Schizophr. Bull.* **4**, 473–475.

Buchsbaum, M. S. and Ludwig, A. M. (1980). Effects of sensory input and alcohol administration on visual evoked potentials in normal subjects and alcoholics. *In* "Biological Effects of Alcohol" (H. Begleiter, ed.), pp. 561–571. Plenum, New York.

Buchsbaum, M. S. and Pfefferbaum, A. (1971). Individual differences in stimulus-intensity response. *Psychophysiology* **8**, 600–611.

Buchsbaum, M. S. and Silverman, J. (1968). Stimulus intensity control and the cortical evoked response. *Psychosom. Med.* **30**, 12–22.

Buchsbaum, M. S., Goodwin, F. K., Murphy, D. L. and Borge, G. (1971). AER in affective disorders. *Am. J. Psychiat.* **128**, 19–25.

Buchsbaum, M. S., Landau, S., Murphy, D. L. and Goodwin, F. K. (1973). Average evoked response in bipolar and unipolar affective disorders: relationship to sex, age of onset, and monoamine oxidase. *Biol. Psychiat.* **7**, 199–212.

Buchsbaum, M. S., Henkin, R. I. and Christiansen, R. L. (1974). Age and sex differences in average evoked responses in a normal population with observations of patients with gonadal dysgenesis. *Electroenceph. Clin. Neurophysiol.* **37**, 137–144.

Buchsbaum, M. S., Coursey, R. D. and Murphy, D. L. (1976). The biochemical high-risk paradigm: behavioral and familial correlates of low platelet monoamine oxidase activity. *Science* **194**, 339–341.

Buchsbaum, M. S., Davis, G. C. and Bunney, W. E., Jr. (1977a). Naloxone alteration of pain perception and somatosensory evoked potentials in normal subjects. *Nature* **270**, 620–622.

Buchsbaum, M. S., Post, R. M. and Bunney, W. E., Jr. (1977b). AER in a rapidly cycling manic–depressive patient. *Biol. Psychiat.* **12**, 83–99.

Buchsbaum, M. S., Lavine, R. A., Davis, G. C., Goodwin, F. K., Murphy, D. L. and Post, R. M. (1979). Effects of lithium on somatosensory evoked potentials and prediction of clinical response in patients with affective illness. *In* "International Lithium: Controversies and Unresolved Issues" (T. B. Cooper, S. Gershon, N. S. Kline and M. Schou, eds), pp. 685–702. Excerpta Medica, ICS Series, New Jersey.

Buchsbaum, M. S., Davis, G. C., Goodwin, F. K., Murphy, D. L. and Post, R. M. (1980). Psychophysical pain judgments and somatosensory evoked potentials in patients with affective illness and normal adults. *In* "Recent Advances in Biological Psychiatry" (C. Perris, L. von Knorring, and D. Kemali, eds), pp. 63–72. Karger, Basel.

Buchsbaum, M. S., Davis, G. C., Coppola, R. and Naber, D. (1981). Opiate pharmacology and individual differences. I Psychophysical pain measurement. *Pain* **10**, 357–366.

Buchsbaum, M. S., Rigal, F., Coppola, R., Cappelletti, J., King, C. and Johnson, J. (1982). A new system for gray-level surface distribution maps of electrical activity. *Electroenceph. Clin. Neurophysiol.* **53**, 237–242.

Chen, A. C. N. and Chapman, C. R. (1980). Aspirin analgesia evaluated by event-related potentials in man: possible central action in brain. *Expl. Brain Res.* **39**, 359–364.

Coger, R. W., Dymond, A. M. and Serafetinides, E. A. (1976). Classification of psychiatric patients with factor analytic EEG variables. *In* "Proceedings of the San Diego Biomedical Symposium" (J. I. Martin, ed.), pp. 279–284. Academic Press, New York and London.

Coger, R. W., Kenton, B., Pinsky, J. J., Crue, B. L., Carmon, A. and Friedman, Y. (1980). Somatosensory evoked potentials and noxious stimulation in patients with intractable, non-cancer pain syndromes. *Psychiatry Res.* **2**, 279–294.

Coursey, R. D., Buchsbaum, M. S. and Frankel, B. L. (1975). Personality measures and evoked responses in chronic insomniacs. *J. Abnorm. Psychol.* **84**, 239–249.

Davis, G. C., Buchsbaum, M. S. and Bunney, W. E., Jr. (1978). Naloxone decreases diurnal variation in pain sensitivity and somatosensory evoked potentials. *Life Sci.* **23**, 1449–1460.

Davis, G. C., Buchsbaum, M. S., van Kammen, D. P. and Bunney, W. E., Jr. (1979). Analgesia to pain stimuli in schizophrenics reversed by naltrexone. *Psychiatry Res.* **1**, 61–69.

Davis, G. C., Buchsbaum, M. S., Naber, D. and van Kammen, D. P. (1980). Effect of opiates and opiate antagonists on somatosensory evoked potentials in patients with schizophrenia. *In* "Clinical Neurophysiological Aspects of Psychopathological Conditions" (C. Perris, L. von Knorring and D. Kemali, eds), pp. 73–80. Karger, Basel.

Duff, T. A. (1980). Topography of scalp recorded potentials evoked by stimulation of the digits. *Electroenceph. Clin. Neurophysiol.* **49**, 452–460.

Friedman, J., and Meares, R. (1979). Cortical evoked potentials and severity of depression. *Am. J. Psychiatry* **136**, 1218–1220.

Gershon, E. S. and Buchsbaum, M. S. (1977). A genetic study of average evoked response: augmentation/reduction in affective disorders. *In* "Psychopathology and Brain Dysfunction" (C. Shagass, S. Gershon and A. J. Friedhoff, eds), pp. 279–290. Raven Press, New York.

Haier, R. J., Buchsbaum, M. S., Murphy, D. L., Gottesman, I. I. and Coursey, R. D. (1980a). Psychiatric vulnerability, monoamine oxidase and the average evoked potential. *Arch. Gen. Psychiatry* **37**, 340–345.

Haier, R. J., Buchsbaum, M. S. and Murphy, D. L. (1980b). An 18-month follow-up of students biologically at risk for psychiatric problems. *Schizophr. Bull.* **6**, 334–337.

Hall, R. A., Rappaport, M., Hopkins, H. K., Griffin, R. and Silverman, J. (1970). Evoked response and behaviour in cats. *Science* **170**, 998–1000.

Hall, R. A., Rappaport, M., Hopkins, H. K. and Griffin, R. (1973). Tobacco and evoked potential. *Science* **180**, 212–214.

Kaskey, G. B., Salzman, L. F., Klorman, R. and Pass, H. L. (1980). Relationships between stimulus intensity and amplitude of visual and auditory event-related potentials. *Biol. Psychol.* **10**, 115–125.

Knott, V. J. and Venables, P. H. (1978). Stimulus intensity control and the cortical evoked response in smokers and non-smokers. *Psychophysiology* **15**, 186–192.

Knorring, von, L. (1974). An intra-individual comparison of pain measures, averaged evoked responses and clinical ratings during depression and after recovery. *Acta Psychiat. Scand.* **255**, 109–120.

Knorring, von, L. (1975). The experience of pain in depressed patients: a clinical and experimental study. *Neuropsychobiology* **1**, 155–165.

Knorring, von, L. (1976). Visual averaged evoked responses in patients suffering from alcoholism. *Neuropsychobiology* **2**, 233–238.

Knorring, von, L. (1978). Visual evoked responses in patients with bipolar affective disorders. *Neuropsychobiology* **4**, 314–320.

Knorring, von, L., Monakhov, K. and Perris, C. (1978). Augmenting/reducing: an adaptive switch mechanism to cope with incoming signals in healthy subjects and psychiatric patients. *Neuropsychobiology* 4, 150–179.

Knorring, von, L., Almay, B. G. L., Johansson, F. and Terenius, L. (1979). Endorphins in CSF of chronic pain patients, in relation to augmenting–reducing response in averaged evoked response. *Neuropsychobiology* 5, 322–326.

Kuster, G., Harrow, M. and Tucker, G. (1975). Kinesthetic figural after-effects in acute schizophrenia: a style of processing stimuli? *Percept. Mot. Skills* 41, 451–458.

Landau, S. G., Buchsbaum, M. S., Carpenter, W., Strauss, J. and Sacks, S. (1975). Schizophrenia and stimulus intensity control. *Archs Gen. Psychiat.* 32, 1239–1245.

Larmore, K., Ludwig, A. M. and Cain, R. L. (1977). Multiple personality – an objective case study. *Brit. F. Psychiat.* 131, 35–40.

Ludwig, A. R., Cain, R. B. and Wikler, A. (1977). Stimulus intensity modulation and alcohol consumption. *J. Studies Alcohol* 38, 2049–2056.

Lukas, J. H. and Siegel, J. (1977). Cortical mechanisms that augment or reduce evoked potentials in cats. *Science* 198, 83–75.

Martin, D. C., Becker, J. and Buffington, V. (1978). An evoked potential study of endogenous affective disorders in alcoholics. *In* "Evoked Brain Potentials and Behavior" (H. Begleiter, ed.), pp. 401–418. Plenum, New York.

McCarthy, G. and Donchin, E. (1981). A metric for thought: A comparison of P300 latency and reaction time. *Science* 211, 77–80.

Mushin, J. and Levy, R. (1974). Averaged evoked response in patients with psychogenic pain. *Psychol. Med.* 4, 19–27.

Nebylitsyn, V. D., (1972). Fundamental Properties of the Human Nervous System. Plenum, New York.

Petrie, A. (1960). Some psychological aspects of pain and the relief of suffering. *Ann. N.Y. Acad. Sci.* 86, 13–27.

Petrie, A. (1974). Reduction or augmentation? Why we need two "planks" before deciding. *Percept. Mot. Skills* 39, 460–462.

Petrie, A. (1978). Comment on "augmentation-reduction and pain experience" by Elton *et al. Percept. Mot. Skills* 47, 589–590.

Petrie, A., Collins, W. and Solomon, P. (1958). Pain sensitivity, sensory deprivation and susceptibility to satiation. *Science* 128, 1431–1433.

Petrie, A., Holland, T. and Wolk, I. (1962). The perceptual characteristics of juvenile delinquents. *J. Nerv. Ment. Dis.* 134, 415–421.

Petrie, A., Holland, T. and Wolk, I. (1963). Sensory stimulation causing subdued experience: audio-analgesia and perceptual augmentation and reduction. *J. Nerv. Ment. Dis.* 137, 312–321.

Pfefferbaum, A., Roth, W., Tinklenberg, J., Rosenbloom, M. J. and Kopell, B. S. (1979). The effects of ethanol and meperidine on auditory evoked potentials. *Drug and Alcohol Dependence* 4, 371–380.

Pfefferbaum, A., Horvath, T., Roth, W., Tinklenberg, J. and Kopell, B. S.(1980). Auditory brain stem and cortical evoked potentials in schizophrenia. *Biol. Psychol.* 15, 209–223.

Rappaport, M., Hopkins, H. K., Hall, K., Belleza, T. and Hall, R. A. (1975). Schizophrenia and evoked potentials: Maximum amplitude frequency of peaks, variability and phenothiazine effects. *Psychophysiology* 12, 196–207.

Redmond, D. E., Murphy, D. L. and Baulu, J. (1979). Platelet monoamine oxidase activity correlates with social affiliative and agonistic behaviours in normal rhesus monkeys. *Psychosom. Med.* 42, 87–100.

Ryan, E. D. and Foster, R. (1967). Athletic participation and perceptual augmentation and reduction. *J. Personality Soc. Psychol.* **6**, 472–476.

Schooler, C., Buchsbaum, M. S. and Carpenter, W. T. (1976). Evoked response and kinesthetic measures of augmenting/reducing in schizophrenics: replications and extensions. *J. Nerv. Ment. Dis.* **163**, 221–232.

Schooler, C., Zahn, T. P., Murphy, D. L. and Buchsbaum, M. S. (1978). Psychological correlates of monoamine oxidase in normals. *J. Nerv. Ment. Dis.* **16**, 221–232.

Shagass, C. (1972) "Evoked Brain Potentials in Psychiatry". Plenum, New York.

Silverman, J., Buchsbaum, M. S. and Stierlin, H. (1973). Sex differences in perceptual differentiation and stimulus intensity control. *J. Pers. Soc. Psychol.* **25**, 309–318.

Silverman, J. (1972). Stimulus intensity modulation and psychological disease. *Psychopharmacologia* **24**, 42–80.

Sitaram, N., Buchsbaum, M. S. and Gillin, J. C. (1977). Physostigmine analgesia and somatosensory evoked responses in man. *Eur. J. Pharmacol.* **42**, 285–290.

Spitzer, R., Endicott, J. and Robins, E. (1978). Research diagnostic criteria: Rationale and reliability. *Arch. Gen. Psychiat.* **35**, 773–782.

Zuckerman, M., Murtaugh, T., and Siegel, J. (1974). Sensation seeking and cortical augmenting–reducing. *Psychophysiology* **11**, 535–542.

Zuckerman, M., Buchsbaum, M. S. and Murphy, D. L. (1980). Sensation seeking and its biological correlates. *Psychol. Bull.* **88**, 187–214.

9 Pavlov's Nervous System Typology and Beyond

J. Strelau

Abstract This chapter outlines the main features of Pavlov's typology of the nervous system and the principal trends in the development of the theory, with special emphasis on the study of man. Attention is drawn to the contribution of the Teplov and Nebylitsyn school which has come to approach nervous system strength as a bipolar property (sensitivity/endurance), identifies additional nervous system properties (e.g. dynamism, lability), and focuses on nervous system properties rather than types. In proposing a psychological interpretation of Pavlov's typology, the author concentrates upon the dimensions of temperament that reflect individual differences in the energy level of behaviour. The two traits identified in this respect, **reactivity** and **activity**, perform important regulative functions in human behaviour. The chapter ends with a discussion of the relationships between some Eastern European notions of nervous system properties and Western personality dimensions such as extraversion–introversion, neuroticism, and anxiety.

I. Pavlov's Theory of Nervous System Types

As their research on conditioned reflexes in dogs progressed, Pavlov and his co-workers became more and more sensitive to individual differences observed in the behaviour of their experimental animals. In particular, they were concerned with differences in the efficiency and speed with which both positive and negative (inhibitory) conditioned responses were formed and differences in the magnitude and durability of such responses.

Basing his approach on the concept of "nervism", according to which any behaviour is governed by the nervous system, Pavlov hypothesized that these individual differences in conditioning in dogs are determined by what he called the basic properties of the nervous system. By this he meant the strength of the processes of excitation and inhibition, the mobility of these processes, and the balance or equilibrium of nervous processes. A particular configuration of these properties constituted the *type of the nervous system*,

PHYSIOLOGICAL CORRELATES OF HUMAN BEHAVIOUR
ISBN 0-12-273901-9

or *type of higher nervous activity*. The first experiments on nervous system types in dogs were conducted by Pavlov's student, Nikiforovsky.

Pavlov's idea of nervous system types was subject to incessant modification in the course of his untiring programme of research. It received its most comprehensive and consistent treatment in *General Types of Higher Nervous Activity in Animals and Man*, a paper published in 1935 (Pavlov, 1951–1952).

In analysing the fundamental properties of nervous processes as a basis of nervous system type Pavlov relied on anatomical and physiological data much less than on behavioural evidence.

Pavlov argued that the most essential property of the nervous system, namely, **strength of excitation**, reflects the functional capacity of the nerve cell. Its principal manifestation is the cell's capacity to withstand either a prolonged or a short-lived but exceedingly strong excitation without slipping into protective inhibition, which closes the cell down completely. The strength of excitation can be estimated by recording the organism's responses to powerful, prolonged, or recurrent stimulation. The "excitatory" strength of a nervous system is the minimal intensity of the stimulus that releases protective inhibition. Pavlov conceived of excitation strength as a property, rather than as a process or current state of the nervous system. It is to be seen as a property of the nerve cell responsible for individual differences in the intensity of the excitation process evoked by one and the same stimulus at a particular level of cortical activation.

By **strength of the inhibition process** Pavlov referred to the nervous system's functional capacity in the realm of inhibition, meaning conditioned, rather than unconditioned inhibition, as revealed in processes of extinction, delay and differentiation. Described without due precision, this property was of secondary importance in Pavlov's typology; it was used chiefly to characterize individuals in terms of the balance of nervous processes. Strength of inhibition is expressed in the capacity for developing various conditioned inhibitory responses, as in the case of extinction, differentiation, or delay. In behavioural terms, we might say that strength of inhibition reveals itself in all situations in which the individual is confronted with negative injunctions, i.e. has to refrain from action, or delay action. Similarly, as in the case of strength of excitation, strength of inhibition was viewed by Pavlov as a property, rather than as the current state of the nervous system.

When speaking of **balance (equilibrium) of nervous processes**, Pavlov had in mind the equilibrium between processes of excitation and inhibition. The relative strength of these two kinds of process tells us whether the given individual is balanced or not, i.e. whether his nervous system is dominated by excitation or by inhibition. In order to determine the balance of nervous processes, investigators used to juxtapose the data reflecting strength of excitation with those representing strength of inhibition.

The third property of the nervous system to be discovered was **mobility of nervous processes**. According to Pavlov, mobility is reflected in the speed of switching from one type of process (e.g. excitation to inhibition or vice versa). At the behavioural level, mobility of nervous processes reveals itself in the capacity for rapid changes in behaviour parallel to changes in stimulation; hence mobility can be estimated from the speed with which the individual switches from one action to another.

Firmly adhering to the types of temperament proposed by Hippocrates and Galen, Pavlov identified four types of nervous system, each based on a particular configuration of the basic properties of nervous processes. Pavlov's nervous system typology is displayed in Fig. 1. As can be seen from this characterization, Pavlov did not construct his classification in a mechanical manner by simply combining the three basic properties of the nervous system. Had he done so, he would have had to distinguish twenty-four types of nervous system in all. Commenting on his limited choice of possible alternatives Pavlov argued that the existence of the four types had been vindicated in his many years of study of the behaviour of dogs in both laboratory and natural conditions.

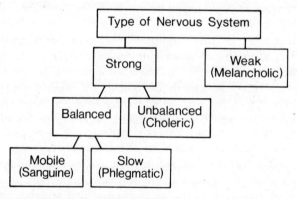

Fig. 1 *Pavlov's typology of the nervous system.*

Pavlov conceptualized nervous system type as being *innate*, and hence relatively immune to environmental influences, including rearing. He referred to it as the genotype, in contradiction with the traditional meaning of the term, thus giving rise to various misinterpretations of his position. For genotype means the genetic programme inherited by a given individual, whereas innate traits are the result of genotype and prenatal environment. Pavlov conceived nervous system type as a physiological basis of temperament, the latter being simply a psychological manifestation of nervous system type.

The investigations into nervous system types in dogs, undertaken by Pavlov in his laboratory at Koltushe near Leningrad, have been continued since on various other animals.

II. Early Studies into Nervous System Types in Man

The first attempts to apply Pavlov's theory of nervous system type in the study of man were made by Ivanov-Smolensky and Krasnogorsky, two students of the great physiologist, in the 1930s. The two worked on higher nervous activity in children but arrived at two different classifications of nervous system types.

Using his technique of verbal "reinforcement", Ivanov-Smolensky (1953) concentrated on the speed and facility of conditioned response elaboration (CRs of the motor and vegetative kind) and proposed the following four types of "temporal connection formation".

(i)   Mobile type: both positive and inhibitory temporal connections are formed easily and quickly.
(ii) Slow type: both positive and inhibitory connections are formed slowly, with difficulty.
(iii) Excitable type: positive temporal connections are formed easily and quickly, and inhibitory connections slowly and with difficulty.
(iv) Inhibited type: positive temporal connections are formed slowly, inhibitory connections easily and quickly. (We should note that Ivanov-Smolensky's technique of verbal reinforcement uses verbal encouragement in place of the UCS; after considerable criticism, this technique was abandoned).

Ivanov-Smolensky leaves no room for what Pavlov thought to be the most fundamental property of the nervous system, namely, strength of nervous processes. In the light of contemporary research on the basic properties of the nervous system, Ivanov-Smolensky's classification, where speed of conditioning is the most crucial factor, can be seen to rest squarely on the *dynamism* of nervous processes (see p. 144 below) and on the *balance* between excitation and inhibition in dynamism.

Krasnogorsky was likewise concerned with conditioned responses in children, but in his search for types he drew a distinction between cortical and subcortical processes, and the balance between these two kinds of process became a major criterion of his typology. Offering the following definitions of his four types of nervous system, Krasnogorsky (1958) referred again to the ancient classification of temperament.

(i) Strong type, with optimal excitation, balanced and quick; harmonious co-operation of all segments of the brain (sanguine).
(ii) Strong type, with optimal excitation, balanced and slow (phlegmatic).
(iii) Strong type, excitable, immoderate, unbalanced; due to the domination of excitation in the subcortical centres (choleric).
(iv) Weak type, with low excitation of both cortical and subcortical centres, and lack of balance between excitation and inhibition (melancholic).

Both Ivanov-Smolensky and Krasnogorsky agreed on the magic number four in their typologies of nervous system, although they differed from each other as well as from Pavlov so far as the criteria of classification were concerned.

III. The contribution of the Teplov-Nebylitsyn School

Pavlov's theory of nervous system types thrived afresh when the research was extended to human subjects, resulting in new discoveries. Undoubtedly, the most comprehensive contribution was made in this field by Teplov and Nebylitsyn and their co-workers.

Whenever they justify their methodological strategy Teplov (1961) and Nebylitsyn (1972a) assert that the crux of the problem lies in the investigation of the basic properties of the nervous system, the distinction of types being a secondary issue. Nervous system properties ought to be studied by laboratory investigation of vegetative responses and involuntary movements, which are thought to reflect the basic properties of the nervous system in their original, innate form, relatively undisguised by postnatal influences of the environment. The methods developed by Teplov and Nebylitsyn for the investigation of basic nervous properties are described in detail in Gray (1964) and Nebylitsyn (1972a).

Evidence accumulated in the course of many years led Teplov and Nebylitsyn to the conclusion that the strength of the nervous system in an excitatory sense (by which they mean the functional capacity of the nerve cell) is related in a particular way to sensitivity, i.e. response threshold. This relationship is expressed by the following formula: R/r const., where R is endurance (the upper threshold of reaction, measured by the maximum-intensity stimulus to which there is an adequate response) and r is sensitivity (lower threshold of reaction).

The **endurance** of nerve cells and their **sensitivity** can be viewed as two facets of one nervous system property, namely strength of the nervous system. Hence, Teplov and Nebylitsyn have come to consider excitatory strength of nervous processes as a bipolar property that can be designated in terms of either endurance or sensitivity.

Exploring the notion of mobility of nervous processes, Teplov found mobility as conceived by Pavlov to fall into two separate properties, both relating to temporal features of behaviour. **Mobility** in a narrow sense of the term is described as the nervous system's capacity for passing from one state to another. It is expressed in the speed of reversing the signal value of stimuli, i.e. reversing a positive stimulus into an inhibitory one, and vice versa. Pavlov introduced the method of altering the signal value of a pair of stimuli for measuring mobility of nervous processes and it has preserved its classical function to this day.

The other property of nervous processes of a temporal character is the speed of onset and termination of nervous processes. Teplov calls it **lability** of the nervous system. Testing the interrelations between 36 indices which characterize the activity of the nervous system in the temporal plane, Borisova *et al.* (1963) found, in a factor analytic study, that there is no interrelation between mobility, in the narrow sense of the term, and lability. The same view is held by Nebylitsyn (1972a).

In addition to these three classical properties of the nervous system, Russian investigators have identified other traits. Examining the evidence obtained in a number of studies, Teplov and Nebylitsyn (1963) singled out one more nervous system property, which they call **dynamism** of nervous processes. This is in essence the speed and facility with which excitatory and inhibitory processes are generated during the formation of conditioned responses. The main index of this property is the efficiency of positive (dynamism of excitation) and negative (dynamism of inhibition) classical conditioned response formation.

In an earlier publication (Strelau, 1969) I expressed my doubts as to the qualifications of dynamism as an autonomous property of the nervous system, on the evidence that speed of conditioning correlates negatively with nervous system strength, and in view of the fact that the USSR Academy of Medical Sciences' standard for the investigation of nervous system type in dogs cites speed of conditioning as an index of nervous system strength (Podkopayev, 1952). For Ivanov-Smolensky and some other authors speed of conditioning was an index of nervous system mobility.

Nebylitsyn (1972a) was of the opinion that balance of nervous processes, just like strength and mobility, is not an independent property of the nervous system; rather it amounts to a general classification of nervous processes (excitation and inhibition) in relation to the various properties of the nervous system. Hence, balance applies not only to the strength of excitation and inhibition processes, as claimed by Pavlov, but also to the mobility and dynamism of excitation and inhibition processes.

According to Nebylitsyn, a full programme for investigating nervous system properties comprises nine properties, six of them being basic:

strength, mobility and dynamism, each for excitation and inhibition taken separately. The remaining three are secondary properties and they all refer to the balance between excitation and inhibition in the domains of strength, mobility and dynamism of nervous processes. In the literature we find some other properties of the nervous system. Two of these deserve to be discussed here: concentratability and "aktivirovannost". The latter term could be translated as activatability. Both are viewed as self-contained properties, i.e. independent of strength, mobility and dynamism.

Concentratability is understood by Borisova (1972, p. 38), the author of the concept, as a "certain *facility* of concentration", or as a "tendency of the nervous processes to concentration"; its measure is the discrimination threshold. The immediate reason for identifying it as an independent property (i.e. independent of all other nervous system properties) is the finding that discrimination threshold does not correlate with sensitivity threshold, the latter being considered by Teplov as one of the major indices of nervous system strength. Neither did discrimination threshold correlate, in Borisova's study, with mobility of nervous processes. An additional argument for including concentratability among the basic properties of the nervous system is, for Borisova (1978), the fact that people differ vastly in this respect and also that these differences are relatively stable. Nevertheless, there is nothing in the literature (including the contributions by Teplov and Nebylitsyn's former associates) that would give support to Borisova's claim.

One more property which Soviet psychologists tend to count with increasing frequency among the basic nervous system properties is "activatability" or aktivirovannost. This property has been extensively investigated by Golubeva and co-workers (see Golubeva *et al.*, 1974; Izyumova *et al.*, 1977; Leites, *et al.*, 1980; Izyumova, 1980). According to them **activatability** is a relatively stable property of the nervous system and it reveals itself in a characteristic level of activation for a given individual. At first glance it resembles Gray's (1964) notion of **arousability**, which is a determinant of individual differences in activation level. As long as all other determinants are held constant, this level is indeed a function of arousability thus conceived. The term has been coined by Gray in an effort to point out the convergences between the concept of nervous system strength and the theory of activation level. Gray says that "the weak nervous system is more easily or more highly *aroused*; and the personality dimension known as 'strength of the nervous system' could be described as a dimension of *levels of arousal* or of *arousability*" (ibid., p. 289).

Reverting to the notion of activatability, we are reminded that it came to be formulated on the basis of EEG studies which have been pursued with great zest at Nebylitsyn's laboratory ever since the late 1960s. The syndrome of activatability as a property of the nervous system has been found to comprise the following indices of the brain's bioelectric activity: the amplitude, frequency, and total energy of alpha waves, the alpha index, the energy of theta waves, and the driving response of high frequency components.

Individuals scoring high on activatability display a low overall energy of the alpha rhythm as well as the theta rhythm, a low amplitude and a high frequency of alpha waves. Individuals scoring low on activatability display the opposite characteristics. These features coincide to a great extent with Nebylitsyn's (1972a) characterization of dynamism in excitation processes; at the same time, the literature contains nothing that could tell us conclusively how the two properties are related to each other.

Over recent years there has been a growing number of studies aimed at the genetic determination of the basic properties of the nervous system. However, evidence obtained by I. V. Ravich-Shcherbo and her co-workers from comparisons of pairs of monozygotic (MZ) and dizygotic (DZ) twins is by no means conclusive. For example, measurements of nervous system strength by extinction with reinforcement (a widely accepted method of this domain; See Gray 1964 and Nebylitsyn, 1972a) have shown that MZ twins do not differ from DZ twins in the extent of diagnostic convergence. On the other hand, such measures of nervous system strength as low-frequency photic driving and the motor RT curve have revealed a high measure of genetic determination of these reactions (Shlakhta and Panteleyeva, 1978).

Comparing MZ and DZ twins in terms of nervous process mobility, Vasilets (1978) used three measures of this nervous system property: (i) alteration of the signal value of a pair of stimuli, (ii) after-effect of positive stimuli, and (iii) after-effect of inhibitory stimuli. Vasilets found conclusive evidence in favour of genetic determination of the nervous system property only for the last of these indices. But the data obtained for the other two indices, including the classical signal alternation technique, have failed to confirm the assumption.

Discussing evidence compiled in her laboratory, Ravich-Shcherbo (1978) concluded that the syndrome of basic properties of the nervous system comprises indices of two different kinds: those that are genetically determined and those that are subject to environmental influences. Without going into the details of the argument it must be pointed out that this evidence speaks against the notion put forward by Pavlov and reinforced by Teplov: that the basic properties of the nervous system are innate.

IV. An Attempt to Give a Psychological Interpretation to Pavlov's Theory of Basic Properties of the Nervous System

The theory of basic properties of the nervous system, developed by Pavlov and widely accepted in the Soviet Union, has inspired large-scale research of an innovative kind both there and elsewhere.

After a few years of preoccupation with the theory in its conventional form (Strelau, 1969), my team in Warsaw turned towards a psychological interpretation of Pavlovian notions. We have come to underline the regulative functions of the identified properties, these properties being assigned to the sphere of temperament. By **temperament** we mean a set of formal, relatively stable traits of the individual, that are displayed in the energy level of behaviour and in the temporal characteristics of reactions. We conceive of temperament as being the result of biological evolution, but this does not imply that temperament is fully determined genetically. In our studies of temperament we have concentrated upon the energy level of behaviour, covering all those traits that are determined by relatively stable individual differences in physiological mechanisms responsible for the accumulation and release of energy in the organism.

Our analysis of the energy level of behaviour has led us to single out two basic properties: reactivity and activity of behaviour. By **reactivity** we mean a property which determines a given individual's characteristic, and relatively stable, intensity (magnitude) of reaction. Reactivity constitutes a dimension that runs from sensory or emotional sensitivity at one end to extreme endurance to strong stimulation at the other. Thus conceived, reactivity resembles strength of the nervous system.

We decided to abandon the notion of nervous system strength for a number of reasons (cf. Strelau, 1974). One reason was that nervous system strength is essentially an explanatory concept of rather limited scope. Pavlov and his students used to ascribe this property to cortical processes almost exclusively; more recently, notably at Nebylitsyn's laboratory, some attention has been paid also to subcortical processes. To quote Nebylitsyn: "the regulatory brain system, including the fronto-central cortex together with the connected complex of paleocortex and subcortical nuclei, forms the morphological substrate of the general properties" (1972b, p. 411). Our view is that the physiological mechanism of reactivity is even more complex than that, being an amalgam of several systems: the endocrine system, the autonomic nervous system, certain neural centres in the brain stem, and some features of the cortex – a combination of relatively stable structures within the given individual (Strelau *et al.*, 1972). Individuals differ in the functioning of each of the systems, these differences being the source of the partial differences that have been thoroughly described in the literature (Nebylitsyn, 1972b; Strelau, 1972a).

Another reason for giving up the notion of nervous system strength has been our desire to underline the *behavioural* aspect of our interest in temperament. Furthermore, both strength of excitation and strength of inhibition are ambiguous terms, in that they are used in a variety of ways, on one occasion to designate a *process*, in other cases to designate a *property*, and this has given rise to numerous misunderstandings (see Nebylitsyn, 1972a; Strelau, 1969). Finally, the notion of nervous system strength is saddled, as are all the other nervous processes properties, with a certain typological tradition. One drawback of this tradition is an emphasis on the innateness or even immutability of the properties (cf. Pavlov, 1951–1952; Teplov, 1961); such a claim appears doubtful in the light of recent evidence, including our own (Eliasz, 1979).

Speaking of reactivity itself, our notion is that an individual's reactivity is the greater the weaker the stimulus that evokes a just noticeable reaction (and hence the higher the person's sensitivity) and, also, the weaker the stimulus needed to disrupt efficient responding (and hence the lower the person's endurance), and vice versa. A person with low reactivity displays low sensitivity and high endurance.

Setting aside details of the physiological mechanism of reactivity, we simply suggest that in highly reactive individuals this mechanism tends to reinforce stimulation: both external and internal stimuli evoke in these persons stronger reactions than in low reactive individuals. A high-reactive individual has therefore a high stimulation processing coefficient (SPC). Low-reactive individuals possess a physiological mechanism that tends to depress stimulation: a stimulus of a given intensity evokes in them a weaker response than in high-reactive persons. Hence, the former have a low SPC (Matysiak, 1980).

Besides reactivity we have isolated another property that bears testimony to the energy level of a person's behaviour, namely, **activity**, which is conceived of as a property on which individuals vary in the intensity or frequency with which they undertake actions or engage in tasks. Irrespective of its specific character or direction, which depend on the person's task or goal, activity functions also as a *regulator* of the amount of stimulation, the demand for which is determined by the person's reactivity level. High-reactive persons (with high SPC) are able with weaker stimulation to reach what is for them an optimal level of activation (Hebb, 1955). Hence, their demand for stimulation, and naturally also their activity in searching for such stimulation, is lower than in low-reactive persons. The latter need strong stimulation, being driven by the desire to function at an optimal activation level. Thus, low-reactive individuals (with low SPC) have a strong demand for stimulation and also for activity as a regulator of that demand.

Activity may serve as either a direct or an indirect source of stimulation. It is a direct source in the sense that the person's motor activity results in an activation of the receptors, and the latter pass on this activation to higher nervous centres. This type of stimulation arises on the basis of the well-known mechanism of feedback afferentation. Moreover, a behaviour that arouses certain emotions for the performed action possesses a particular stimulating capacity itself, in that the excitation-inducing factor is the emotional process accompanying the given action. Activities may thus be a source of stimulation chiefly because they generate certain emotions which in turn elicit a particular state of activation.

Activity is an indirect source of stimulation mainly because it serves the person to choose those situations, surroundings, and tasks that supply the desired amount of stimulation. Evidence, obtained in our laboratory from studies of rats (Matysiak, 1979), suggests that the above mentioned relationship between activity and reactivity applies only to activities that generate stimulation in a direct fashion, i.e. through feedback afferentation or by generating emotions. High-reactive individuals may manifest a great deal of activity in their behaviour, providing the goal of their activity is to reduce or avoid stimulation. On the one hand, we have positively oriented activity (stimulation seeking) and, on the other, negatively oriented activity (stimulation avoidance), as shown by Matysiak (1979).

A detailed discussion of reactivity and activity, the relationships between the two concepts, and the temporal characteristics of behaviour can be found elsewhere (Eliasz, 1973; Strelau, 1974; Gorynska and Strelau, 1979).

Working with a conception of temperament that focuses on reactivity as the principal dimension we have carried out a series of studies into the regulative functions of temperament in man's activities. Among other things, it has been shown that reactivity is decisive for the formation of the person's *style of action* (Strelau, 1975), that reactivity co-determines *tolerance to stress* (e.g. Strelau and Maciejczyk, 1977), that it determines *preferences* for actions supplying the necessary amount of *stimulation* (e.g. Kozlowski, 1977), and that it shows a definite relationship with the individual's *personality*, being a factor in the formation of this personality (Eliasz, 1973; Strelau, 1983).

A similar line of study has been pursued by Soviet investigators, notably by V. S. Merlin and his students. Their research has shown that properties of the nervous processes greatly affect a person's behaviour, determining individual style of action (e.g. Klimov, 1969), tolerance to stress in occupational settings (e.g. Gurevich, 1970), in sporting activities (Vyatkin, 1978), and in school work (e.g. Merlin, 1973).

The finding that basic properties of the nervous system, as well as the temperamental traits of a person, greatly affect the person's behaviour has given fresh impetus to research in this area.

V. Nervous System Properties and Biologically Determined Dimensions of Personality

Since the mid-1960s, investigators have shown increasing interest in possible relationships between nervous system properties identified by Pavlov and the

Teplov school (initially strength of the nervous system) and the well-known dimensions of personality discussed in the literature. This interest has centred upon the dimensions with a strong biological component, dimensions commonly interpreted with the help of physiological mechanisms, i.e. extraversion–introversion and neuroticism as proposed by H. J. Eysenck, anxiety level as proposed by Taylor or Spielberger, and, more recently, also sensation seeking as proposed by Marvin Zuckerman, and stimulus intensity modulation as proposed by Petrie. Because of space limitations, we can deal with only a few of the relevant interrelations (but see Chapters in this volume by H. J. Eysenck, Zuckerman, and Buchsbaum, Haier and Johnson).

By far the greatest number of studies has been devoted to the relationship between nervous system strength and extraversion–introversion. Addressing the International Congress of Psychology in Moscow in 1966, Eysenck pointed out that the strong type of nervous system resembles the extravert and the weak type resembles the introvert. In drawing this parallel, Eysenck referred to underlying physiological mechanisms as well as evidence in terms of indices (Eysenck and Levey, 1972).

Diagnosing the basic properties of the nervous system with Strelau's Temperament Inventory, the STI (Strelau, 1972b), we were able to demonstrate, repeatedly and with great consistency, a positive relationship (correlations ranging from $0 \cdot 349$ to $0 \cdot 548$) between nervous system strength (in excitation) and extraversion–introversion, in line with Eysenck's predictions.

Some investigators have reported evidence to the contrary, however (Mangan and Farmer, 1967; Zhorov and Yermolayeva-Tomina, 1972; Loo, 1979), to the effect that introversion coresponds to strength and extraversion to weakness of the nervous system.

The reason for this contradiction may lie in the methodological basis of these studies. In our investigations we compared both strength of nervous system and extraversion–introversion as measured by inventory. In their studies, on the other hand, extraversion–introversion was measured by inventory while nervous system strength was measured by motor RT.

Our research has yielded quite consistent evidence of a fairly high positive correlation ($0 \cdot 448$–$0 \cdot 692$) between extraversion–introversion and mobility of nervous processes (Strelau, 1983). Measured by the STI, mobility is viewed as the capacity for switching from one activity to another, in accordance with the changing situation. Similar results have been obtained by Mangan (1978) employing different techniques.

In the above study (Strelau, 1983), we also showed that neuroticism is negatively related to nervous system strength in excitation and in inhibition, which refers to acquired (conditioned) inhibition. Neuroticism was measured by the Maudsley Personality Inventory and the basic nervous system properties on the STI. White and Mangan (1972) have likewise reported evidence of a negative relationship between neuroticism and nervous system strength, the latter trait being measured by transmarginal inhibition.

In our laboratory (Strelau, 1983), we have obtained some data bearing on the relationship between the basic properties of the nervous system, as measured on the STI, and anxiety, as measured on Taylor's MAS or the Spielberger STAI (X2 - trait anxiety scale). The results concur in revealing a negative relationship between nervous system strength in excitation and anxiety level (in five studies correlation coefficients ranging from -0.394 to -0.617 were obtained). It will be recalled here that Pavlov (1951–1952) himself found dogs of the weak nervous system type to show a very pronounced passive-defensive reaction, which might be assumed to be an indicator of anxiety. Theoretical arguments for a relationship between nervous system strength and anxiety level have been presented elsewhere (Strelau, 1969). A similar relationship, though on a smaller scale, has been obtained in all our studies where anxiety was correlated with strength of inhibition as measured on the STI (from -0.202 to -0.581).

Our cursory survey of research on the basic properties of the nervous system has shown that the nervous system typology developed by Pavlov and his associates, whereby individually stable features of behaviour are accounted for by particular configurations of strength, mobility, and balance of nervous processes, has born fruit over the decades. The idea that the physiological mechanisms of various personality dimensions are contained in those properties of the nervous system that are responsible for individual differences in activation level or level of arousal has been pursued by investigators in many different ways, as dictated by the specific character of each dimension.

Initially expounded seventy years ago and chiefly promoted in the Soviet Union, Pavlov's typology of the nervous system has clearly withstood the test of time and seems to attract growing interest nowadays among personality psychologists in many countries.

Further Reading

Strelau, J., Farley, F. and Gale, A. (eds), (1983). "The Biological Bases of Personality and Behavior". Hemisphere, New York.
This is the proceedings of two conferences held at the Institute of Psychology, University of Warsaw, Poland. It contains contributions by a number of international authorities, and includes theoretical, empirical and applied papers. There are several papers by Eastern European workers; the book therefore provides an opportunity for the Western reader to see how Pavlovian theories have evolved since the publication, in 1964, of *Pavlov's Typology*, edited by J. A. Gray.
Mangan, G. L. (1981). "The Biology of Human Personality". Pergamon Press, Oxford.

This is a comparative study of Russian and Western work on temperament and personality. The author attempts to integrate Western personality theory with Soviet differential psychology. Different theories, models and typologies are compared and a number of psychophysiological studies are reported which test for similarities between the two approaches. The author was one of the pioneers in the West to test for comparisons between Western and Eastern theories by experimental means.

Strelau, J. (in press). "Temperament Personality Activity". Academic Press, London and New York.

This is a summary of the author's work over a period of fifteen years. A large portion of the book deals with Pavlovian typology, focusing in particular on current research in the area. Part of the book is also devoted to the discussion of the Strelau Temperament Inventory (STI).

References

Borisova, M. N. (1972). Concentration of nervous processes as an individual typological feature of higher nervous activity. *In* "Biological Bases of Individual Behaviour" (V. D. Nebylitsyn and J. A. Gray, eds). Academic Press, New York and London.

Borisova, M. N. (1978). The investigation of inherent determined discrimination threshold. *In* "Problems of Genetic Psychophysiology in Man" (B. F. Lomov and I. V. Ravich-Shcherbo, eds). Nauka, Moscow. (In Russian).

Borisova, M. N., Gurevich, K. M., Yermolayeva-Tomina, L. B., Kolodnaya, A. Y., Ravich-Shcherbo, I. V. and Shvarts, L. A. (1963). Materials to comparative investigation of different indices of nervous system's mobility in man. *In* "Typological Features of Higher Nervous Activity in Man", (B. M. Teplov, ed.), Vol. 3, Akad. pedagog. Nauk RSFSR, Moscow, (In Russian).

Eliasz, A. (1973). Temperament traits and reaction preferences depending on stimulation load. *Polish Psychol. Bull.* 4, 103–114.

Eliasz, A. (1979). Temporal stability of reactivity. *Polish Psychol. Bull.* 10, 187–198.

Eysenck, H. J. and Levey, A. (1972). Conditioning, introversion–extraversion and the strength of the nervous system. *In* "Biological Bases of Individual Behavior". (V. D. Nebylitsyn and J. A. Gray, eds). Academic Press, New York and London.

Golubeva, E. A., Izyumova, S. A., Trubnikova, R. S. and Pechenkov, V. V. (1974). Relationship between EEG rhythms and basic nervous system properties. *In* "Problems of Differential Psychophysiology" (V. D. Nebylitsyn, ed.), Vol. 8, Nauka, Moscow. (In Russian).

Goryńska, E. and Strelau, J. (1979). Basic traits of the temporal characteristics of behavior and their measurement by an inventory technique. *Polish Psychol. Bull.* 10, 199–207.

Gray, J. A. (1964). "Pavlov's Typology". Pergamon Press, Oxford.

Gurevich, K. M. (1970). "Vocational Fitness and Basic Nervous System Properties". Nauka, Moscow. (In Russian).

Hebb, D. O. (1955). Drives and the CNS (conceptual nervous system). *Psychol. Rev.* 62, 243–254.

Ivanov-Smolensky, A. G. (1953). On the investigation of types of higher nervous activity in animals and man. *Zhurnal vysshei nervnoi Deyatelnosti*, 3, 36–54.

Izyumova, S. A. (1980). Features of arousability and processes of information storing and transformation in man. *In* "Psychophysiological Investigations of Intellectual Self-regulation and Activity" (V. M. Rusalov and E. A. Golubeva, eds). (In Russian).

Izyumova, S. A., Golubeva, E. A., Guseva, Ye. P., Trubnikova-Morgunova, R. S. and Pechenkov, V. V. (1977). Statistical analysis of some background and reactive indices of the electroencephalogram. *In* "Problems of Differential Psychophysiology" (Borisova *et al.*, eds), Vol. 9. Pedagogika, Moscow. (In Russian).

Klimov, Ye. A. (1969). "Individual style of action as conditioned by the typological properties of the nervous system". Izdatelstvo Kazanskogo Universiteta, Kazan. (In Russian).

Kozłowski, C. (1977). Demand for stimulation and probability preferences in gambling decisions. *Polish Psychol. Bull.* 8, 67–73.

Krasnogorsky, N. I. (1958). "Higher Nervous Activity in Children". Medgiz, Leningrad. (In Russian).

Leites, N. S., Golubeva, E. A. and Kadyrov, B. R. (1980). The dynamic aspect of mental activity and arousablity of the brain. *In* "Psychophysiological Investigation of Intellectual Self-regulation and Activity". (V. M. Rusalov, and E. A. Golubeva, eds). Nauka, Moscow. (In Russian).

Loo, R. (1979). Neo-Pavlovian properties of higher nervous activity and Eysenck's personality dimensions. *Int. J. Psychol.* 14, 265–274.

Mangan, G. L. (1978). The relationship of mobility of inhibition to rate of inhibitory growth and measures of flexibility, extraversion, and neuroticism. *J. Gen. Psychol.* 99, 271–279.

Mangan, G. L. and Farmer, R. G. (1967). Studies of the relationship between neo-Pavlovian properties of higher nervous activity and Western personality dimensions: I. The relationship of nervous strength and sensitivity to extraversion. *J. Exp. Res. Personality* 2, 101–106.

Matysiak, J. (1979). Activity motivated by sensory drive. *Polish Psychol. Bull.* 10, 209–214.

Matysiak, J. (1980). "Różnice indywidualne w zachowaniu zwierząt w świetle koncepcji zapotrzebowania na stymulację" (Individual differences in animal behavior in the light of the need of stimulation theory). Ossolineum, Wrocław.

Merlin, V. S. (ed.), (1973). "Outline of the theory of temperament" 2nd edn. Permskoye knizhnoye izdatelstvo, Perm. (In Russian).

Nebylitsyn, V. D. (1972a). "Fundamental Properties of the Human Nervous System". Plenum, New York and London.

Nebylitsyn, V. D. (1972b). The problem of general and partial properties of the nervous system. *In* "Biological Bases of Individual Behavior" (V. D. Nebylitsyn and J. A. Gray eds). Academic Press, New York and London.

Pavlov, I. P. (1951–1952). "Complete Works" 2nd edn. Akademia Nauk SSSR, Moscow and Leningrad. (In Russian).

Podkopayev, N. A. (1952). "Method of Conditioned Reflex Study" 3rd edn. Akademia Nauk SSSR, Moscow and Leningrad. (In Russian).

Ravich-Shcherbo, I. V. (1978). The twins method in psychology and psychophysiology. *In* "Problems of Genetic Psychophysiology in Man" (B. F. Lomov and I. V. Ravich-Shcherbo, eds). Nauka, Moscow. (In Russian).

Shlakhta, H. F. and Panteleyeva, T. A. (1978). The investigation of genotypically determined strength of the nervous system syndrome. *In* "Problems of Genetic Psychophysiology in Man" (B. F. Lomov and I. V. Ravich-Shcherbo, eds). Nauka, Moscow. (In Russian).

Strelau, J. (1969). "Temperament i typ układu nerwowego" (Temperament and type of nervous system). Państwowe Wydawnictwo Naukowe, Warszawa.

Strelau, J. (1972a). The general and partial nervous system types – data and theory. In "Biological Bases of Individual Behavior" (V. D. Nebylitsyn and J. A. Gray, eds). Academic Press, New York and London.

Strelau, J. (1972b). A diagnosis of temperament by non-experimental techniques. Polish Psychol. Bull. 3, 97–105.

Strelau, J. (1974). Temperament as an expression of energy level and temporal features of behaviour. Polish Psychol. Bull. 5, 119–127.

Strelau, J. (1975). Reactivity and activity style in selected occupations. Polish Psychol. Bull. 6, 199–206.

Strelau, J. (1983). Temperament and personality. Pavlov and beyond. In "The Biological Bases of Personality and Behavior" (J. Strelau, F. Farley and A. Gale, eds). Hemisphere, New York.

Strelau, J. and Maciejczyk, J. (1977). Reactivity and decision making in stress situations in pilots. In "Stress and Anxiety" (C. D. Spielberger and I. G. Sarason, eds), Vol. 4. Hemisphere, New York.

Strelau, J., Klonowicz, T. and Eliasz, A. (1972). Fizjologiczne mechanizmy cech temperamentalnych (Physiological mechanisms of temperament traits). Przegląd Psychologiczny 15, 25–51.

Teplov, B. M. (1961). "Problems of Individual Differences". Akademia pedagogicheskikh Nauk RSFSR, Moscow. (In Russian).

Teplov, B. M. and Nebylitsyn, V. D. (1963). The study of basic properties of the nervous system and their significance in psychology of individual differences. Voprosy psikhologii 5, 38–47. (In Russian).

Vasilets, T. V. (1978). Mobility as a trait of nervous processes. The genetical aspect of the problem. In "Problems of Genetic Psychophysiology in Man" (B. F. Lomov and I. V. Ravich-Shcherbo, eds). Nauka, Moscow. (In Russian).

Vyatkin, B. A. (1978). "The Role of Temperament in Sports Activity". Fizkultura i sport, Moscow. (In Russian).

White, K. D. and Mangan, G. L. (1972). Strength of the nervous system as a function of personality type and level of arousal. Behav. Res. Therapy 10, 139–146.

Zhorov, P. A. and Yermolayeva-Tomina, L. B. (1972). Concerning the relation between extraversion and the strength of the nervous system. In "Biological Bases of Individual Behavior" (V. D. Nebylitsyn and J. A. Gray, eds). Academic Press, New York and London.

10 Anxiety and Depression

M. Lader

Abstract Anxiety and depression are closely related emotions. They can be normal responses to life events or abnormally severe, persistent or all-pervasive. Both conditions are accompanied by a variety of physical as well as psychological symptoms. The physical symptoms are mediated by psychophysiological changes. Thus, in anxious patients the pulse rate is elevated, salivation decreased, muscle activity augmented and corticosteroids and adrenal catecholamines raised. In depression the psychophysiology is more complex, because the bodily changes themselves are more variable, often extreme, and poorly understood. Laboratory experiments designed to make normal subjects anxious are useful, but the induction of depression is not.

Anxiety and depression are closely related emotions, moods or affects. Both can be so unpleasant in terms of severity, duration or pervasiveness that people suffering from these conditions may seek medical help. Before discussing the psychophysiology of these conditions, a brief outline of the features of each will be given.

I. Anxiety

A. *Clinical Features*

Anxiety is an emotion and as such is an irreducible phenomenon, that is, its subjective aspects are not susceptible to analysis in any other terms. However, anxiety is accompanied by a wide variety of physiological changes which underlie bodily symptoms. These alterations can be studied by the psychophysiologist as a way of quantifying anxiety. However, such physiological measures must be calibrated against other aspects of anxiety (Krause, 1961): (i) subjective reports of the presence and the intensity of the emotion of anxiety; (ii) observations of the behaviour, gestures and facial expression by an independent witness; and (iii) indirect inferences from alterations in psychological performance. Physiological changes alone cannot prove that the person is experiencing anxiety, but they do allow the observer to estimate the severity of the anxiety which the person reports or complains of.

PHYSIOLOGICAL CORRELATES OF HUMAN
BEHAVIOUR   ISBN 0-12-273901-9

Anxiety can be state or trait in type: state anxiety is the feeling of anxiety at any one time; trait anxiety is the longterm predisposition towards feeling anxious. Physiological measures can only detect directly state anxiety. High trait anxiety makes the person more likely to be experiencing state anxiety at the time of recording but otherwise cannot be detected physiologically, only by questionnaire. There are many manoeuvres to make normal subjects anxious in the laboratory.

In clinical terms, a person becomes a patient when he can no longer tolerate his anxiety symptoms and seeks medical help (Lader, 1972). This is an operational definition and the process of diagnosis goes no further than acquiescing in the person's self-labelling as anxious. Different types of clinical anxiety can be delineated. In normal anxiety, the person is responding with symptoms of anxiety to the pressures of life – work, physical health, family problems, etc. – and his response seems understandable in the circumstances. It is normal for a man who has recently survived a serious operation to feel anxious. Neurotic anxiety is an exaggerated anxiety reaction bound up with symbolic subconscious strains in the person's ego structure. Often it is very difficult to discern any cause for the neurotic anxiety.

Anxiety can also be divided into phobic and "free-floating". In the former, the anxiety is attached to a situation or an object, and is usually termed "fear"; in the latter case, the anxiety is all-pervasive, ineffable and related vaguely to ill-defined future catastrophes. Anxiety and fear are very closely related and the physiological changes accompanying these two emotional states are indistinguishable.

B. *Physiological Changes in Normal Subjects made Anxious*

Academic examinations form a convenient real-life situation to assess the induction of anxiety. Blood pressure becomes slightly elevated, the heart rate raised by about 20 beats/minute and peripheral blood vessels constrict. Sport-parachuting provides another structured situation (Fenz and Epstein, 1967). Skin conductance levels and heart rate are similar in novices and veterans in the time before arriving at the airport and during take-off. Thereafter, curves diverge: the novices show a marked rise in these measures with the maxima at the time of jump; the experienced parachutists show maximal activation at the time of landing, the most dangerous part of the exercise.

. Threat of electric shock is often used in the laboratory to induce anxiety. The heart rate accelerates in the 30 s before an expected shock except for the very last few seconds when it slows. Subjects without prior experience of the shock show more heart-rate increase than sophisticated subjects.

Several studies have looked at the relationship between anxiety-proneness (trait anxiety) and psychophysiological measures. High scorers on trait anxiety have higher muscle activity and more eye blinks than phlegmatic subjects. Similarly, high scorers on Test Anxiety Questionnaires have higher skin conductance levels than subjects who are not bothered by tests.

Habituation refers to the decrement in response to repeated identical stimuli (see Chapter 4 by O'Gorman for a detailed account). Trait anxiety is associated with slowing of habituation of some physiological responses. Also, normal subjects made anxious by threat of shock or by impending examinations showed delayed habituation of GSR's (sweat-gland responses).

An interesting series of studies examined the properties of potentially phobic stimuli. Pictures of snakes and spiders were shown to students and compared with the effects of neutral stimuli such as houses. Subjects took significantly longer to habituate to the phobic stimuli with respect to GSR's (Öhman *et al.*, 1974). When potentially phobic stimuli were used as conditioned stimuli, with electric shocks as unconditioned stimuli, the conditioned sweat gland response was acquired after one trial and extinguished slowly. Potentially phobic stimuli produced conditioned defence responses, whereas the neutral stimuli resulted in conditioned orienting responses.

As well as physiological measures, neuroendocrine responses have been extensively evaluated in states of anxiety. Adrenocortical and adrenomedullary function have been most commonly used, either by measuring plasma levels, or by estimating urinary excretion. Taking blood from a vein or the anticipation of it raises plasma cortisol levels, so careful experimental procedures must be used to control for this. Stressful real-life situations have included soldiers in combat or in parachute training. In one study (Berkun *et al.*, 1962), soldiers in training were exposed to five simulated situations: (i) an aircraft emergency during flight; (ii) the disruption of a military exercise by misdirected incoming shells; (iii) a forest fire; (iv) apparently radioactive fallout; and (v) a soldier was made to feel responsible for a comrade's accidental injury. Situations 3 and 4 had little effect on urinary corticosteroid excretion, 1 and 2 produced definite increases, whereas situation 5 had the greatest effect. College examinations are associated with marked increases in cortisol excretion in the urine. The pattern of steroid excretion differs from that following exercise.

A poignantly tragic situation is that of parents of children dying of leukaemia. Urinary corticosteroid excretion is higher in parents with high scores on a personality defensiveness scale than those with low scores, suggesting that elevated adrenocortical activity is related to curtailed verbal expression of anxiety. In another study, involving patients undergoing elective surgery, those who used defences of intellectualization had lower rates of cortisol production than those who relied on defences of denial, displacement or projection.

Admission to hospital may itself elevate cortisol production, which may persist for a week or even more. This has to be taken into account in assessing cortisol levels in newly admitted psychiatric patients. Also, some drugs such as barbiturates alter cortisol production.

Adrenocortical activity is not clearly related to personality variables such as trait-anxiety. High scores on the Taylor Manifest Anxiety Scale and the Nowlis Hostility Score tend to be associated with high urinary corticosteroid excretion but the relationship is not strong.

Adrenomedullary function has been evaluated in detail because of the importance of the catecholamines, adrenaline and noradrenaline, in emotional states. That adrenaline is released in states of anxiety and fear is now a cliché of the advertising copywriter. Both plasma adrenaline and noradrenaline levels and urinary excretion of these catecholamines and their metabolites can be measured, although earlier work concentrated on the latter.

Motion pictures have provided the stimulation situation in several experiments. For example, Levi (1972) screened four different films on four consecutive evenings to 20 female office clerks. Bland natural scenery films were associated with an increase in the rating of "boredom" and catecholamine excretion was significantly decreased as compared with control periods. The second film was Stanley Kubrick's "Paths of Glory" depicting the unjust court-marshalling and execution of three members of a French infantry regiment during the 1914–18 war. "Fright", "aggression" and "despondency" ratings all increased significantly during this film; adrenaline but not noradrenaline excretion also increased. The farcical comedy, "Charlie's Aunt", shown on the third evening, was accompanied by an increase in "amusement" and "laughter", and by similar adrenaline increases as on the previous night. Finally, a typical horror film, "The Mark of Satan", increased "fright" and "despondency" and the excretion of both hormones. Thus, adrenaline excretion was responsive to *all* forms of emotional arousal, while noradrenaline excretion increased only during states of marked fear. In a similar study, films with a sexual content were shown to male and female medical students. Catecholamine excretion increased in both sexes, but more in the males. Other studies have shown females to be less responsive in general than males with respect to catecholamine excretion.

Industrial situations have also been examined. Female invoicing clerks on day-rate pay excreted less catecholamines than on days when the conditions of pay were piece-work. Work output was twice as high on piece-work days. In one study, the amount of noradrenaline excreted correlated positively with the improvement in performance.

Paratroop training provides a usefully graded series of stresses (Bloom *et al.*, 1963). During training in jumping from a tower, adrenaline and noradrenaline excretion of trainees doubled over values during routine ground duties. During the period of the first jump from an airplane, adrenaline excretion remained high but noradrenaline excretion returned to its base-line levels. By the sixth jump, the noradrenaline had risen again to the tower training level and by the eighth jump, at night, levels had stabilized. Personality traits did not correlate with catecholamine excretion. Thus, patterns of excretion are complex being influenced both by the emotional effects of the task and the physical demands.

Urinary adrenaline, but not noradrenaline, excretion increases before and during important examinations. Some relationship is detectable between these increases and self-ratings of concern and anxiety.

Several studies have evaluated the relationship between catecholamines and emotions by examining the effects of injections of these compounds. For example, some hospital doctors were interviewed to catalogue any previous specific reactions to stress, such as apprehension, palpitations and tremor. Adrenaline was then infused intravenously and its effects compared with those of saline. Adrenaline increased blood pressure and heart rate. Palpitations were the commonest symptoms. Symptoms were reported on saline occasions as well as adrenaline occasions, but only half as frequently and usually when saline was the first of the two infusions. Adrenaline produced symptoms resembling those listed in the first interview. In emotionally labile subjects, excess symptoms but few cardiovascular changes occurred; in rigid personalities, no symptoms but marked physiological changes were apparent.

Schachter (1966) has examined the interactions between cognitive factors and physiological arousal by injecting small doses of adrenaline; some subjects were warned what effects to expect, while others remained in ignorance. The subjects were then left with a stooge who behaved either angrily or in a euphoric manner. Subjects ignorant of the expected effects showed and felt more emotional experience, anger or euphoria, than informed subjects. Thus, awareness of physiological arousal might provide the basis for cognitive clues to induce a specific emotion. If the clues are threatening then fear will be experienced. If arousal occurs for internal reasons, following subconscious transactions, in the absence of external cognitive clues free-floating anxiety might result.

C. *Physiological Changes in Anxious Patients*

1. *Cardiovascular measures*

The pulse rate is generally raised in anxious patients. Increases at rest of 10–20 beats per minute are generally found. With the onset of sleep, the pulse rate of anxious patients drops to normal. Spider phobics have exaggerated pulse rate responses to slides of spiders. Heart rate feedback techniques have been used to attempt to treat anxious patients, in particular those complaining of palpitations. However, it is doubtful whether such techniques are of much practical value in anxious patients. Often, patients can lower their heart rate just as effectively by sitting quietly as by using active feedback methods, and even when the heart rate is reduced, clinical anxiety may not be helped. See chapter 14 by Beatty for a full discussion of biofeeedback techniques.

Anxious patients show vasoconstriction of the skin especially of the face and hands. Again, vasodilatation to normal levels occurs with the onset of sleep. Conversely, muscle blood flow is increased. Typically, anxious patients have forearm muscle blood flows twice or more as great as those of relaxed subjects. Even so these flows are still only a fraction of those in subjects exercising their forearms. During stressful mental arithmetic the forearm blood flows of both anxious and calm individuals increases, the latter more than the former, so that group differences at rest are cancelled out.

Blood pressure is raised in anxious subjects, the systolic rather more than the diastolic. In a laboratory situation, anxious patients' blood pressures rise before a stressful task and remain elevated for some time after the task has finished; relaxed subjects have less rise in blood pressure with a marked drop after the task.

2. Pupil

Pupil size at rest is slightly dilated in anxious subjects, due to sympathetic overactivity. Following stress, the pupils of normal subjects quickly return to base-line values, whereas those of anxious subjects remain dilated for some time.

3. Sweat-gland activity

This function, measured as skin conductance, has been the most widely studied of all physiological measures. Anxious patients have high skin conductance levels (increased sweat-gland activity), small responses and high rates of spontaneous activity. Habituation of GSR's (sweat gland responses) has been evaluated in several studies. Anxious patients have smaller responses than normal to the first few of a series of stimuli. Then, normal subjects habituate, typically giving no responses to the later stimuli whereas anxious patients continue to respond. Therefore, anxious subjects are initially less responsive than normal (because they are at higher levels already and are restrained from large responses); but, later after the normals have habituated, they are more responsive (Lader and Wing, 1966).

Skin conductance fluctuation rate is probably the most sensitive of all these variables. Ratings of overt anxiety, and to a lesser extent self-ratings of anxiety, correlate with spontaneous fluctuation rate; the higher the anxiety the more frequent the fluctuations.

Habituation and spontaneous fluctuation rate can also be used to evaluate different groups of patients. Thus, anxious, agoraphobic (fears of crowds and open spaces) and socially phobic (fears of social situations, such as eating in public) patients have slow habituation rates and high frequency of fluctuations; subjects with specific phobias (birds, spiders, snakes, etc.) tend to be normal psychophysiologically. Physiological monitoring can be used during behaviour therapy, such as systematic desensitization and exposure (see Chapter 15 by Crits-Christoph and Schwartz). Heart rate, skin conductance and subjective anxiety ratings all differentiate between phobic and neutral imagery. Lessening of physiological responses is generally followed by decreases in phobic anxiety and in avoidance.

4. Electromyogram

Patients have higher resting muscle tension than normal subjects and this, measured electrically as the EMG, increases with stress. Interviews touching on sensitive topics seem particularly effective at inducing major increases in EMG levels, especially in muscles in the forehead and neck. Patients with complaints of anxious tension in various groups of muscles have abnormally high EMG levels in those muscles. Tremor activity is also raised in anxious patients and may constitute a disabling symptom.

5. Electroencephalogram

The EEG findings in anxiety states have focused on alpha activity. In normal subjects the dominant alpha frequency is about 10 Hz; in patients it tends to be $0 \cdot 5 - 1 \cdot 5$ Hz higher and less abundant alpha is seen. Beta activity predominates in the anxious. Alpha blocking to repeated stimuli tends to persist longer in anxious individuals.

The contingent negative variation (CNV) is a negative-going EEG wave which develops between a warning and an imperative stimulus. Patients with anxiety states have small CNV's which are likely to disappear when distracting stimuli are introduced. Anxious patients also show slower habituation of the CNV than normal.

6. Neuroendocrine measures

Adrenocortical function is elevated in anxious patients, plasma cortisol being about 50–100% above normal levels. Stressful interviews increase plasma cortisol levels even more. Detailed analysis of affective changes accompanying such increases suggest that the total emotional intensity is the closest correlate rather than any specific emotion. When the anxiety is "disintegrative" in type, with fear of loss of sanity or of self-control, cortisol levels are exceptionally high. The secretion of plasma cortisol is controlled by ACTH, and the latter substance is higher in anxious subjects; the levels tend to fluctuate with the intensity of the anxiety.

Surprisingly few studies have addressed themselves to catecholamine levels in anxiety. In general, adrenaline but not noradrenaline levels in plasma and urine are elevated in anxious subjects, especially after such stimuli as probing interviews. The correlation in patients with depression as well as anxiety tends to be with the intensity of the anxiety component rather than with the total affect.

When adrenaline is injected or infused into normal subjects, they tend to report not genuine anxiety but "feeling as if I were anxious". In patients, by contrast, the symptoms closely mimic those of spontaneous anxiety (Breggin, 1964). Two factors seem important: first, the strength of the subject's previously learned association between psychological feelings of acute anxiety and sympathomimetic symptoms, such as palpitations; second, the degree of anxiety produced by the experiment. Thus, anxious patients are made even more anxious by the experimental situation, which together with the physiological effects of the adrenaline produces real anxiety. Lactate injections seem to have similar effects to adrenaline, inducing somatic symptoms evocative of anxiety.

II. Depression

A. *Clinical Features*

Clinical anxiety only differs from normal anxiety in matter of degree. By contrast, many patients with clinical depression show psychological and physiological features which are qualitatively different from normal. Thus, normal subjects can be made anxious in laboratory situations and studying these changes throws light on abnormal anxiety; making normals depressed does not help understand the changes in really depressed patients.

Normal depression can be regarded as an understandable response to life's problems, especially those of loss such as bereavement or redundancy. Neurotic depression is an exaggeration of such a response – the stimulus is not easily apparent. Depression can be a personality attribute like trait anxiety. The additional factor in the more serious cases of depression is the biological or "endogenous" one, that is, a presumed biochemical predisposition to develop bodily abnormalities and psychological aberrations. This complication makes the psychophysiology of depression confusing.

The physiological changes in depressed patients are varied but not easily related to normal upsets. Sleep is broken, less satisfying and the patient wakes early. Appetite is lost and weight drops so that the patient's clothes hang loosely on him. Sexual libido and performance are impaired. Women become frigid and their menstrual periods become scanty or stop. Physical symptoms such as dry mouth and constipation are bitterly complained of. The depressed patient also complains of aches and pains especially of the face and abdomen. Pre-existing symptoms such as indigestion and backache become much worse.

Bodily functions in general slow down and the patient shows psychomotor retardation. Thus, he answers questions slowly after a delay and his voice is monotonous. Sometimes he is anxious or even agitated as well and this may mask the underlying retardation.

Severe psychological changes also occur. The patient is deeply depressed, cannot see any future and may be actively suicidal. He blames himself for his predicament and is excessively guilty about past peccadilloes. His powers of attention, concentration and memory are poor. He lacks energy, interest and any joie de vivre. His morbid thoughts may become delusional in intensity so that he truly believes he is the worst sinner on earth or that everyone's hand is against him. He may fear he has cancer or an incurable disease. He may hallucinate, hearing accusatory voices.

Patients with these features are generally termed "endogenous" in type, in distinction to "neurotic" and "reactive" depressives. Mixed types, however, are quite common, some external event precipitating a depressive illness in a biologically predisposed individual. Typically, recurrent illnesses occur: patients who suffer only depressive episodes are termed "unipolar"; those with both depressive and manic episodes are called "bipolar" in type. Mania in many but not all respects is the opposite of depression, with elevation of mood and over-activity.

B. *Physiological Changes in Depressed Patients*

Because of the complexity of the qualitative differences between normal subjects and patients with endogenous depression, there is little point in laboratory studies designed to induce depression in normal subjects. Minor degrees of depression, really despondency, can be produced by various manipulation, but the intensity of the emotion is minimal and psycho-physiological changes are undetectable. At the other extreme, that of study-ing moderately and severely depressed patients, another complication arises. Because of the general retardation of bodily functions, many of the effector systems such as sweat-glands are themselves diminished in function, and no longer truly reflect central states. With these provisos in mind, the various systems will be briefly reviewed.

1. Cardiovascular measures

These tend to reflect the degree of anxiety or agitation in the depressed patient. The pulse rate is increased in agitated but not in retarded depressives. Forearm blood flow is increased in agitated depressives (mean $3 \cdot 2$ ml/100 ml arm volume/minute), as compared with non-agitated depressives ($2 \cdot 1$) and normals ($2 \cdot 2$). After electroconvulsive therapy the forearm blood flow of severely depressed patients rises significantly.

2. Salivation

This measure has been extensively studied in depressed patients, because one of their complaints is of dry mouth. Several studies have shown the salivary flow rate to be abnormally low in depressives, although the reduction in salivation correlates poorly with subjective complaints. Salivary inhibition is greater in depressive patients with psychomotor retardation than in those without (Brown, 1970). When patients with reduced salivation are treated and their depression lifts, the salivary flow rate returns to normal; when depressed patients with normal salivation recover, there is either no change or a slight drop in salivation. More detailed studies have established a clinical rhythm in salivary flow. In normal subjects, the flow is maximal in the morning; in depressives it is highest in the evening. As depressed patients recover the clinical pattern reverts to normal.

3. Sweat-gland activity

Studies of skin conductance levels, responses and spontaneous fluctuations have been few and often used small numbers of patients or mixed groups. In general, sweat-gland activity is low in depressed patients and increases with recovery. Studies of GSR reactivity have been inconsistent, but most studies report a decrease in the amplitude of GSR's in depressed patients. In the definitely retarded patients GSR reactivity may be abolished, that is, the patient fails to respond at all. By contrast, agitated patients show persistent small responses. Spontaneous fluctuation rate also shows differences: retarded patients may have few if any responses, the skin conductance tracing being flat; agitated patients have recordings like those of severe anxiety states with frequent fluctuations.

4. Electromyogram

Studies of EMG levels in depression are not consistent but there is some evidence that depressive illness, especially if severe, is associated with increased levels of muscle activity (Goldstein, 1965). Some claims have been made that muscle activity is markedly raised in association with retardation, suggesting that retardation may result from too much muscle activity rather than too little.

5. Sedation and sleep thresholds

The sedation threshold is the amount of barbituate in mg per kg body weight needed on slow intravenous injection to produce a characteristic EEG change or slurring of speech. The sleep threshold is the amount required to produce sleep. These thresholds are low in severe depressives and high in neurotic depressives and in anxious patients. However, severe depressives tend to be elderly and the elderly are more sensitive to drugs anyway. Also the end-point, e.g. sleep, is often not distinct.

6. Electroencephalogram

No consistent EEG changes have been found in depressives. Some diminution in alpha and increased beta which has been described reflects concomitant anxiety.

7. Sleep studies

Attention has been focused on patterns of sleep in depressives, because sleep is often so disrupted. When compared with normal control subjects, depressives usually show less total sleep, absent or negligible stage 4, increased stage 1 and more frequent transitions between sleep stages. Rapid eye movement (REM) sleep is either normal or marginally reduced. Awakenings during the night are more frequent and more prolonged than normal.

8. Neuroendocrine measures

There has been a longstanding interest in several aspects of neuroendocrine function in depressed patients. Patients with endocrine diseases such as Cushing's Syndrome (overactivity of the adrenal cortex) often have affective changes and patients administered cortisone for rheumatic conditions sometimes develop psychological symptoms.

Urinary corticosteroid excretion is generally raised in depressed patients. Steroid excretion is particularly elevated in patients undergoing emotional turmoil. Behavioural deterioration and increased urinary corticosteroids generally occur on the same day especially when psychological conflict is high. Patients who improve tend to show some diminution in urinary level. Plasma cortisol estimations allow a much finer analysis. Very high cortisol levels are associated with intense emotional distress especially of a depressive nature in the presence of retardation. Plasma cortisol levels show a pronounced diurnal rhythm with peak levels in the early morning. Depressed patients have higher levels and they tend to be maximal during the night, thus setting the cycle back a few hours. Cortisol is secreted during the late evening and early morning when in normals secretion is negligible. Cortisol is secreted into the blood in a series of bursts. These bursts are longer in depressives accounting for the attainment of higher levels on average, as reflected by urinary excretion or of a single plasma sample. On recovery, cortisol secretion patterns return to normal. The biological half-life of cortisol remains normal suggesting that the utilization of cortisol in the periphery proceeds at the normal rate.

The adrenal cortex is under the control of the hypothalamic–pituitary axis. The integrity of these systems can be evaluated using injections of the synthetic steroid, dexamethasone. In normal subjects this substance inhibits ACTH secretion and cortisol levels are suppressed. In many depressed patients, especially the more severely ill and retarded, such suppression does not take place. Thus, the increased adrenocortical function in many depressives reflects increased ACTH production which in turn suggests insensitivity of the feedback mechanism, which normally controls this cycle by inhibiting ACTH release. Noradrenergic neurones play an important part in this control and it has been suggested that the primary deficit lies in the functioning of these neurones.

Adrenomedullary function has been less extensively studied in depressives than in stress and anxiety responses. Catecholamines in plasma and urine are generally normal in concentration in depressed patients although the admixture of anxiety in such patients is associated with minor increases.

III. Summary

Anxiety and depression are closely related emotions, moods or affects but the distinction between them is worth making both on clinical and scientific grounds. Clinical anxiety differs from normal anxiety in matters of degree, persistence and pervasiveness only. Consequently, much can be learned from studying normal subjects made anxious as well as the anxious patients themselves. Psychophysiological changes are those of over arousal – increased pulse rate, blood-pressure, muscle blood flow and electromyogram, decreased skin blood flow and EEG alpha activity, enhanced adrenomedullary and adrenocortical responses.

Depression is more complex, both clinically and psychophysiologically. The secondary features of retardation and agitation greatly influence physiological levels and responses. Also, the depressive process itself seems to alter the peripheral mechanisms of some psychophysiological measures. Regulatory mechanisms, for example in the hypothalamic–pituitary–adrenocortical axis, are often disturbed. For all these reasons, the interpretation of the undoubted psychophysiological changes which take place in depressed patients is controversial.

Further Reading

Van Praag, H. M., Lader, M. H., Rafaelsen, O. J. and Sachar, E. J. (Eds), (1980).
"Handbook of Biological Psychiatry: Part II – Brain Mechanisms and Abnormal
Behavior – Psychophysiology". Marcel Dekker, New York.
This is the best and most detailed, up-to-date account of the psychophysiology of
psychiatric conditions.
Lader, M. (1975). "The Psychophysiology of Mental Illness". Routledge and Kegan
Paul, London.
A simpler account of the whole topic of abnormal psychophysiology. Extensive
reference list.
Fann, W. E., Karacan, I., Pokorny, A. D. and Williams, R. L. (Eds), (1979).
"Phenomenology and Treatment of Anxiety". SP Books, New York.
Wide-ranging series of chapters on many aspects of anxiety; particular emphasis on
clinical aspects.
Gallant, D. M. and Simpson, G. M. (Eds), (1976). "Depression: Behavioral, Biochemi-
cal, Diagnostic and Treatment Concepts". SP Books, New York.
Useful account of many aspects of depression.
Martin, I. and Venables, P. H. (Eds), (1980). "Techniques in psychophysiology".
Wiley, Chichester.
Best account of psychophysiological methods.

References

Berkun, M. M., Bialek, H. M., Kern, R. P. and Yagi, K. (1962). Experimental studies of
psychological stress in man. *Psychol. Monogr.* **76**, No. 15, Whole No. 534.
Bloom, G., Euler, U. S. V. and Frankenhaeuser, M. (1963). Catecholamine excretion
and personality traits in paratroop trainees. *Acta Physiol. Scand.* **58**, 77–89.
Breggin, P. R. (1964). The psychophysiology of anxiety with a review of the literature
concerning adrenaline. *J. Nerv. Ment. Dis.* **139**, 558–68.
Brown, C. C. (1970). The parotid puzzle: a review of the literature on human
salivation and its applications to psychophysiology. *Psychophysiol.* **7**, 66–85.
Fenz, W. D. and Epstein, S. (1967). Gradients of physiological arousal of experienced
and novice parachutists as a function of an approaching jump. *Psychosom. Med.* **29**,
33–51.
Goldstein, I. B. (1965). The relationship of muscle tension and autonomic activity to
psychiatric disorders. *Psychosom. Med.* **27**, 39–52.
Krause, M. S. (1961). The measurement of transitory anxiety. *Psychol. Rev.* **68**,
178–89.
Lader, M. H. (1972). The nature of anxiety. *Br. J. Psychiat.* **121**, 481–91.
Lader, M. H. and Wing, L. (1966). "Physiological Measures, Sedative Drugs, and
Morbid Anxiety". Oxford University Press, London.
Levi, L. (1972). Psychological and physiological reactions to and psychomotor
performance during prolonged and complex stressor exposure. *Acta Med. Scand.*
Suppl. **528**, 119–42.
Öhman, A., Eriksson, A., Fredriksson, M., Hugdahl, K. and Olofsson, C. (1974).
Habituation of the electrodermal orienting reaction to potentially phobic and
supposedly neutral stimuli in normal human subjects. *Biol. Psychol.* **2**, 85–93.
Schachter, S. (1966). The interaction of cognitive and physiological determinants of
emotional state. *In* "Anxiety and Behavior" (C. D. Spielberger, ed.), pp. 193–224.
Academic Press, New York and London.

11 Psychosomatic Disorders: Theories and Evidence

L. A. Warwick-Evans

Abstract We illustrate how our thoughts and feelings influence our physiological activity, and consider the view that psychosomatic disorders are a manifestation of this process. First we ask the question, what kind of data would count as evidence for this view? The main theories of the development of psychosomatic disorders are then outlined. Finally, currently available evidence is evaluated. Relevant observations come from a number of disparate sources: introspection, single case studies, epidemiological analysis, prospective studies, stress interviews, and experimental laboratory work with animals and man. It is concluded that, in spite of the methodological difficulties of each approach, the combined weight of evidence supports the view that psychological factors are, at least partly, responsible for many diseases.

Psychosomatic disorders are physical disorders of the body which are caused by psychological factors. A psychosomatic ulcer is not an imaginary hole in the head but a real hole in the gut. The concepts of cause and of psychological factors deserve further comment. It is unlikely that any psychosomatic disorder has a single unique cause, it is probably multifactorial in origin or multiply caused. The concept of cause is here used in a broad sense to include any factor which contributes to the onset, the severity or the duration of a disorder or which causes its reappearance after a period of remission. It is also useful to distinguish long term or predisposing causes from short-term or precipitating causes. The meaning of "psychological factors" should become clear from the following examples: peeling onions or reading poetry may both bring tears to one's eyes but only reading poetry is a psychological factor; evading members of the opposing team to score the winning touch down will cause adrenaline to be secreted and the heart rate to increase, but the same effect may be produced in the excitement of merely watching one's team hero do this. In the latter case there are no physiological demands which require these responses, they are due to one's psychological involvement.

PHYSIOLOGICAL CORRELATES OF HUMAN
BEHAVIOUR   ISBN 0-12-273901-9

When an asthma patient inhales the pollen to which he is allergic then he may experience respiratory problems, but these problems may also be experienced if he looks at a photograph of the pollen source, in the former case the stimulus is external and biochemical in the latter case the cause is internal and psychological.

The World Health Organisation guide to classification of diseases (WHO, 1968) and its English counterpart (HMSO, 1968) both list the following under the heading "Physical disorders of presumably psychogenic origin" (the examples are provided by the present writer): skin (eczema, hives); musculo-skeletal (tension headache, tics and muscle spasms); cardiovascular (arrhythmias, essential hypertension); haematic and lymphatic (disturbance of the lymph system or of the blood); gastro-intestinal (ulceration or dyspepsia); genito-urinary (amenorrhoea, impotence); endocrine (some disorders of the pituitary or adrenal glands, diabetes mellitus); organs of special sense (hysterical deafness or anaesthesia); and other.

The list is not only extensive, it is controversial. Some authors would include certain cases of muscular weakness, tremor, arthritis, disorders of the immune system and even death. Evidence for psychological causes of death come from four areas: (i) well-authenticated instances of voodoo death; (ii) the phenomenon of sudden death in animals; (iii) statistical data showing a correlation between time of death and the achievement of important life objectives; (iv) numerous clinical observations on loss of the will to live. It is not claimed that these effects are always psychologically caused, either wholly or partly, but that psychological factors can produce these effects in some people. The central issue of this chapter is whether there is sufficient evidence to justify such a claim or hypothesis. First I shall briefly outline what would be the best possible evidence for the hypothesis, then the currently available data will be compared with the demands of this ideal proof.

I. An Ideal Proof

A brief statement of the experimental hypothesis is: psychological factors (that is thoughts and feelings evoked by current stimuli, or by the anticipation of future stimuli or by the remembrance of past stimuli) cause, in the previously defined sense, physiological or biochemical changes in some people which are serious enough to be classified as disorders.

First, there must be an adequate theory to explain how mental events could lead to bodily disorders, including a detailed description of the pathways and mechanisms involved. Second, the appropriate empirical data should be found across the range of all possible approaches. These may be classified as follows.

A. *Correlational Studies*

A strong association must be shown between the disorder under investigation and a psychological factor or set of factors. The latter could be assessed at an individual level, by interview or questionnaire, or at a group level, by trying to identify the psychological demands of different occupations or the psycho-social demands of different societies. This type of study presents two problems of interpretation. Firstly, the existence of an association does not establish which is the *cause* and which the *effect*, or whether each is both cause and effect of the other. Secondly, a particular psychological feature may characterize an occupation or society and may be associated with a particular physical disorder but the interpretation is in practice still uncertain. In the case of occupational disease it may be the result of *pre-existing* psychological or physiological differences between the subjects and the controls, or it may be due to some other aspect of the occupation which the researcher has ignored or dismissed. In the case of the societal disease it may again be due to other differences between the societies being compared, such as genetic factors, diet, exercise, the structure of the economy, drug habits and so on. Perfect matching of control groups is virtually impossible and there are no practical *objective* criteria for deciding how rigorously controls must be matched.

B. *Quasi-experimental Studies*

An improvement on these cross-sectional correlational studies is the longitudinal or prospective approach. In theory, a group of healthy subjects is selected and studied for months or years; psychological and physiological factors are continuously monitored and cause and effect are not confused because of their order or appearance. In practice, a limited number of variables are recorded only intermittently and the problems of initial differences and of additional confounding variables remain. But with the increasing availability of telemetry, continuous physiological recording is possible while the subject goes about his daily routine. However, the managerial problems in terms of time, money and skills are considerable.

A second approach which is intermediate between the correlational and the fully experimental is the so-called "stress interview". In this the interviewer manipulates a psychological variable, e.g. the subject's feelings of anger or resentment, by suitable questions and comments, while simultaneously looking for physiological changes, e.g. in blood pressure or respiratory function. The procedure rarely satisfies the requirements of a rigorous experiment: there are usually no controls for order effects, no control groups, no quantification of either stimulus or response, no statistical tests of significance and it is not double-blind. There are also ethical considerations which, if not outlawing the technique, certainly restrict the duration and severity of the manipulation. Practical considerations also limit its use to physiological variables which are quick to respond and easy to measure. With patients whose disorder has remitted it may be used to show that a psychological change can precipitate an attack – one of the types of causation mentioned earlier. With healthy normal subjects the best it can do is illustrate, yet again, that psychological factors can produce some physiological changes. The outstanding unanswered question is whether these are trivial, transient and reversible, or whether, if they are repeated frequently enough, they will lead to serious, lasting pathology. Ethical considerations form an insuperable barrier to the direct investigation of this question.

C. *Laboratory Experiments*

The most direct test of the psychosomatic hypothesis would use human subjects in controlled experimental designs with psychological independent variables and physiological dependent variables. This would enable us to identify the crucial stimuli, measure their effects, quantify the relationship between them, see if the findings are true for all subjects or if only certain people are susceptible and, if so, to list their identifying characteristics. But, as in the case of the stress interview, ethical constraints prohibit or severely restrict this approach. Nevertheless, a few experimenters have reported using controlled experimental procedures to evoke asthmatic attacks in patients, with dramatic results. And similarly, a number of experimenters have produced in normal subjects a range of physiological changes which arguably, if sustained, could lead to pathology.

By contrast, ethical considerations have not deterred researchers from using animals in experiments which have produced pathological changes in almost all the systems in the WHO list, including death. There are two perennial questions here. Firstly, are the physiological and biochemical processes in the animal world sufficiently similar to our own to justify extrapolating the results from animals to man? Before such extrapolation can be made the results must be shown to be consistent across a wide range of species including those closest to man. This condition is not often satisfied. Secondly, are the animals' cognitive and emotional processes sufficiently similar to our own to allow us to analyse meaningfully the situation without the benefit of either close evolutionary kinship or linguistic communication? That is a subjective decision which the reader must make for himself. This is perhaps a suitable point at which to invite the reader to consider a hitherto unmentioned and currently unfashionable source of evidence, introspection. Consider whether psychological influences seem to initiate, intensify or prolong your own physiological disorders. It may in scientific terms be inadmissible evidence, but it may also be illuminating.

D. *Miscellaneous*

Finally, there is a potentially rich line of evidence which cuts across this classificatory system. Most approaches contain data on control groups which show little or no physiological deterioration. The systematic study of animals and men who lead lives comparatively free from illness or disease might allow us to identify their physiological and psychological characteristics and those of the physical and social environment which confer on them this benefit of health. This could provide insight into possible techniques of prevention rather than cure.

II. Current Evidence

A. *Theory*

1. *Genetic Factors*

It is not in doubt that there are genetic influences on susceptibility to psychosomatic disorders. This does not mean that genotype is the sole determinant of whether one develops ulcers or high blood pressure, rather what is inherited is the disposition to become ill if the appropriate circumstances arise. Evidence is plentiful, but not above criticism. Selective breeding experiments have produced strains of rats which are either resistant to or susceptible to stress-induced ulcers (Mikhail, 1969); strains of hypertensive or normotensive rats have also been bred (Frohlich, 1977), although the mechanism underlying spontaneous hypertension in animals may be quite different from that responsible for essential hypertension in humans. First degree relatives have similar blood pressure; Pickering (1977) reports a figure of $0 \cdot 25$ for the heritability of hypertension. It is, however, possible that at least part of this correlation can be accounted for by shared non-genetic factors, such as similarities in diet, smoking habits, attitudes to exercise or family social relationships; after all the correlation in blood pressure between husband and wife can hardly be due to their shared genotype!

2. *Evolutionary theory*

But there is a more elaborate theory which may explain how man's genetic heritage predisposes him to psychosomatic diseases. During the course of human evolution the ability to respond swiftly and effectively to environmental threats and demands must have evolved and been genetically transmitted.

More specifically, those animals survived which were best fitted (i) to escape from predators, (ii) to do battle with competitors or, (iii) to react effectively to bodily insults, such as wounds, infection or extremes of temperature. The first two are known as the emergency or fight and flight reactions, the third is called, as a result of the work of the endocrinologist Hans Selye, the general adaptation syndrome (GAS). Both these adaptations involve intense widespread physiological activity. The fight or flight reaction is mainly mediated by the autonomic nervous system (ANS) as energy resources for escape or conflict are mustered; heart rate and stroke volume increase while blood is diverted to the major skeletal muscles (thereby increasing blood pressure) and adrenaline secreted from the adrenal medulla reinforces these effects. It is important to notice that these are not responses to *physical* activity (for they occur in anticipation of physical activity), but occur in response to the perception of a situation which will require action. If they take place only *after* the canines of the sabre-toothed tiger have penetrated the carotid artery it is already too late, they would have no survival value. By contrast the GAS mainly involves the endocrine system, is much slower and lasts longer. Selye (1956) has shown that a wide variety of severe noxious stimuli (electric shock, burns, infections, cold and forcible restraint) produce the same threefold syndrome of (i) enlargement of the adrenal cortex and increased corticosteroid output due to adrenocorticotrophic hormone (ACTH), (ii) ulceration of the gastro-intestinal tract, and (iii) atrophy of the thymus and lymphatic system. Selye reasoned that if such disparate stimuli produced the same syndrome they must share a common property; this he identified as "the stress of any change in the environment" (Selye, 1956, p. 29). Although the stressors Selye applied were physical and not psychological it seems reasonable to assume that they were accompanied by psychological changes in the form of pain, suffering and even anxiety over the future course of events. Psychologists have tended to assume that purely psychological factors such as prolonged stress can elicit the same pathological changes. There is some evidence that prolonged grief (Hofer *et al.*, 1972) or sustained exposure to front line battle conditions (Rose *et al.*, 1969) can lead to changes in the direction of the syndrome outlined by Selye (and to other endocrine disturbances), but it is difficult to ascribe the effect solely to psychological factors independent of such conditions as loss of sleep or excessive physical effort. Finally, it is worth recalling that the emergency reaction is coordinated by the hypothalamus, that the hypothalamus also controls the GAS, via the pituitary gland, and most importantly that cortical influences operate on the hypothalamus, thus allowing cognitive factors to exert an effect.

A theory which invokes the emergency reaction and the GAS in a psychological explanation of myocardial infarction (heart attack) has been proposed by Raab (1971). He suggests that three processes converge on their common victim, the myocardial cells. These are: (i) a reduction in blood flow, due for example to atherosclerosis; (ii) long term stress, which increases adrenal corticoid output (cf. the GAS) and disturbs the electrolytic environment of myocardial cells; and (iii) a large increase in heart rate due to the emergency reaction, which requires more oxygen and hence more blood flow to myocardial cells. But because the blood supply is already poor (factor 1) and the electrolyte environment already inadequate (factor 2), this sudden energy demand (factor 3) cannot be satisfied and the myocardial cells cease to respond. The theory is very speculative but is consistent with current evidence, which implicates a number of variables, some psychological, some non-psychological in the genesis of ischaemic heart disease, e.g. smoking, age, maleness, obesity, diet and lack of exercise.

3. Specific attitudes

The "specific attitudes" theory forms part of the traditional psychophysiological theory that each emotion or attitude is characterized by a specific bodily response pattern. The idea occupies a central role in the psychosomatic theorizing of Graham and of Alexander. Graham (Grace and Graham, 1952) has suggested that each psychosomatic disorder is associated with a particular attitude, for example, the patient with essential hypertension "feels threatened with harm and has to be ready for anything". Suggestive evidence comes from studies in which sufferers from psychosomatic disorders were shown cartoons representing different attitudes and were required to select the cartoon which best expressed how they felt (Graham *et al.*, 1962); in another series of studies (Graham *et al.*, 1958; Graham and Kunish, 1965) it was suggested to normal subjects that they were experiencing certain emotional attitudes. There was a significant tendency for a particular attitude to evoke a specific pattern of physiological responding as required by the theory. Although frequently quoted, the theory has received very little recent support, and a failure to replicate was reported by Peters and Stern (1971).

4. Psychodynamic theory

Graham's specific attitudes theory has its origins in the more complex psychodynamic theory of Alexander (1950). According to this theory, three conditions are necessary for the development of a psychosomatic disorder; a "psychodynamic constellation", or specific attitude; an "onset situation", or distressing life situation or event; and the "X factor" or vulnerability in a particular organ system. For example someone who (i) experiences a "continuous struggle against expressing hostile aggressive feeling and ... difficulty in asserting himself", (ii) is involved in a divorce and (iii) has a pre-existing weakness in his cardiovascular system, is likely to develop essential hypertension. In spite of extensive clinical research by Alexander and his colleagues (Alexander *et al.*, 1968), unambiguous empirical support did not emerge and the theory has received little recent interest.

5. Type A and type B

On the other hand, the extensive research programme of Rosenman (Rosenman *et al.*, 1975) clearly establishes that a specific complex of attitude, behaviour and emotion does tend to accompany ischaemic heart disease. They describe the typical sufferer as "engaged in a relatively chronic struggle to obtain an unlimited number of poorly defined things from their environment in the shortest period of time, and, if necessary, against the opposing effects of other things or persons in this same environment" (Friedman, 1969, p. 84).

6. Response specificity

The theory of "response specificity" holds that some people regularly respond maximally in one particular body system regardless of the nature of the stimulus. The concept is central to Sternbach's analysis of the development of psychosomatic disorders (Sternbach, 1966). Three conditions must be met: firstly, an individual must show response specificity or stereotypy; secondly, the response system must show inadequate homeostatic restraint (cf. Alexander's concept of organ weakness); thirdly, he must be repeatedly exposed to the activating situation. The theory resembles, but is not identical with, the specific attitudes theories of Graham and Alexander. But Sternbach goes on to speculate that this process can be set in motion not just by exposure to the real activating situation but also by imagining such a situation, or by misperceiving a harmless situation as a threatening one. Although the theory seems plausible, supporting evidence is in short supply. Individuals certainly differ in the efficiency of their homeostatic mechanisms, but experiments show that response specificity is slight (Wenger *et al.*, 1961) and not very reliable over time (Oken *et al.*, 1962). Also, there are no longitudinal data on whether repeated exposure results in a reduction or an increase in response magnitude.

Since not everyone suffers from psychosomatic disorders, the idea that only people with a *specific* personality pattern succumb is attractive. It is, however, not consistently supported by the evidence, except for the recurrent theme of an association between repressed anger and cardiovascular disorders.

7. Learning models

Both classical and instrumental learning theories have been invoked to explain the occurrence of psychosomatic disorders. If classical conditioning is to take place, there must first be a naturally occurring response (UCR) which is evoked by a stimulus (UCS). For example, if an increase in blood pressure is the repeated response to conflict with a colleague at work, this may become conditioned and generalize to the mere appearance of the person or even to arriving at work. Repetition of this transient response may then lead to sustained high blood pressure. Although the cardiovascular system is very amenable to classical conditioning (Wilson, 1969), there is no evidence that this results in changes of clinical significance. But if the naturally occurring response is already a psychosomatic one (e.g. an asthmatic attack in response to pollen), then it may generalize to the previously neutral stimulus (e.g. the sight of imitation flowers, (MacKenzie, 1886). But on the other hand, some experimental attempts to transfer asthmatic responses to neutral stimuli (e.g. Dekker *et al.*, 1957) have been unsuccessful.

Instrumental conditioning has also been suggested as a mechanism involved in the acquisition of asthma at least for some asthmatics. During the course of development it may well be rewarding for some children to wheeze and struggle for breath; the performance attracts attention and sympathy; it provides a powerful weapon for manipulating parents and siblings. In later life, an asthmatic attack conspicuously authenticated by wheezing and paroxysms is an effective way of claiming the *sick role* and temporarily opting out of the responsibilities of the social contract. But this instrumental conditioning analysis requires that the patient has at least some voluntary control over his asthma, which may be true only for a small subgroup of asthmatics (Dekker and Groen, 1956) and which may be reduced in adulthood. But in those people for whom the asthmatic response is rewarding, it should be possible to extinguish it by removing its reward value e.g. by ignoring it. There is some evidence (Greer, 1970) that this treatment is effective. However, an operant conditioning analysis has not been widely advocated for other psychosomatic disorders except for migraine or tension headaches.

Clearly there is no shortage of theories which could explain how the central nervous system, in particular the higher mental processes, can exercise a malign influence over physiological functioning.

B. *Correlational Studies*

Diseases such as essential hypertension and myocardial infarction are much more frequent in some societies than in others. This could be due to a number of differences between the societies, e.g. genetic, occupational, dietary, exercise, social or family structure. In Europe and the USA blood pressure increases steadily with age, whereas for Navajo Indians on reservations and for the Samburu, a Kenyan gerontocracy, blood pressure remains stable with age. It is difficult to identify which factors are responsible for this, but more systematic information is available for Roseto (Stout *et al.*, 1964), an Italian community in Pennsylvania, where the incidence of myocardial infarction is only half that found in control communities. Their inhabitants were similar to Rosetans in terms of serum cholesterol and smoking habits, although Rosetans were in fact *more* overweight and consumed *more* animal fats. The distinguishing features of Roseto are social and psychological; it is a mutually supportive, caring community with little poverty and crime, family structure is close and unambiguous, with the elderly occupying a respected role, and the people are described as vigorous and fun-loving. Two minor criticisms of this study are that there were inevitably some differences in occupation between Rosetans and controls and that the genetic control data from relatives living away from Roseto are not presented quantitatively.

Similarly, peptic ulcers and hypertension are more frequent in some occupations than in others, for example, both are more prevalent among air traffic controllers than among airmen (Cobb and Rose, 1973). These and similar findings have been interpreted as showing that responsibility, decision making, time pressure or some other psychological variable is at least partly responsible for the disorder. But it is almost impossible to rule out alternative explanations in terms of pre-existing differences between groups, or other differences between the experimental and control occupations.

The possible association between important life changes (e.g. marriage, loss of job, death of a relative) and a wide variety of illnesses has been explored by Rahe (1972, 1974). He developed a schedule of recent life events questionnaire (SRE), in which events were measured in terms of life change units (LCU). Small ($r = 0.12$ to 0.09), but highly significant ($p < 0.001$) correlations were consistently found. On the other hand, recent experimental work by Totman *et al.* (1980) found no correlation between susceptibility to cold viruses and SRE scores, although a correlation did emerge between a revised scale (Totman's change index) and susceptibility. But in addition to the slightness of this relation, it is again difficult to disentangle the psychological effect of life changes from possible accompanying changes in work, diet, exercise, sleep and so on.

The most striking associations of psychological changes and physiological dysfunction come from single case studies, although these do not usually meet the requirements of scientific rigour. A small number of people have suffered accidents which resulted in their having a lifelong gastric fistula, which allows direct observation of stomach activity. Wolf (1971) reports that emotional turmoil, such as feelings of frustration and conflict, are reliably accompanied by enhanced blood flow, greater contractility, more acid secretion and an increase in the fragility of the membrane, conditions which if sustained could well lead to ulceration. It is worth noting that these responses are for once under *parasympathetic* rather than sympathetic control. More systematic studies (e.g. Sales and House, 1971) report that myocardial infarction is often immediately preceded by an intense emotional upset. Traumatic events such as violent rows with superiors, witnessing a serious car accident, the death of a spouse or even the anniversary of the death of a spouse are typical events which may precipitate a cardiovascular incident. Greene, *et al.* (1972) describe the case of a 50 year old man with no previous history of cardiovascular disease who, on the evening after an operation, suffered a myocardial infarction from which he recovered. Three months later he took his first convalescent stroll in his garden where he saw "an arborway, which he had built earlier that summer and of which he was very proud, had been sprayed with tar-paint". The patient apparently just looked at this while his wife expressed her anger. He walked 20 yards back towards the house, collapsed and died.

C. *Quasi-experimental Studies*

There are relatively few longitudinal studies of the development of psychosomatic disorders. One widely quoted study (Weiner *et al.*, 1957; Yessler *et al.*, 1959) screened 2073 army draftees for signs of duodenal ulcer, first at induction, then at 8–16 weeks and again after 2 years. It was designed to test Alexander's hypothesis that an "onset situation" (the army induction course) plus "the X factor" (high pepsinogen levels) will produce ulcers in people with the appropriate "psychodynamic constellation". The study is too complex to evaluate here, but 5 out of 63 men with high initial pepsinogen levels developed ulcers after 16 weeks and no further ulcers were present within this group after 2 years.

The eight year, blind, prospective study of coronary heart disease (CHD) by Rosenman and colleagues (Rosenman *et al.*, 1975) was more fruitful. At initial interview, a number of physiological, biochemical and socio-economic measures were recorded. Subjects with enhanced aggressiveness, ambitiousness, competitive drive and chronic sense of time urgency (p. 872) were classified as type A, and subjects with low scores on these measures, type B. Of 1500 type A's 178 developed CHD, but only 79 out of 1500 type B's. This relationship remained even after statistical adjustments had been made to allow for any possible contributory effects of smoking, parental CHD, blood pressure, cholesterol, triglyceride or lipoprotein concentrations.

The stress interview has sometimes been used to demonstrate physiological change to psychological stress, particularly in the rapidly responding cardiovascular system. The blood pressures of a group of normotensive medical students were recorded continuously during an oral examination. When a student was singled out for questioning blood pressure increased by up to 20 mm Hg (von Uexküll and Wick, 1962; cited by Herrman *et al.*, 1976). Wolf (1965) describes a patient with a gastric ulcer who had been deeply disturbed to find her husband molesting her twelve year old daughter. Although her gastric acid flow was unresponsive to histamine injections, merely asking her about her rejection of her husband was sufficient to produce gastric acid to 40 mEq/l.

Recording the physiological activity of people with stressful occupations has also produced impressive results. The heart rates of television announcers, in the few seconds before they are on the air, can rise to 200 beats per minute. (Baxter, 1979). Carruthers (1974, p. 41) reports the same figure in racing drivers during a race. More important, perhaps, is his finding that during the race large amounts of fat appeared in their blood plasma. This, he argues, is not due to recent food intake and must therefore be being manufactured by the drivers themselves, and could be the link connecting emotional stress and coronary heart disease.

D. *Laboratory Experiments*

In spite of ethical considerations, some experimental work has been done with human volunteer subjects. The anticipation of electric shock or the fear of failure has often been used as the psychological variable, with a range of dependent variables including catecholamine or corticoid levels and most components of the autonomic nervous system (e.g. Patkai, 1974). As before, it has been shown that the changes are statistically significant, not that they are clinically significant. But a few experiments have produced clinically significant changes in patients already suffering from a disorder. Luparello (Luparello *et al.*, 1968) suggested to 40 asthmatics and 40 controls that they were inhaling an allergen in polluted air. They actually inhaled a spray of physiological saline. Twelve asthmatics developed "full-blown clinical attacks of asthma with dyspnea and wheezing" (ibid., p. 822); no respiratory changes were recorded in controls. The effect was reversed by inhaling a placebo.

Numerous experiments with animals have manipulated stressors such as electric shock, forcible restraint, food deprivation or immersion in water. These produced a variety of effects, including stomach ulceration, 30% increases in systolic pressure, ectopic heart beats and myocardial infarctions. In most of these experiments it is not possible to decide whether the effects are due simply to the physical treatments, or to some psychological change such as fear or anxiety which may accompany them, or to the combination. But some work with psychological disruption and with the yoked control design does go some way towards identifying the crucial independent variable. Studies of overcrowding (social density) in laboratory and wild populations reliably find adrenal gland hypertrophy, involution of the thymus, hypertension and lowered resistance to infection (cf. the GAS). It is arguable that in many of these studies the results are indirect, they are mediated by increased fighting, inadequate food and greater opportunity for transmitting infection. But in a few studies (see Thiessen and Rodgers, 1961) adequate food was consumed and little fighting occurred and was unrelated to the severity of the effects, although the criticism concerning possible infection remains. Careful work by Henry and Stephens (1977) and Henry *et al.* (1967) in the USA confirms that both crowding and altering the social structure of caged mice produced elevations of blood pressure. Although increased fighting may be partly responsible for the effect in some of the groups he used, he reports that one group of female mice developed high blood pressure even in the absence of fighting. Russian work described by Lapin and Cherkovich (1971) shows even more serious effects of social manipulation. The dominant male baboon was removed from his troop of females and juveniles, who were then caged alongside. A new mature male was introduced to this cage and the occupants were fed first, before their previous leader, who eventually suffered hypertension, coronary insufficiency and myocardial infarction.

A more orthodox experimental procedure is the yoked control paradigm used to study the causes of ulcers in mice, rats and monkeys. The experimental animal and its yoked control are treated identically, usually by being connected together in an in-series electrical circuit. Both animals are exposed to the same aversive stimulus; the only difference is that the experimental animal is able to delay or prevent the stimulus to both animals by making the appropriate response. Most results (e.g. Weiss, 1968) show that the helpless animal suffers significantly more ulceration. This is usually interpreted as showing that either the ability to predict the onset of the aversive stimulus or the mastery of the coping response are important psychological variables in the development of ulcers. But the design itself (Church, 1964) and the interpretation of the results (Murison, 1980) are not without their critics. Moreover, before generalizing these results to humans, it is important to note that the pathology is not due just to a psychological factor but its combination with a purely physical treatment, such as shock or hunger.

III. Summary and Conclusions

The chapter began with a definition of the term psychosomatic, and with a consideration of what is meant by a cause and by a psychological factor. This was followed by a list of disorders which are conventionally classified as of psychogenic origin. Although in practice it may be acceptable to divide illnesses into those which are psychosomatic and those which are not, it is *logically* unjustifiable. Each particular occurrence of a disorder in an individual must be evaluated separately; one man's migraine or heart attack may be caused on one occasion by an allergen or by heavy exercise and on another occasion by fear or extreme anger. The original list is simultaneously over-inclusive and under-inclusive and also misguided in principle.

There may be considerable agreement about what is required as definitive proof of the hypothesis that the paramyxovirus has caused a particular case of measles or that the clostridium tetani bacillus caused tetanus. But there is no such agreement about what, even in theory, would be an acceptable proof that psychological factors have caused an attack of asthma or are responsible for the development of an individual's essential hypertension. Nevertheless, it is suggested both that the psychosomatic hypothesis can be clearly stated and that criteria for its acceptance or rejection can be made explicit. The hypothesis is that psychological factors cause (either alone or in combination with other factors) a number of physiological disorders. The criteria are, first, that this is predictable from an acceptable theory which relates psychological activity to physiological functioning, and, second, that there is adequate empirical evidence showing an association between the two. A powerful explanatory theory is available by combining the following three propositions: (i) in the course of evolution elaborate reflex mechanisms of the nervous and endocrine systems have become inextricably linked with subjective mental events, such as emotion, memory and expectation; (ii) these obey the laws of operant and classical conditioning; (iii) there are crucial biochemical, physiological and psychological differences between individuals. This theory affords an adequate explanation of how psychological factors could cause physiological disorders. Empirical evidence comes from the following disparate approaches: (i)introspection; (ii) correlational studies of the association between psychological stress and physiological dysfunction in single clinical cases, in some occupations and professions and in certain types of society; (iii) quasi-experimental research using "stress interviews" and prospective rather than cross-sectional approaches; (iv) controlled laboratory experiments with animals and man. Although each separate type of research may be constrained by ethical considerations, limited by scarcity of research resources, open to alternative explanations or liable to "scientific" criticisms, it is argued that, collectively, the whole body of evidence is most parsimoniously explained in terms of the psychosomatic hypothesis. However, two outstanding problems remain: first, how to evaluate in any given case the importance of the physiological contribution relative to other possible causes such as diet, lack of exercise, environmental pollution or smoking; second, how to devise techniques of prevention or, failing that, of cure.

The implication of the psychosomatic hypothesis is that prevention may be achieved in several ways: the real world may be altered so as to remove a source of threat or stress, e.g. by a change of employment, by restructuring the social environment or even society itself; alternatively, it is one's subjective experience of the world which can be changed, e.g. by denial or repression, by better reality orientation, or by acquiring cognitive, emotional or behavioural coping strategies (as in yoked control experiments). Additionally, it should be noted that, if a disorder is psychologically caused, it must also be psychologically preventable, but the fact that it is psychologically caused does not entail that it must be psychologically curable (e.g. death). Finally, unlike the traditional medical explanation which often requires chemical or surgical intervention, the psychosomatic explanation credits man with much greater autonomy and independence; the individual has responsibility for his own bodily condition, since by purely psychological means he can, in theory, always prevent and often cure a disorder, as is so dramatically illustrated by the placebo effect and by faith healing.

Further Reading

A collection of short review articles ranging over most aspects of psychosomatic medicine may be found in the two books:
Hill, O. H. (ed.), (1976). "Modern Trends in Psychosomatic Medicine – 3". Butterworths, London.
Levi, L. (ed.), (1971). "Society, Stress and Disease: Vol. 1 – The psychosocial environment and psychosomatic disease". Oxford University Press, London.
More detailed treatments of physiological aspects and of social aspects may be found respectively in;
Weiner, H. (1977). "Psychobiology and Human Disease". Elsevier, New York.
Insel, P. M. and Moore, R. H. (1974). "Health and the Social Environment". Heath, Lexington.
Detailed reports on contemporary research are contained in:
Levine, S. and Ursin, H. (eds), (1980). "Coping and Health". Plenum, London.
Two major journals are devoted to psychosomatic topics, and contain articles representing a wide variety of theoretical and practical approaches. The journals are:
Journal of Psychosomatic Research, published bimonthly. Pergamon Press, Oxford.
Psychosomatic Medicine, published bimonthly. Elsevier/North Holland, Amsterdam.

References

Alexander, F. (1950). "Psychosomatic Medicine". Norton, New York.
Alexander, F., French, T. M. and Pollock, G. H. (eds), (1968). "Psychosomatic Specificity". University of Chicago Press, Chicago.
Baxter, R. (1979). Public performance from the point of view of the performer. Paper presented at the meeting of the Society for Psychosomatic Research, London, in November, 1979.
Carruthers, M. (1974). "The Western Way of Death". Davis-Poynter, London.

Church, R. M. (1964). Systematic effect of random error in the yoked control design. *Psychol. Bull.* **62**, 122–131.

Cobb, S. and Rose, R. M. (1973). Hypertension, peptic ulcer and diabetes in air traffic controllers. *J. Am. Med. Assoc.* **224**, 489–492.

Dekker, E. and Groen, I. I. (1956). Reproducible psychogenic attacks of asthma. *J. Psychosom. Res.* **1**, 58–67.

Dekker, E., Pelse, H. E. and Groen, J. (1957). Conditioning as a cause of asthmatic attacks. *J. Psychom. Res.* **2**, 97–108.

Friedman, M. (1969). "Pathogenesis of Coronary Artery Disease". McGraw-Hill, New York.

Frohlich, E. D. (1977). Hemodynamics of hypertension. *In* "Hypertension" (I. Genest, E. Koiw and O. Kuchel, eds). McGraw-Hill, New York and London.

Grace, W. J. and Graham, D. T. (1952). Relationship of specific attitudes and emotions to certain bodily diseases. *Psychosom. Med.* **14**, 243–251.

Graham, F. K. and Kunish, N. O. (1965). Physiological responses of unhypnotized subjects to attitude suggestions. *Psychosom. Med.* **27**, 317–329.

Graham, D. T., Stern, J. A. and Winokur, G. (1958). Experimental investigation of the specificity of attitude hypothesis in psychosomatic disease. *Psychosom. Med.* **20**, 446–457.

Graham, D. T., Lundy, R. M., Benjamin, L. S., Kabler, J. D., Lewis, W. C., Kunish, N. O. and Graham, F. K. (1962). Specific attitudes in initial interviews with patients having different "psychosomatic" disease. *Psychosom. Med.* **24**, 257–266.

Greene, W. A., Goldstein, S. and Moss, A. J. (1972). Psychosocial aspects of sudden death. *Arch. Intern. Med.* **129**, 725–731.

Greer, T. L. (1970). The use of a time-out from positive reinforcement procedure with asthmatic children. *J. Psychosom. Res.* **14**, 117–120.

Henry, J. P. and Stephens, P. M. (1977). Stress, Health and the Social Evnironment: a sociological approach to medicine. Springer-Verlag, New York.

Henry, J. P., Meehan, J. P. and Stephens, P. M. (1967). The use of psychosocial stimuli to induce prolonged systolic hypertension in mice. *Psychosom. Med.* **29**, 408–431.

Herrmann, H. J. M., Rassek, M., Schoffer, N., Schmidt, Th. and von Uexküll, Th. (1976). Essential hypertension: problems, concepts and an attempted synthesis. *In* "Modern Trends in Psychosomatic Medicine – 3" (O. W. Hill, ed.). Butterworth, London.

HMSO (1968). "A Glossary of Mental Disorders". In the series "Studies on Medical and Population Subjects" No. 22. HMSO, London.

Hofer, M. A., Wolff, C. T., Friedman, S. B. and Mason, J. W. (1972). A psycho-endocrine study of bereavement. *Psychosom. Med.* **34**, 481–491.

Lapin, B. A. and Cherkovich, G. M. (1971). Environmental changes causing the development of neurosis and corticovisceral pathology in monkeys. *In* "Society, Stress and Disease" (L. Levi, ed.), Oxford University Press, London.

Luparello, T., Lyons, H. A., Bleecker, E. R. and McFadden, E. R., Jr. (1968). Influence of suggestion on airway reactivity in asthmatic subjects. *Psychosom. Med.* **30**, 819–825.

MacKenzie, J. N. (1886). The production of "rosa asthma" by an artificial rose. *Am. J. Med. Sci.* **91**, 45–57.

Mikhail, A. A. (1969). Genetic Predisposition to stomach ulceration in emotionally reactive strains of rats. *Psychonom. Sci.* **15**, 245–247.

Murison, R. (1980). Experimentally induced gastric ulceration: a model disorder for psychosomatic research. *In* "Coping and Health" (S. Levine and H. Ursin, eds). Plenum, New York.

Oken, D., Grinker, R. R., Heath, H. A., Heretz, M., Korchin, C. J., Sabshin, M. and Schwartz, N. B. (1962). Relation of physiological response to affect expression. *Arch. Gen. Psychiat.* **6**, 336–351.

Patkai, P. (1974). Laboratory studies of psychological stress. *Int. J. Psychiat. Med.* **5**, 575–585.

Peters, J. E. and Stern, R. M. (1971). Specificity of attitude hypothesis in psychosomatic medicine: a re-examination. *J. Psychosom. Res.* **15**, 129–135.

Pickering, Sir. G. (1977). Personal views of mechanisms of hypertension. *In* "Hypertension" (J. Genest, E. Koiw and O. Kuchel, eds). McGraw-Hill, New York and London.

Raab, W. (1971). Cardiotoxic biochemical effects of emotional-environmental stressors – Fundamentals of Psychocardiology. *In* "Society, Stress and Disease: Vol. 1 – The Psychosocial Environment and Psychosomatic Diseases" (L. Levi, ed.). Oxford University Press, London and New York.

Rahe, R. H. (1972). Subjects' recent life changes and their near-future illness reports. *Ann. Clin. Res.* **4**, 250–255.

Rahe, R. H. (1974). A model for life-changes and illness research. *Arch. Gen. Psychiat.* **31**, 172–177.

Rose, R. M., Bourne, P. G., Poe, R. O., Mougey, E. H., Collins, D. R. and Mason, J. W. (1969). Androgen response to stress. *Psychosom. Med.* **31**, 418–436.

Rosenman, R. H., Brand, R. J., Jenkins, C. D., Friedman, M., Strauss, R. and Wurm, M. (1975). Coronary heart disease in Western Collaborative Group study: final follow-up experience of 8½ years. *J. Am. Med. Ass.* **233**, 872–877.

Sales, S. M. and House, J. (1971). Job dissatisfaction as a possible risk factor in coronary heart disease. *J. Chron. Dis.* **23**, 861–873.

Selye, H. (1956). "The Stress of Life". McGraw-Hill, New York.

Sternbach, R. A. (1966). "Principles of Psychophysiology". Academic Press, New York and London.

Stout, C., Morrow, J., Brandt, E. N., Jnr. and Wolf, S. (1964). Unusually low incidence of death from myocardial infarction. *J. Am. Med. Ass.* **188**, 845–849.

Thiessen, D. D. and Rodgers, D. A. (1961). Population density and endocrine function. *Psychol. Bull.* **58**, 441–451.

Totman, R., Kiff, J., Reid, S. E. and Craig, J. W. (1980). Predicting experimental colds in volunteers from different measures of recent life stress. *J. Psychosom. Med.* **24**, 155–163.

Weiner, H., Thaler, M., Reiser, M. F. and Mirsky, I. A. (1957). Etiology of duodenal ulcer: I. Relation of specific psychological characteristics to rate of gastric secretion (serum pepsinogen). *Psychosom. Med.* **19**, 1–10.

Weiss, J. M. (1968). Effects of coping responses on stress. *J. Comp. Physiol. Psychol.* **65**, 251–260.

Wenger, M. A., Clemens, T. L., Coleman, D. R., Cullen, T. D. and Engel, B. T. (1961). Autonomic response specificity. *Psychosom. Med.* **23**, 185–193.

WHO (1968). "International Statistical Classification of Diseases, Injuries and Causes of Death" 8th revision. World Health Organization, Geneva.

Wilson, R. S. (1969). Cardiac response: Determinants of conditioning. *J. Comp. Physiol. Psychol.* **68**, 1–23.

Wolf, S. (1965). "The Stomach". Oxford University Press, New York.

Wolf, S. (1971). Psychosocial influences in Gastrointestinal Function. *In* "Society, Stress and Disease: Vol. 1 – The Psychosocial Environment and Psychosomatic Diseases" (L. Levi, ed.), Oxford University Press, London.

Yessler, P. G., Reiser, M. F. and Rioch, D. M. (1959). Etiology of duodenal ulcer: 11. Serum pepsinogen and peptic ulcer in inductees. *J. Am. Med. Ass.* **169**, 451–456.

12 Psychopathy, Delinquency and Crime

R. Blackburn

Abstract Learning and organismic variables can be seen to interact to produce behaviour which violates legal and moral codes. The predisposition within the nervous system to engage in socially unacceptable behaviour may lie within mechanisms concerned with socialization, and in particular in those involved with passive avoidance learning. A variety of definitions of psychopathy are employed by researchers, and it is clear that reliability of diagnosis and interrelationships among measurement instruments are low. Studies concerned with autonomic correlates of psychopathy have focused upon avoidance learning, fear of punishment and measures of arousal. There is also a long history of research into electrocortical correlates of criminal behaviour, with a particular emphasis upon the relationship between abnormalities in the EEG and dispositions to violence and aggression. Earlier studies were often deficient from a methodological point of view, but recent work indicates relationships between cortical arousal and primary psychopathy. A tentative conclusion from these studies is that psychopaths are under-aroused and unresponsive to threats of punishment; yet psychopaths are distinguished from other offenders in other ways and it is not clear that a full account of psychopathy could be couched in terms of passive avoidance mechanisms alone.

I. The Role of Learning and Organismic Variables in Criminality

Although crime is defined by culturally relative legal criteria, behavioural scientists have typically been concerned with criminality as a disposition on the part of individuals to violate the legal and ethical codes of the society to which they belong. It has been proposed, for example, that people can be ordered along a continuum of socialization according to the extent to which societal norms have been internalized and modulate behaviour (Gough, 1960; Aronfreed, 1968). This chapter is concerned with the intra-organismic variables which might mediate such a disposition.

Some contemporary learning theorists (Burgess and Akers, 1966; Ullmann and Krasner, 1975), as well as many sociologists, locate the sources of

PHYSIOLOGICAL CORRELATES OF HUMAN
BEHAVIOUR   ISBN 0-12-273901-9

criminal behaviour virtually exclusively in social environmental processes. It is, however, unlikely that the individual is a mere passive recipient of such influences. While it is true that crime flourishes in culturally and economically disadvantaged environments, not all those exposed to such conditions become delinquent or criminal (Trasler, 1973). Moreover, studies of criminality in twins and in the biological parents of adoptees who become criminal (Mednick and Hutchings, 1978) clearly indicate that biological endowment must enter into any account of antisocial behaviour. What it is about inheritance which might predispose an individual to engage in criminal behaviour is obscure, but stable properties of the nervous system determining individual differences in response to the social learning process seem probable candidates for this role.

Now, it has been argued that since crime involves universal human needs, a theory of criminality must also be an account of why the majority of people refrain from committing crimes (Trasler, 1973; Eysenck, 1964). Criminality, in these terms, reflects the relative absence of restraints against behaviour which attracts legal and social sanctions. The acquisition of behavioural restraints has therefore been seen as central to the socialization process.

An analogue of this process can be found in the laboratory phenomenon of *passive avoidance learning*, which involves learning to inhibit punished behaviour. According to two-factor learning theory (see Trasler, 1973), suppression of a punished response is accomplished in two stages. First, through a process of classical conditioning, cues associated with the aversive stimulus (punishment) come to arouse fear or anxiety, an emotional state accompanied by autonomic arousal. Second, this conditioned fear response functions as an aversive state which is reduced by an inhibitory response. The act of not responding therefore avoids punishment, and is reinforced by the reduction of fear. There is evidence that behavioural suppression of this kind represents the activity of an important brain system governing mammalian emotional behaviour (Gray, 1970, 1975). This is described as the behavioural inhibition system (BIS), and it is responsive to conditioned stimuli for punishment or the absence of anticipated reward (i.e. it responds to warnings of impending punishment rather than to punishment itself). This is distinguished from a behavioural activation system (BAS), which responds to conditioned stimuli for reward or non-punishment, and which controls active avoidance behaviour. Both systems have reciprocal relations with the reticular system of the brainstem and produce generalized arousal. Sensitivity to *unconditioned* aversive stimuli appears to be a function of general arousal level. Gray suggests that the BIS may mediate anxiety-proneness and the BAS impulsivity, two personality variables which have been particularly implicated in antisocial behaviour. (A full account of the theory is provided by Gray in Chapter 3).

Applying the passive avoidance model to human socialization, both Trasler and Eysenck point to the role of punishment in child training. Refraining from behaviour which has previously been punished avoids further parental chastisement or withdrawal of approval, and it seems reasonable to suppose that this is governed by conditioned fear or anxiety responses to cues signalling the imminence of punishment. As Eysenck puts it, "Conscience is a conditioned reflex". Through generalization and second-order conditioning, the cues eliciting such anticipatory fear may come to extend to a range of socially disapproved behaviours. Furthermore, conditioned fear can be acquired vicariously, through observing the receipt of punishment by others (Bandura and Rosenthal, 1966), and through symbolic processes, it can also come to be aroused by internal cues (Aronfreed, 1968). Direct experience of punishment for illegal acts is therefore not a necessary condition of refraining from them.

A disposition to engage in antisocial behaviour can in these terms be seen as representing a failure to respond to internal or external cues which signal the probability of punishing consequences for such behaviour. As Trasler emphasizes, however, this deficit in socialization could arise for several reasons. At one extreme, socialization may fail because the appropriate conditions for learning (e.g. parental discipline) are lacking. At the other extreme, it may fail because the child is insensitive to punishment cues. Eysenck proposes that this will happen if the individual is relatively lacking in the ability to form conditioned responses *in general*, an attribute hypothesized to be a function of low cortical arousal and extraverted personality. But there is little evidence for a generalized trait of "conditionability", and since extraverts are in any case poor conditioners only under very precisely controlled laboratory conditions, it is unlikely that variations in conditionability are the principal sources of real life differences in susceptibility to social training (Gray, 1970). According to the passive avoidance model, the latter are more likely to be related to insensitivity to punishment or weak formation of conditioned *fear* responses. Physiological under-reactivity to unconditioned and/or conditioned *aversive* stimuli might, then, be significant organismic factors contributing to a failure of socialization.

It must be stressed that this would not be predicted to characterize all criminals. Although the passive avoidance model offers a general account of how criminality as a disposition might emerge, an inadequately socializing environment seems sufficient to account for this disposition in many offenders. Moreover, some who commit crimes are "situational" offenders, who have broken the law under temporary provocation, and who are not otherwise disposed to engage in criminal behaviour. In short, the extent to which organismic variables (including temperament) mediate crime is likely to vary for different categories of offender. The heterogeneity of criminal populations is, in fact, well established. Quay (1972), for example, has shown that young offenders can be differentiated in terms of psychopathy, inadequacy, neurotic delinquency and subcultural delinquency. Psychopathic offenders are the most incorrigible, and if there are indeed organismic factors which retard the development of socialization, it is in this group that they are most likely to be identified. The remainder of this chapter will therefore focus on the characteristics of psychopaths.

II. Psychopathic Personality

A. *The Concept of the Psychopath*

The term psychopath (or sociopath) is a psychiatric concept for which a universally agreed definition remains lacking. It is nevertheless used widely to describe deviant individuals appearing in both psychiatric and penal institutions. In clinical and medico-legal use in Britain, it continues to be regarded as a discrete category of "mental disorder". Continental European (Schneider, 1923) and American use of the term (now antisocial personality disorder: American Psychiatric Association, 1979), however, gives greater recognition to the distinction between mental disorder or illness and personality disorder. Where mental "illness" denotes a disruption or discontinuity in the individual's life-style, psychopathy is a disposition inferred from the early appearance and persistence of unsocialized behaviour. Its "symptoms" are, in fact, *typical* behaviours or personality characteristics. Clinical use of the term, however, suffers from the general unreliability of psychiatric diagnosis, and in Britain at least, those diagnosed clinically as psychopaths appear to be a heterogeneous group with little more in common than a history of socially undesirable behaviour (Blackburn, 1975a).

Research usage generally involves employing operational measures which aim to tap the personality characteristics described by such writers as McCord and McCord (1964) or Cleckley (1964). The McCords describe the psychopath as "an asocial, aggressive, highly impulsive person, who feels little or no guilt and is unable to form lasting bonds of affection with other human beings". A rather more heterogeneous list of characteristics is suggested by Cleckley, who offers the following as salient: (i) superficial charm; (ii) absence of psychotic signs; (iii) absence of nervousness; (iv) unreliability; (v) untruthfulness and insincerity; (vi) lack of remorse or shame; (vii) inadequately motivated antisocial behaviour; (viii) failure to learn from experience; (ix) egocentricity and incapacity for love; (x) emotional poverty; (xi) lack of insight; (xii) unresponsiveness to interpersonal relations; (xiii) uninviting behaviour, sometimes with alcohol; (xiv) empty suicide threats; (xv) impersonal sex life; (xvi) failure to follow a life plan.

The concept of the psychopath is, then, most appropriately viewed as referring to a personality type representing deviations on certain personality variables. Gray (1970) has suggested that these may be reducible to a combination of high impulsivity and low anxiety, a notion for which there is some empirical support (Blackburn, 1975a, 1979). It must be emphasized that the term refers to personality deviation and not to antisocial behaviour or criminality *per se*. Many psychopaths are habitual offenders, but not all recidivists nor all violent offenders exhibit psychopathic personality characteristics. Conversely, there are individuals displaying these characteristics who do not come to the attention of criminal justice or psychiatric agencies (Widom, 1977).

B. *Primary and Secondary Psychopathy*

Psychopaths may not form a homogeneous group, and several researchers have distinguished between *primary psychopaths*, who broadly display the characteristics listed above, and *secondary or neurotic psychopaths*, who are similar except that they do in fact show signs of neurotic anxiety and emotional reactions, such as guilt or shame. The distinction has been objected to on the grounds that the antisocial behaviour of secondary psychopaths is motivated by neurotic conflicts (Hare, 1970). Unfortunately, we do not know for certain what motivates the behaviour of psychopaths, and the distinction has been found to be necessary on empirical grounds (Blackburn, 1975a). However, it will be noted that the identification of the secondary psychopathic group raises difficulties for theories which attribute antisocial behaviour in the psychopath to a *lack* of anxiety. This point will be discussed later.

C. *Research Definitions of Psychopathy*

While some investigations rely on clinical criteria of unknown reliability, the bulk of recent work has employed one of the following as the independent variable.

(i) *Cleckley's criteria* Hare and other North American researchers have been guided by Cleckley's description in deriving global ratings of psychopathy from case history records.
(ii) *MMPI* (Minnesota Multiphasic Personality Inventory) This clinically oriented self-report test contains two scales, *Pd* (psychopathic deviate) and *Ma* (hypomania), joint elevations of which are commonly found in offenders or psychiatric patients clinically described as psychopaths. *Pd* seems more a general measure of lack of socialization, since high scores

are not necessarily associated with other psychopathic personality traits. *Ma* seems primarily a measure of impulsivity. Some researchers have employed *Pd* alone, others rely on both *Pd* and *Ma*.

(iii) *Quay's dimensions of psychopathy and neurotic withdrawal* Quay (1972) has identified these dimensions in factor analytic studies of case history data, behaviour ratings and self-report questionnaires in young offenders. They have been employed singly, or in combination, to identify psychopaths and neurotic delinquents (not secondary psychopaths).

(iv) *So* (socialization) This self-report scale was developed by Gough (1960) to measure role playing deficits which he proposed as central to psychopathy. It has been favoured in particular by Schalling and her associates (Schalling, 1978), who have used an earlier version of the scale (*De*: delinquency). Low scores on *So* are held to reflect psychopathic traits.

D. *Methodological Issues*

The major methodological problem in research on the psychophysiology of psychopathy is to integrate research findings from investigations using different criteria of psychopathy. Unfortunately technical sophistication of psychophysiological recording is not always matched by judicious consideration of the psychometric niceties of reliability and validity. Some investigators continue to employ clinical criteria of unknown reliability and highly questionable validity. The measures described above have the advantage of good reliability (reproducibility), and all can claim some evidence of construct validity. However, what evidence there is suggests that the intercorrelations between them tend to fall in the region of 0·4 to 0·5, which indicates moderate overlap, but certainly not identity. It is little consolation to observe that psychopathy research is no worse in this respect than other areas of research in the clinical area.

III. Autonomic Correlates of Psychopathy

Psychophysiological studies of psychopaths first appeared in the form of clinical EEG studies, in the late 1930s, but these early investigations are difficult to evaluate because of poor methodology. The current era of research can be traced to the 1950s, when investigators introduced reproducible operational criteria of psychopathy. Although by no means all studies have been guided by the passive avoidance learning model, many, if not a majority, have centred on the hypothesis that the psychopath is relatively insensitive to punishment, and that this is a consequence of a failure to generate a mediating state of fear arousal. The initial question to be considered is, therefore, whether psychopaths are indeed deficient in learning to avoid punishment.

A. *Avoidance Learning*

The paradigm for punishment typically employed is the application of a response contingent noxious stimulus, usually electric shock. Lykken (1957) devised a "mental maze" for the study of passive avoidance. The subject's task in this experiment was to learn a sequence of 20 choices, each choice involving the selection of one of 4 levers (manifest task). At the same time, depression of one of the 3 incorrect levers produced a shock, and the subject could therefore learn to avoid shock by making an alternative choice (latent task). Subjects were non-offender controls and offenders classified by Cleckley's criteria as primary (*P*) or secondary (*S*) psychopaths. All groups learned the manifest task equally well, indicating that psychopaths do not have any intrinsic generalized learning disability, but both *P* and *S* performed significantly less well on the latent task. Both groups of psychopaths therefore demonstrated relatively poor passive avoidance.

Lykken's design has now been used, with comparable results, by several other investigators. Schachter and Latané (1964) confirmed that primary psychopaths learn the manifest task as well as controls, but that they are poorer in learning shock avoidance. Schmauk (1970) also provided results consistent with the earlier studies. Schmauk, however, introduced two additional punishments, one being social punishment (*SP*: disapproval), the other tangible punishment (*TP*: loss of money). In addition, he recorded electrodermal activity, and obtained ratings of subjective anxiety concurrently with the avoidance task. Subjects categorized as primary and secondary psychopaths were inferior in avoidance learning when shock and SP were employed but no differences were found in comparison with controls in their performance under TP conditions. Anticipatory electrodermal responses and subjective anxiety ratings broadly followed a similar pattern. This study, then, demonstrates that psychopaths do not have any absolute inability to avoid unpleasant contingencies. Schmauk suggests that when the punishment is relevant to their value system, they can be motivated to learn as well as non-psychopaths.

In the study of Schachter and Latané (1964), it was found that an injection of adrenaline improved the avoidance learning of psychopaths. One possibility is that increased sensitivity to the threat of shock or to shock itself resulted from an increase in arousal. Chesno and Kilmann (1975) achieved a similar result by introducing loud background noise into a shock avoidance task. However, these authors argue that a somewhat different interpretation of the data is possible. They suggest that psychopaths are typically in a low state of arousal, and "stimulus hungry". The avoidance learning task may be particularly boring for psychopaths and hence shock may actually serve the non-aversive function of increasing sensory input. The arousal-increasing effect of intense noise would reduce this "need for stimulation". Quay (1965), in fact, proposed that much of the impulsive, thrill-seeking behaviour of the psychopath represents "pathological stimulation-seeking", a hypothesis which has received some degree of support. For example, some studies have found that psychopaths, relative to non-psychopathic offenders, score higher on a test of "sensation seeking" (see Blackburn, 1978; and Chapter 7 by Zuckerman).

B. *Anticipation of Punishment*

In the avoidance learning situation, the subject has to respond to cues preceding the aversive stimulus, if he is to avoid punishment. The dual-process learning model hypothesises that this anticipatory reaction involves the arousal of conditioned fear or anxiety. Lykken (1957) examined autonomic conditioning in psychopaths, using shock as UCS, and recorded electrodermal responses (EDRs). Primary psychopaths showed less evidence of fear conditioning, while secondary psychopaths performed at a level midway between that of primary psychopaths and controls. Psychopaths thus failed to learn to anticipate punishment. Hare (1965a) has also demonstrated poorer EDR conditioning to a shock UCS in psychopaths. An illustration of the potential relevance of this kind of laboratory response to behaviour outside the experimental situation is provided by the work of Tong (1959) at an English maximum security hospital. Offenders who produced few conditioned EDRs to a buzzer, with mildly aversive eyelid stimulation as the UCS, were more likely than rapid conditioners to reoffend following release. They also tended to have been convicted of their first offence at an earlier age. Tong felt justified in identifying his poor conditioners as primary psychopaths.

Only one study (Fenz *et al.*, 1974) has found a slower conditioning of cardiac responses (HRRs) during anticipation of a noxious stimulus. Other evidence suggests that poor autonomic conditionability in psychopaths may be confined to EDRs. Hare and Quinn (1971) recorded both EDR and HRR while presenting subjects with two UCSs, one aversive (shock), the other pleasant (slide of a nude female). Psychopaths exhibited smaller conditioned anticipatory responses to shock, though not to slides, but this was found only for EDRs, and not for HRRs. This finding contradicts Eysenck's hypothesis of a generalized trait of conditionability. On the other hand, if the activity of Gray's BIS is reflected in electrodermal but not cardiac responsiveness, as

Fowles (1980) has recently suggested, the results are consistent with the hypothesis that psychopaths have a specific deficit in anticipatory fear responses. This might also account for the findings of poorer vicarious EDR conditioning shown by primary and secondary psychopaths when observing aversive stimulation delivered to others (Aniskiewitz, 1979).

A procedure analogous to the conditioning experiment is the "count-down" situation, where the subject is forewarned that a particular number in a series will be followed by a noxious stimulus. Using this paradigm, Hare (1965b) found that primary psychopaths produced less electrodermal arousal than either controls or non-psychopathic criminals while anticipating shock. Lippert and Senter (1966) also found less increase in electrodermal spontaneous fluctuations in psychopaths in a similar situation. Hare interprets this phenomenon in terms of a temporal gradient of fear arousal: psychopaths, he suggests, are less likely to experience anticipatory fear unless warning signals are temporally very close to an aversive event.

As with the conditioning data, however, there is evidence that the weak anticipatory electrodermal activity of psychopaths in the face of threat of an aversive stimulus is not due to any generalized autonomic hyporesponsive-ness. In a study by Hare and Craigen (1974), pairs of subjects participated in a "game" which involved administration of shock to each other in turn. Psychopaths gave smaller EDRs during the 10 second periods prior to both receipt and administration of shock, but *larger* HRRs. Fenz (1971) also found both primary and secondary psychopaths to exhibit larger anticipatory HRRs prior to forewarned shock. Hare suggests that this dissociation of cardiac and electrodermal responding may reflect not so much the subject's state of emotional arousal to the threat of aversive stimulation as the opera-tion of sensory modulation related to coping processes. He draws on the "sensory rejection" hypothesis of Lacey (Lacey and Lacey, 1974), which proposes that heart rate acceleration reduces cortical arousal via baroreceptors in the carotid sinus, and thereby attenuates the effect of subse-quent sensory input. In terms of this model, then, psychopaths may have an efficient protective mechanism which enables them to reduce the emotional impact of an aversive situation. How far this might relate to the operation of the BIS does not seem to have been investigated.

A recent study by Hare *et al.* (1978), which used a loud (120db) noise as the aversive stimulus, yields partial confirmation of these findings. Cleckley defined psychopaths produced significantly larger anticipatory HRRs. How-ever, smaller accompanying EDRs were found only for those who achieved low scores on Gough's *So* scale. While it is speculated that these subjects represent a more "pure" group of primary psychopaths, Hare (1978a) reports MMPI score patterns which suggest a similarity to offenders identified as *secondary* psychopaths by others (e.g. Fenz, 1971; Blackburn, 1979).

C. Autonomic Reactivity

The preceding evidence suggests that psychopaths are less likely to be aroused, at least electrodermally, by cues signalling impending noxious events. This is consistent with the passive avoidance model, and with the notion of a deficiency in the responsiveness of the BIS (Fowles, 1980). However, it still remains to be explained why psychopaths fail to *acquire* conditioned anticipatory fear responses. As we have seen, they do not display any general deficit in conditionability (Hare and Quinn, 1971), but it is possible that their *unconditioned* responses to aversive stimuli are not sufficiently strong for conditioned fear to develop. Quay (1965), in fact, proposed that the "stimulation-seeking" of psychopaths might be motivated by a need to augment a basically low level of responsiveness to sensory input in general.

There is, however, little firm evidence that psychopaths are typically under-reactive to simple, non-aversive stimulation. A few studies (e.g. Borkovec, 1970) have found smaller electrodermal orienting responses (OR) to auditory stimuli in psychopaths, but others (e.g. Hare, 1968; Blackburn, 1979) have not. On the other hand, evidence regarding the cardiac OR of psychopaths is contradictory. Hare found a smaller cardiac OR to a tone (Hare, 1968), but not to a visual stimulus (Hare and Quinn, 1971). Blackburn (1978) found larger cardiac ORs in psychopaths, although this finding did not reach statistical significance when subjects were classified by more stringent criteria (Blackburn, 1979).

Alternatively, Quay (1965) suggested that psychopaths might be prone to habituate rapidly to sensory events and hence to seek out more varied stimulation. Rate of habituation of the OR is to some extent independent of autonomic reactivity (Martin and Rust, 1976), and probably a function of higher cortical processes (Gray, 1975). However, habituation of the electrodermal OR was not found to be related to psychopathy by either Hare (1968) or Borkovec (1970). On the other hand, Hare (1968) found that primary psychopaths habituated more slowly in their cardiac ORs. Since this dissociation of electrodermal and cardiac habituation is a characteristic of drowsiness (McDonald *et al.*, 1964), this may reflect a low level of cortical alertness. Blackburn (1979) found evidence for this uncoupling of cortical and autonomic activity when subjects became drowsy, but rapid electrodermal habituation and slow cardiac habituation characterized *secondary* psychopaths. As there is other evidence which suggests that the MMPI criteria used to identify secondary psychopaths in this study may be closely related to both Cleckley and *So* criteria of psychopathy (Blackburn, 1980), these findings may be less inconsistent than they seem.

One aspect of electrodermal responsiveness in psychopaths which has attracted recent interest is EDR *recovery time*. Mednick (Mednick and Hutchings, 1978) has suggested that slow autonomic recovery would lead to a failure of reinforcement of passive avoidance responses by fear reduction, and that psychopaths might accordingly be characterized by slower EDR recovery times. Although there are other explanations for the significance of EDR recovery (see Hare, 1978b; and Venables' discussion in Chapter 13), evidence to date lends some support to this hypothesis. While not using explicit criteria of psychopathy, Siddle *et al.* (1976) found that more "anti-social" delinquents exhibited slower EDR recovery, and this also character-ized "high risk public offenders" when compared with "domestic offenders" (Hinton *et al.*, 1980). Levander *et al.* (1980) have also produced evidence that slow recovery may be related to low scores on the *So* scale. However, Hare (1978a) found this relationship only for responses to high intensity stimula-tion, and only in the left hand. Hare (1978b), therefore, suggests that slow EDR recovery times among offenders may not be specific to psychopaths.

The clearest evidence for autonomic under-responsiveness in psychopaths comes from studies of the effects of noxious stimulation. Thresholds for shock detection in psychopaths tend to be high, and although they typically tolerate no more shock than non-psychopaths, they can be induced to do so with material incentives (Hare and Thorvaldson, 1971). In several of the studies already described, EDRs to shock were found to be lower in psychopaths (Lykken, 1957; Hare and Quinn, 1971; Hare and Craigen, 1974), and recent findings indicate that electrodermal unresponsiveness to aversive stimulation may be particularly related to low *So* scores (Ward, 1976; Hare, 1978a). Hare (1978b) suggests that this may reflect the opera-tion of a mechanism for "tuning-out" intense noxious stimulation, similar to that found when aversive stimulation follows a warning signal. Whether this is also related to cardiac effects is not clear, but Fenz (1971) did find greater cardiac acceleration to shock in both primary and secondary psychopaths.

D. *Autonomic Arousal Level*

It has been a consistent finding that psychopaths do not differ from non-psychopaths in "resting" cardiac activity. There has, however, been a tendency for psychopaths to exhibit lower electrodermal tonus at rest. Sum-marizing the results of eight of his own investigations, Hare (1978b) notes that although psychopaths differed significantly from non-psychopaths in only two studies, combined results indicate a highly significant tendency towards lower electrodermal levels at rest in psychopaths. However, the influence of classification criteria here is illustrated in an unpublished study by Milner (see Blackburn, 1979). She applied both Cleckley and MMPI criteria to her subjects, and found that there was a significant association between high Cleckley ratings of psychopathy and lower electrodermal levels at rest, as found by Hare. In contrast, MMPI criteria emphasizing impulsivity correlated with higher electrodermal arousal.

It is probably the case that electrodermal "resting" tonus is influenced not only by a generalized reaction to the experimental situation, but also by local properties of the skin. Perhaps more significant psychophysiologically is the appearance of non-specific responses (NSRs) in the unstimulated subject. It will be recalled that electrodermal NSRs tend to be lower in psychopaths during the anticipation of a stressor (Lippert and Senter, 1966). Schalling *et al.* (1973) also found that criminals scoring low on Gough's *So* scale produced fewer NSRs during auditory stimulation and during the post-stimulation period, suggesting lower arousal and more rapid recovery. However, some investigators have found that psychopaths emit fewer NSRs under resting conditions (Fox and Lippert, 1963), although Blackburn (1979) found that secondary psychopaths showed the least arousal in this respect.

Schalling (1978) has pointed out that NSRs are related to the level of cortical arousal via a common brainstem excitatory mechanism. She suggests that NSRs might also reflect imaginal activity and that the tendency of psychopaths to produce fewer NSRs could indicate a weak vividness of imagery. If this were the case, it would permit a rapprochement between psychophysiological research on psychopaths and the phenomenological approach of Gough (1960), who argues that psychopaths are unable to take the role of "the generalized other". Such a role-taking deficit could well arise in individuals who were unable to experience in fantasy the emotional effects of their behaviour on others. A study by Gillham (Blackburn, 1980) has in fact demonstrated that weak vividness of imagery is a characteristic of secondary, but not primary psychopathic delinquents. It is also correlated with low scores on the *So* scale.

E. *Catecholamine Secretion and Psychopathy*

The apparent unresponsiveness of psychopaths to cues signalling punishment might also be expected to be reflected in reduced adrenaline secretion in anticipation of stress. Lidberg *et al.* (1976) have found evidence which supports this idea. Among a group of criminals awaiting trial, the most psychopathic, as assessed by low *So* scores and high impulsivity, produced less increase in urinary adrenaline immediately prior to the stress of trial than did non-psychopaths. Woodman *et al.* (1978) have also identified a group of assaultive offenders among patients of a security hospital who are physiologically unresponsive when anticipating laboratory stressors, and who show very high ratios of noradrenaline to adrenaline in both plasma and urine. If, as the authors acknowledge, it is the low excretion of adrenaline which is significant, then the response of this group might also be an indication of reduced anticipatory fear reactions. However, measures of psychopathy were not obtained in this study.

IV. Electrocortical Correlates of Psychopathy

Some of the earliest studies of psychopathy involved examinations of the EEG characteristics of patients clinically diagnosed as psychopaths, particularly those displaying aggressive behaviour. For example, Hill and Watterson (1942) found that among psychiatrically disordered combat troops, EEG abnormalities were displayed by 65% of aggressive psychopaths, 32% of inadequate psychopaths and 26% of neurotics, compared with 15% of non-patient controls. Similar findings have been reported more recently by others (see Syndulko, 1978). The notion of EEG "abnormality" is unfortunately somewhat arbitrary, although the most common kind of "abnormality" observed is diffuse slow-wave activity in the theta band. This has been interpreted as indicative of a maturational "lag", since such records are relatively common in young children. In some studies, however, abnormalities have been seen particularly in temporal lobe areas, leading to the suggestion of limbic dysfunction.

For the most part, these clinically oriented studies are methodologically unsound, and are uniformly deficient in reliable criteria of psychopathy, quantification and statistical evaluation of EEG data, and controlled experimental manipulation (Ellingson, 1954; Syndulko, 1978). While it is tempting to see a relationship between the putative limbic dysfunction and the findings on peripheral autonomic activity in psychopaths described above, it must be emphasized that the former is an inference based on very tenuous evidence.

An equally plausible interpretation is that the diffuse slow-wave activity, claimed to be a common characteristic of psychopaths in the clinical literature, reflects a state of low cortical arousal generated by relatively monotonous conditions. In these terms, psychopaths may be in a chronic state of under-arousal, and hence more easily become drowsy during EEG recording. This would in fact be consistent with the improvement in avoidance learning in psychopaths found when background intensity of stimulation is increased (Chesno and Kilmann, 1975), and with the failure of their cardiac ORs to habituate (Hare, 1968; Blackburn, 1979). It might also relate to the stimulation seeking behaviour of psychopaths (Quay, 1965).

A quantitative study of EEG parameters and aggressive dispositional measures by Blackburn (1975b) failed to yield evidence of an association between aggressiveness and EEG arousal in offenders. However, when primary and secondary psychopaths were examined, relatively clear differences emerged between these two subgroups, the secondary psychopaths showing the lowest level of arousal in EEG indices, including a greater amount of slow wave (theta) activity (Blackburn, 1979). They also become drowsy more rapidly. Primary psychopaths, in contrast, were more alert during "resting" conditions and tended to remain so. As was noted earlier, the secondary psychopaths in this study resemble the undifferentiated psychopaths identified in some other studies.

One specific electrocortical measure which has attracted some recent attention in relation to psychopathy is the contingent negative variation (CNV) found preparatory to a motor response in a signalled reaction time experiment. McCallum (1973) reported smaller amplitude CNVs prior to a button pressing task for psychopaths, but this was not confirmed by Syndulko *et al.* (1975). Fenton *et al.* (1978) found *higher* CNV amplitudes in psychopaths than in non-psychopathic offenders, and CNV amplitude also correlated positively with MMPI measures of impulsivity and psychopathy. However, it is clear from questionnaire data provided in these studies that McCallum's subjects and those of Syndulko *et al.* were predominantly secondary or neurotic psychopaths, while those of Fenton *et al.* were primary psychopaths.

The functional significance of the CNV remains in dispute, but it is obtained under conditions which parallel the "count-down" experiment in which an aversive stimulus is forewarned. Howard *et al.* (1980) have recently recorded CNVs in psychopaths during a task requiring active and passive avoidance of aversive noise. Psychopaths in this study did not show any deficit in avoidance behaviour, but produced significantly higher CNVs during passive avoidance. This is interpreted as indicating a deficit in inhibitory processes. However, it would appear that these subjects were again predominantly primary psychopaths.

V. Conclusions

Any attempt to make firm generalizations about the psychophysiological characteristics of psychopaths would be premature at the present stage of research. A case can be made for concluding that psychopaths are physiologically under-aroused and under-responsive to threats of punishment, as well as to punishment itself, and that this is due to a deficiency in the mechanisms governing fear arousal and passive avoidance (Gray, 1970; Hare, 1970; Fowles, 1980). There are, however, several reasons for regarding this as no more than a working hypothesis with modest support, and at best, only a partial explanation for the under-socialized behaviour of psychopaths.

First, there are a number of inconsistencies in the data. In part, this reflects the continued problem of the use of different criteria to identify subjects as psychopaths, but one review (Mawson and Mawson, 1977) suggests that the available findings might be construed as reflecting a tendency of psychopaths to oscillate from a state of low (e.g. rapid sleep onset) to high (e.g. aggressiveness) arousal and reactivity. Additionally, psychopaths do not seem to form a homogeneous group, and primary and secondary psychopaths do not show the same patterns of psychophysiological activity. On the other hand, there are intriguing similarities, both psychometric and psychophysiological, in the subgroups identified by (i) high Cleckley ratings together with low *So* scores; (ii) low *So* and high impulsivity scores; and (iii) MMPI criteria of *secondary* psychopathy. Although theories of psychopathy aim to account for the behaviour of primary psychopaths, it seems to be these subgroups which provide the most consistent evidence of cortical and electrodermal under-arousal and under-responsiveness to threat and aversive stimulation.

Whether or not this is the case, findings from secondary psychopaths pose a problem for current theories of psychopathy. Central to the passive avoidance model is the assumption that successful avoidance is mediated by conditioned fear or anxiety. But the secondary psychopath, who is identified by a *high* degree of anxiety-proneness, nevertheless shows deficits in avoidance and threat reactions. Furthermore, the primary psychopath is not typically found, on psychometric scales, to be *less* anxiety-prone than non-psychopaths, yet he displays similar deficits in avoidance of punishment.

It seems likely that a lack of anxiety or conditioned fear has been made to carry an undue theoretical burden in accounting for the under-socialization of psychopaths, and that more attention needs to be paid to the *motivation* for their behaviour. The passive avoidance model assumes that we do not need to account for the motivation of antisocial behaviour, but simply why some individuals give uninhibited expression to common human motives. But if the only difference between psychopathic and non-psychopathic offenders was that the former cannot *learn* to avoid punishment while the latter have not been *trained* to avoid it, there would be no way of distinguishing between them at a behavioural level. Yet psychopaths are distinguished from other offenders by their callousness, impulsivity and, not infrequently, the commission of bizarre and brutal crimes. It is difficult for example to see sadistic assaults as simply a universal human need expressed in the absence of socialized restraints. In short, it seems unlikely that the impulsive, aggressive, callous attributes of psychopaths can be derived simply from lack of fear. There may not only be something unusual about the responsiveness of psychopaths to punishment, there may also be something unusual about the kinds of event which reinforce their behaviour. Some of the data on low arousal and "stimulation-seeking" are suggestive in this respect.

Finally, there is a need to examine the possibility that the deviations of the psychopath lie less in deficiencies of physiological mechanisms of arousal or reactivity than in the central decision processes which activate, or fail to activate them. The evidence that psychopaths may be able to "tune-out" aversive stimulation is relevant in this context. The psychophysiological characteristics of the psychopath are likely to make sense only when we understand how far they are a cause and how far a consequence of his appraisals of the world.

Further Reading

Trasler, GB. (1973). Criminal Behaviour. *In* "Handbook of Abnormal Psychology" (H. J. Eysenck, ed.), 2nd edn. Pitman, London.
A general discussion of the psychology of crime.

Shah, S. A. and Roth, L. H. (1974). Biological and psychophysiological factors in criminality. *In* "Handbook of Criminology" (D. Glaser, ed.). Rand McNally, Chicago.
A survey of the biological correlates of crime, notably the role of brain and hormonal abnormalities, genetics and chromosome disorders, and perinatal complications; their treatment of psychophysiological studies is rather cursory.

Blackburn, R. (1980). Aggression (physiological). *In* "Encyclopedia of Clinical Assessment" (R. H. Woody, ed.). Jossey-Bass, San Francisco.
A short review of the physiological correlates of human aggression.

Hare, R. D. (1970). "Psychopathy: Theory and Research". Wiley, New York.
Still the most readable introduction to research on psychopathy. Hare surveys most of the earlier experimental work, including psychophysiological research.

Hare, R. D. and Schalling, D. (eds), (1978). "Psychopathic Behaviour: Approaches to Research". Wiley, New York.
This monograph contains surveys and research reports by most of the active researchers in this area. Particularly relevant to the research discussed in this chapter are the contributions by Hare and Cox, Schalling, Hare, Syndulko, Blackburn, Mednick and Hutchings, and Trasler.

As a sample of original research, the following papers can be recommended as representative of work in this area.

Hare, R. D. (1965). Temporal gradient of fear arousal in psychopaths. *J. Abnorm. Psychol.* 70, 442–445.

Schmauk, F. J. (1970). Punishment, arousal and avoidance learning in sociopaths. *J. Abnorm. Psychol.* 76, 325–335.

Hare, R. D. and Quinn, M. (1971). Psychopathy and autonomic conditioning. *J. Abnorm. Psychol.* 77, 223–235.

Chesno, F. A. and Kilmann, P. R. (1975). Effect of stimulation intensity on sociopathic avoidance learning. *J. Abnorm. Psychol.* 84, 144–150.

Levander, S. E., Schalling, D. S., Lidberg, L., Bartjai, A. and Lidberg, Y. (1980). Skin conductance recovery time and personality in a group of criminals. *Psychophysiology* 17, 105–111.

References

American Psychiatric Association (1979). "Diagnostic and Statistical Manual of Mental Disorders" 3rd edn. Washington, D.C.

Aniskiewitz, A. (1979). Autonomic components of vicarious conditioning and psychopathy. *J. Clin. Psychol.* **35**, 60–67.

Aronfreed, J. (1968). *Conduct and Conscience*. Academic Press, New York and London.

Bandura, A. and Rosenthal, T. L. (1966). Vicarious classical conditioning as a function of arousal level. *J. Personality Soc. Psychol.* **3**, 54–62.

Blackburn, R. (1975a). An empirical classification of psychopathic personality. *Br. J. Psychiat.* **127**, 456–460.

Blackburn, R. (1975b). Aggression and the EEG: a quantitative analysis. *J. Abnorm. Psychol.* **84**, 358–365.

Blackburn, R. (1978). Psychopathy, arousal, and the need for stimulation. *In* "Psychopathic Behaviour: Approaches to Research" (R. D. Hare and D. Schalling, eds). Wiley, New York.

Blackburn, R. (1979). Cortical and autonomic arousal in primary and secondary psychopaths. *Psychophysiology* **16**, 143–150.

Blackburn, R. (1980). Personality and the criminal psychopath: a logical analysis and some empirical data. *In* "Lo Psicopatico Delinquente" Facolta di Giurisprudenza, Universita di Messina, Giuffre, Milan.

Borkovec, T. D. (1970). Autonomic reactivity to sensory stimulation in psychopathic and normal juvenile delinquents. *J. Consult. Clin. Psychol.* **35**, 217–222.

Burgess, R. L. and Akers, R. L. (1966). A differential association-reinforcement theory of criminal behaviour. *Soc. Problems.* **14**, 128–147.

Chesno, F. A. and Kilmann, P. R. (1975). Effect of stimulation intensity on sociopathic avoidance learning. *J. Abnorm. Psychol.* **84**, 144–150.

Cleckley, H. (1964). "The Mask of Sanity" 4th edn. Mosby, St. Louis.

Ellingson, R. J. (1954). Incidence of EEG abnormality among patients with mental disorders of apparently nonorganic origin: a critical review. *Am. J. Psychiat.* **111**, 263–275.

Eysenck, H. J. (1964). "Crime and Personality" 1st edn. Routledge and Kegan Paul, London.

Fenton, G. W., Fenwick, P. B. C., Ferguson, W. and Lam, C. T. (1978). The contingent negative variation in antisocial behaviour: a pilot study of Broadmoor patients. *Br. J. Psychiat.* **132**, 368–377.

Fenz, W. D. (1971). Heart rate responses to a stressor: a comparison between primary and secondary psychopaths and normal controls. *J. Exp. Res. Personality* **5**, 7–13.

Fenz, W. D., Young, M. J. and Fenz, H. G. (1974). Differences in the modulation of cardiac activity between psychopaths and normal controls. *Psychom. Med.* **36**, 488–502.

Fowles, D. C. (1980). The three arousal model: implications of Gray's two-factor learning theory for heart rate, electrodermal activity, and psychopathy. *Psychophysiology* **17**, 87–104.

Fox, R. and Lippert, W. (1963). Spontaneous GSR and anxiety level of sociopathic delinquents. *J. Consult. Psychol.* **27**, 368.

Gough, H. G. (1960). Theory and measurement of socialisation. *J. Consult. Psychol.* **24**, 23–30.

Gray, J. A. (1970). The psychophysiological basis of introversion–extraversion. *Behav. Res. Therapy* 8, 249–266.

Gray, J. A. (1975). "Elements of a Two-process Theory of Learning". Academic Press, New York and London.

Hare, R. D. (1965a). Acquisition and generalisation of a conditioned fear response in psychopathic and nonpsychopathic criminals. *J. Psychol.* 59, 367–370.

Hare, R. D. (1965b). Temporal gradient of fear arousal in psychopaths. *J. Abnorm. Psychol.* 70, 442–445.

Hare, R. D. (1968). Psychopathy, autonomic functioning, and the orienting response. *J. Abnorm. Psychol. Monogr. Suppl.* 73, No. 3, 1–24.

Hare, R. D. (1970). "Psychopathy: Theory and Research". Wiley, New York.

Hare, R. D. (1978a). Psychopathy and electrodermal responses to nonsignal stimulation. *Biol. Psychol.* 6, 237–246.

Hare, R. D. (1978b). Electrodermal and cardiovascular correlates of psychopathy. *In* "Psychopathic Behaviour: Approaches to Research" (R. D. Hare and D. Schalling, eds). Wiley, Chichester.

Hare, R. D. and Craigen, D. (1974). Psychopathy and physiological activity in a mixed-motive game situation. *Psychophysiology* 11, 197–206.

Hare, R. D. and Quinn, M. (1971). Psychopathy and autonomic conditioning. *J. Abnorm. Psychol.* 77, 223–235.

Hare, R. D. and Thorvaldson, S. A. (1971). Psychopathy and response to electrical stimulation. *J. Abnorm. Psychol.* 76, 370–374.

Hare, R. D., Frazelle, J. and Cox, D. N. (1978). Psychopathy and physiological responses to threat of an aversive stimulus. *Psychophysiology* 15, 165–172.

Hill, D. and Watterson, D. (1942). Electroencephalographic studies of the psychopathic personality. *J. Neurol. Psychiat.* 5, 47–64.

Hinton, J. W., O'Neill, M., Hamilton, S. and Burke, M. (1980). Psychophysiological differentiation between psychopathic and schizophrenic abnormal offenders. *Br. J. Soc. Clin. Psychol.* 19, 257–269.

Howard, R., Fenton, G. W. and Fenwick, P. B. (1980). Slow cerebral potentials in a 'go-no go' avoidance situation: a study on special hospital patients. *In* "Evoked Potentials" (C. Barber, ed.). MTP Press.

Lacey, J. I. and Lacey, B. C. (1974). On heart rate responses and behaviour: a reply to Elliott. *J. Personality Soc. Psychol.* 30, 1–18.

Levander, S. E., Schalling, D. S., Lidberg, L., Bartfai, A. and Lidberg, Y. (1980). Skin conductance recovery time and personality in a group of criminals. *Psychophysiology* 17, 105–111.

Lidberg, L., Levander, S. E., Schalling, D. and Lidberg, Y. (1976). Excretion of adrenaline and noradrenaline as related to real life stress and psychopathy. "Reports from the Laboratory for Clinical Stress Research", Stockholm, No. 50.

Lippert, W. W. and Senter, R. J. (1966). Electrodermal responses in the sociopath. *Psychonom. Sci.* 4, 25–26.

Lykken, D. T. (1957). A study of anxiety in the sociopathic personality. *J. Abnorm. Soc. Psychol.* 55, 6–10.

McCallum, C. (1973). The CNV and conditionability in psychopaths. *Electroenceph. Clin. Neurophysiol. Suppl.* 33, 337–343.

McCord, W. and McCord, J. (1964). "The Psychopath: an Essay on the Criminal Mind". Van Nostrand, Princeton, New Jersey.

McDonald, D., Johnson, L. C. and Hord, D. J. (1964). Habituation of the orienting response in alert and drowsy subjects. *Psychophysiology* 1, 163–173.

Martin, I. and Rust, J. (1976). Habituation and the structure of the electrodermal system. *Psychophysiology* 13, 554–562.

Mawson, A. R. and Mawson, C. D. (1977). Psychopathy and arousal: a new interpretation of the psychophysiological literature. *Biol. Psychiat.* 12, 49–74.

Mednick, S. A. and Hutchings, B. (1978). Genetic and psychophysiological factors in asocial behaviour. *In* "Psychopathic Behaviour: Approaches to Research" (R. D. Hare and D. Schalling, eds). Wiley, New York.

Quay, H. C. (1965). Psychopathic personality as pathological stimulation seeking. *Am. J. Psychiat.* 122, 180–183.

Quay, H. C. (1972). Patterns of aggression, withdrawal, and immaturity. *In* "Psychopathological Disorders of Childhood" (H. C. Quay and J. S. Werry, eds), 1st edn. Wiley, New York.

Schachter, S. and Latané, B. (1964). Crime, cognition and the autonomic nervous system. *In* "Nebraska Symposium on Motivation" (D. Levine, ed.). University of Nebraska Press, Lincoln.

Schalling, D. (1978). Psychopathy – related personality variables and the psychophysiology of socialisation. *In* "Psychopathic Behaviour: Approaches to Research" (R. D. Hare and D. Schalling, eds). Wiley, New York.

Schalling, D., Lidberg, L., Levander, S. E. and Dahlin, Y. (1973). Spontaneous autonomic activity as related to psychopathy. *Biol. Psychol.* 1, 83–97.

Schmauk, F. J. (1970). Punishment, arousal, and avoidance learning in sociopaths. *J. Abnorm. Psychol.* 76, 325–335.

Schneider, K. (1923). "Psychopathic Personalities". Deuticke, Vienna.

Siddle, D. A. T., Mednick, S. A., Nicol, A. R. and Foggit, R. H. (1976). Skin conductance recovery in antisocial adolescents. *Br. J. Soc. Clin. Psychol.* 15, 425–428.

Syndulko, K. (1978). Electrocortical investigations of sociopathy. *In* "Psychopathic Behaviour: Approaches to Research" (R. D. Hare and D. Schalling, eds). Wiley, New York.

Syndulko, K., Parker, D. A., Jens, R., Maltzman, I. and Ziskind, E. (1975). Psychophysiology of sociopathy: electrocortical measures. *Biol. Psychol.* 3, 185–200.

Tong, J. E. (1959). Stress reactivity in relation to delinquent and psychopathic behaviour. *J. Ment. Sci.* 105, 935–956.

Trasler, G. (1973). Criminal behaviour. *In* "Handbook of Abnormal Psychology" (H. J. Eysenck, ed.), Pitman, London.

Ullmann, L. P. and Krasner, L. (1975). "A Psychological Approach to Abnormal Behaviour". Prentice-Hall, Englewood Cliffs, New Jersey.

Ward, W. M. (1976). Skin conductance response to both signalled and unsignalled noxious stimulation predicts level of socialisation. *J. Personality Soc. Psychol.* 34, 923–929.

Widom, C. S. (1977). A method for studying non-institutionalised psychopaths. *J. Consulting Clin. Psychol.* 45, 674–683.

Woodman, D. D., Hinton, J. W. and O'Neill, M. T. (1978). Plasma catecholamines and aggression in maximum security patients. *Biol. Psychol.* 6, 147–154.

13 Some Problems and Controversies in the Psychophysiological Investigation of Schizophrenia

P. H. Venables

Abstract Rather than presenting a review of psychophysiological findings in work on schizophrenic patients, this chapter aims to outline some of the areas where there are uncertainties and where more work is required before firm statements can be made. The examples are almost all taken from work using electrodermal measures, and consider the topics of non-responsivity versus hyper-responsivity, lateral asymmetry of responsivity, the recovery time of the electrodermal response and the problems raised by apparent non-replication in high-risk studies.

I. Introduction

In recent years, there has been considerable coverage of the psychophysiology of schizophrenia (Lader, 1975; Venables, 1975a, b; Buchsbaum, 1977a, b; Holzman and Levy, 1977; Venables, 1977; Zahn, 1977; Itil, 1977; Shagass, 1977; Roth, 1977; Venables, 1979, 1980a, b; Saletu, 1980; Spohn and Patterson, 1979). Some of these papers attempt to cover all the various areas of psychological measurement, while others concentrate on particular fields, such as electrodermal activity or evoked cortical potentials. Collectively, the coverage of available knowledge is extensive.

This chapter will attempt to outline some of the difficulties and problems present in the field, and to identify some of the points where knowledge is limited and where it is impossible to make firm statements until further work has been completed.

In this instance, consideration will be concentrated almost entirely around issues raised by abnormality of the electrodermal orienting response. Figure 1 shows a schematic skin conductance orienting response, with the various

PHYSIOLOGICAL CORRELATES OF HUMAN
BEHAVIOUR   ISBN 0-12-273901-9

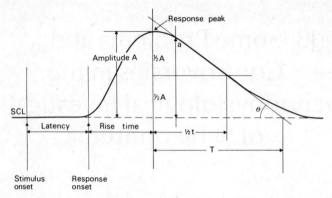

Fig. 1 *A schematic diagram of the parameters of the skin conductance response.*

components which will be referred to in later sections. This omits a major area of work concerned with electro-cortical activity where considerable advances have been made recently. This area has, however, been reviewed recently by Venables (1981) and, consequently, further coverage would be redundant at this time.

One of the areas to be examined is concerned with the issue of hyper- and hypo-responsivity of schizophrenic patients to simple stimuli. Another skein of interest is the identification of lateral cerebral dysfunction and the extent to which unilateral disorder involving the left hemisphere may be characteristic of schizophrenia.

A development which has become increasingly apparent over the last decade is represented by the extent to which workers on the general topic of schizophrenia feel that it is important to extend the study of this subject, beyond that of the identified at-present-ill-patient, to: (i) the patient in remission; (ii) his/her relatives; (iii) normal subjects with "schizotypic" characteristics and; of course, to (iv) the "bandwagon" (Rosenthal, 1974) of "high-risk" studies of children who might become schizophrenic. In this last case, the success with which the pioneering work of Mednick and Schulsinger (e.g. 1968) in Copenhagen has or has not been replicated by other workers is a matter of interest. Factors of subject selection, methodology and other potentially interacting factors require careful consideration.

A further important development, which needs to be taken into account in considering psychophysiological approaches to schizophrenia, is the current diagnostic trend (exemplified in a particularly strong way by Kety, 1980), which appears to have moved away from the use of the currently present symptoms as the main means of identification of "schizophrenia" (e.g. Wing *et al.*, 1974). This latter procedure, which stems from the impetus of Schneider (1959), and emphasizes the importance of the identification of critical "first-rank" positive symptoms (particularly, hallucinations and delusions), is being called into question. A return to the original formulations of Kraepelin (1913) and Bleuler (1911) is proposed. As Bleuler (1911) said, "Hallucinations and delusions are partial phenomena of the most varied diseases. Their presence is often helpful in making the diagnosis of a psychosis, but not in diagnosing the presence of schizophrenia." The emphasis of those who advocate a return to a more limited description of schizophrenia, nearer to that of Kraepelin and Bleuler, is on negative aspects of the disease (i.e. lack of social relationships and competence, poverty of speech, etc.), on slowness of onset and poorness of prognosis. This is important to the psychologist for several reasons: (i) it leads to a more circumscribed definition by which a schizophrenic group may be selected for experimental study; (ii) it suggests different hypotheses of underlying aetiology than those resulting from a definition which includes positive symptoms; (iii) it suggests that some of the within group differences, shown in so many instances of psychophysiological and behavioural data from "schizophrenic" groups, may reflect real differences between more narrowly defined "nuclear" schizophrenics and those at present showing "schizophrenic" symptoms, who are possibly not truly schizophrenic. It should be noted that these distinctions are perhaps no more than those which have been current for many years, i.e. between process and reactive, and poor and good pre-morbid schizophrenia (Strauss *et al.*, 1977). However, the current trends, away from reliance on current symptoms, do re-emphasize the importance of a longitudinal view of the disorder.

Underlying the discussion of all these areas in this chapter, there is an implicit bias. That is, that it is, or should be, the prime concern of psychophysiological studies of schizophrenia to help to unravel ideas about the mechanisms of the disorder, rather than merely to make statements about differences between schizophrenics and normals. Consequently, studies which just show that schizophrenics are more (or less) "aroused" than normals do not necessarily advance the subject to any extent. In general, the preferred approach views psychophysiological measures as indirect indices of underlying physiological or biochemical dysfunction. In consequence, unless findings are integrated with behavioural or neuropsychological studies which produce convergent support, there is likely to be little resultant progress. One of the main reasons why psychophysiological measures are important in this area is that they are capable of providing psychological evidence from intact human subjects. It must, however, be recognized that these measures are an *indirect* reflection of underlying activity and perhaps their major value is that they are covert. Thus, while "significant others" may react in important ways if speech is disturbed in a patient or patient to be, the fact that he/she shows an abnormality of electrodermal activity does not elicit a social response. For this reason, it may be possible to identify early aspects of the disorder before the cycle of overt disturbance (social response) reaction to that response sets in. Thus, the patient, as he arrives before the psychiatrist, is an amalgam of primary and secondary features, and where it is possible the secondary features are more clearly identified as "the disease".

II. Responsivity to Simple Stimuli

A. *Examples of Patterns of Responsivity from Different Studies on Adult Schizophrenics*

In 1968, Zahn *et al.* provided data which suggested that schizophrenic patients gave larger responses and showed less habituation than normal subjects. Around the same time, Bernstein (1964, 1970), replicating Russian work, reported data providing evidence for a *hypo*-responsive pattern in schizophrenics.

Some reconciliation between these apparently opposed positions was achieved in 1972 when Gruzelier and Venables, testing a group of schizophrenics with a series of stimuli to which orienting responses would normally be given, reported a bimodal pattern of responses. About 50% of schizophrenic subjects showed a total, apparent electrodermal non-responsivity. The remainder tended to exhibit hyper-responsivity, i.e. high amplitude, fast-recovery SCRs which did not habituate. (See, for instance, Venables, 1977, for a more complete coverage).

Subsequent work has not entirely cleared up this position. The bimodal distribution of responsivity has been independently replicated by Rubens and Lapidus (1978) and is also reported in later studies by Gruzelier (see, for example, Gruzelier and Connolly, 1979; Gruzelier *et al.*, 1981). However, Zahn (1976), re-analysing his 1968 and other data, could find no evidence for a bimodal distribution of responsivity. Apart from these data, the pattern of response which is reported tends to emphasize hypo-responsivity. Patterson (1976), for instance, reported that 46% of chronic schizophrenics are non-responders, while Straube (1979) reported 40% of non-responders in an acute schizophrenic population. In contrast to the Gruzelier–Venables (1972) and Rubens-Lapidus (1978) data, neither Patterson's nor Strube's material appear to show an excess of hyper-responding and non-habituation in comparison to normals. A current exception to the consistent report of an abnormally large number of non-responders in all schizophrenic populations is that of Frith *et al.* (1979), who report only 4 out of 45 patients as non-responders, while 22 gave a non-habituating pattern of response to 14, 85 dB 1000 Hz tones. In this study, no patient received neuroleptic drugs in the four weeks prior to testing. In this connection, Gruzelier and Hammond

(1978) showed no clear connection between neuroleptic drug status and hypo- or hyper-responsivity. Furthermore, Zahn (1976), in his paper discussing the bimodal issue, suggests that differences in results between experiments are unlikely to be directly due to differences in drug status.

Why is this issue important? Firstly, these studies suggest the possibility that there are sub-groups within the total "schizophrenic" population who react autonomically in different ways. Secondly, they make possible suggestions about the underlying mechanisms involved.

B. *Possible Factors Affecting Results*

1. *Technical and subject factors*

Before considering these possibilities, it is necessary to ask how far the results reported may be artefactual, or result from different experimental procedures. From the outset it is possible to say that probably all recent studies use good standard techniques for measuring electrodermal activity, and no differences are likely to arise from that source. O'Gorman (1978) raised the possibility that apparent non-responsivity might result from differences in gain of recording systems, particularly when different studies use constant current or constant voltage systems. However, Zahn (1978) suggests that amounts of non-responsivity reported are unlikely to be due to different criteria having been used to set limits for the point at which a response may be scored.

In the studies so far reviewed, the stimuli used have been those which might be considered to elicit orienting responses (i.e. 65–85 dB tones with relatively slow rise and fall-times). A factor clearly affecting responsivity is, of course, intensity. In recent papers, for instance, (Gruzelier *et al.*, 1980; Gruzelier *et al.*, 1981) it was reported that the majority of recently admitted schizophrenic patients who were non-responsive to moderate intensity, 70 dB tones, responded to tones at an intensity of 90 dB. Data on 640 normal subjects, aged 5–25 years (Venables *et al.*, 1984) show that 32·8% responded to a 60 dB stimulus, 79·5% to a 75 dB stimulus and 88·9% to a 90 dB stimulus.

In addition to the need to pay attention to the intensities of stimulation used in different studies, it may be important to take account of the age of the subjects involved, particularly in the case where studies of children at risk are involved. Venables (1978), for instance, reports percentages of responding to a 75 dB stimulus as follows: Age 3, 43·8%; Age 5, 74·4%; Age 10, 86·9%; Age 15, 95·1%; Age 20, 90·1%; Age 25, 87·5%. During adulthood, however, data from an unpublished study from the author's laboratory on subjects between age 18 and 69 showed no relation between age and responsivity. Thus, in the studies on adult schizophrenics which have been received, age may not be a significant variable.

2. *Instructions and the setting of the experiment*

The other major experimental factors which may influence the extent of responsivity are, the nature of the instructions given to the subject and the experimental setting in which the study is carried out. This issue is discussed critically by Iacono and Lykken (1979), who point out that the degree of signal value invested in the stimuli presented modifies responsivity and rate of habituation. They further indicate that the type of instruction to "just ignore the tones", so frequently used in this type of experiment, leaves the subject free to place his own interpretation on what is required of him. It is, however, somewhat difficult to relate the actual instructions used in studies with different outcomes to those outcomes. For instance, in a study obtaining no hyper-responsivity (Straube, 1979) "the subjects were told that they would hear some tones but that they did not have to do anything; they should not pay attention to these tones, but should try and remain relaxed." In studies by Gruzelier and Venables (1974) and Rubens and Lapidus (1978), where bimodality of responding was reported, the instructions were respectively "to sit and listen to the tones, not to fall asleep and not to attach any importance to them" and "there was nothing to do except relax and listen to the tones." In the studies reported by Gruzelier *et al.* (1981), where bimodality of responsivity was found in undrugged patients, the recording session was explained as a routine procedure to assess the patient's state of relaxation. The patient was told not to bother about the occasional sounds he might hear. In the study by Frith *et al.* (1979), where minimal non-responsivity was reported, the subject was told "that he did not have to respond in any way to the noises." There would not appear to be such a difference in the value of these instructions that they are likely, *of themselves*, to produce large differences in responsivity. Rather it seems appropriate to suggest that more subtle influences, such as the setting of the study, the familiarization of the subject with the setting, and the attitude of the experimenter, may be of importance in influencing the extent of responsivity shown.

Gruzelier *et al.* (1981) point out that the consistent reporting of a bimodal distribution of responses from his laboratory is present in a range of studies with patients on and off neuroleptic drugs, with experimental conditions which vary considerably and with 8 different experimenters at different times. They suggest that "an important factor is the patient's attitude to the task which is formed from the moment the patient is invited for testing." The recognition that the effectiveness with which a stimulus elicits a response is not merely a function of the characteristics of that stimulus, but is also a function of the circumstances in which that stimulus may previously have been presented and the more immediate setting (including instructions) in which it is now presented is emphasized, for instance, in the theories of Wagner (1976) and Öhman (1979), but has not so far been adequately taken into account by workers on the orienting response in schizophrenic patients. Studies do not, for instance, report on the extent to which any practice trials may have been given, or whether the subjects have been used in previous similar studies. It is factors of this type that may be of critical importance.

The subjective reaction of the subject to the stimulus as a factor effecting responsivity is also important, and is shown in a study by Thayer and Silber (1971). Subjects were presented with 85 dB tones. No overall differences in responsivity was shown between schizophrenic and normal groups. The main factor effecting responsivity was the tonic level of conductance characteristic of the subject, subjects with high tonic levels being more responsive than those with low levels (this is, of course, in line with data showing a higher tonic level of conductance in responder than non-responder patients, e.g. Gruzelier and Venables, 1972). A factor having a major effect on electrodermal responsivity was, however, the subject's subjective reaction to the stimulus. These reactions were classified as (i) "experiencing startle"; (ii) "feeling anxiety"; and (iii) remarks which indicated that the subject did not pay attention. There was a major difference between the electrodermal responsivity of the subjects in the first two categories and those in the last. In the last case responsivity was minimal and of such a size that non-responsivity would often be reported by currently used criteria.

With the apparently single exception of the study by Frith *et al.* (1979), there does, however, appear to be a fairly universal report of 40–50% of non-responsivity in groups of schizophrenic patients. With this in mind it becomes necessary to examine the other major factor which modifies responsivity which has already been alluded to, namely diagnosis, or perhaps in this instance, so as not to blur the issue, subject characteristics.

C. *Sub-groupings among the Schizophrenic Population*

It is noteworthy that Frith *et al*'s (1979) patients, who were diagnosed as schizophrenic by the use of the "present state examination" (PSE) (an instrument as its name implies using current symptoms as material), were all experiencing the "positive" symptoms hallucinations and/or delusions "rather fewer showed thought disorder and incongruity of affect. The negative symptoms of schizophrenia (muteness, retardation etc.) were relatively little in evidence." Frith *et al.* also note that about half the patients would not meet the Feighner *et al.* (1972)criteria. "In every case this was due to the onset of current symptoms being acute (less than 6 months of symptoms prior to admission)". It is possible, therefore, that Frith *et al*'s patients were akin to those diagnosed as "acute schizophrenic reaction" (e.g. Kety *et al.*, 1976), which would appear to form a separate group of schizophrenic-like disorders from that formed by those having "chronic", "uncertain" or "latent" diagnoses, which may be shown to be genetically interrelated (Kety *et al.* 1976). It should be noted, however, that a study with the most contrasting result to that of Frith *et al.* (1979), (Straube, 1979), also used patients with a diagnosis of acute schizophrenic symptomatology – "such as severe delusions or hallucinations as well as thinking disorders or affective abnormalities." But it is possible that an attempt to relate electrodermal responsivity to standard diagnoses is not a fruitful exercise.

Straube (1979) extended his study to note particular characteristics of schizophrenic non-responders as compared to responders. Non-responders were significantly higher on ratings of "emotional withdrawal", "conceptual disorganization", "somatic concern", "depressive mood" and "motor retardation". They were lower on ratings of "excitement". A somewhat similar flavour of rated behaviour is reported by Gruzelier (1976), who showed that non-responders had significantly lower ratings than responders on "manic state", "anxiety", "psychotic belligerence", "attention demanding behaviour" and "assaultive behaviour". His patients did not differ significantly on depression, withdrawal, or affective flatness. Thus, while there is some similarity between the two studies it is not complete. Although Gruzelier's data are also drawn from a non-institutionalized group, it is possible that differences in hospital regime may have an effect on rated behaviour. Some light is thrown on the position by a recent report of Simons (1980), in which groups of normal subjects were selected on the basis of high and low score on the physical anhedonia scale of Chapman, Chapman and Raulin (1976). Subjects scoring high on this scale would probably have some of the characteristics of emotional withdrawal, lack of excitement and mania and depressive mood, described by Gruzelier and by Straube. Simon reported that approximately 50% of his high anhedonic normals were electrodermal non-responders.

D. *Degrees of Responsivity in other Response Modalities*

Work in this area is extremely sparse. A study of direct relevance is that of Gruzelier (1975), who reported that electrodermally responsive schizophrenics showed heart rate acceleration in response to 75 dB neutral tones, while electrodermal non-responders showed a minimal deceleration with a rapid return to the initial level of heart rate. In passing it should be noted that schizophrenics' heart rate acceleration to tones which would be expected to produce a deceleratory orienting response has been reported in other studies (Zahn *et al.*, 1968; Dykman *et al.*, 1968). In the study by Simons (1980) referred to above, anhedonic patients were also less responsive in their phasic heart rate measures than non-anhedonic normal subjects. Patterson (1976), in a study examining pupillary responsivity in groups of schizophrenics defined by their electrodermal responsivity, provides parallel confirmatory evidence to that of Gruzelier (1975), in showing that schizophrenic electro-dermal non-responders display minimal pupillary responsivity.

A further report of possible relevance is that of Roth and Cannon (1972), who show that in a study in which event related cortical potentials to frequent and infrequent tones were measured there is a deficiency of the late positive component of the ERP in their schizophrenic group. With a mean latency of 238 ms, this component may be identified as P3a of Squires *et al.* (1975), suggesting that it has affinities with the orienting response. The patients in this instance were not, however, identified as to their electrodermal responsivity status.

While these data are sparse, they do suggest that electrodermal non-responsivity is not an isolated phenomenon but extends to other areas of function. A more extended review of this area is presented by Straube (1979).

E. *Mechanisms of Responsivity*

Arguments for the proposal that autonomic responsivity is related to limbic system balance have been reviewed previously by Gruzelier and Venables (1972), Venables (1973, 1975), Gruzelier (1978, 1979). The basis for much of the theorizing lies in the work from Pribram's laboratory, reported initially by Bagshaw *et al.* (1965) and recently in detail by McGuinness and Pribram (1980). In essence, the proposal is that, as bilateral amygdalectomy results in an electrodermally hypo-responsive animal while hippocampectomy produces autonomic hyperresponsivity, it is possible that the hypo- and hyper-responsivity shown by schizophrenic patients reflects a functional state of relative amygdalectomy or hippocampectomy in these patients. Spohn and Patterson (1979) suggest a biochemical substrate for these functional "lesions", on the basis of disturbed balance of cholinergic activity. It is also possible to link limbic dysfunction with the more fashionable dopamine hypothesis of schizophrenia, in so far as the meso-limbic pathway is a suggested system by which dopamine imbalance may produce psychotic symptoms (e.g. Meltzer and Stahl, 1976). A much more speculative proposal for a mechanism of schizophrenic disturbance was put forward by Mesulam and Geschwind (1978) and involves both dopaminergic and cholinergic pathways. Its main hypothesis, however, is the suggestion that right parietal lobe dysfunction is involved in schizophrenia. Some arguments in support of a fundamental right hemispheric dysfunction in schizophrenia have been presented by Venables (1980b). It is possible, however, to tentatively suggest the relevance of other material to align the notion of right hemispheric dysfunction with electrodermal non-responsivity.

The most direct evidence is that of Heilman *et al.* (1978), who show that 7 patients with right hemisphere lesions had a mean skin resistance response of $0\cdot5$ kΩ. However, this mean value represents only the response data for 2 patients, as the other 5 had no recordable GSR. What the data do emphasize is the general hypo-responsivity of right hemisphere lesion patients, as the mean GSR of those patients who did respond was only $0\cdot175$ kΩ. On the other hand, patients with aphasic symptoms involving left sided disturbances had mean GSRs of $4\cdot30$ kΩ, which were larger than those shown by a non-lesion control group. These responses were to shock stimuli presented to the forearm ipsilateral to the lesion. It has already been suggested that electrodermally non-responsive patients are likely to be those who show "anhedonia", "motor-retardation", withdrawal, etc. It is worth noting that Howes and Boller (1975) report right hemisphere lesioned patients as having markedly impaired simple reaction times, with values comparable to those exhibited by severely ill schizophrenics, and that left lesioned patients, while evidencing some impairment, are not so motorically impaired as right lesioned patients. In a possible analogue to "anhedonia", Heilman *et al.* (1975) report that patients with right hemisphere dysfunction have a defect in the comprehension of affective speech.

Thus, these few pieces of evidence raise the possibility that, in addition to pursuing the hypothesis of limbic dysfunction underlying autonomic responsivity and its associated patterns of behaviour, it may also be worthwhile considering the role of lateral hemispheric balance in this context. While the data in favour of right hemispheric dysfunction have been proposed as underlying the pattern of non-responsiveness, anhedonia, retardation and thus possibly the type of schizophrenia originally defined by Kraepelin and Bleuler, the general tenor of work on lateral dysfunction in schizophrenia has pointed toward a left hemispheric disturbance (Gruzelier and Flor-Henry, 1979).

III. Lateral Dysfunction

The strongest data supporting a left-located cerebral dysfunction in schizophrenia are those for EEG, neuropsychological and behavioural studies. These are available in the volume edited by Gruzelier and Flor-Henry (1979). Flor-Henry *et al.* (1979), for example, provide data showing greater 13–20 Hz EEG power from the left temporal region in schizophrenics and from the right in depression. As an example from neuropsychology, Abrams and Taylor (1979) provide evidence, using the aphasia screening test, that schizophrenics show errors indicating dominant temporal and temporo-parietal defects. On the behavioural side, Gur (1978) describes a tachistoscopic experiment indicating that there is left hemisphere dysfunction in schizophrenics in the initial processing of verbal information. However, as some of the initial impetus for the proposals of disturbed asymmetry of function in schizophrenia arose from examination of electrodermal data (Gruzelier, 1973; Gruzelier and Venables, 1974), it is worthwhile considering this area in greater detail.

A. *Lateral Differences in Electrodermal Activity*

It is probably important to state at the outset that data presently available to relate lateral recording of electrodermal activity at the hands to lateral cerebral activity are inconclusive and represent an area where major research effort is required..

Important, but somewhat conflicting statements of this position are made by Shimkunas (1978) and by Gruzelier (1979). The original position adopted by Gruzelier and Venables was to suggest homolateral connections between hands and hemispheres, on the basis of work by Luria and Homskaya (1970) and Sourek (1965). The clearest support for a homolateral position comes from this latter author who, in providing data on skin potential activity after cortical lesions, states ". . . constant changes in the SPR were found only in patients from whom we removed medial and basal parts of the frontal lobe or the medial parts of the temporal lobe . . . In all patients in whom post operative recording produced asymmetrical results the SPRs were reduced on the homolateral extremities." However, Sourek goes on to say "as an SPR could be much better provoked after the operation than before it and had greater amplitude, we cannot exclude even the possibility that this is the case of contralateral increase in the SPR caused by the loss of inhibitory influence of the removal of the brain hemispheres." Other data on human subjects reported by Holloway and Parsons (1969) give some support to the notion of a contralateral inhibitory process. And animal work by Wilcott and his colleagues (e.g. Wilcott and Bradley, 1970) gives rise to the statement ". . . it is reasonable to conclude that the anterior cortex contains inhibitory as well as excitatory systems for SP (skin potential) and other components of arousal. It further appears that the inhibitory system is mainly contralateral while the excitatory system seems to affect both sides to the same extent."

These results would appear to suggest that any lateral asymmetry of electrodermal activity is likely to be due to contralateral inhibitory influences. However, as Gruzelier (1979) cautions, there is need to take into account the known facts of the hierarchy of segmental influences from spine to cortex in the determination of electrodermal responsivity (see Venables and Christie,

1973, for a review); and in addition it is important to separate lateral influences on tonic and phasic activity.

Experiments to elucidate the position, by the device of attempting differential cortical activation by using alternative verbal or spatial types of stimulation, have provided conflicting results. Myslobodsky and Rattock (1977) showed that with a verbal task larger right than left hand responses were recorded, while with a visual task larger left than right responsivity was the case. These results are in accord with the authors' expectations that activation of one hemisphere would result in greater responsivity on the contralateral hand. It should, however, be noted that Myslobodsky and Rattock's recording method was such that level and response aspects of electrodermal activity may well have been confounded. In contrast to this result, Lacroix and Comper (1979), who also used verbal and spatial tasks to activate left and right hemispheres respectively, reported results showing that responses were *smaller* on the hand contralateral to the hemisphere stimulated, a result more in accord with the contralateral inhibitory mechanism reviewed above. This result was replicated by Smith *et al.* (1980) and by Comper and Lacroix (1980). In this latter study, in addition to the use of material designed to activate left or right hemispheres as in their previous study, the authors also presented the data to the right and left visual hemi-fields. Again where steps were taken to activate the left hemisphere selectively a diminution of right hand response was seen and vice versa.

The dependence of these studies on particular stimulus material to obtain maximum activation in one cerebral hemisphere or the other is itself liable to produce equivocal results. The instructions concerning the desired approach to the stimulus material may produce differential responding. Thus, for instance, it may be important to take into account the distinction between the orienting responses produced in conditions of "voluntary" and "involuntary" attention (Maltzman *et al.*, 1977). An example of the voluntary OR is that of the CR in a GSR conditioning paradigm, while the UCR would be classed as an involuntary OR. Maltzman *et al.* suggest that "the physiological basis for the two kinds of ORs may be the hemisphere asymmetry of the cerebral control mechanisms for the GSR. The involuntary OR is largely determined by the right hemisphere, whereas the voluntary OR is primarily under left hemisphere control."

In summary, therefore, as far as amplitude of phasic response is concerned, the weight of present evidence appears to be in the direction of models of contralateral cortical inhibition or of ipsilateral cortical excitation. These cannot be distinguished in our present state of knowledge. However, with conflicting results in the literature, the position is by no means firm. While the data reviewed relate to possible influences of cortical mechanisms on handedness of response, there is only limited data available which would enable interconnection between hands and sub-cortical mechanisms to be assessed. Toone *et al.* (1979) measured the bilateral electrodermal responsivity of patients having unilateral temporal lobectomies. No differences could be detected between operated and non-operated sides within the parietal group. However, the ability of patients to give electrodermal responses even with the major sensory pathways absent is exemplified by a study by Zihl *et al.* (1980), who showed that even with patients where stimuli are presented to the blind part of the visual field after damage to the geniculo-striate pathway an electrodermal orienting response may be elicited. Thus, higher lesions may lead to dependence on lower level mechanisms of response. Knowledge of the laterality of connections involved at all levels would, of course, be important to throw further light on the limbic mechanisms of responsivity which are currently thought to be directly involved as possible areas of disturbance in schizophrenia. Even more obscure is the position with regard to the lateral control of the temporal components of the skin conductance response. Bearing in mind the data from Bell *et al.* (1977) from a study of twins, which shows a high degree of heritability of the SCR recovery time from the left but not the right hand, it would be valuable to know if these data indicate heritability of right or left cerebral function.

With these caveats in mind, the data on electrodermal asymmetry in schizophrenics needs to be looked at carefully. The data are reviewed extensively by Gruzelier (1979). In electrodermally responsive schizophrenic patients the general finding is of higher right than left responsivity. In some instances total absence of left hand responsivity is reported. As far as tonic electrodermal levels are concerned, subjects who gave responses showed higher right than left levels, while non-responders tended to show the reverse pattern. It should be noted that depressive subjects tend to show opposite patterns of activity. The data reviewed by Gruzelier (1979) suggest that among schizophrenics higher right than left responsivity is found in patients with poor prognosis and the reverse is noted in patients in whom a better outcome may be expected. This would be in accord with the notion that the inclusion of an affective element in the symptomatology is conducive to a better prognosis. A report by Gruzelier (1980) relates later differences in electrodermal responsivity to individual symptoms exhibited by patients selected to have a Catego diagnosis of schizophrenia. (Catego is a computer program for producing standardized diagnoses, using as its input symptoms for the present state examination (PSE), Wing *et al.*, 1974). Gruzelier states "there is a striking resemblance between the profile of the R>L patients and the classical description of schizophrenia by Kraepelin and Bleuler with its interpersonal disturbance, lack of affect and motivation and thought disorder." On the other hand florid symptoms characterize the L>R patients and are characteristic of a manic or schizo-affective psychosis.

On the basis of these results, Gruzelier proposes that "classical schizophrenia with its retarded mobility, impoverished speech and sometimes muteness involves reduced left hemisphere activation. The florid psychotic syndrome with its pressure of speech and flight of ideas involves enhanced left hemisphere activation." This result, if replicated, advances our knowledge of this complex area a stage further, and suggests that the behavioural and EEG data showing lateral differences between schizophrenic and other patients and normals should be re-examined in the light of more closely defined symptomatology.

It should be noted that the hypothesis of right hemisphere dysfunction raised in Section IIE gives rise to directly opposite postulates. It was suggested at that point that there was limited evidence leading to an idea of the occurrence of negative symptoms in right hemisphere dysfunction patients and that these would also be electrodermal hypo-responders. While this fits with the general view, reviewed in Section IIC, that hypo-responders might show non-florid symptoms, it also leads to the view that left hemisphere enhanced activities would be found in these patients, which is opposite to the suggestion made by Gruzelier. At this stage, it is evident that more data must be gathered before strong statements can be made.

IV. Skin Conductance Response Recovery and Schizophrenic Psychopathology

Another area of considerable contention concerns the extent to which the recovery time of the skin conductance response may be related to schizophrenic pathology. This topic is of importance, because the earliest of the studies of children at risk for schizophrenia (e.g. Mednick *et al.*, 1978) showed electrodermal recovery to be possibly the best indicator of later schizophrenic breakdown. Since the review of this area presented by Venables in 1977, the main area of controversy has been outside the field of schizophrenia and has revolved around the issue of the independence of the recovery component of the SCR from other aspects of electrodermal responsivity. This point is important because, on the one hand, Edelberg (e.g. 1970) considered that the recovery aspect of the SCR might involve a separate effector mechanism from response amplitude, and, on the other hand, empirical use of the recovery component had shown that it appeared to be related to aspects of individual subject characteristics in ways that were different from other components.

The work which called into question the independence of recovery time was that of Bundy and Fitzgerald (1975); this showed that recovery time was closely related to the electrodermal activity prior to the response on which recovery time was measured. In the work reported, this relation approached unity and thus gave reason for disquiet concerning the independent nature of recovery. While subsequent work by Edelberg and Muller (1977) essentially supports the Bundy position, the issue is on the whole concerned with the extent of the relation between recovery and general responsivity. Venables and Fletcher (1981), while providing data which could be taken as some support for Bundy, nevertheless, show that the relation is weak and variable. At this point, it is still worthwhile to consider skin conductance recovery time as a relatively independent variable, for practical purposes. This is also the position adopted by Levander *et al.* (1980).

Thus, it is still possible to consider as valid the several studies which indicate that skin conductance recovery time is faster in schizophrenics than normals (for example, Ax and Bamford, 1970; Gruzelier and Venables, 1973; Zahn *et al.*, 1975; and the study of Neilsen and Petersen, 1976, showing a correlation between "schizophrenism" and fast SCR recovery in normal subjects). However, data of Maricq and Edelberg (1975) suggest that recovery time is longer in schizophrenics than normals. In this context, it may be noted that Patterson and Venables (1978) identified a group of schizophrenic patients who were characterized by particularly fast habituation of their orienting responses. These patients had recovery times which were markedly longer than both schizophrenic and normal subjects, who gave responses which habituated over a period longer than the first two trials. In a later study by Patterson and Venables (1980), it was shown that these "fast habituator" patients, although not distinguishable from other schizophrenics on the diagnostic criteria used, were nevertheless, indistinguishable from normals on an auditory vigilance task; while other non-responding and responding schizophrenics did show impaired performance. These experiments suggest that there is a need to consider carefully sub-classifications of patients labelled as schizophrenic when attempting to establish relationships with length of recovery time, in the same way as has been found necessary when considering responsivity or lateral asymmetry.

As with the other electrodermal indices which have been discussed in this chapter, one of the greatest requirements is for further knowledge concerning the mechanism of recovery. Venables (1974) reviews some possibilities of peripheral factors which might be involved, suggesting that sodium reabsorption in the epidermal duct, triggered by electrolyte concentration and hydrostatic pressure, might be responsible. The reabsorptive process might be passive or might be due to the increased ductal hydrostatic pressure, caused by myo-epithelial squeezing of the duct which may have sympathetic innervation. Passive control of reabsorption could probably only be by amount of sweat secretion, and would suggest that a very high relation would be always present between ongoing electrodermal activity and speed of recovery as suggested by Bundy and Fitzgerald (1975). That this is not the case is indicated by Venables and Fletcher (1981). Venables (1974) also reviews the limited material which points to central factors involved in SCR recovery. In brief, it can be shown that hippocampectomized animals have shorter recovery times than controls (see McGuinness and Pribram, 1980), while lesions of the dorsolateral frontal cortex lead to longer recovery times, although response amplitudes do not differ from normal.

Mednick (1974, 1977) has hypothesized that the length of the skin conductance response before it returns to base-line is an index of the extent to which there is maintenance of central (fear) arousal elicited by the stimulus producing the response, and in consequence is related to the extent of reinforcement of avoidance responding in the setting involved. A somewhat similar view, i.e. that SCR recovery time indicates the length of time of a central process, is suggested by McGuinness and Pribram (1980) when they state, "It appears from this that hippocampectomized monkeys re-equilibriate more rapidly than normal subjects, whose slower GSR recovery may indicate a more prolonged processing time." Either of these ideas requires that long recovery is indicative of maintenance of the process which brought about the orienting response. The most obvious candidate is that of continuous sweat secretion, resulting from continuing sympathetic innervation of the sweat glands.

This somewhat theoretical discussion does have repercussions in practical questions of measurement. At the moment, it is common to consider the measurement of SC recovery as half recovery time as valid only when the fall to a value of half the peak amplitude follows a relatively smooth quasi-exponential course (Venables, 1974). Measurement of half recovery is not undertaken when subsequent secondary "responses" supervene before half amplitude is reached. If, however, these can be considered as "real" indications of continuing "arousal" or "processing", then it may be that recovery measurement should not be abandoned in the presence of secondary responsivity. Practical tests of this position may be undertaken by using standard measures of half recovery time and measures where secondary responsivity is present in relation to other variables, either of a "task" or "individual difference" kind.

In summary, while the measure of recovery time appears to have potential usefulness as an index showing a relation to schizophrenic tendency (and to delinquent tendency when excessively long, e.g. Mednick, 1977), its controlling mechanism is poorly understood and, in consequence, its ultimate usefulness limited.

V. Electrodermal Activity in High-risk Studies

High-risk for schizophrenia studies are those in which behaviour is measured in the pre-morbid state and the subjects followed up longitudinally until some of them breakdown psychiatrically as adults. The studies are designated as high-risk as in most the experimental group has an elevated chance of breakdown because one or both parents have a schizophrenic diagnosis. When schizophrenia in one parent is involved the lifetime morbid risk is raised from about 1%, as in the general population, to between 10 and 15%. The only real test of the success of pre-morbid measures as indicators of later breakdown is by their relation to actual breakdown. Only one study, that of Mednick and Schulsinger conducted in Copenhagen on subjects of mean age 15 years in 1962, is in a position to meet this test. Other studies have attempted to show differences in the pre-morbid indices between groups designated as high and low-risk, the latter having no familial tendency to develop schizophrenia. Although such a comparison is unlikely to produce strong results, as 90% of the high risk population is possibly indistinguishable from the low risk population, the early success of Mednick and Schulsinger (e.g. Mednick, 1967) in distinguishing high and low risk groups has led others to make the attempt.

Mednick and Schulsinger used an electrodermal conditioning paradigm in their work, in order to test a theory of schizophrenic development outlined by Mednick (1958). This procedure used eight 1000 Hz desensitization tones, of duration ranging from 5–11 s, followed by 14 conditioning trials. The UCS was a 96 dB irritating noise, presented for 4·5 s and following half a second after the onset of the 54 dB CS. Nine of the trials were reinforced and there were five interspersed test trials of the CS alone. Inter-trial intervals ranged from 17 to 77 s. Following the conditioning trials were generalization trials, with stimuli of 1311 and 1967 Hz.

It should be noted that with such a small CS–UCS interval there is no possibility of distinguishing the three types of responses which are measured in paradigms currently employed (e.g. Prokasy and Kumpfer, 1973). Only single response data are therefore reported for each trial. The data reported by Mednick (1967) show that the latency of the response is significantly shorter for the experimental (high-risk) group than the control group in almost all the desensitization, conditioning and test trials and for the generalized trials, with the exception of those to the 1967 Hz stimulus where the latency is reversed. (This rather unusual finding has echoes in a report by Gruzelier and Hammond, 1976, which says that schizophrenics have lower absolute auditory thresholds than controls at frequencies "up to 1000 or 2000 Hz, whereas above this the hearing of the controls was superior"). The amplitude of responses shown by the experimental group was in nearly all cases significantly larger than the control group. Most surprising to Mednick (but not now with knowledge of more recent data) was the finding of a tendency for the high-risk group to show a shorter rather than longer half recovery time of the electrodermal response than controls. This finding on recovery time was opposite to that predicted by Mednick's (1958) theory. It is interesting that recovery time was, however, significantly different between groups on the response made to the fitting of the earphones at the start of the session and to the last of the reinforced trials.

What in many ways is striking about these findings is that evidence of pre-morbid electrodermal responsivity which is different from normal is shown. This difference is apparent even when the data from the relatively small group of "to-be-sick" subjects are diluted by those from the larger group of high-risk subjects who will remain well. To some extent the non-replications of the original Mednick and Schulsinger findings need to be examined with this in mind, as later reports (e.g. Mednick and Schulsinger, 1968; Mednick et al., 1978) show that there are differences in response characteristics of the "to-be-sick" and those of the "at risk but remaining well" and control subjects.

Two studies, in New York and in Rochester, provide apparently close methodological replications of the Mednick and Schulsinger study; however, at this stage none have reported the relation of pre-morbidly collected indices to later breakdown, so that the comparison must be with the high risk/low risk data presented by Mednick in 1967.

Erlenmeyer-Kimling (1975) and Erlenmeyer-Kimling et al. (1979) report preliminary electrodermal results from a study on children between the ages of 7 and 12. Those in risk groups had either a schizophrenic father, or a schizophrenic mother, or both parents schizophrenic. There were two control groups one with other than schizophrenic psychiatric illness in the parent and one with normal parents. In this study there was almost complete non-replication of the Copenhagen findings and it is necessary to seek reasons for the differences reported.

Erlenmeyer-Kimling et al. (1979) report that high-risk subjects had slower responses to UCS than controls. The groups did not differ on response amplitude or recovery rate. The children of schizophrenic mothers, however, showed a slightly faster recovery rate than the low-risk children, while those with schizophrenic fathers showed a rather slower recovery rate. Thus, the recovery data are at least in the same direction as the Copenhagen data where children of schizophrenic mothers were involved. It should, however, be pointed out that the Copenhagen data were not strong on the recovery variable. If the initial response to fitting headphones is discarded, as it may well not have been measured by Erlenmeyer-Kimling, then on only one trial is there reported a significantly faster recovery in the high risk group.

The slower latency and lack of amplitude differences are more of a problem. At least one possibility is that there were differences in parental diagnosis, or that there will be differences in breakdown characteristics in the

New York and Copenhagen groups. It is known from the Mednick *et al.* (1978) report that the relationship of the hyper-responding pre-morbid pattern of electrodermal response (of the males in the sample at least) is to symptoms showing a fairly florid set of characteristics with little emphasis on negative aspects of schizophrenia. The New York data are only presented in summary, but there is at least the possibility of a wide distribution of hypo- to hyper-responsivity, leading to mean values giving the results reported.

Perhaps most important is the selection of the New York sample on the basis of family intactness. Mednick (1978) shows, very convincingly, that in intact families in the Copenhagen material there is very little difference in latency, amplitude or recovery rate between high-risk and low-risk groups, whereas in the portion of the sample from non-intact families there are marked differences in the directions of responsivity already reported.

In addition there is a difference in age between the New York and the Copenhagen samples. Unpublished data from the author's laboratory suggest that, for intense stimuli (as the UCS in the studies reported) amplitude of response increases with age, between age 5 and 15, in females, but not in males, while latency and half recovery also increase in age to approximately the same degree in both sexes. These differences tend to level out after age 15, which appears to be a time of maximal responsiveness. How age differences interact with risk status is not known. It could, however, be that the fact that no non-responsiveness is reported in either high- or low-risk groups in Copenhagen is a function of their testing at age 15, when non-responsiveness is likely to be minimal.

Finally, a possibly very important interacting factor is the approach to the subject which differs in the two studies. This factor has already been dealt with at some length in Section IIB above, when Gruzelier is quoted as saying in this connection "an important factor (in relation to responsivity) is the patient's attitude to the task which is formed from the moment the patient is invited for testing." In Copenhagen the subjects' testing day was one of considerable pressure, and there was little attempt made to ease any worries as a tight schedule had to be kept. In the New York study, as Erlenmeyer-Kimling points out, the psychophysiology session was not a stressor. Under these circumstances it would be expected (i) that there would be more hyper-responsivity in the Danish setting and also (ii) that the labile autonomic nervous system, that could characterize pre-schizophrenic subjects, would interact with a stressfully presented stimulus setting to produce hyper-responsivity.

The Rochester material is presented in Salzman and Klein (1978). Salzman and Klein's stimulation paradigm follows very closely that of Mednick's original, except that the CS–UCS interval is extended to allow the measurement of all aspects of conditioned responsivity. Salzman and Klein's data showed no significant differences in latency, or recovery between high- and low-risk groups. However, as far as responses to the UCS were concerned, high-risk subjects were significantly more responsive than the low-risk subjects, thus replicating the Mednick findings.

Although the recovery times overall were not significantly different in high- and low-risk groups, it is noteworthy that graphical representation of the data does show an apparently longer SCR recovery in the low-risk than in the high-risk group on the first 3 trial block. It is possible that this early occasion on which a recovery time difference is shown is akin to that shown by Mednick's subjects on headphone placement. Otherwise, the facts that the subjects in this study were ten year olds and the study was carried out in a more leisurely fashion, in which the subjects were "given a tour of the laboratory", may account for other differences.

In summary, it is suggested that the two most direct "replications" of the Copenhagen study, which are on occasions used to suggest that that study is likely to be replicated, may be unlikely to produce similar results. The factors which are not replicated and which may be of major rather than trivial importance are (i) the setting of the study and the form of its introduction to the subjects, (ii) the age of the subjects and (iii) the intactness of the subjects' families.

Two final points, bearing in mind the bias against getting a statistically significant result when many subjects are not going to succumb psychiatrically, the fact that the Mednick (1967) material reported any results is remarkable rather than that the "replications" did not provide confirmation. However, there are other aspects of the study as reported in 1967 which appear to have been exaggerated on the basis of later findings in relation to actual breakdown; in particular, the short recovery time in the "to-be-sick" subjects. This was only a minor finding in the 1967 report. It is suggested that as both the Mednick and the Salzman and Klein data appear to show that it is early responsivity on which recovery time differences are shown that this may be a clue worth following up. Venables (1981) makes the suggestion that the longer recovery time in the normal subjects may reflect initial global pre-attentive processing before later sequential verification takes place. This early global processing might be absent in schizophrenics and pre-schizophrenics.

Further Reading

Perhaps the best up-to-date coverage of the area is given in a single number of *Schizophrenia Bulletin*. Edited and introduced by M. S. Buchsbaum, it presents chapters by a variety of authors, all well known in particular branches of this area of research.
Schizophrenia Bull. 3, No. 1. (1977).

A more recent review brings the field almost to the present.
  Spohn, H. E. and Patterson, T. (1979). Recent studies of psychophysiology in schizophrenia. *Schizophrenia Bull.* 5, 581–611.
A more extensive coverage of all areas of the application of psychophysiological techniques to psychiatric research is in a series of books in six parts. Part II is particularly pertinent to the material covered in this chapter.
  Van Praag, H. M. (ed.), (1980). "Handbook of Biological Psychiatry: part II – Brain Mechanisms and Abnormal Behaviour – Psychophysiology". Marcel Dekker, New York.

References

Abrams, R. and Taylor, M. A. (1979). Laboratory studies in the validation of psychiatric diagnoses. *In* "Hemisphere Asymmetries of Function in Psychopathology" (J. Gruzelier and P. Flor-Henry, eds). Elsevier/North Holland, Amsterdam.

Ax, A. F. and Bamford, J. L. (1970). The GSR recovery limb in chronic schizophrenia. *Psychophysiology* 7, 145–147.

Bagshaw, M. H., Kimble, D. P. and Pribram, K. H. (1965). The GSR of monkeys during orienting and habituation and after ablation of the amygdala, hippocampus and inferotemporal cortex. *Neuropsychologia* 3, 111–119.

Bell, B., Mednick, S. A., Gottesman, I. I. and Sergeant, J. (1977). Electrodermal parameters in male twins. *In* "Biosocial Bases of Criminal Behaviour" (S. A. Mednick and K. O. Christiansen, eds). Gardner Press, New York.

Bernstein, A. S. (1964). The galvanic skin response orienting reflex among chronic schizophrenics. *Psychonom. Sci.* 1, 391–392.

Bernstein, A. S. (1970). Phasic electrodermal orienting response in chronic schizophrenics. *J. Abnorm. Psychol.* 75, 146–156.

Bleuler, E. (1911). "Dementia Praecox or the Group of Schizophrenias" (Translated by H. Zirkin). International Universities Press, New York.

Buchsbaum, M. S. (1977a). Psychophysiology and schizophrenia. *Schizophrenia Bull.* 3, 7–14.

Buchsbaum, M. S. (1977b). The middle evoked response components and schizophrenia. *Schizophrenia Bull.* 3, 93–104.

Bundy, R. S. and Fitzgerald, H. E. (1975). Stimulus specificity of electrodermal recovery time: An examination and reinterpretation of the evidence. *Psychophysiology* 12, 406–411.

Chapman, L. J., Chapman, J. P. and Raulin, M. L. (1976). Scales for physical and social anhedonia. *J. Abnorm. Psychol.* 85, 374–382.

Comper, P. and Lacroix, J. M. (1980). Further evidence of lateralization in the electrodermal system as a function of relative hemisphere activation. Paper presented to the 20th Annual Meeting of the Society for Psychophysiological Research, Vancouver.

Dykman, R. A., Reese, W. G., Galbrecht, C. R., Ackerman, P. T. and Sunderman, R. S. (1968). Autonomic responses in psychiatric patients. *Ann. N. Y. Acad. Sci.* 147, 237–303.

Edelberg, R. (1970). The information content of the recovery limb of the electrodermal response. *Psychophysiology* 6, 527–539.

Edelberg, R. and Muller, M. (1977). The status of the electrodermal recovery measure: a caveat. Paper presented to the 17th Annual Meeting of the Society for Psychophysiological Research, Philadelphia.

Erlenmeyer-Kimling, L. (1975). A prospective study of children at risk for schizophrenia: Methodological considerations and some preliminary findings. In "Life History Research in Psychopathology" (R. D. Wirt, G. Winokur and M. Roff, eds), Vol. 4. University of Minnesota Press, Minneapolis.

Erlenmeyer-Kimling, L., Cornblatt, B. and Fleiss, J. (1979). High-risk research in schizophrenia. Psychiat. Ann. 9, 79–99.

Feighner, J. P., Guze, S. B., Woodruff, R. A. Winokur, G. and Munoz, R. (1972). Diagnostic criteria for use in psychiatric research. Arch. Gen. Psychiat. 26, 57–63.

Flor-Henry, P., Koles, Z. J., Howarth, B. G. and Burton, L. (1979). Neurophysiological studies of schizophrenia, mania and depression. In "Hemisphere Asymmetries of Function in Psychopathology" (J. Gruzelier and P. Flor-Henry, eds). Elsevier/North Holland, Amsterdam.

Frith, C. D., Stevens, M., Johnsone, E. C. and Crow, T. J. (1979). Skin conductance responsivity during acute episodes of schizophrenia as a prediction of symptomatic improvement. Psychol. Med. 9, 101–106.

Gruzelier, J. H. (1973). Bilateral asymmetry of skin conductance activity and levels in schizophrenia. Biol. Psychol. 1, 21–42.

Gruzelier, J. H. (1975). The cardiac responses of schizophrenics to orienting, signal and non-signal tones. Biol. Psychol. 3, 143–155.

Gruzelier, J. H. (1976). Clinical attributes of schizophrenic skin conductance responders and non-responders. Psychol. Med. 6, 245–249.

Gruzelier, J. H. (1978). Bimodal states of arousal and lateralized dysfunction in schizophrenia: effects of chlorpromazine. In "The Nature of Schizophrenia" (L. C. Wynne, R. L. Cromwell and S. Matthyse, eds). Wiley, New York.

Gruzelier, J. (1979). Lateral asymmetries in electrodermal activity and psychosis. In "Hemispheric Asymmetries of Function in Psychopathology" (J. Gruzelier and P. Flor-Henry, eds). Elsevier/North Holland, Amsterdam.

Gruzelier, J. H. (1980). Paper presented at 2nd International Symposium on "Clinical-Neurophysiological Aspects of Psychopathological Conditions". Capri. September 1980.

Gruzelier, J. H. and Connolly, J. F. (1979). Differential drug action on electrodermal orienting responses as distinct from nonspecific responses and electrodermal levels. In "The Orienting Reflex in Humans" (H. D. Kimmel, E. H. Van Olst and J. F. Orlebeke, eds). Erlbaum, Hillsdale, New Jersey.

Gruzelier, J. and Flor-Henry, P. (eds), (1979). "Hemisphere Asymmetries of Function in Psychopathology." Elsevier/North Holland, Amsterdam.

Gruzelier, J. and Hammond, N. V. (1976). Schizophrenia: A dominant hemisphere temporal-limbic disorder? Res. Communications Psychol. Psychiat. Behav. 1, 33–72.

Gruzelier, J. H. and Hammond, N. V. (1978). The effect of chlorpromazine upon psychophysiological, endocrine and information processing measures in schizophrenia. J. Psychiat. Res. 14, 167–182.

Gruzelier, J. H. and Venables, P. H. (1972). Skin conductance orienting activity in a heterogenous sample of schizophrenics. J. Nerv. Ment. Dis. 155, 277–287.

Gruzelier, J. H. and Venables, P. H. (1973). Skin conductance responses to tones with and without attentional significance in schizophrenic and non-schizophrenic psychiatric patients. Neuropsychologia 11, 221–230.

Gruzelier, J. H. and Venables, P. H. (1974). Bimodality and lateral asymmetry of skin conductance orienting activity in schizophrenics: Replication and evidence of lateral asymmetry in patients with depression and disorder of personality. *Biol. Psychiat.* **8**, 55–73.

Gruzelier, J. H., Connolly, J. F. and Hirsch, S. R., (1980). Altered brain functional organisation in psychosis: Brain behaviour relationships. Paper presented at 2nd International Symposium On Clinical-Neurophysiological Aspects of Psychopathological Conditions, Capri.

Gruzelier, J., Connolly, J., Eves, F., Hirsch, S., Zaki, S., Weller, M. and Yorkston, N. (1981). Effect of propranolol and phenothiazines on electrodermal orienting and habituation in schizophrenia. *Psychol. Med.* **11**, 93–108.

Gur, R. E. (1978). Left hemisphere dysfunction and left hemisphere overactivation in schizophrenia. *J. Abnorm. Psychol.* **87**, 226–238.

Heilman, K. M., Scholes, R. and Watson, R. T. (1975). Auditory affective agnosia. *J. Neurol. Neurosurg. Psychiat.* **38**, 69–72.

Heilman, K. M., Schwartz, H. D. and Watson, R. T. (1978). Hypoarousal in patients with neglect syndrome and emotional indifference. *Neurology* **28**, 229–232.

Holloway, F. A. and Parsons, O. A. (1969). Unilateral brain damage and bilateral skin conductance levels in humans. *Psychophysiology* **6**, 138–148.

Holzman, P. S. and Levy, D. L. (1977). Smooth pursuit eye movements and functional psychoses; a review. *Schizophrenia Bull.* **3**, 15–27.

Howes, D. and Boller, F. (1975). Simple reaction time: evidence for local impairment for lesions of the right hemisphere. *Brain* **98**, 317–332.

Iacono, W. G. and Lykken, D. T. (1979). The orienting response: importance of instructions. *Schizophrenia Bull.* **5**, 11–14.

Itil, T. M. (1977). Qualitative and quantitative EEG findings in schizophrenia. *Schizophrenia Bull.* **3**, 61–79.

Kety, S. S. (1980). The syndrome of schizophrenia: unresolved questions and opportunities for research. *Br. J. Psychiat.* **136**, 421–426.

Kety, S. S., Rosenthal, D., Wender, P. H. and Schulsinger, F. (1976). Studies based on a total sample of adopted individuals and their relatives: why they were necessary, what they demonstrated and failed to demonstrate. *Schizophrenia Bull.* **2**, 413–428.

Kraepelin, E. (1913). "Dementia Praecox and Paraphrenia" (translated by R. M. Barclay). Livingstone, Edinburgh.

Lacroix, J. M. and Comper, P. (1979). Lateralization in the electrodermal system as a function of cognitive/hemispheric manipulations. *Psychophysiology* **16**, 116–129.

Lader, M. H. (1975). "The Psychophysiology of Mental Illness". Routledge and Kegan Paul, London.

Levander, S. E., Schalling, D. S., Lidberg, L., Bartfai, A. and Lidberg, Y. (1980). Skin conductance recovery time and personality in a group of criminals. *Psychophysiology* **17**, 105–111.

Luria, A. and Homskaya, E. D. (1970). Frontal lobe and regulation of arousal processes. *In* "Attention: Contemporary Theory and Research" (D. Mostovsky, ed.). Appleton-Century-Crofts, New York.

McGuiness, D. and Pribram, K. (1980). The neuropsychology of attention: emotional and motivational controls. *In* "The Brain and Psychology" (M. C. Wittrock, ed.). Academic Press, New York and London.

Maltzman, I., Langdon, B., Pendery, M. and Wolff, C. (1977). Galvanic skin response – orienting reflex and semantic conditioning and generalisation with different unconditioned stimuli. *J. Exp. Psychol. Gen.* **106**, 141–171.

Maricq, H. R. and Edelberg, R. (1975). Electrodermal recovery rate in a schizophrenic population. *Psychophysiology* 12, 630–641.

Mednick, S. A. (1958). A learning theory approach to research in schizophrenia. *Psychol. Bull.* 55, 316–327.

Mednick, S. A. (1967). The children of schizophrenics: Serious difficulties in current research methodologies which suggest the use of the "High-risk-group" method. *In* "Origins of Schizophrenia" (J. Romano, ed.), pp. 179–200. Exerpta Medica, Amsterdam.

Mednick, S. A. (1974). Electrodermal recovery and psychopathology. *In* "Genetics, Environment and Psychopathology" (S. A. Mednick, F. Schulsinger, J. Higgins and B. Bell, eds). Elsevier/North Holland, Amsterdam.

Mednick, S. A. (1977). A bio-social theory of the learning of law-abiding behaviour. *In* "Biosocial Bases of Criminal Behaviour" (S. A. Mednick and K. O. Christiansen, eds). Gardner Press, New York.

Mednick, S. A. (1978). Berkson's Fallacy and high risk research. *In* "The Nature of Schizophrenia" (L. C. Wynne, R. L. Cromwell and S. Matthysse, eds). Wiley, New York.

Mednick, S. A. and Schulsinger, F. (1968). Some pre-morbid characteristics related to breakdown in children with schizophrenic mothers. *In* "The Transmission of Schizophrenia" (D. Rosenthal and S. S. Kety, eds), pp. 267–291. Pergamon Press, New York.

Mednick, S. A., Schulsinger, F., Teasdale, T. W., Schulsinger, H., Venables, P. H. and Rock, D. R. (1978). Schizophrenia in high-risk children: Sex differences in predisposing factors. *In* "Cognitive Defects in the Development of Mental Illness" (G. Serban, ed.). Brunner/Mazel, New York.

Meltzer, H. Y. and Stahl, S. M. (1976). The dopamine hypothesis of schizophrenia: A review. *Schizophrenia Bull.* 2, 19–76.

Mesulam, M.-M. and Geschwind, N. (1978). On the possible role of the neo-cortex and its limbic connections in attention and schizophrenia. *In* "The Nature of Schizophrenia" (L. C. Wynne, R. L. Cromwell and S. Matthyse, eds). Wiley, New York.

Myslobodsky, M. S. and Rattock, J. (1977). Bilateral electrodermal activity in waking man. *Acta Psychol.* 41, 273–282.

Neilsen, T. C. and Petersen, K. E. (1976). Electrodermal correlates of extraversion, trait anxiety and schizophrenia. *Scand. J. Psychol.* 17, 73–80.

O'Gorman, J. G. (1978). Method of recording: a neglected factor in the controversy over the bimodality of electrodermal responsiveness in schizophrenic samples. *Schizophrenia Bull.* 4, 150–152.

Öhman, A.(1979). The orienting response, attention and learning: An information processing perspective. *In* "The Orienting Reflex in Humans" (H. D. Kimmel, E. H. Van Olst and J. F. Orlebeke, eds). Erlbaum, Hillsdale, New Jersey.

Patterson, R. (1976). Skin conductance responding/nonresponding and pupillometrics in chronic schizophrenia: a confirmation of Gruzelier and Venables. *J. Nerv. Ment. Dis.* 163, 200–209.

Patterson, T. and Venables, P. H. (1978). Bilateral skin conductance and skin potential in schizophrenia and normal subjects. The identification of the Fast Habituator group of schizophrenics. *Psychophysiology* 15, 556–560.

Patterson, T. and Venables, P. H. (1980). Auditory vigilance: Normals compared to chronic schizophrenic subgroups defined by skin conductance variables. *Psychiat. Res.* 2, 107–112.

Prokasy, W. F. and Kumpfer, K. L. (1973). Classical conditioning. *In* "Electrodermal

Activity in Psychological Research" (W. F. Prokasy and D. C. Raskin, eds). Academic Press, New York and London.

Rosenthal, D. (1974). Issues in high-risk studies of schizophrenia. *In* "Life History Research in Psychopathology" (D. F. Ricks, A. Thomas and M. Roff, eds), Vol. 3. University of Minnesota Press, Minneapolis.

Roth, W. T. (1977). Late event-related potentials and psychopathology. *Schizophrenia Bull.* 3, 105–120.

Roth, W. T. and Cannon, E. H. (1972). Some features of the auditory evoked reponse in schizophrenics. *Arch. Gen. Psychiat.* 27, 466–471.

Rubens, R. L. and Lapidus, L. B. (1978). Schizophrenic patterns of arousal and stimulus barrier functioning. *J. Abnorm. Psychol.* 78, 199–211.

Saletu, B. (1980). Central measures in schizophrenia. *In* "Handbook of Biological Psychiatry: Part 2" (H. M. Van Praag, ed.). Marcel Dekker, New York.

Salzman, L. F. and Klein, R. H. (1978). Habituation and conditioning of electrodermal responses in high-risk children. *Schizophrenia Bull.* 4, 210–222.

Schneider, K. (1959). "Clinical Psychopathology" (translated by M. W. Hamilton). Grune and Stratton, New York.

Shagass, C. (1977). Early evoked potentials. *Schizophrenia Bull.* 3, 80–92.

Shimkunas, A. (1978). Hemispheric asymmetry and schizophrenic thought disorder. *In* "Language and Cognition in Schizophrenia" (S. Schwartz, ed.). Erlbaum, Hillsdale, New Jersey.

Simons, R. F. (1980). Anhedonia as a risk factor in schizophrenia. Paper presented to the 20th Annual Meeting of the Society for Psychophysiological Research, Vancouver.

Smith, B. D., Ketterer, M. W. and Concannon, M. (1980). Hemisphere variables in bilateral electrodermal activity. *Psychophysiology* 17, 305.

Sourek, K. (1965). The nervous control of skin potential in man. Praha. Nakladalelství Československé Akadamie Věd.

Spohn, H. E. and Patterson, T. (1979). Recent studies of psychophysiology in schizophrenia. *Schizophrenia Bull.* 5, 581–611.

Squires, N. K., Squires, K. C. and Hillyard, S. A. (1975). Two varieties of long-latency positive waves evoked by unpredictable auditory stimuli in man. *Electroenceph. Clin. Neurophysiol.* 38, 387–401.

Straube, E. R. (1979). On the meaning of electrodermal non-responding in schizophrenia. *J. Nerv. Ment. Dis.* 167, 601–611.

Strauss, J. S., Kokes, R. F., Klorman, R. and Sacksteder, J. L. (1977). Premorbid adjustment in schizophrenia: concepts measures and implications. *Schizophrenia Bull.* 3, 182–185.

Thayer, J. and Silber, D. E. (1971). Relationship between levels of arousal and responsiveness among schizophrenic and normal subjects. *J. Abnorm. Psychol.* 77, 162–173.

Toone, B. K., Cooke, E. and Lader, M. H. (1979). The effect of temporal lobe surgery on electrodermal activity: implications for an organic hypothesis in the aetiology of schizophrenia. *Psychol. Med.* 9, 281–285.

Venables, P. H. (1973). Input regulation and psychopathology. *In* "Psychopathology" (M. Hammer, K. Salzinger and S. Sutton, eds). Wiley, New York.

Venables, P. H. (1974). The recovery limb of the skin conductance response in 'high-risk' research. *In* "Genetics Environment in Psychopathology" (S. A. Mednick, F. Schulsinger, J. Higgins and B. Bell, eds). Elsevier/North Holland, Amsterdam.

Venables, P. H. (1975a). A psychophysiological approach to research in schizophrenia. *In* "Clinical Applications of Psychophysiology" (D. C. Fowles, ed.). Columbia University Press, New York.

Venables, P. H. (1975b). Psychophysiological studies of schizophrenic pathology. *In* "Research in Psychophysiology" (P. H. Venables and M. J. Christie, eds). Wiley, London.

Venables, P. H. (1977). The electrodermal physiology of schizophrenics and children at risk for schizophrenia: Current controversies and developments. *Schizophrenia Bull.* 3, 28–48.

Venables, P. H. (1978). Psychophysiology and psychometrics. *Psychophysiology* 15, 302–315.

Venables, P. H. (1979). The psychophysiology of schizophrenia. *In* "Current Themes in Psychiatry – 2" (R. N. Gaind and B. L. Hudson, eds). Macmillan, London.

Venables, P. H. (1980a). Peripheral measures of schizophrenia. *In* "Handbook of Biological Psychiatry, Part 2" (H. M. Van Praag, ed.). Marcel Dekker, New York.

Venables, P. H. (1980b). Primary dysfunction and cortical lateralization in schizophrenia. *In* "Functional States of the Brain: Their Determinants" (M. Koukkou, D. Lehmann and J. Angst, eds). Elsevier/North Holland, Amsterdam.

Venables, P. H. (1981). Psychophysiology of abnormal behaviour. *In* "Psychobiology" (A. Summerfield, ed.). *Brit. Med. Bull.* 37, 199–203.

Venables, P. H. and Fletcher, R. P. (1981). The status of skin conductance recovery time: an examination of the Bundy effect. *Psychophysiology* 18, 10–16.

Venables, P. H. and Christie, M. J. (1973). Mechanisms, instrumentation, recording techniques and quantification of responses. *In* "Electrodermal Activity in Psychological Research" (W. F. Prokasy and D. C. Raskin, eds). Academic Press, New York and London.

Venables, P. H., Fletcher, R. P., Mednick, S. A., Schulsinger, F. and Cheeneebash, R. (1984). Aspects of development of electrodermal and cardiac activity between 5 and 25 years. In preparation.

Wagner, A. R. (1976). Priming in STM: An information processing, mechanism for self-generated or retrieval generated depression in performance. *In* "Habituation. Perspectives from Child Development, Animal Behaviour and Neurophysiology" (J. J. Tighe and R. N. Leaton, eds). Erlbaum, Hillsdale, New Jersey.

Wilcott, R. C. and Bradley, H. H. (1970). Low frequency electrical stimulation of the cat's anterior cortex and inhibition of skin potential responses. *J. Comp. Physiol. Psychol.* 72, 351–355.

Wing, J. K., Cooper, J. E. and Sartorius, N. (1974). "The Measurement and Classification of Psychiatric Symptoms" Cambridge University Press, London.

Zahn, T. P. (1976). On the bimodality of the distribution of electrodermal orienting responses in schizophrenic patients. *J. Nerv. Ment. Dis.* 162, 195–199.

Zahn, T. P. (1977). Autonomic nervous system characteristics possibly related to a genetic predisposition to schizophrenia. *Schizophrenia Bull.* 3, 49–60.

Zahn, T. P. (1978). Sensitivity of measurement and electrodermal "nonresponding" in schizophrenic and normal subjects. *Schizophrenia Bull.* 4, 153.

Zahn, T. P., Rosenthal, D. and Lawlor, W. G. (1968). Electrodermal and heart rate orienting reactions in chronic schizophrenia. *J. Psychiat. Res.* 6, 117–134.

Zahn, T. P., Carpenter, W. T. and McGlashan, T. H. (1975). Autonomic variables related to short-term outcome in acute schizophrenic patients. Paper presented to Society of Psychophysiological Research, Toronto.

Zihl, J., Tretter, F. and Singer, W. (1980). Phasic electrodermal responses after visual stimulation in the cortically blind hemifield. *Behav. Brain Res.* 1, 197–203.

14 Biofeedback in Theory and Practice

J. Beatty

Abstract What is biofeedback? In many kinds of systems, both man-made and biological, the return of information to the system concerning its output or performance is an important influence in controlling the future behaviour of that system (Beatty and Legewie, 1977). This returning information is feedback. Biofeedback is a term coined in the 1960s, and refers to the presentation of information to an organism concerning some aspect of its physiology. Biofeedback has come to refer to methods for learning to control internal physiological events using immediate feedback from electronic sensing devices, with the intention of producing significant changes in bodily function. There have been claims that one might learn to cure hypertension by voluntarily lowering blood pressure, or learn to stop migraine headaches by using biofeedback to reduce extracranial blood flow and improve vascular tone. All this is the promise of using simple principles of learning theory to obtain control of previously uncontrolled or dysfunctional physiological systems (Miller, 1969). Just how much of this image is fact and how much is fiction is the topic of this chapter.

I. Visceral Learning: some historical background

The idea that biofeedback might be useful in modifying the activity of physiological systems stemmed from a series of exciting, and now quite controversial, experiments performed by Neal Miller and his students. They attempted to demonstrate a common type of learning for both the skeletal musculature and the visceral functions (Miller, 1969). Miller was challenging the widely held view that visceral functions, such as heart rate, blood pressure, vasomotor tone, gastrointestinal activity, renal function, etc, could only be classically, not operantly, conditioned.

Pavlov's famous dogs provide an example of classical conditioning of a visceral function, saliva excretion. In classical conditioning, an unconditioned reinforcing stimulus, such as meat powder, is employed that automatically elicits the desired response, here salivation, without training. By pairing a previously neutral stimulus, such as a ringing bell, with the uncon-

PHYSIOLOGICAL CORRELATES OF HUMAN
BEHAVIOUR   ISBN 0-12-273901-9

ditioned stimulus, the meat powder, the animal will slowly learn to salivate to the sound of the bell alone, a so-called conditioned response. The range of behaviours that might be learned by classical conditioning is quite limited; it is necessary to find an appropriate unconditioned stimulus that already elicits the desired response before conditioning can be undertaken.

In contrast, operant or instrumental conditioning is a flexible method well suited to learning of responses by our skeletal musculature, the organs that directly affect our interactions with the environment. In instrumental conditioning, a reinforcement or reward is employed that has the property of strengthening any immediately proceeding response. Thus, one might train a dog to jump through a hoop by first giving meat powder as he approaches the hoop, then when he touches it, and finally, only when he jumps through. This graduated procedure is termed shaping, and is a useful way of operantly training successive approximations to the desired behaviour. It is easy to see that operant conditioning is in many ways a more powerful procedure than classical conditioning. Operant methods allow the acquisition of novel behavioural acts.

Much of the current interest in biofeedback was generated by Miller's argument that operant procedures could be used to train visceral responses, that is, that a common principle of learning extends to the visceral or autonomic nervous system as well as to the skeletal system. The implications of his hypothesis are far reaching, in that it not only suggests a powerful explanation for the development of psychosomatic disorders (that they may be operantly conditioned by unknown environmental reinforcing contingencies) but also a new and potentially powerful method for their treatment, the retraining of bodily responses by operant conditioning.

A major problem in testing the idea that visceral events can be operantly conditioned is the fact that activities in the somatic or skeletal musculature exert profound effects on the viscera. Just as heart rate increases when running up stairs, so can other, less obvious, types of motor responses induce changes in visceral functions. Therefore, precautions must be taken when testing for operant conditioning effects on visceral responses to be sure that any observed effects are not simply consequences of accidental operant conditioning of unknown skeletal responses. This is one form of the question of response mediation. Miller and his students tried to solve this problem by using the drug curare, which selectively paralyses the skeletal musculature while leaving the muscles of the autonomic system unaffected. They reasoned that, in an animal whose skeletal muscles are completely blocked by curare, any effect of operant conditioning procedures on visceral variables, such as heart rate or blood pressure, must represent genuine instances of instrumental visceral learning.

The initial experiments were highly successful. It appeared that operant procedures do modify visceral responses as predicted. Moreover, the learning appeared not only to be sizeable in magnitude, but remarkably specific as well. In these initial experiments using curarized rats, there was evidence that training to raise or lower heart rate produced the expected changes in heart rate without affecting other aspects of cardiovascular functioning (Miller and DiCara, 1967). Parallel studies showed similar specificity for blood pressure conditioning (DiCara and Miller, 1968a). Other papers demonstrated learned control of renal blood flow and even specific regulation of blood flow in the ears of the rat: increasing flow in one ear and decreasing it in the other (DiCara and Miller, 1968b). All of these results had major implications not only for learning theory, but for physiology and medicine as well.

When these data became known to psychologists and psychiatrists in the late 1960s, it appeared that the foundations were firmly laid for a new approach to behavioural psychosomatic medicine. The implications of Miller's experiments were not lost on the clinical community. Biofeedback appeared to provide a much needed tool for the treatment of cardiovascular and, particularly, stress-related disorders. For these reasons, the clinical use of biofeedback methods grew rapidly in the early 1970s. However, this rush to therapeutic application was premature. There were troubles with the early experiments, difficulties that emerged as experiments were repeated, both in Miller's laboratories and elsewhere. Only the initial experiments provided clear evidence for instrumental visceral learning. In each succeeding experiment, the size of the learned response inexplicably decreased. By the early 1970s, it was impossible to obtain evidence of instrumental conditioning of visceral responses in curarized animals. These increasing failures to replicate or reproduce the original results were disquieting. A number of procedures were employed to resurrect the original phenomenon, but none succeeded. Miller, in a review published a decade after his original work in the field, was led to the conclusion that "in the face of the much more extensive, careful studies that have failed to replicate the results of the original ones, it is prudent not to rely on any of the experiments on curarized animals for evidence on the instrumental learning of visceral responses" (Miller, 1978, p. 376).

Unfortunately, the exclusion of the curare data leaves the issue of instrumental visceral conditioning in a precarious state, since the question of somatic mediation still must be resolved in some manner. And it is to that crucial question that we now turn our attention.

II. Skeletal Mediation of Operant Visceral Conditioning Effects

The curarized animal seemed an ideal control for simple skeletal motor mediation of visceral responses in testing for operant visceral learning, because any direct mechanical effect of skeletal muscle activation could be eliminated, at least in principle. There are several ways in which a subject being tested for visceral learning might produce the desired responses by use of his skeletal musculature, either with or without explicit awareness on the part of the learner. For example, many biological sensors are accurate only when placed in an exactly correct position, as is the case for mechanical sensors of arterial pulsation. A slight movement or displacement of the sensor results in a marked loss in sensitivity. Thus, when attempting to reduce blood flow in a particular region, mechanically shifting the position of the sensor would yield data that appear to reflect decreased flow and therefore conditioning, but in fact reflect only an experimental artifact unintentionally introduced by the learner.

Other types of skeletal mediation are more biological in nature, but nonetheless provide false indications of visceral learning. Small changes in skeletal muscle tension can induce a variety of variations in cardiovascular variables, including heart rate, blood pressure and peripheral circulation. If attempts to operantly condition one or several of these parameters result in the desired changes, but these changes are actually a direct result of shifting patterns of skeletal motor activity, no true evidence of visceral learning has been obtained. In this context, it might be mentioned that early reports of Indian Yogis being able to stop then restart their own heart beat were the result of a simple skeletal motor procedure called the val salva manoeuvre. This manoeuvre is accomplished by holding the breath and increasing pressure within the chest cavity by tightening the diaphragm, until the intra-thoracic pressure exceeds that produced by cardiac contraction. Under these conditions, the heart continues to beat but at a pressure insufficient to force the venous return of blood to the heart; therefore no blood moves. Since it is the movement of blood through the arteries that produces the sound of the heartbeat, the val salva manoeuvre stops heart sounds but not heart beat. This is an extreme example, but it must be taken seriously. The use of the val salva manoeuvre escaped the detection of a distinguished French cardiologist and Yogic heart stopping was reported as fact in the medical literature for over a decade. Unfortunately, the possible mediating effects of the skeletal musculature are many and devious, severely taxing the ingenuity of the investigator to devise a convincing demonstration that any learned change in visceral function is not simply a consequence of relatively uninteresting changes in skeletal motor activity (Miller and Dworkin, 1977).

More complicated problems arise when issues concerning the central integration of skeletal and visceral functions are considered, and here even the curarized animal could not help disentangle the skeletal component (Obrist, et al., 1974). It is widely believed that many sorts of visceral and skeletal events are coordinated at higher levels of the central nervous system. Evidence for such a view comes from demonstrations that an attempt to move a paralysed arm results in no movement, but produces appropriate changes in heart rate and blood pressure. These changes may be introduced by brain motor systems in advance of the actual movement in order to assure adequate vascular support for the intended motor action. But such issues are really beside the point when evaluating the present evidence for operant visceral learning: the more primitive, muscular types of skeletal motor mediation have yet to be ruled out.

Thus, the idea that visceral events may be operantly controlled is far from demonstrated. The evidence presently available, from basic experimental studies, is contradictory at best. There is simply very little data that would lead one to conclude that the old view of autonomic events as being refractory to instrumental conditioning is wrong. Yet it is precisely the assumption that instrumental visceral learning is possible which provides the scientific basis for much of the biofeedback therapy seen in psychological clinics today. It is for this reason that the question of skeletal mediation is so important.

III. Learned Control of Central Nervous System Events

Another area of basic research using biofeedback method is the learned control of signs of central nervous system activity and its effects on behaviour. Here also the focus of interest has shifted over the short lifetime of biofeedback research. Much of the original work was concerned with operant control of human alpha activity, a regular 10 cycle per second wave that occurs frequently in electroencephalographic recordings taken from the posterior regions of the human scalp. Alpha activity in humans is largest over visual cortex and may be blocked fairly reliably by presentation of visual stimuli. For this reason, alpha activity is more abundant with the eyes closed and in darkness (Adrian, 1944).

An early interest in alpha activity and its enhancement by biofeedback methods was based on the observation that some meditators showed increased levels of alpha activity while meditating. This observation led to the conjecture that by learning to increase alpha activity one might achieve a central state like that of an experienced meditator. Alpha biofeedback training was viewed by some as a technologically advanced method of achieving an altered inner mental state (Kamiya, 1969).

It is not difficult to see the problems with such logic. Most obvious is the assumption that an increase in alpha activity physiologically defines a unique mental state. If such an hypothesis were true, then dimming the lights should produce more profound psychic effects than actually occur in most of us. Still, the hypothesis was testable, and a number of attempts were undertaken to demonstrate the psychological consequences of regulated alpha activity. The net result of this work was quite clear: controlling alpha activity had no consistent effects on self-reported mental state (Beatty, 1977). Nonetheless, this failure to show any evidence for alpha-induced meditative states had little effect on the sale of alpha biofeedback machines to an eager, if somewhat gullible, public.

In this context, it is interesting to note that although operant procedures can be used to increase or decrease the abundance of alpha frequency EEG activity in the appropriate directions, these effects can also be obtained by simple instructions without the use of feedback procedures (Beatty, 1972). Similar results have been noted when comparing feedback and instructions on the control of heart rate in normal human volunteers. Thus, the idea that the mere use of operant procedures produces operant learning is not something that can be accepted at face value. As always, when dealing with a poorly understood phenomenon or set of phenomena, the use of appropriate control procedures can often be revealing.

Other attempts to utilize operant training procedures to study brain/behaviour relationships have met with more success. One example involves the posterior theta rhythms, a low voltage 4 to 7 cycle per second irregular waveform that characteristically marks the transition between waking and sleeping in the human nervous system. Operant procedures have been used to increase or decrease the power of theta frequency activity in normal volunteers with reasonable success; individuals reinforced for increasing theta frequency activity do so, whereas those reinforced for the opposite contingency show the reverse pattern. In this work, the question of mediation, while interesting, is far less crucial. No claim is being made that the measured responses themselves are the object of conditioning, as was the case in visceral learning. The contention is only that, by reinforcing changes in one reliable indicator of systemic arousal, the value of that indicator may be modified in an orderly fashion.

Are such changes in theta activity of behavioural consequence? Apparently not, under the normal conditions of daily life. Volunteers trained to regulate theta activity for short periods of time report no unusual subjective phenomena. However, the effects of learned control are important in arousal-sensitive situations. Under monotonous monitoring conditions, as when watching a radar display for a prolonged period in search of infrequent targets, the control of the posterior theta rhythms becomes behaviourally significant; augmenting theta induces a profound deterioration of detection performance whereas suppressing theta activity maintains detection ability at alerted levels (Beatty et al., 1974). The mechanism by which alertness is maintained under such circumstances is only poorly understood.

Thus, there is some good evidence that operant procedures can induce systematic and predictable changes in electrical indicators of central nervous system function. Whether or not these changes represent instrumental conditioning of the brain rhythms is beyond the scope of available data. Nonetheless, biofeedback procedures may provide a useful tool in some instances for the investigation of central nervous system functions.

IV. Evaluating Biofeedback as a Clinical Treatment

In evaluating the use of biofeedback methods as treatment for any disorder, disease or dysfunction, a number of questions must be answered. Some are by now familiar, such as the problem of a mediating mechanism. If the nature of the process by which a procedure, such as biofeedback, effects its action is known, a more rational judgement concerning its use as a therapeutic intervention may be made. Such is the case in the best examples of clinical medicine, but it is not yet possible in evaluating any biofeedback procedure directed towards visceral or central nervous system function. Knowing why a procedure may work is important knowledge, if only that it suggests the range of useful application and perhaps indicates some conditions under which the treatment might be inappropriate.

Yet it is often said that it is not necessary in medicine to know why a treatment works, only that it does work. Such a proposition cannot be wholly true, given the benefits of understanding the therapeutic mechanism mentioned above. Nonetheless, it is important, and surprisingly difficult, to disentangle the beneficial effects of a particular treatment from several other factors present in the context of clinical evaluation. A clear and critical determination of clinical effectiveness must distinguish between treatment-specific and other, more general, effects in evaluating any therapeutic intervention, including the clinical use of biofeedback.

Perhaps the most difficult problem in evaluating any particular therapeutic procedure derives from the fact that few disorders are permanent; most disease processes have a particular and usual course and show spontaneous recovery or remission. Worse yet for analysis purposes, many disorders are sporadic – they simply come and go rather unpredictably. This means that the condition of the patient following some therapeutic intervention may not depend simply upon the treatment, but upon other factors that vary with time. The fact that the body tends to heal itself and that disorders tend to be transitory means that great care must be taken in evaluating any particular treatment.

These problems are even more exaggerated in a clinical setting. People tend to seek help when they are feeling worse; the very time that patients present themselves for treatment is likely to be the time at which the disorder is most disabling. One implication of this non-random sampling of patients for treatment is that, given time, the disorder is much more likely to diminish rather than progress. Statisticians call this situation an example of regression toward the mean. It is a serious problem in treatment evaluation and is one reason why controlled group studies are necessary in assessing treatment efficacy. One type of control for these remission and regression effects is the waiting list control procedure, if ethically defensible. By randomly assigning some patients to a treatment group and others to a waiting list for later treatment, any improvement shown by the controls represents the beneficial effects of time, not treatment, whereas the improvement shown by the treatment group(s) reflect both factors. This is just one issue, but a major issue, in the critical evaluation of clinical treatment, including biofeedback treatments.

A second issue is the magical effect of being treated, as distinct from the specific therapeutic benefits produced by the therapy. These placebo effects, as they are called, may not be trivial; under the proper conditions they may give the impression of an impressive recovery. But placebo effects are never long lasting, so that the illusion of recovery from a placebo treatment is transitory. Today, a fair amount is known about factors governing placebo effects in treatment, but rather little is known about the physiological mechanisms through which these short-term beneficial effects are mediated (Stroebel and Glueck, 1973). First, placebo effects, being products of social interaction, grow with the authority of the practitioner and the impressiveness of the treatment procedure. In this respect, biofeedback methods might be expected to elicit large placebo effects, in that the machinery often used appears complex and sophisticated. Shiny biofeedback devices may appear to represent to the patient the very promise of modern technology to cure age-old problems of disease and ill health. Second, the size of the placebo effect has been shown to increase with the enthusiasm of the practitioner. It is for this reason that common medical cynicism holds that every new treatment works at least for a few years, while those who believe in the method are testing it on their patients. There is certainly no lack of enthusiasm among contemporary therapists who utilize biofeedback procedures in treating their clients. Finally, the degree of benefit obtained from a placebo treatment increases with the cost that the patient must pay to receive the new therapy. In some sense, the human psyche seems to insist on getting its money's worth. All of these factors contribute to the production of a placebo effect in biofeedback therapy.

To properly evaluate a particular biofeedback therapy for a particular class of disorders, both remission/regression and placebo factors must be experimentally controlled. Unfortunately, remarkably few published clinical research efforts meet even the rudimentary standards for scientific treatment evaluation. These research efforts fall into several categories.

(i) *Anecdotal case reports* In these extended treatment notes there is no attempt to account for remission/regression or placebo effects. For this reason, they contribute almost nothing toward rational treatment evaluation. Unfortunately, such reports are reasonably common in the biofeedback literature.

(ii) *Systematic case reports* These reports make a gesture toward quantitative evaluation, in that pre-treatment baseline data are obtained against which treatment effects may be contrasted. But such designs are more deceptive than useful, in that they offer no help in assessing the specific effects of the treatment.

(iii) *Single group outcome studies* These reports are like the systematic case reports, but report data from more than one patient. Such designs offer the illusion of scientific evaluation, in that conventional statistics may be computed to describe the reliability of change, but offer no help in distinguishing between general and specific treatment effects.

(iv) *Controlled group outcome studies* Controlled group studies, in which two or more experimentally defined procedures are compared, constitute the minimum formal requirement for scientific treatment evaluation. The actual value of any particular study is a function of the appropriateness of the factors varied between the several groups. Thus, if an experimental treatment group and a waiting list control group are employed, the data obtained would be relevant to the question of the effects of remission/regression, but not to the issue of placebo effects in treatment. If two treatments are contrasted, one the experimental treatment and the other a procedure known to be ineffective, the intention of the study might be to exclude the effects of placebo from that of the experimental treatment. Here, problems may arise from the dependence of the placebo effect on the impressiveness of the treatment. If the control condition is unimpressive, or if offered unenthusiastically, differences in the effectiveness of the two treatments may only reflect differing strengths of the placebo effect between groups. These are important issues, and ones that may only be resolved in the context of a particular problem. It is distressing to note that very little of the published literature on biofeedback treatment reports between-group comparisons of any sort.

(v) *Double-blind controlled outcome group studies* These types of investigations are among the clearest possible in assessing the specific effects of therapeutic treatments. They involve testing two or more groups of randomly assigned patients in which neither patient nor therapist knows

which treatment is administered to which patient. Double-blind evalua-
tions are routinely used in pharmacological research and are possible
in biofeedback research as well, although they are seldom actually
employed. The fact that not even the therapist knows which treatment
he is administering is an attempt to assure that the placebo effects will
not differ between groups. However, even here there can be problems. In
pharmacological studies, if the experimental drug produces subjectively
detectable sensations (e.g., flushing, nausea, tremors) and the placebo
does not, the best laid plans for a double blind experiment may be foiled.
It is not uncommon, particularly when the study is conducted in a
hospital ward, for all the patients to know who is receiving the active
treatment while all the staff remain blind to the treatment conditions. In
such cases, a powerful placebo effect may be operating selectively in the
experimental condition despite the attempt to achieve double blind
control.

There are no formulae for perfectly controlled evaluation studies. There are
only guidelines drawn from experience and the use of careful logic in experimental design. The purpose of any treatment evaluation study is to distinguish between any specific treatment effects, should they exist, and other
non-specific factors. With this principle in mind, we now briefly summarize
the clinical studies of biofeedback as behavioural medicine.

V. Clinical Applications of Biofeedback

It has been more than a decade since biofeedback methods were first applied
to the treatment of clinical disorder. Biofeedback therapies have received
widespread attention and have become increasingly popular. Nonetheless,
there is very little solid evidence that these procedures constitute effective
therapy. In evaluating clinical research in several areas, we will adopt a
standard clinical criterion for the acceptance of a treatment: is the new
procedure better (in any sense) than the best available, commonly accepted
treatment for the disorder. Judging the published data, it is difficult to justify
the continued clinical application of biofeedback in most instances.

A. Hypertension

Hypertension is a physiological state in which elevated blood pressure places
the hypertensive individual at risk for a variety of specific disorders.
Hypertension can result from definite pathological processes, such as kidney
dysfunction, or may arise for unknown reasons, in which case the hyperten-

sion is said to be essential. A number of treatments are available for essential hypertension, the most dramatically successful of which are pharmacological. However, dietary changes and stress management regimens may also be therapeutically important (see Chapter 11 by Warwick-Evans).

Because of the early animal work on blood pressure conditioning, it is not surprising that essential hypertension should provide an initial and enduring focus for cardiovascular biofeedback therapy (DiCara and Miller, 1968a). It would seem reasonable that a patient might be trained to lower his resting blood pressure and thereby effect a treatment without the complicating side effects often associated with pharmacological therapy. Unfortunately, the accumulated data do not support this early hope. Despite a number of concerted attempts to produce large stable reductions in diastolic blood pressure, only relatively small (5–15 mm Hg), variable decreases have been obtained. Moreover, in the few comparative studies available, the biofeedback treatments have been neither more nor less effective than a variety of other non-specific treatments, like relaxation, psychotherapy, hypnosis and placebo therapy (Legewie, 1977). Thus, there is little reason to suggest that operant training is a useful approach to the treatment of essential hypertension.

B. *Migraine Headache*

Migraine is a painful disorder of the arteries of the head, primarily those outside the cranial cavity. No one really understands the mechanism by which a migraine is triggered, but the result is a marked loss of tone or strength in the arterial walls. As a result, the arteries expand dramatically as each heart beat forces a wave of blood through this flaccid vasculature. Since the extracranial arteries lack the tone necessary to withstand the pressure wave, they are momentarily stretched, producing the initial, pulsatile pain of a migraine headache. The fault, however, is not in the arteries themselves, but rather in the neuronal systems that control cardiovascular tone.

In treating migraine, the most successful pharmacological treatments act to increase vasomotor tone, thereby constricting the extracranial arteries and preventing the painful distension that results in headache. However, the agents that are most effective in restoring vasomotor tone, primarily derivatives of ergotamine alkaloids, have a number of unpleasant side effects. Some people prefer the headache to the discomfort of the cure. For this reason, a behavioural method of specifically inducing extracranial vasoconstriction would represent a significant advance in the treatment of migraine headache.

The early evidence of learned control of vasomotor tone in curarized animals offered the promise of a rational, behavioural treatment for migraine, but this promise has remained unfulfilled (DiCara and Miller,

1968b). In one of few controlled studies that attempted to train vasoconstriction of the extracranial arteries, there was some evidence of a specific effect of training on vasomotor tone (Friar and Beatty, 1976). However, the size of these effects was too small to suggest that the procedure would be clinically useful.

Most attempts to use operant procedures to treat migraine have taken a less direct approach, primarily for experimental ease. Migraine headache is often accompanied by an extreme peripheral vasoconstriction, at the same time as the extracranial arteries are dilated. Thus, the hands of a migraine patient are often cold and cyanosed during the period of the headache. This suggested to some workers that trained hand warming might lead to suppression of migraine headache. (By the way, warming the hands in a basin of water does not alter migraine headache.) However, evidence for learned hand warming in treating migraine is not positive. For example, a large recent controlled study compared learned hand warming and a number of other control procedures. Little support for the efficacy of the treatment was found; the physiological effects were very small and unrelated to headache outcome (Cohen *et al.*, 1980). Similar results have been obtained in the other, well-controlled studies of learned hand warming treatment of migraine headache (Jessup *et al.*, 1979).

C. *Muscle Tension Headache*

In contrast to the vascular origin in migraine, it is the muscles of the forehead and neck that are the sites of tension headache. Relaxation of these muscles removes the source of the tension headache. Thus, a reasonable behavioural approach to the treatment of tension headache would be to record the level of muscular activation at the site of headache and train the patient to reduce this level, resulting in muscular relaxation. Electrically recording muscular activation is a simple procedure, and biofeedback trainers for electromyographic (EMG) activity have been widely used in treating tension headache. When compared with no-treatment or other non-therapeutic control groups, the effects of EMG biofeedback on muscle tension and muscle tension headache have been consistent and positive. Biofeedback training reliably has beneficial effects on tension headache.

But when compared against other types of treatment, these results are less impressive. When EMG biofeedback for tension headaches is compared with simple relaxation instructions, the instructional procedures are consistently as effective as biofeedback and, like biofeedback, superior to control conditions (Jessup, *et al.*, 1979). Thus, the external biofeedback component appears to be unnecessary in achieving behavioural treatment in patients with tension headache.

VI. Some Conclusions

Both the experimental and clinical results summarized above provide a disappointing realization of a field once bright with promise. Nonetheless, the story of biofeedback is instructive. It illustrates the importance of experimental test in the development of science, and it provides an example of the self-corrective nature of the scientific enterprise; when initial positive results could not be replicated, more extensive and detailed tests were undertaken to help clarify the question of the instrumental visceral learning. Gradually, scientific opinion has returned to the view that there may be fundamental differences in the ways in which the environment produces plastic change in skeletal and visceral responses. Such a conclusion has serious consequences for the continued use of biofeedback methods in clinical settings.

Further Reading

Beatty, J. and Legewie, H. (1977). "Biofeedback and Behaviour". Plenum, New York. This volume is the published proceedings of an international conference on biofeedback held in Munich. It contains contributions by nearly all major researchers active at that time.

Miller, N. E. (1978). Biofeedback and visceral learning. *A. Rev. Psychol.* **29**, 373–404. This article provides a critical re-evaluation of the question of visceral learning after a decade of research.

Schwartz, G. E. and Beatty, J. (1977). "Biofeedback: Theory and Research". Academic Press, New York and London. This was planned to provide a comprehensive overview of the area of biofeedback, with chapters contributed by major workers.

Yates, A. J. (1980). "Biofeedback and the Modification of Behaviour". Plenum, New York. A recent critical review of biofeedback as therapy.

References

Adrian, E. D. (1944). Brain rhythm. *Nature.* **153**, 360–362.

Beatty, J. (1972). Similar effects of feedback signals and instructional information of EEG activity. *Physiol. Behav.* **9**, 151–154.

Beatty, J. (1977). Contributions of biofeedback methods to the understanding of visceral and central nervous system functions. *In* "Biofeedback and Behaviour" (J. Beatty and H. Legewie, eds). Plenum, New York.

Beatty, J. and Legewie, H. (1977). "Biofeedback and Behaviour" Plenum, New York.

Beatty, J., Greenberg, A., Diebler, W. P. and O'Hanlon, J. F. (1974). Operant control of occipital theta rhythm affects performance in a radar monitoring task. *Science* **183**, 871–873.

Cohen, M. J., McArthur, D. L. and Rickles, W. H. (1980). Comparison of four biofeedback treatments for migraine headache: Physiological and headache variables. *Psychosom. Med.* **42**, 463–480.

DiCara, L. V. and Miller, N. E. (1968a). Instrumental learning of systolic blood pressure responses by curarized rats: dissociation of cardiac and vascular changes. *Psychosom. Med.* **30**, 489–494.

DiCara, L. V. and Miller, N. E. (1968b). Instrumental learning of vasomotor responses by rats: learning to respond differentially in the two ears. *Science* **159**, 1485–1486.

Friar, L. R. and Beatty, J. (1976). Migraine: management by trained control of vasoconstriction. *J. Consult. Clin. Psychol.* **44**, 46–53.

Jessup, B. A., Neufeld, R. W. J. and Merskey, H. (1979). Biofeedback therapy for headache and other pain: an evaluative review. *Pain* **7**, 225–270.

Kamiya, J. (1969). Operant control of the EEG rhythm and some of its reported effects on consciousness. *In* "Altered States of Consciousness" (C. Tart, ed.). Wiley, New York.

Legewie, H. (1977). Clinical implications of biofeedback. *In* "Biofeedback and Behaviour" (J. Beatty and H. Legewie, eds). Plenum, New York.

Miller, N. E. (1969). Learning of visceral and glandular responses. *Science* **163**, 434–445.

Miller, N. E. (1978). Biofeedback and visceral learning. *A. Rev. Psychol.* **29**, 373–404.

Miller, N. E. and DiCara, L. V. (1967). Instrumental learning of heart rate changes in curarized rats: shaping and specificity to discriminative stimulus. *J. Comp. Physiol. Psychol.* **63**, 12–19.

Miller, N. E. and Dworkin, B. R. (1977). Critical issues in therapeutic applications of biofeedback. *In* "Biofeedback: Theory and Research" (G. E. Schwartz and J. Beatty, eds). Academic Press, New York and London.

Obrist, P. A., Black, A. H., Brener, J. and DiCara, L. V. (1974). "Cardiovascular Psychophysiology". Aldine, Chicago.

Stroebel, C. F. and Glueck, B. C. (1973). Biofeedback treatment in medicine and psychiatry: An ultimate placebo? *In* "Biofeedback: Behavioural Medicine". Grune and Stratton, New York.

15 Psychophysiological Contributions to Psychotherapy Research: a Systems Perspective

*P. Crits-Christoph
and G. E. Schwartz*

Abstract As part of a growing interest in the psychobiological foundations of human behaviour, psychotherapists have become increasingly interested in the application of psychophysiological approaches to intervention. Therapies as diverse as psycho-dynamically oriented psychotherapy, behaviour modification, biofeedback, autogenic training, hypnosis, feeling therapy and progressive relaxation have all been used clinically or experimentally in conjunction with some form of psychophysiological assessment or treatment.

This spurt of interest in psychobiology as it applies to psychotherapy is seen in several recent developments within psychology and medicine. Formal training in clinical psychophysiology is now offered in a substantial number of graduate programmes in clinical psychology and clinical internships in the United States (Feuerstein and Schwartz, 1977). The establishment of the interdisciplinary field of behavioural medicine, and the new sub-discipline of health psychology, within the last few years, has provided conferences and journals as an outlet for research and theory concerned with the interface of biology and behaviour change. A new "biopsycho-social" orientation towards traditionally medical or psychiatric disorders has been proposed (Engel, 1977; Leigh and Reiser, 1980), integrating biological, psychological and social dimensions of health and illness.

This chapter will review the current status of the contribution of psychophysiology to the field of psychotherapy. The focus will be on the more recent theoretical and empirical advances in this area, with an emphasis on a general systems, psycho-biological perspective on psychotherapy (Schwartz, 1978). The problems and limita-tions of a psychophysiological view of psychotherapy will be explored and speculation about the potential future course of this topic will be presented.

I. Conceptual Issues

The scientific study of psychotherapy and behaviour change from a psychophysiological perspective has been hindered by a number of factors.

PHYSIOLOGICAL CORRELATES OF HUMAN
BEHAVIOUR   ISBN 0-12-273901-9

One major problem has been the practical difficulties associated with monitoring physiological variables during psychotherapy. In addition to the expense of instrumentation, the process of attaching electrodes on different parts of a patient's body is rather intrusive. Thus, many clinicians have felt that physiological monitoring interferes with the normal therapy process. Technological advances bearing on this issue will be discussed later in this chapter.

The lack of a conceptual framework which would allow an integration of knowledge from psychophysiology and psychotherapy has also been a stumbling block. Two frequently cited and interrelated barriers to integration of knowledge from these fields are the mind/body issue and the specialization of disciplines and professions in their training, language, and domains of interest.

Schwartz (1977, 1978) has proposed that there is a fundamental property of the brain that has contributed to the creation of the classical mind/body dichotomy and consequently has interfered with the development of a psychobiological view of psychotherapy and behaviour change. He has termed this property "the brain self-regulation paradox." Briefly, Schwartz has proposed that the brain has evolved to process information in three-dimensional space, with the goal of localizing stimuli in the environment or in the body as being "external" to the brain. Consequently, the brain has no direct awareness that it is involved in the construction of conscious experience and is fundamentally responsible for the regulation of bodily processes as well as imagery and emotion.

Lacking direct conscious experience of these essential neuropsychological processes, therapists and clients alike erroneously conclude that they directly control their "hands" or their "thoughts" rather than control the neural processes in their brains. As Powers (1973) points out, the control of behaviour is actually a side effect of the control of perception, and the latter is *constructed* by the brain via processes that are not accessible to direct awareness. This normal tendency to *experience* control of both mind and body as being independent of the control of the brain strongly interferes with our ability to view overt behaviour and subjective experience as manifestations of integrated, psychobiological processes. Since body and mind are subjectively experienced as being relatively separate entities (and not connected by the brain), this has promoted the separation of the biological and behavioural sciences, including the specific separation of physiological research from research on psychotherapy.

The specialization of disciplines and training of professions has traditionally encouraged the separation of psychotherapy from psychophysiology. In the past, psychotherapists rarely have had any training in recording and interpreting psychophysiological data. Likewise, experts in psychophysiology have confined most of their activities to laboratory experimentation on non-clinical populations. As a consequence of specialized training, limited theories of the aetiology and treatment of "disease" and "mental illness" have been propagated within each discipline. For example, the traditional medical model has ignored behavioural and psychological effects and most psychological theories have ignored knowledge from the biological sciences.

Psychophysiology as it applies to psychotherapy has been defined in certain restricted ways because of the above issues. For example, sometimes psychophysiology is defined in terms of its methods or procedures: if one uses electronic equipment to monitor physiological processes, one is practising the techniques of psychophysiology. The artificiality of this definition was discussed by Schwartz (1978), using the measurement of eye movements as an example.

> If a therapist asks a patient the following question: "Picture your father's face. What emotion strikes you?" and notes that the patient's eyes move to the left while reflecting on the answer, the eye movement is defined as "behaviour" and is typically the province of psychology. . . . However, the therapist who wanted to obtain a more complete and accurate measure of eye movement would consider using modern procedures that extend these biological capacities for continuously monitoring and scoring signals of this sort. . . . When employing these biomedical procedures, the therapist would no longer simply be recording behaviour as a psychologist, but rather would be recording psychophysiological changes as a psychophysiologist. Note that although the theoretical questions might well be the same, the therapist's field and label could change simply because of the difference in method used (ibid., p. 65).

Psychophysiology has also been defined in terms of a desired outcome or goal for psychotherapy. The field of psychosomatic medicine has used this approach. For instance, patients with specific psychophysiological disorders such as headaches or hypertension might be monitored physiologically during therapy in order to document improvement.

A different definition of psychophysiology has been espoused by Schwartz (1978). He suggests that psychophysiology as it relates to behaviour can be viewed in terms of its underlying mechanisms. This functional definition allows one to view all behaviours as having psychophysiological components. Behaviour and physiology are not separate, but rather are different levels of analysis of the same system. Thus, if one takes this perspective, psychotherapy is ultimately biotherapy. Applying psychophysiology to psychotherapy is not simply using certain methods of measuring certain outcomes, but it is a frame of mind, a level of analysis of the phenomenon of interest.

An important book by Miller (1978), *Living Systems*, provides a comprehensive meta-theory which clarifies the conceptual issues involved in multi-level problems. This theory has been applied to the field of behavioural medicine by Schwartz (1980). A complete description of Miller's theory is beyond the scope of this chapter; however, certain key concepts can be extracted that have obvious relevance to our topic.

Deriving his principles from general systems theory (von Bertalanffy, 1968), Miller outlines seven different levels of living systems – cellular, organ, organism, group, organization, societal and supranational. According to Miller, there must be nineteen different functional subsystems present at each level in order for the system to be a healthy, living system. The theory is designed so that each level can be discussed using the same language and concepts. This ability to translate across levels allows one to use living systems theory to integrate theory and research across multiple disciplines: a necessary condition for a psychobiological perspective on psychotherapy.

Another key concept in living systems theory is the notion of emergence and interaction. The properties of a system at a given level emerge out of the interactions of the components comprising the system. No one component equals the whole system. Thus, for example, the response of an organ (e.g. the heart) to a stressful situation cannot be expected to equal (correlate 100% with) the response of the organism at another level (e.g. subjective experience of emotion by the organism). Only when multiple variables (patterns of variables) at each level are examined can we describe how one level influences another. Studies examining the physiological correlates of emotional reactions during psychotherapy have typically failed to address this issue.

Miller (1978) also explains the importance of feedback mechanisms and the role they play in a self-regulating system. Feedback mechanisms are inherent in all systems that attempt to maintain their variables in homeostatic balance. The breakdown of appropriate negative feedback loops has been described by Schwartz (1977) as leading to a state of "disregulation." Such a breakdown in feedback loops is seen, for example, with the psychological defence mechanism of repression. Repressors learn to block out of consciousness symptoms of anxiety and pain (feedback from peripheral organs to the brain). As a result of not attending to these important feedback cues, the person may remain in the stressful environment, placing continued strain on his body, instead of generating more adaptive, health-oriented behaviour. In systems terms, a therapist's goal with such a patient, therefore, might be to facilitate the reconnection of the feedback loops that are not functioning. It is for this reason that systems theorists such as Schwartz (1978) propose that biological feedback is a fundamental component, not only in psychotherapy (e.g. helping people to become better aware of their emotional states by having them correctly label their facial expressions, visceral reactions, etc.), but in all therapies requiring self-regulation of the client (e.g. taking medication).

The multi-level, multi-disciplinary view of Miller (1978), Schwartz (1980), and others appears to be necessary for a complete understanding of the role of psychophysiology within psychotherapy. This new attitude has just begun to carry over into the research realm. Accordingly, studies reported in the literature have not taken an integrative systems approach. The next section will describe some of the empirical work that has been done to date. Early studies of the psychophysiology of psychotherapy have been extensively reviewed elsewhere (Lacey, 1959; Lang, 1971) and will not be covered here. Instead, a selection of representative work over the last ten years will be discussed to give the reader an overview of the types of questions that have been addressed in the literature. Examples of research taken from diverse types of psychotherapy will be presented to illustrate the range of applications that have been attempted.

II. Empirical Developments

A. *Traditional Psychotherapy*

Most of the early research on insight-oriented or psychoanalytically oriented psychotherapy looked for physiological changes which were correlated with the expression of affect or conflicts during psychotherapy sessions (Lacey, 1959; Lang, 1971). This trend has continued to the present. Some examples are described below.

Roessler *et al.* (1975) correlated global ratings of affect intensity with eight physiological parameters over four psychotherapeutic interviews with one patient. The measure of affect intensity was obtained by instructing raters (experienced clinicians) to judge the intensity of the patient's emotional responsiveness, regardless of the specific type of emotion, for twenty second intervals from videotapes of the therapy sessions. Significant correlations were found for respiratory amplitude, respiratory rate, pulse volume, skin conductance and number of galvanic skin responses. In all cases greater affect intensity was associated with greater autonomic arousal.

McCarron (1973) investigated the relationship between speech disturbance and skin resistance response in 20 patients during psychotherapy interviews. The results indicated that a disruption in the finely coordinated motor activity of speech was significantly associated with higher amplitude skin resistance responses. Increased autonomic arousal and more speech disturbance were also found during periods when the therapist was talking. When patients were allowed to continue a sequence of verbalizations, there was a reduction in both speech disturbance and skin resistance response.

A study by Stanek *et al.* (1973) investigated the heart rates of 32 cardio-phobic patients and the interviewers during the initial psychoanalytic session. The authors report that "psychic agitation" in patients during the session manifested itself in changes in mean heart rate and variability of heart rate. They also found that concordance between patient and therapist heart rates was found during certain psychodynamically meaningful phases of the session, particularly transference–countertransference communications.

These representative studies illustrate how physiological and behavioural levels of analysis can be integrated in the therapy situation. It would be valuable in future research if an attempt was made to integrate these different levels more closely by, for example, preselecting those physiological parameters that are most directly involved in the behavioural processes of interest (e.g. selecting forearm muscle tension and diastolic blood pressure as two component processes underlying anger behaviour – see Schwartz et al., 1981).

The possibility of combining biofeedback with more traditional talking psychotherapy has been proposed by a number of writers (Legalos, 1973; Stephenson, 1976; Toomin and Toomin, 1975; Werbach, 1977). Two interesting studies have been done by Edwin (1979) and Giles (1978) and will be described here.

As an empathy-training device, Edwin (1979) used galvanic skin response biofeedback to provide clues about a client's underlying affective state to beginning psychotherapists. Twenty graduate psychology students were matched and assigned to an experimental (GSR biofeedback) or control (no client physiological information) group as therapists. The results indicated that the experimental group showed significantly greater verbal attention to client affect than the control group. Significant positive trends in "perceptual sensitivity" were also identified for the experimental group.

Giles (1978) examined the separate and combined effects of biofeedback training and brief individual psychotherapy in the treatment of gastrointestinal disorder. Forty subjects were randomly assigned to a biofeedback training group, brief individual psychotherapy, a combination of biofeedback and psychotherapy, or a waiting list control group. Subjects in the treated groups showed improved physical and emotional well-being at the end of treatment and eight-month follow-up compared to the control group. The biofeedback-only group showed superior results on symptom and relaxation variables, and the individual psychotherapy group manifested better psychiatric adjustment. The combined treatment was found to be superior to either treatment alone. Without psychotherapy, however, biofeedback was found to reinforce obsessiveness, perfectionism, and preoccupation with somatic concerns.

These studies illustrate how biofeedback can be potentially used in a creative yet focused manner to complement and extend more traditional psychotherapy. The Giles study, in particular, illustrates the concept of emergent property, since the biofeedback and verbal psychotherapy processes tended to act upon different processes, and when combined, produced a unique combination of effects. The need to examine the interactions (and, therefore, emergent properties) of different therapeutic techniques (both within and across levels, such as within psychological levels or between psychological and biological levels) is a major challenge for future psychophysiological research on psychotherapy.

B. *Behavioural Approaches*

The contribution of behaviour therapies to the role of psychophysiology in psychotherapy and behaviour change has been substantial. In particular, the development of biofeedback as a clinical intervention has brought psychophysiology directly within the realm of many behaviour therapies. Excellent reviews of research on biofeedback as treatment for a variety of disorders exist elsewhere (e.g. Ray *et al.*, 1979; Yates, 1979) and, therefore, will not be discussed here (but see Chapter 14 by Beatty).

The role of psychophysiology in relation to other behavioural treatments such as systematic desensitization and progressive muscle relaxation has also been investigated in many studies. Most of this research has been done within the context of changes in physiology as one "index" of anxiety or fear.

One notable exception, arising from a behavioural perspective, is the theory of emotional imagery and behaviour change proposed by Lang (1977, 1979). In trying to understand the effects of systematic desensitization, an imagery-based therapy, Lang has suggested that we focus on the verbal instruction given to clients concerning their fear images used in desensitization therapy. The extent to which clients follow instructions about what to imagine is the extent to which they are recreating the neural patterns suggested by the verbal instructions. More specifically, fearful images are conceptualized within this theory as propositional structures rather than "pictures in the head." These propositional structures consist of both stimulus and response components. Stimulus propositions are essentially descriptive of a scene, e.g. a black snake moving on the ground. Response propositions involve assertions about the individual's behaviour in response to the stimulus. These can involve verbal responses ("I scream"), overt motor responses ("I run away"), and/or physiological responses ("My heart is pounding").

Lang (1979) states that the response propositions play a central role in the fear process and that the way to reduce fear is to change the response propositions of the fear image. In order to change a physiological fear response in a client, for example, a therapist should include visceral response propositions within the imagery script read to a client. Initially, the therapist would want to elicit the fear response in the client with certain phobic response propositions (e.g. "My heart is racing"), and would then replace these with non-fear response propositions (e.g. "My heart is slow and regular").

Lang and colleagues have conducted a number of experiments which support aspects of his bio-informational theory of emotional imagery. For example, subjects trained in generating emotional images, which include somato-visceral response propositions, generate greater physiological activity during imagery (Lang, 1979). Studies have also indicated that greater covariation between verbal and physiological indices of fear can be obtained through response proposition training (Lang, 1979). The work by Lang and associates provides an important framework for translating psychological concepts into patterns of physiological processes. A major challenge for the future will be to link the verbal and physiological levels of analysis with neuropsychological levels of analysis and research methodology (e.g. do response propositions involve the regulation of premotor and motor cortical regions which in turn are expressed peripherally as increased physiological responding?).

A study by Grayson and Borkovec (1978) assessed whether different response propositions influence subjective and physiological measures of fear in speech-phobic college students. In their one-session study, subjects who imagined themselves behaving in a relaxed and competent manner had lower subjective ratings of fear to phobic images than subjects who either imagined being anxious and incompetent or imagined themselves avoiding the phobic situations. However, no difference between the groups was found for heart-rate response to images.

At present, the research method proposed by Lang (1979) is in its infancy and contradictory data are likely to be uncovered. It seems probable, however, that the systematic analysis of imagery into its components, as proposed by Lang, will prove to be a useful tool for asking meaningful questions about underlying physiological mechanisms of imagery as a psychotherapeutic device.

The trend towards examining more specific physiological and subjective components of treatments is seen in the theory described by Davidson and Schwartz (1976). These authors have proposed a multiprocess psychobiological model to account for the effects of relaxation and related states. They claim that different self-regulation therapies involve different patterns of psychobiological systems. Taking anxiety as an example, Davidson and Schwartz hypothesized that different activities affect different components of anxiety; i.e. high- and low-cognitive versus somatic manifestations of anxiety. The predictions concerning which self-regulation practices affect which psychobiological systems are presented in Table 1.

Schwartz *et al.* (1978) conducted a study to test some of the predictions made by the Davidson and Schwartz model. Their research addressed the

Table I: Cognitive and somatic components of anxiety and associated activities hypothesized to reduce such anxiety. The activities in each of the cells maximally engage the system(s) in which anxiety is high. Thus, for example, both progressive relaxation and hatha yoga maximally engage the somatic system with little effect on the cognitive system, while reading and watching television are hypothesized to have the opposite effect. Active sports are thought to maximally engage both modes, while meditation is hypothesized to engage each of the two modes minimally (adapted from Davidson and Schwartz, 1976).

		Somatic anxiety Low	Somatic anxiety High
Cognitive anxiety	Low	Meditation	Progressive relaxation Hatha yoga
	High	Reading Watching television	Active sports

question of whether subjects who regularly practise physical exercise (emphasizing skeletal muscle regulation) would show less somatic versus cognitive anxiety than subjects who practise a cognitively oriented activity (meditation). Anxiety was assessed by a scale which separately tapped cognitive (e.g. "I can't keep anxiety-provoking thoughts out of my mind") and somatic (e.g. "My heart beats faster") components of self-reported anxiety. Results supported the basic hypothesis. Although there was no difference between the groups on overall anxiety assessed globally, meditators showed a pattern of relatively less cognitive and more somatic anxiety than did exercisers.

Using physiological measures, a study by Warrenburg *et al.* (1980) also supported the model proposed by Davidson and Schwartz (1976). It was found that progressive muscle relaxation (a somatic technique) produced larger overall decreases in two somatic measures (oxygen consumption and heart rate) compared to transcendental meditation.

If, as Davidson and Schwartz (1976) suggest, "relaxation is not relaxation is not relaxation" in terms of patterns of cognitive and underlying somatic processes, then future research examining patterns of changes in relevant physiological systems accompanying different relaxation procedures and in different individuals may help us to understand what kinds of relaxation procedures work best for whom, and why.

C. Group Psychotherapy

Silbergeld *et al.* (1975) report the results of a psychobiological investigation of group psychotherapy. The authors conducted a pilot study examining the relationship between dopamine-B-hydroxylase (DBH) activity and a variety of psychological variables in five married couples participating in 15 sessions of brief group therapy. The main results indicated that: (i) group therapy produced significant increases in DBH from pre-session to post-session; and (ii) analyses for each subject predicting pre- to post-session changes in DBH from psychological variables revealed that specific affect and behaviour variables (obtained by self-report and content analysis of a free-association test at the beginning and end of the group sessions) were highly related to the DBH changes. However, the particular psychological stressors which were related to DBH were idiosyncratic to specific individuals. Although physiological monitoring in couples or groups is more difficult than in individual therapy, the potential research and clinical significance of such data could be great.

Research by Gottman (1979) using sophisticated time-series analysis of the interactive behaviour of couples can readily be applied to the study of interactive physiology of couples. The jump in levels from physiology to organism to group (i.e. the couple in the above instance) should be accompanied by unique interactions that emerge as part of the process of therapy. Parenthetically, the therapist/client relationship can be conceptualized in systems terms as the formation of a biopsychosocial "group" system. The research methods developed by Gottman (1979) can be directly extended to both the behavioural and physiological levels of interaction between therapist and client.

D. Research on Novel Therapies

The psychophysiological effects of "functional psychotherapy" (Hart *et al.*, 1980) have been investigated by a group of therapists in Los Angeles, California. Functional therapy is a humanistically oriented therapy and, as described by Karle *et al.* (1980), it

> . . .emphasizes the development of matched expression of emotions, defined as the congruence of inner sensate and cognitive experience with outer behavioral expression. The therapist systematically examines both how a person feels and the behavioural dynamics that influence how he feels. There is a threefold emphasis on: (1) emotions as basic mediators of behaviour, (2) practical programs for inducing change, and (3) the need for sustained social support to maintain therapeutic changes (ibid., p. 1).

Karle *et al.* (1980) report on a series of investigations, including studies showing the following.

(i) Individual therapy sessions produce greater reductions from pre- to post-session on pulse, blood pressures, and rectal temperature than control subjects showed in an "autobiographical interview" (Woldenberg *et al.*, 1976).

(ii) Experienced clients had lower levels in general on all of these physiological variables than beginning clients, suggesting that the effects of therapy are maintained (Karle *et al.*, 1976).

(iii) Instances of psychological defensiveness during sessions were associated with different patterns of EEG than non-defensive periods in one client (Woldenberg *et al.*, 1979).

(iv) Therapy seems to affect patterns of sleep, producing lower REM time and shorter REM latencies (Karle *et al.*, 1977), and influencing the spontaneous K-complex (Scott *et al.*, 1978).

(v) Increases in cardiovascular measures (heart rate, blood pressure) were directly related to the emergence of emotionally stressful material during sessions, and subsequent expression of feelings and gaining insight into one's behaviour resulted in decreases in these measures, sometimes below baseline levels (Karle *et al.*, 1980).

Without going into a detailed critical analysis of these studies on functional psychotherapy, it should be noted that most of them used small numbers of subjects and lacked appropriate controls and, consequently, the results have limited generality. These studies, however, represent a unique attempt by a group of practising clinicians to view their therapy from a psychophysiological perspective and to use the feedback obtained from their own research results to influence their future practice. The authors report that a more comprehensive five-year psychophysiological study on a large group of clients is currently in progress (Karle *et al.*, 1980).

III. Problems of Interpretation of Data

There are several important methodological issues which cut across the different studies that have been reviewed in this chapter. The earlier discussion of conceptual problems in this field briefly raised some of these issues. In this section we will present theory and research results which have specifically elucidated the important problems associated with the interpretation of data from investigations of the role of psychophysiology in psychotherapy.

Psychophysiological manifestations of emotional states have been a central theme for many of the studies reported in this chapter. This is not surprising given the key role that emotion plays in almost all forms of psychotherapy. Several factors have made it difficult to interpret physiological measures of emotion during therapy. The first of these factors is the often found lack of agreement between physiological indices and self-report measures of emotion. The measurement of anxiety, for example, has been separated into physiological, behavioural and verbal components (Lang, 1977) which tend to be weakly correlated with each other.

Schwartz (1978) has proposed that desynchrony between these different components or subsystems involved in emotion can be analyzed in terms of underlying psychobiological mechanisms. For example, if a person showed high physiological components of anxiety but verbally reported little or no anxiety, this would imply that the person was not accurately processing the state of his or her peripheral physiology and thus was engaging in denial or repression. A study by Weinberger *et al.* (1979) investigated the distinction between truly low-anxious subjects, who report low trait anxiety on the Taylor manifest anxiety scale and low defensiveness on the Marlowe–Crown social desirability scale, and repressors who report low anxiety but high defensiveness. Repressors showed higher heart rate, spontaneous skin resistance responses and forehead muscle tension during a phrase-association task compared to the low-anxious group. In fact, repressors tended to show greater physiological changes than a high-anxious group as well. This pattern of dissociation between self-report and physiology has obvious importance for psychotherapy research.

A second major problem has been the use of only single physiological variables. Many studies have assumed that increases or decreases in one particular psychophysiological measure gives an index of general emotional response. The frequent use of frontalis EMG biofeedback for the treatment of anxiety disorders is an example. Recent evidence strongly criticizes the single parameter approach. For example, Friedlund *et al.* (1980) have found that the decreases in frontalis EMG produced by frontalis EMG biofeedback are not accompanied by decreases in the muscle tension at other sites.

In place of single measures, investigators have begun to examine *patterns* of physiological responses and their relation to subjective experience of emotion. In biofeedback studies, where subjects are taught to decrease both heart rate and blood pressure simultaneously, more reports of sensations of relaxation were found compared to subjects who learned to decrease only one function. Similarly, when subjects generated a pattern of high frontalis muscle tension and high heart rate they reported greater anxiety than when increasing each function separately (reviewed in Schwartz, 1977). This emphasis on emergent properties produced by interactions between components follows from the systems theory approach mentioned earlier and from a general psychobiological perspective.

The suggestion that researchers examine multiple physiological systems and their interactions does not mean that one should blindly collect data on every measure that one can obtain in an experiment. The selection of measures should be guided by theory on the psychobiological mechanisms underlying the theory process of interest. Holding this view leads one to the conclusion that more basic research is needed on the psychobiology of emotions and other phenomena involved in psychotherapy. Once advances are made in these basic research areas, we can begin to apply these concepts to psychotherapy.

One final methodological note concerns the difficulty of doing research in a highly uncontrolled situation: that of the typical psychotherapy session. Even the most structured of therapies takes place in an interpersonal context where the number of variables operating is very large. It is known, for example, that just the process of talking alone can have large effects of physiological measures such as blood pressure (Lynch *et al.*, 1980). Attempting to control for some of these variables in an experiment would interfere with the normal course of therapy. Some investigators have used unusual experimental designs such as P-technique (repeated intra-individual measurements), especially for examining the context of psychosomatic symptoms during therapy sessions (Luborsky and Mintz, 1972). Also, as pioneered by Gottman (1979), time-series analyses can be performed to examine temporal patterns and constraints within the group system defined as psychotherapy. These and other more fine-grained approaches to data may help to unravel the complexities inherent in psychotherapy research.

IV. Future Directions

The future course of scientific investigation of the psychophysiological foundations of psychotherapy will be profoundly influenced by advances in technology. New computer systems have already made the collection and storage of large amounts of physiological data possible. As these computers and physiological-monitoring equipment become easier to use and are less expensive, a continuation of the growth of interest in psychophysiological research is likely. In addition to researchers, more and more practising psychotherapists will be able to incorporate physiological monitoring into their clinical work. In fact, comprehensive, computer-based "behavioural medicine" systems such as the Biolab system (developed by Cyborg, which collects, stores, and graphically displays physiological data, as well as handles administration of tests, patient billing, and therapy progress notes) are becoming available. Also, the development of portable and unobtrusive equipment will reduce the therapist's resistance to obtaining psychophysiological information during psychotherapy session. One spin-off of these advances is the possibility of monitoring physiology, not only during sessions, but during the daily life of a patient as well. A wealth of important data on changes in a patient's physiology produced by naturally occurring stress can then be used to direct the course of treatment.

The extent to which clinicians make physiological monitoring an active part of their work will depend, of course, on the research and theoretical developments that indicate the potential benefits of taking a psychobiological view of psychotherapy. Based on our review of the current work in the field, we can speculate on the possibile directions that research may lead and the subsequent broader ramifications of the greater acceptance of a psychobiological perspective with regard to behaviour change.

It seems likely that the trend towards viewing psychophysiology in terms of underlying mechanisms and the emphasis on specificity and patterning (Davidson, 1978; Schwartz, 1978) will continue. A potentially fruitful topic of inquiry is hemispheric activation during different therapeutic techniques. By examining asymmetry in any of a number of peripheral physiological measures, one can infer whether the left or right side of the brain is more activated and, consequently, obtain data on the type of information/emotional processing that is being called into play. One goal of such research is to link the biocognitive mode of the intervention to the mode of the psychophysiological or psychosocial problem for which the patient is seeking treatment.

A second important line of research will be on the interaction of pharmacological and behavioural or psychosocial treatments. Myslobodsky and Weiner (1978) have examined the personality and situational factors in drug responses and discussed how clinical psychologists can consequently participate in and share responsibility for the outcome of pharmacotherapy. By examining the psychobiological mechanisms of psychotherapeutic techniques, a therapist can potentially predict whether a given technique will facilitate or interfere with a specific drug treatment.

One implication of drug/behavioural interactions and a psychobiological view of psychotherapy is that they raise questions about legal ramifications and professional limitations in clinical work. If we begin to uncover that "psychological" techniques inherently involve certain changes in peripheral organs that can influence health and illness, are those who employ such techniques practising "medicine"? The usual definitions of medical versus psychological treatments break down when one learns to examine the interface and interaction of multiple levels of analysis. Thus, these issues ultimately involve legal, ethical and moral questions that must be addressed on the broader social level as well. Psychophysiological research on psychotherapy from a systems perspective will probably play an important role in guiding this emerging paradigm shift (see DeRosnay, 1979) about the biobehavioural basis of all levels of therapy.

Further Reading

DeRosnay, J. (1979). "The Macroscope". Harper and Row, New York.
This book provides a broad introduction to general systems theory. It is comprehensive, covering theory and applications in the physical, biological, behavioural and social sciences. The book is unique for its clarity, organization, and elucidation of the philosophical as well as scientific implications of the approach.
Garfield, S. and Bergin, A. (eds), (1978). "Handbook of Psychotherapy and Behavior Change" 2nd edn. Wiley, New York.
This book provides detailed reviews of the psychotherapy research literature as well as chapters on basic methodology and orientation including one on the psychobiological foundations of psychotherapy. Probably the most comprehensive, empirical analysis of the field, it is recommended to any reader who is interested in the scientific study of psychotherapy.
Maser, J. and Seligman, M. E. P. (eds), (1977). "Psychopathology: Experimental Models". W. H. Freeman, San Francisco.
Further advances in the treatment of behavioural, psychological, and psychobiological disorders will hinge upon developments in the understanding of the etiology and course of these problems. In this book, several biobehavioural models of pathology originating out of laboratory research are presented, and the implications of these theories for treatment are discussed.
Miller, J. G. (1978). "Living Systems". McGraw Hill, New York.
A monumental work that provides a theoretical approach to the study of living systems at all levels – from the single cell to supra-national systems. It is particularly useful for integrating ideas across different levels, e.g. a psychophysiological analysis of psychotherapy. Recommended reading for students and scientists in any discipline.
Lacey, J. I. (1959). Psychophysiological approaches to the evaluation of psychotherapeutic process and outcome. *In* "Research in Psychotherapy" (E. A. Rubinstein and M. B. Parfoff, eds), Vol. 1. American Psychological Association, Washington, D.C.
The extensive early work on the application of psychophysiology to psychotherapy is reviewed in this excellent chapter. Since this was written before the advent of the behavioural therapies, the focus is on the more traditional, psychodynamic therapies that were prevalent at that time. Conceptual issues in psychophysiology are also discussed.

References

Bertalanffy, von, L. (1968). "General Systems Theory". Braziller, New York.
Davidson, R. J. (1978). Specificity and patterning in biobehavioral systems: Implications for behavior change. *Am. Psychol.* 33, 430–436.
Davidson, R. J. and Schwartz, G. E. (1976). The psychobiology of relaxation and related states: A multi-process theory. *In* "Behavior Control and Modification of Physiological Activity" (D. I. Mostofsky, ed.). Prentice Hall, Englewood Cliffs, New Jersey.
DeRosnay, J. (1979). "The Macroscope". Harper and Row, New York.
Edwin, S. I. (1979). "Galvanic Skin Response as an Adjunct to Psychotherapy: Effects upon Accurate Emphatic Understanding". Unpublished doctoral dissertation, United States International University.

Engel, G. L. (1977). The need for a new medical model: A challenge for biomedicine. *Science* **196**, 129–136.

Feuerstein, M. and Schwartz, G. E. (1977). Training in clinical psychophysiology: Present trends and future goals. *Am. Psychol.* **32**, 560–568.

Fridlund, A. J., Fowler, S. C. and Pritchard, D. A. (1980). Striate muscle tensional patterning in frontalis EMG biofeedback. *Psychophysiology* **17**, 47–55.

Giles, S. L. (1978). Separate and Combined Effects of Biofeedback Training and Brief Individual Psychotherapy in the Treatment of Gastrointestinal Disorders. Unpublished doctoral dissertation, University of Colorado at Boulder.

Gottman, J. (1979). "Marital Interaction: Experimental Investigations". Academic Press, New York and London.

Grayson, J. B. and Borkovec, T. D. (1978). The effects of expectancy and imagined response to phobic stimulus on fear reduction. *Cognit. Ther. Res.* **2**, 11–24.

Hart, J., Corriere, R. and Karle, W. (1980). Functional psychotherapy. *In* "Handbook of Innovative Psychotherapies" (R. Corsini, ed.). Wiley, New York.

Karle, W., Corriere, R., Hart, J., Gold, S., Maple, C. and Hopper, M. (1976). Maintenance of psychophysiological changes in feeling therapy. *Psychol. Rep.* **39**, 1143–1147.

Karle, W., Hopper, M., Corriere, R., Hart, J. and Switzer, A. (1977). Two preliminary studies on sleep and psychotherapy. *Physiol. Behav.* **19**, 419–423.

Karle, W., Woldenberg, L. and Corriere, R. (1980). Physiological Methods in Psychotherapy Research: A Review of the Psychotherapy Research Program at The Center Foundation in Los Angeles. Paper presented at the meeting of the Society for Psychotherapy Research, Pacific Grove, California.

Lacey, J. I. (1959). Psychophysiological approaches to the evaluation of psychotherapeutic process and outcome. *In* "Research in Psychotherapy" (E. A. Rubinstein and M. B. Parloff, eds), Vol. 1. American Psychological Association, Washington, D.C.

Lang, P. J. (1971). The application of psychophysiological methods to the study of psychotherapy and behavior change. *In* "Handbook of Psychotherapy and Behavior Change" (A. E. Bergin and S. L. Garfield, eds). Wiley, New York.

Lang, P. J. (1977). Imagery in therapy: An information processing analysis of fear. *Behav. Ther.* **8**, 862–886.

Lang, P. J. (1979). A bio-informational theory of emotional imagery. *Psychophysiology* **6**, 495–512.

Legalos, C. N. (1973). Biofeedback and psychotherapy. *Seminars Psychiat.* **5**, 529–533.

Leigh, H. and Reiser, M. F. (1980). "The Patient: Biological, Psychological, and Social Dimensions of Medical Practice" Plenum, New York.

Luborsky, L. and Mintz, J. (1972). The contribution of P-technique to personality, psychotherapy, and psychosomatic research. *In* "Multivariate Analysis: Essays in Honor of Raymond B. Cattell" (R. M. Dreger, ed.). Claitor's Publishing Division, Baton Rouge.

Lynch, J., Thomas, S., Long, J., Malinow, K., Chickadonz, G., and Katcher, A. (1980). Human speech and blood pressure. *J. Nerv. Ment. Dis.* **168**, 526–534.

McCarron, L. T. (1973). Paralanguage and autonomic response patterns in psychotherapy. *Psychother: Theory, Res. Practice* **10**, 229–230.

Miller, J. G. (1978). "Living Systems". McGraw Hill, New York.

Msylobodsky, M. and Weiner, M. (1978). Clinical psychology in the chemical environment. *Psychol. Rep.* **43**, 247–276.

Powers, W. T. (1973). "Behavior: The Control of Perception". Aldine, Chicago.

Ray, W. J., Raczynski, J. M., Rogers, T. and Kimball, W. H. (1979). "Evaluation of Clinical Biofeedback". Plenum, New York.

Roessler, R., Bruch, H., Thum, L. and Collins, F. (1975). Physiologic correlates of affect during psychotherapy. *Am. J. Psychother.* **29**, 26–36.

Schwartz, G. E. (1977). Psychosomatic disorders and biofeedback: A psychobiological model of disregulation. *In* "Psychopathology: Experimental Models" (J. D. Maser and M. E. P. Seligman, eds). W. H. Freeman, San Francisco.

Schwartz, G. E. (1978). Psychobiological foundations of psychotherapy and behavior change. *In* "Handbook of Psychotherapy and Behavior Change" (S. L. Garfield and A. E. Bergin, eds), 2nd edn. Wiley, New York.

Schwartz, G. E. (1980). Behavioral medicine and systems theory: A new synthesis. National Forum, Winter 1980, p. 25–30.

Schwartz, G. E., Davidson, R. J. and Goldman, D. (1978). Patterning of cognitive and somatic processes in the self-regulation of anxiety: Effects of meditation versus exercise. *Psychosom. Med.* **40**, 321–328.

Schwartz, G. E., Weinberger, D. and Singer, J. A. (1981). Cardiovascular differentiation of happiness, sadness, anger, and fear following imagery and exercise. *Psychosom. Med.*

Scott, R., Karle, W., Switzer, A., Hart, J., Corriere, R. and Woldenberg, L. (1978). Psychophysiological correlates of the spontaneous K-complex. *Percept. Mot. Skills* **46**, 271–287.

Silbergeld, S., Manderscheid, R. W., O'Neill, P., Lamprecht, F. and Ng, L. (1975). Changes in serum dopamine-B-hydroxylase activity during group psychotherapy. *Psychosom. Med.* **37**, 352–367.

Stanek, B., Hahn, P. and Mayer, H. (1973). Biometric findings on cardiac neurosis: Changes in ECG and heart rate in cardiophobic patients and their doctor during psychoanalytical initial interviews. *Psychother. Psychosom.* **22**, 289–299.

Stephenson, N. L. (1976). Two cases of successful treatment of Raynaud's Disease with relaxation and biofeedback training and supportive psychotherapy. *Biofeedback and Self-regulation* **1**, 318–319.

Toomin, M. K. and Toomin, H. (1975). GSR biofeedback in psychotherapy: Some clinical observations. *Psychother: Theory, Res. Practice* **12**, 33–38.

Warrenburg, S., Pagano, R., Woods, M. and Hlastala, M. (1980). A comparison of somatic relaxation and EEG activity in classical progressive relaxation and transcendental meditation. *J. Behav. Med.* **3**, 73–93.

Weinberger, D. A., Schwartz, G. E. and Davidson, R. J. (1979). Low-anxious, high-anxious, and repressive coping styles: Psychometric patterns and behavioral and physiological responses to stress. *J. Abnorm. Psychol.* **88**, 369–380.

Werbach, M. R. (1977). Biofeedback and psychotherapy. *Am. J. Psychother.* **31**, 376–382.

Woldenberg, L., Karle, W., Gold, S., Corriere, R., Hart, J. and Hopper, M. (1976). Psychophysiological changes in feeling therapy. *Psychol. Rep.* **39**, 1059–1962.

Woldenberg, L., Karle, W. and Corriere, R. (1979). An electroencephalographic investigation of psychological defensiveness in psychotherapy. Paper presented at the meeting of the American Psychological Association, New York.

Yates, A. J. (1979). "Biofeedback and the Modification of Behaviour". Plenum, New York.

16 Psychophysiology, Psychopathology and the Social Environment

G. Turpin

Abstract The use of psychophysiological measures for investigating the influence of social factors on psychiatric relapse is reviewed. In particular, the effect of the emotional atmosphere in the home upon the relapse rate of schizophrenic patients is described. A model is outlined which relates the incidence of relapse to the patient's level of physiological arousal. The model also states that a patient's arousal level is determined by a number of factors including medication, the occurrence of stressful life events and the expressed emotion of the patient's relatives.

A number of studies are examined which have explored the above model using psychophysiological techniques. The problems associated with studying social interaction within a laboratory setting and the stressful nature of this situation for psychiatric patients are also discussed.

I. Introduction

The psychophysiology of mental illness is perhaps a misnomer. The wide variety of psychophysiological techniques which have been applied to the study of psychological dysfunction reflects the many disparate approaches to mental illness in general, rather than any theoretical diversification of psychophysiology as a particular field of study. Psychophysiology has usually been exploited as a convenient collection of techniques with which to examine hypotheses from within completely separate theoretical frameworks.

Several different approaches to the study of mental illness which have employed psychophysiological techniques may be identified. Of these, the diagnostic approach is perhaps the oldest and the most easily recognized. For many years, psychophysiological measures have been employed in attempts to classify and discriminate between various clinical groups of patients.

PHYSIOLOGICAL CORRELATES OF HUMAN BEHAVIOUR
ISBN 0-12-273901-9

Unfortunately, the low degree of success encountered in these studies probably reflected the lack of clarity and precision of the clinical methods which had been applied in order to select the patient groups. A similar approach has used psychophysiological indices to chart the longitudinal development of psychiatric disturbance in the population as a whole. Such studies are usually known as "high risk studies", since they concentrate on individuals prone to psychiatric disorder. It is claimed that psychophysiological techniques provide a reliable, efficient and unbiased method with which to screen large numbers of individuals (see Venables' discussion in Chapter 13). Finally, psychophysiological measures are sometimes employed in an attempt to elucidate the mechanisms responsible for certain psychological dysfunctions. A good example is the study of the orienting reflex as a means of investigating the attentional deficit exhibited by some schizophrenic patients.

The different approaches described briefly above have been discussed in some detail in the previous chapters. The purpose of this chapter is to examine a relatively new approach to the study of psychiatric disorder, which has also recently employed psychophysiological techniques. This approach examines the importance of social factors in determining the onset and course of psychiatric disorder. In particular, the influence of these factors on the relapse of schizophrenic patients will be reviewed.

Although the study of social factors has tended to be based upon poor empirical evidence, recent studies have reversed this trend (Hirsch and Leff, 1975). This is probably due to a change in emphasis, whereby social factors are not considered as the sole aetiological explanation of mental disorder. Instead, the current opinion is to stress the contribution of social influences to a multi-factorial explanation of psychiatric morbidity, which embraces both environmental and genetic determinants. This change in emphasis may be attributed to the growth of interest in the social environment of the psychiatric patient, and a shift away from institutionalized to community care. The maintenance of patients within the community has necessitated the study of those factors said to precipitate or increase the probability of a patient's relapse and readmission to a psychiatric hospital. Some important factors which have been identified include: longterm medication, the extent and quality of family interaction and the occurrence of life events. Many researchers have attempted to construct a model which can account for the effects of these disparate influences upon the incidence of psychiatric relapse. One of these models has employed the notion of physiological arousal as a hypothetical construct between the precipitating factors and the occurrence of relapse. Put very simply, this model states that, if the level of physiological arousal exceeds some threshold value, the patient's psychiatric symptoms either return or are exacerbated, resulting in readmission to hospital. Factors such as medication, life events of the social milieu are all said to modify the arousal level of the patient and hence determine the probability of relapse. The use of the concept of a "physiological arousal level" obviously demands the adoption of psychophysiological methods in any attempt to investigate this model empirically.

II. The Influence of Social Factors on the Course of Psychiatric Disorder

Before discussing the possible mediating effects of physiological arousal on the incidence of psychiatric relapse, the research strategies used to investigate the nature of social influences on mental disorder need to be described. Much of this research has been concerned with the quality of family life, and originates mainly from the work of Brown and his colleagues. These researchers were originally interested in identifying those factors associated with good adaptation of the long-term patient to life outside the hospital. In a number of follow-up studies of long-term, male schizophrenics (Brown *et al.*, 1958; Brown *et al.*, 1962), a surprising relationship between relapse and the patient's social conditions emerged. Contrary to popular belief, patients who were discharged and returned to live either in the marital or parental home were *more* likely to relapse, showed more disturbed behaviour, and remained unemployed longer than patients living either by themselves or in hostels. Moreover, for those patients living with relatives, if the quality of their social relationship was rated as "highly emotionally involved", then the incidence of their relapse was even greater.

The approach used by Brown in the studies above was to interview a key informant who was in close contact with the patient. This person was usually a parent, spouse, landlady or, in the case of socially isolated patients, the patient himself. It was feasible, therefore, that the differential effect of family environment on relapse might be due to the accuracy of the information supplied by the key informant. In an attempt to improve both the reliability and validity of these studies, a structured interview was developed (Brown and Rutter, 1966). The aim of this interview was to ascertain the events, attitudes and emotions experienced by the patient three months prior to admission to hospital. The relative's emotional behaviour was rated by the interviewer using a number of scales concerning such emotions as warmth, dissatisfaction, hostility and emotional over-involvement. These ratings were based on the content of the relative's speech and also on its rate, intensity and tone. In addition, the number of hostile or critical comments made by the relative about the patient was also recorded.

The techniques described above were employed by Brown *et al.* (1972) in a further prospective follow-up study of 101 schizophrenic patients, who on discharge returned to live with their relatives. The contribution of various factors in determining relapse at a 9 month follow-up period was examined. Relapse was defined as either a transition back to a carefully defined diagnosis of schizophrenia, or a marked deterioration of the patient's chronic schizophrenic symptomatology. The different variables examined included the degree of behavioural disturbance, work impairment, psychiatric symptomatology, social withdrawal and the amount of emotional involvement with the relative. This last factor was assessed as an overall index of the relative's emotional behaviour derived from the previously described individual rating scales. This index was termed the "expressed emotion" (EE) of the relative and was the major variable associated with the incidence of relapse (Kuipers, 1979). Of the patients living in homes with relatives rated high in EE, 58% relapsed, whereas only 16% relapsed from low EE homes. The incidence of relapse and the EE of the relative were also associated with the degree of work impairment and degree of behaviour disturbance.

An obvious explanation of these findings is that the relationship between EE and relapse is spurious, and can be attributed to the severity of the patient's behavioural disturbance. Thus, the more disturbed the patient, the more likely the occurrence of relapse and the greater degree of EE experienced within the home. Brown *et al.* (1972) carefully explored this possibility but concluded that the incidence of relapse is directly related to the EE of the patient's relative and not mediated by any of the other variables which they had measured. Hence, the incidence of relapse should be modified by changing the EE of the patient's relative.

The implications of the Brown *et al.* (1972) study for the management of psychiatric patients within the community were obviously very important. Thus, in 1976, a replication of their study was reported by Vaughn and Leff. These authors extended the original study, and included depressed as well as schizophrenic patients in their sample. In addition, since the Camberwell Family Interview which had been employed in the Brown *et al.* study could take up to 6 hours to administer, a shortened version of the interview was developed. Essentially, the findings from this study were identical to those reported by Brown *et al.* (1972). Twenty eight percent of the total number of schizophrenic patients relapsed. These accounted for 48% of the patients living with a high EE relative and only 6% of patients living with a low EE relative. A similar pattern of results was obtained for depressed patients, although it would appear that they were even more sensitive to criticism than schizophrenic patients.

Using regression analysis, Vaughn and Leff (1976) examined the relative importance of EE to other possible mediating variables in predicting relapse. Even when the degree of behavioural disturbance was partialled out, EE significantly predicted relapse. In addition, several other factors said by Brown *et al.* (1972) to moderate relapse were examined. These included the effects of medication, face to face contact between the patient and relative and also the degree of social withdrawal. This analysis revealed a series of interactions between these variables and the EE of the relative. Hence, the effects of medication and the extent of face to face contact are more pronounced in high EE patients than low EE patients. These findings are outlined in Fig. 1. Once again these authors emphasized the therapeutic implications of their findings for the patient living within the community. For instance, it can be seen that for patients living in low EE homes the protective effect of medication over the 9 month period studied is minimal compared with patients from high EE homes. Similarly, the degree of face to face contact between the patient and relative can seriously affect the probability of relapse in high EE patients, but not in low EE patients. Hence, a possible therapeutic intervention for high EE families might be the use of long-term medication and a reduction in the extent of the face to face contact between the relative and the patient.

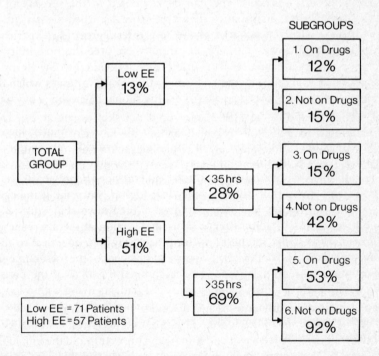

Fig. 1 *Percentage of patients from each group who relapsed during a nine month follow up. (Adapted, with permission, from Vaughn and Leff, 1976. Copyright: British Journal of Psychiatry).*

Finally, the influence of independent life events upon the precipitation of psychiatric illness has been examined by the same groups of researchers. An independent life event is an occurrence in the life of a patient, the onset of which could not have been influenced by the patient's own behaviour. Therefore, the marriage or death of a friend or relative might be an example of an independent life event. Leff and Vaughn (1980) have detailed a complex interaction between life events, EE and psychiatric relapse. With regard to schizophrenic patients, they revealed that the distribution of life events prior to admission differed significantly between patients from low EE and high EE homes. Low EE patients were much more likely to have experienced a life event prior to admission than patients from high EE homes.

In summary, the studies described above have established a relationship between the incidence of psychiatric relapse and a number of different facets of the patient's social environment. Of these, the EE of the relative would appear to determine the probability of relapse to a greater degree than the other variables so far studied. However, many of these other variables seem to interact in a multiplicative fashion in determining the eventual outcome.

III. A Psychophysiological Model of Social Reactivity and Psychiatric Relapse

The notion of a relationship between physiological arousal and the degree of social stimulation experienced by the schizophrenic patient is not a recent one. Venables and Wing (1962) measured the skin potential activity of schizophrenic patients and revealed an unexpected association between social withdrawal and high levels of physiological arousal. It was suggested, therefore, that schizophrenic patients possessed an optimum level of arousal, which when exceeded led to a deterioration in their psychological functioning and an exacerbation of their symptoms. It was also suggested that many forms of social interaction would lead to a state of over-arousal. Hence, patients, who were already highly aroused, could protect themselves from excessive stimulation by withdrawing from social situations.

The similarity of the above hypothesis to the proposed moderating influence of both social withdrawal and high face to face contact on the effect of EE upon relapse, led Brown *et al.* (1972) to postulate a similar arousal explanation for the influence of social conditions on schizophrenic relapse. Hence, the emotional milieu within the home, the effects of social contact and withdrawal, the occurrence of stress-inducing life events and the influence of long-term medication were all said to determine the incidence of relapse, via their independent effect upon a patient's level of physiological arousal. A similar model has also been put forward by Vaughn and Leff (1976).

The question arises as to how this model can be tested and whether there exists any evidence in its support. Essentially, the model treats the patient's level of physiological arousal as a hypothetical construct, which mediates the effects of social factors on relapse. Hence, two related predictions can be made. The first predicts that factors such as high EE, social contact and the recent occurrence of life events will give rise to an excessive increase in the patient's level of arousal. The second prediction is that high levels of physiological arousal will be associated with a greater probability of psychiatric relapse. It is essential that both these predictions are examined when testing the overall validity of the model.

A. *Psychophysiological Correlates of Expressed Emotion*

As outlined above, one prediction derived from the arousal model is that the social factors associated with relapse should lead to an excessive state of high arousal. Thus, a simple prediction would be that patients from high EE homes are more highly aroused than low EE patients. However, even with this simple hypothesis, there exists a number of problems. The first of these relates to the general problem of the measurement of physiological arousal in behavioural studies. Accordingly, many researchers have relied upon the measurement of skin conductance activity which they have operationally defined as the arousal level. A second problem concerns the situation and the kind of activity in which the patient is engaged at the time of testing. Although it is usual for psychophysiological studies to employ a laboratory based approach, a number of researchers have criticized the use of such a situation for the study of psychiatric patients. The major objection is that a highly technical laboratory environment will be perceived as stressful and threatening by the majority of patients. Moreover, in the case of institutionalized or socially withdrawn patients this encounter will be even more stressful, due to the relative novelty of the social interaction between experimenter and patient. Furthermore, the type of laboratory task usually employed, such as reaction time or habituation to a sequence of auditory stimuli, has also been criticized as being of little relevance to the patient. Hence, a number of different approaches have been employed to assess the relationship between arousal and the EE of the patient. These have ranged from laboratory based studies to the use of non-laboratory social interview situations.

Most of the research which has examined the relationship between physiological arousal and EE was conducted by Tarrier and coworkers (Tarrier *et al.*, 1978 a, b; Tarrier, *et al.*, 1979). In a series of psycho-physiological studies, Tarrier compared a group of partially remitted schizophrenic patients living in the community with both a group of normal controls and a group of hospitalized chronic schizophrenic patients. The community patients had been recruited from a large sample of patients previously used by Vaughn and Leff (1976) and whose relatives' level of EE had already been determined. A number of physiological measures were employed and these included the electroencephalogram (EEG), heart rate (HR), blood pressure (BP) and skin conductance activity (SC). Since Tarrier was concerned with the social effects of the testing situation on the patient's psychophysiological response, he adopted two different testing conditions. One of these experimental situations was the typical psychophysiological laboratory and involved the use of both a simple habituation series of auditory stimuli and a reaction time test. The second situation involved testing patients in their own homes. Initially, the patient was interviewed alone by the experimenter, for a period of 15 minutes, about his/her experience of mental illness. The patient's key relative was then invited to join the interview for a further 15 minutes. Obviously, Tarrier was unable to conduct this particular test with the chronic hospitalized patients.

The results from the laboratory studies failed to find any differences between community patients and the normal control group in EEG, HR or SC. The community patients also differed very little from the chronic inpatient group. This lack of findings occurred on three separate testing occasions conducted at approximately three monthly intervals. In contrast, the study undertaken in the home provided definite support for a distinction between high and low EE patients. Although these patients did not differ initally whilst talking to the experimenter alone, differences were obtained between the two groups when the key relative entered the room and joined in the conversation. Low EE patients showed a gradual decline in SC activity and BP throughout this second 15 minute period. The high EE patients showed a sustained level of SC and BP activity throughout both the initial and subsequent 15 min periods (see Fig. 2). However, these differences were only apparent on the first testing session and were not obtained on two subsequent sessions.

Tarrier and his coworkers drew a number of conclusions from these studies regarding the effects of EE and social situation on psychophysiological arousal. The first of these was that psychophysiological measures were sensitive to differences in the EE of a patient. The second conclusion was that these differences can only be obtained when an appropriate social setting such as the patient's own home is employed. Thus, the laboratory situation should not be used to study the psychophysiological response of schizophrenic patients to their social environment. They also concluded that the differences between the two EE groups were obtained due to the stressful nature of the interview. Hence, the failure to obtain differences between the groups on the second and third testing occasions was due to the patients being more familiar with the situation, and thus experiencing relatively little stress.

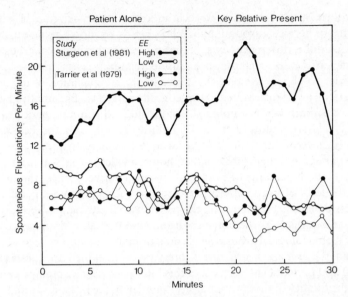

Fig. 2 *Skin conductance activity of schizophrenic patients recorded during an interview. (Adapted, with permission, from Sturgeon* et al., *1981. Copyright: British Journal of Psychiatry).*

Several questions can be raised concerning the generality of some of the conclusions reached by Tarrier *et al.* (1979). The first concerns the specificity of the home environment and asks to what extent the differences in arousal can be attributed to the physical environment rather than to the presence of the key relative *per se.* Similarly, the second issue concerns their conclusion that differences in SC activity between these two EE groups can be obtained only if a social interaction situation in the home is employed. Unfortunately, Tarrier *et al.* (1979) confounded the effects of different testing situations with the order of testing. Patients were always tested first in the home and then on a subsequent occasion in the laboratory. Since no differences were found between the two EE groups on either the two remaining home tests or the three laboratory sessions, it would appear that the effect of EE is dependent upon the novelty of the first testing occasion. Thus, the conclusion regarding the appropriateness of home versus laboratory testing is perhaps unwarranted and premature. The third point concerns the nature of the differences in arousal between the two groups. A number of questions can be raised as to whether this difference is specific to schizophrenia. For instance, do these differences reflect a specific difference in arousal, or do they just reflect differences in the amount of anxiety experienced by the patients? Similarly, it could be argued that these differences merely reflect differences between the two groups in the amount of speech and other overt activities. Lastly, the relationship between arousal and EE has yet to be shown to be causal. The fact that similar differences exist between EE and physiological arousal does not necessarily imply that they are causally related.

In order to clarify some of the above issues, a replication of the original Tarrier study was attempted (Sturgeon et al., 1981). Essentially the same interview situation was employed, comprising a 15 minute period without the key relative followed by a 15 minute period with the key relative. However, several important changes were introduced. Instead of interviewing the patient and the relative in their home, a video studio was used in order to record the behaviour of both patient and relative. Hence, the extent to which the level of overt activity determines the level of physiological arousal could be assessed. Furthermore, the use of the video studio also meant that the separate effects of the home environment and relative's presence on the patient's physiological arousal level could be investigated. The second change involved the use of a structured interview with which to question both relative and patient. The purpose of this interview was to obtain information about the quality of the emotional environment in the home and also to elicit, if possible, criticism of the patient from the patient's key relative. The original study by Tarrier did not elicit critical remarks due to the unstructured nature of the interview. The final and perhaps most important distinction between this and the original Tarrier study was the experimental design. Tarrier tested a group of partially remitted patients several times whilst living in the community. The Sturgeon et al. study tested patients whilst acutely ill and also whilst living back in the community following remission. Only patients living in high contact with their relatives were included in the study since these were at the highest risk of relapse. In addition to testing acutely ill patients, the study also randomly allocated patients living with a high EE relative to one of two groups: a control and an intervention group. The purpose of the intervention group was to lower explicitly either the amount of social contact between the patient and relative or the EE level of the key relative or both. It was predicted that the relapse rate of the intervention group should be considerably reduced. Moreover, this should also be accompanied by a fall in the arousal level of these patients. In order to test this hypothesis, the patient's arousal level was monitored whilst acutely ill and also at a 9 month follow-up.

Only the results of the initial stage of this study, when the patients were acutely ill and hospitalized, have been analysed. Essentially, the same pattern of findings as reported by Tarrier et al. (1979) was obtained. This was irrespective of the fact that these patients were both acutely ill and also interviewed in a video studio rather than in their own homes. Patients living with a high EE relative showed a failure to adapt to the interview when their relative was present, whereas low EE patients demonstrated a gradual decline in SC activity throughout this period (Fig. 2). The difference was not accounted for by differences in the level of the patients' overt behaviour, since an analysis of both speech and looking behaviour revealed no significant differences between the groups.

The only important difference between this and the original Tarrier *et al.* (1979) study concerned the overall level of SC activity. The high EE patients from the Sturgeon *et al.* study possessed a much greater rate of SC responding than the low EE patients from either study or the high EE patients from the original study. This difference was explained by Sturgeon *et al.* by the fact that the patients in their own study were acutely ill, whereas patients in the Tarrier *et al.* study were in remission and living back in the community. Unfortunately, the follow-up study, when the same acutely ill patients are tested again after remission, has yet to be completed. These results should indicate whether these differences in SC activity can be explained in terms of a difference between acutely ill and remitted community patients.

In general, the results from the above experiments support the notion that physiological arousal is associated with social factors such as EE, social contact and life events. Patients whose relatives differ in their degree of EE also demonstrate a correspondingly different pattern of SC activity when interviewed in the presence of the key relative. This finding is irrespective of whether the patient is acutely ill or in remission, and is also independent of whether the interview is conducted in the patient's home or in a video studio.

The differential SC activity displayed by these patients is only evident when they are placed in a fairly stressful situation. Hence, in the studies already described, it was only the first testing occasion when patients were interviewed in their own homes which led to differences between the high and low EE groups. Subsequent testing occasions, both in the home and laboratory, resulted in an overall lower level of arousal and a failure to detect differences between the groups. A similar effect of first time testing upon the ability to detect differences between groups of schizophrenic patients has previously been described (Spratt and Gale, 1979). It would seem, therefore, that differences in arousal attributed to schizophrenic patients may reflect their inability to cope with the social demands of the experimental situation. However, on repeated exposure to this situation, the patients adapt to its stressful nature, and so the difference in arousal level diminishes. Research conducted using college students would tend to support the arousing effects of social interaction.

The interpretation of the specific pattern of SC activity exhibited by the two EE patient groups raised a number of interesting problems. Although the two groups are initially highly aroused, the high EE group remains aroused throughout the entire interview, whereas, the low EE group demonstrates a gradual decline in arousal. This difference may be interpreted in two ways. One obvious explanation is that the actual presence of the relative brings about the difference in SC activity. Thus, the presence of a high EE relative maintains the patient's high level of arousal. In contrast, the low EE relative would be said to facilitate the patient's adaptation to the social situation and help in the dissipation of high arousal. An alternative explanation is that the presence of the relative in the interview situation is irrelevant to the differential pattern of SC activity and that this difference reflects a difference in a more general response to the stress of the interview itself. Hence, it could be argued that low EE patients adapt more easily to stressful situations and exhibit a reduction in arousal, whereas high EE patients do not adapt and remain highly aroused. This difference is not situationally determined since it is suggested that the presence of the relative is not important. However, the difference does require that the situation is initially a stressful one. Thus, the difference in SC activity between the two EE groups reflects a general discrepancy in the ability of the two groups to adapt to social stress and dissipate high arousal. It is also suggested that this inability of the high EE patient to adapt to stressful situations can be attributed to the effects of living in high contact with a high EE relative. A test of these two interpretations which has yet to be investigated involves the differential effect of the relative's presence and absence in the interview situation on the patient's SC activity.

Finally, the actual causal relationship between arousal and social factors, such as EE, has yet to be demonstrated. Provisional results from the intervention study, previously described, suggest that lowering the EE of a relative does in fact alter the probability of psychiatric relapse. However, it is not yet known whether this decrease in EE is also associated with a decrease in the level of physiological arousal.

B. *Physiological Arousal and Psychiatric Relapse*

The use of the concept of arousal to explain the effect of social factors on psychiatric relapse is based upon a major assumption: that increased or excessive arousal leads to a greater probability of psychiatric relapse. Unfortunately, there is little direct evidence to support this proposition. The intervention study previously described should provide some support since reduction in EE and social contact ought to result in both a lowered probability of relapse and a reduced level of arousal. However, the results from this stage of the study have yet to be analysed. Another approach to this problem would be to monitor the arousal level of a group of high risk patients in their homes for several months using either psychophysiological measures or perhaps, even, hormonal indicators of activation. If the assumption relating relapse to excessive arousal is correct, then the occurrence of relapse in these patients should be preceded by an increase in their level of arousal. Furthermore, this increased arousal should also be associated with a change in the patient's social circumstances. A prospective psychophysiological study as has been suggested above has yet to be undertaken.

An alternative to the study of the effects of arousal on psychiatric relapse is to examine the incidence of disturbed behaviour in psychiatric patients. An obvious corollary of the proposition that increased arousal leads to a greater incidence of relapse is that excessive arousal brings about a greater incidence of psychotic behaviour. Although this proposition is a more easily testable hypothesis than that relating arousal to relapse, it has seldom been examined. Lapidus and Schmolling (1975), in their review of the interrelationships between anxiety, arousal and schizophrenia, cite some research which associates the onset of hallucinations with high arousal in psychiatric patients. Gruzelier *et al.* (1972) attempted to alter the arousal level of schizophrenic patients using physical exercise as a stressor. They reported a number of differential effects of this increase in arousal on physiological functioning. However, they did not comment upon its effects on the general pattern of behaviour of these patients.

It can be argued that the laboratory is particularly ill-suited for the investigation of the effects of arousal on the incidence of psychotic behaviour. The stringent demand characteristics of the laboratory situation usually exert a "normalizing effect" on the patient's behaviour which leads to a reduction in the incidence of psychotic behaviour. Moreover, since the tasks involved in the laboratory situation are fairly complex, usually only relatively co-operative and coherent patients are studied. Thus, together with other criticisms which have already been made about the use of the laboratory situation with psychiatric patients, this setting seems inappropriate for the study of the effects of arousal on the incidence of psychotic behaviour.

In order to overcome some of the problems imposed by both the novelty and demand characteristics of the laboratory setting, psychophysiologists have employed miniature, portable physiological recording equipment to obtain data from freely moving patients within naturalistic settings. Such situations have included the hospital ward and occupational and group therapy sessions. Two techniques have generally been employed. These have been either the use of a small radio transmitter and receiver or a portable cassette tape-recorder, which is worn by the subject and is capable of recording the subject's physiological activity. One study by Stevens and her coworkers (Stevens *et al.*, 1979) examined changes in the EEG of psychiatric patients whilst engaged in their daily activities on the ward. The results from this study confirmed the presence of specific patterns of physiological activity which could be identified with the occurrence of different psychotic behaviours. Similarly, an intensive study of a single psychiatric patient by the present author in conjunction with M. H. Lader has also revealed changes in physiological activity which are associated with the onset of specific behaviours. Some results from this study are presented in Fig. 3. If a relative decrease in alpha activity is considered as a measure of increased arousal, it can be seen that the most arousing conditions were in fact prior to and during social interaction. This result supports the suggestion made earlier that social interaction leads to increased arousal. However, relative to the non-psychotic behaviours such as interaction, working on task and moving around the workshop, the abnormal behaviours such as talking to self and shouting aloud seem to be associated with a relative decrease in arousal. This particular finding is not, therefore, in agreement with the notion of increased arousal precipitating psychotic behaviour. However, it should be pointed out that these preliminary findings relate to physiological activity occurring only 1 min prior to or during the relevant activities, and perhaps it is the more long-term, tonic changes in arousal which are important in determining the incidence of psychotic behaviour. These long-term changes are at present being investigated.

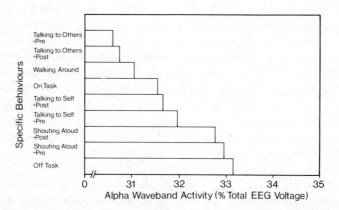

Fig. 3 *EEG alpha waveband activity recorded from a schizophrenic patient whilst working in occupational therapy. Percentages are averaged across each behaviour on 10 separate 2 hour recording sessions.*

In summary, the use of portable recording techniques allows the researcher to study the relationship between physiological arousal and psychotic behaviour in a familiar and naturalistic environment. It is hoped that such techniques will help in the identification of the physiological antecedents and concomitants of abnormal behaviour in psychiatric patients. Such information will aid in the understanding of the many factors which either precipitate or prevent the occurrence of psychiatric relapse.

IV. Summary

These studies have demonstrated the effects of social factors such as expressed emotion, social contact and the incidence of stressful life events upon the incidence of psychiatric relapse. In addition, the use of psychophysiological measures has revealed that patients who live with high EE relatives are more highly aroused than patients living with low EE relatives. It is suggested that this higher level of arousal leads to a greater probability of relapse. The importance of monitoring the arousal level of these patients within naturalistic rather than laboratory settings is emphasized.

Acknowledgement

Preparation of this chapter was supported by an MRC research grant to Professor M. H. Lader. I am also grateful to R. Berkowitz, L. Kuipers, M. H. Lader and J. P. Leff for their helpful comments on an earlier version of this manuscript.

Further Reading

Fowles, D. C. (1975). "Clinical Applications of Psychophysiology". Columbia University Press, New York.
A general review of both theoretical and methodological problems associated with the application of psychophysiology to mental order.
Lader, M. H. (1975). "The Psychophysiology of Mental Illness". Routledge and Kegan Paul, London.
A systematic account of the use of psychophysiological techniques in the study of mental illness.
Leff, J., Kuipers, L., Berkowitz, R., Eberlein, R. and Sturgeon, D. (1982). A controlled trial of social intervention in the families of schizophrenic patients. *Br. J. Psychiat.* **141**, 121–134.
An up-to-date account of the effects of the intervention study referred to in this chapter.
Prokasy, W. F. and Raskin, D. C. (1973). "Electrodermal Activity in Psychological Research". Academic Press, New York and London.
Includes chapters on the use of electrodermal measures for the study of social psychology, psychopathology and the measurement of arousal.
Van Praag, H. M., Lader, M. H., Rafaelsen, O. J. and Sachar, E. J. (1980). "Handbook of Biological Psychiatry, Part II: Brain Mechanisms and Abnormal Behaviour – Psychophysiology". Marcel Dekker, New York.
An up-to-date account of psychophysiological research in Psychiatry.
Venables, P. H. and Christie, M. J. (1975). "Research in Psychophysiology". Wiley, London.
Includes chapters on psychopathology and also the social nature of the psychophysiology experiment.

Wing, J. K. (1978). "Schizophrenia: Towards a New Synthesis". Academic Press, London and New York.
A review of current approaches to schizophrenia. Includes an account of the role of social factors in precipitating the acute attack.

References

Brown, G. W. and Rutter, M. (1966). The measurement of family activity and relationships: a methodological study. *Hum. Relations* **19**, 241–263.

Brown, G. W., Carstairs, G. M. and Topping, G. G. (1958). The post-hospital adjustment of chronic mental patients. *Lancet* **ii**, 685–689.

Brown, G. W., Monck, E. M., Carstairs, G. M. and Wing, J. K. (1962). Influence of family life on schizophrenic illness. *Br. J. Preventative Soc. Med.* **16**, 55–68.

Brown, G. W., Birley, J. L. T. and Wing, J. H. (1972). Influence of family life on the course of schizophrenic disorders: a replication. *Br. J. Psychiat.* **121**, 241–258.

Gruzelier, J. H., Lykken, D. T. and Venables, P. H. (1972). Schizophrenia and arousal revisited: Two-flash thresholds and electrodermal activity in activated and non-activated conditions. *Arch. Gen. Psychiat.* **26**, 427–432.

Hirsch, S. R. and Leff, J. P. (1975). "Abnormalities in Parents of Schizophrenics" Maudsley Monograph No. 22. Oxford University Press, London.

Kuipers, L. (1979). Expressed emotion: A review. *Br. J. Soc. Clin. Psychol.* **18**, 237–243.

Lapidus, L. B. and Schmolling, P. (1975). Anxiety, arousal, and schizophrenia: a theoretical integration. *Psychol. Bull.* **82**, 689–710.

Leff, J. P. and Vaughn, C. E. (1980). The interaction of life events and relative's expressed emotion in schizophrenia and depressive neurosis. *Br. J. Psychiat.* **136**, 146–153.

Spratt, G. and Gale, A. (1979). An EEG study of visual attention in schizophrenic patients and normal controls. *Biol. Psychol.* **9**, 249–270.

Stevens, J. R., Bigelow, L., Denney, D., Lipkins, J. Livermore, A. H., Rauscher, F. and Wyatt, R. J. (1979). Telemetered EEG-EOG during psychotic behaviours of schizophrenia. *Arch. Gen. Psychiat.* **36**, 251–26.

Sturgeon, D., Kuipers, L., Berkowitz, R., Turpin, G. and Leff, J. (1981). Psycho-physiological responses of schizophrenic patients to high and low expressed emotion relatives. *Br. J. Psychiat.* **138**, 40–45.

Tarrier, N., Cooke, E. C. and Lader, M. H. (1978a). Electrodermal and heart-rate measurements in chronic and partially remitted schizophrenic patients. *Acta. Psychiat. Scand.* **57**, 369–376.

Tarrier, N., Cooke, E. C. and Lader, M. H. (1978b). The EEG's of chronic schizophrenic patients in hospital and the community. *Electroenceph. Clin. Neurophysiol.* **44**, 669–673.

Tarrier, N., Vaughn, C., Lader, M. H. and Leff, J. P. (1979). Bodily reactions to people and events in schizophrenics. *Arch. Gen. Psychiat.* **36**, 311–315.

Vaughn, C. E. and Leff, J. P. (1976). The influence of family and social factors on the course of psychiatric illness. *Br. J. Psychiat.* **129**, 125–137.

Venables, P. H. and Wing, J. K. (1962). Level of arousal and the sub-classification of schizophrenia. *Arch. Gen. Psychiat.* **7**, 114–119.

Author Index

The numbers in italics refer to the reference lists at the end of each chapter.

Subject Index